AMERICAN
ESPIONAGE
AND THE
SOVIET
TARGET

AMERICAN ESPIONAGE
AND THE
SOVIET TARGET

JEFFREY RICHELSON

Quill
William Morrow
New York

Library of Congress Cataloging-in-Publication Data

Richelson, Jeffrey.
American espionage and the Soviet target / Jeffrey Richelson.
p.   cm.
Bibliography: p.
Includes index.
ISBN 0-688-07954-7
1. Espionage, American—Soviet Union.   2. United States—
Military relations—Soviet Union.
3. Soviet Union—Military relations—
United States.   I. Title.
E183.8.S65R5 1988   88-4143
327.1′2′0973—dc19   CIP

Printed in the United States of America

First Quill Edition

1 2 3 4 5 6 7 8 9 10

BOOK DESIGN BY MANUELA PAUL

To Lee
who stopped the rain

The Russians escaped while we weren't watching them.

—JACKSON BROWNE
Used by permission

CONTENTS

PREFACE

Since the end of World War II the United States and Soviet Union have eyed each other with suspicion, distrust, and fear. As nations with vastly different domestic policies and the capability to wound the other mortally, such suspicion and fear are hardly surprising. The inevitable result has been that both sides have devoted an enormous amount of resources—in terms of manpower and money—to try to determine the capabilities and intentions of the other side.

Occasionally parts of this effort become publicly known—either because of research or because a public event such as the U-2 or Walker case pushes the efforts into the headlines. This book is an attempt to describe the history of the U.S. effort directed against the Soviet Union from 1945. Obviously it is not the complete story. I have focused largely on *direct* U.S. efforts to collect information on developments *within* the Soviet Union, largely bypassing the intelligence exchange relationship the United States has with numerous countries and events such as the Cuban missile crisis and Berlin Tunnel. Also, thousands of documents remain classified. Many individuals who could provide information have died or simply are unwilling or unable to talk about their activities.

In pulling together the relevant material I have had an enormous amount of help. Wilbert Mahoney of the Modern Military Branch of the National Archives pointed the way to scores of boxes of newly declassified documents. Sergeant Roger Jernigan of the Air Force Office of History aided me in identifying relevant available documents. Staff members of the Truman, Eisenhower, and Kennedy libraries also were quite helpful in my quest to obtain original documents.

Many professional colleagues provided me with hints, documents, and information. I would like to thank John Prados, David Rosenberg, William Arkin, Scott Armstrong, James Bamford, Desmond Ball, William Burrows, Andrew Cockburn, Anthony Kenden, Stan Norris, John Pike, R. Jeffrey Smith, and Paul Stares.

I would also like to thank those at American University and William Morrow who helped turn my work into book form— Evelyn Costelloe, John Martin, and John Tucker, who typed the manuscript, and my editor, Doug Stumpf, who advised me on a number of matters.

AMERICAN ESPIONAGE

AND THE

SOVIET TARGET

I.

A New Enemy

On December 7, 1941, Japanese aircraft bombed the United States naval base at Pearl Harbor. Four days later Japan's ally Nazi Germany declared war on the United States. As a result, the United States found itself allied not only with Great Britain (which Franklin Roosevelt had been aiding as much as possible—often breaking the law) but also with the Soviet Union.

Once actively involved in the war, the United States began to employ a wide range of intelligence assets to acquire vital political, military, and economic information about the Axis powers. Of course, the United States and its allies employed the most traditional of intelligence collection methods—the human agent. But technical collection systems made a major contribution to the success of the Allied effort.

Before the war the United States had begun to set up ground stations to intercept Japanese military and diplomatic communications. Thus it was a Navy listening post on Bainbridge Island in Puget Sound, Washington, that intercepted the Tokyo–Washington, D.C., diplomatic messages—including the note to be delivered to the State Department on December 7 notifying the United States of Japan's decision that further discussions concerning their differences would be useless.[1] With the advent of the war, interception activities were refocused to give priority to military signals, and U.S. intercept units were established at numerous locations, including Corregidor in the Philippines and Townsville in Australia.[2] While the United Kingdom was having notable success in intercepting and deciphering German military signals—an activity that resulted in the now famous ULTRA material—the United States managed some notable achievements against its Pacific enemy. A combination of deception and cryptanalysis allowed the U.S. military to determine that the major Japanese attack to follow Pearl Harbor was to be directed against Midway Island. Armed with that information, the Army and Navy were able to mount a successful defense of the island and deal Japan a decisive setback.[3]

In addition to ground-based interception activities, the United States became heavily involved in aerial reconnaissance. Photographic reconnaissance was employed for target location and damage assessment. In many instances bombers were modified, replacing the bombs with cameras, as in the cases of the B-17 Flying Fortress and the B-24 Liberator. Thus the B-17's became F-9's while the B-24's became F-7's. The F-7's carried six cameras internally, all of them triggered via remote control by an operator placed over the sealed rear bomb-bay doors. Among the cameras was the trimetrogon, mounted in the plane's nose. It consisted of three standard K-17 aerial cameras bolted together but pointed in different directions. The middle camera looked straight down, while the cameras on the left and right sides pointed off in those directions; the result was horizon-to-horizon coverage at thirty thousand feet, with only a slight amount of overlapping coverage. The trimetrogon produced nine-by-nine photos rapidly enough so that a single plane could photograph eight thousand square miles in one hour.[4]

Whereas photographic reconnaissance was not new but simply grew in capability and importance in World War II, airborne electronic reconnaissance was born. It was not until the war that radar (an acronym for *r*adio *d*etection *a*nd *r*anging) was developed and deployed—initially by Britain. Radar systems, by emitting radio signals that would bounce off objects they might encounter (such as airplanes) and back to their point of origin, allowed a defender to determine if enemy bombers were on their way as well as their number and location. To counteract the radars and permit bombers to penetrate, it was necessary to locate the radars and determine their electronic characteristics. That information would then be utilized to develop countermeasures—either active (e.g., jamming, decoys) or passive (avoidance).

The first U.S. "ferret" mission, to search out such radars, involved a B-17 mission of October 31, 1942. The flight of over eleven hours involved a round-trip mission from Espírito Santo to Guadalcanal and Bougainville and back. No enemy signals were found—perhaps because no special effort was made to search for them. That method of operation was to change. An Army Air Forces plane returned from a photographic reconnaissance mission over the Japanese-occupied island of Kiska in the Aleutians with pictures of a pair of structures. The possibility that the structures were radar sets led to a decision to fly a specially equipped plane over the area.[5] A B-24 Liberator bomber was chosen to receive the special intercept equipment as well as to have its engines modified for cold-weather operations. On March 6, 1943, Project Ferret became operational when the modified B-24 lifted off the runway at Adak and headed toward Kiska. This mission did produce enemy signals and additional missions were flown later that month, adding the Japanese-occupied islands of Attu and Agattu to the target list.[6]

Ferret flights also became commonplace in the southern Pacific. One aircraft used on such missions was the four-engine Consolidated-Vultee's PB4Y2 Privateer, the maritime version of Consolidated-Vultee's B-24 Liberator. Each Privateer was a flying radar-interception center—carrying the crew and a dozen operators. Its fuselage was covered with radomes made of a special synthetic material covering the various antennas targeted on enemy radars.[7]

Europe was also an arena for numerous ferret missions. In the summer of 1943 the United States began a series of ferret missions in support of the forthcoming invasion of Sicily, Operation Husky. Flying out of a small airfield at Bilda, near Algiers, a modified B-17F and similar aircraft flew along the Mediterranean and Adriatic coasts of Italy, off southern France and Spain, Yugoslavia, and Albania and to the Islands of Sicily, Sardinia, Corsica, and Crete. To minimize the probability of detection by radar, the missions, some of which lasted eleven hours, were flown at alttitudes of between five hundred to one thousand feet.[8]

The United States also exploited warships and submarines for intelligence collection purposes. An intercept receiver was wired to one of the regular communications antennas of the submarine U.S.S. *Drum*. Despite no special action being taken to search for Japanese signals, the operation produced a considerable amount of information of interest to naval intelligence authorities. Subsequently, in 1944, the main U.S. fleet bases in the Pacific undertook a crash program to install intercept receivers in all warships that might enter the war zone. The receivers were to provide warning of the presence of enemy radars, and allow ships to conduct intercept operations during their regular patrols.[9]

As the alliance with the Soviet Union grew more and more troubled and eventually shattered, the techniques employed against Germany and Japan were further employed and refined against the Soviet Union. It may well have been a sequence of events that was inevitable.

Alliance with the Soviet Union was a product of circumstances, not of ideological or cultural affinity. The initial U.S. reaction to the formation of the Soviet state involved the use of secret agents and troops in an attempt to overthrow Lenin's regime.[10] Subsequently, diplomatic recognition was withheld by three Republican administrations due to Soviet support of revolution and Soviet refusal either to honor financial obligations of the Czarist governments or to make restitution to American businesses for property that had been nationalized.[11] It was only sixteen years after the Bolshevik seizure of power in 1917 that the U.S. government, under the newly elected Franklin Roosevelt, extended diplomatic recognition to the Soviet state.

Recognition of the Soviet Union in 1933 did not imply that U.S. officials were no longer suspicious of Soviet methods and objectives. Nor did events of the next eight years eliminate those suspicions. Particularly disturbing to American representatives were the purge trials of 1936 through 1938—trials that resulted in the liquidation of Communist stalwarts such as Radek, Bukharin, Zinoviev, and Kamenev. As a result, U.S. diplomats gave up earlier hopes of U.S.-Soviet cooperation. Thus Loy Henderson, a Foreign Service officer stationed in Moscow, concluded that the gap between the U.S. and Soviet forms of government was unbridgeable. Likewise, George Kennan wrote that "in view of the frank cynicism with which she [the Soviet Union] views treaty obligations, it may be questioned whether she would even comply with her undertakings regarding military assistance, unless this happened to coincide with her interests at any given moment."[12]

However, the alliance necessitated by the war made cooperation the primary concern and, for many, pushed to a subsidiary level questions concerning the nature of the postwar world. In some cases, the cooperation of World War II produced an optimism concerning the U.S.-Soviet ability to settle amicably issues such as the fate of Germany and Eastern Europe. In the forty-two months in which the United States and the U.S.S.R. battled Germany, the United States provided the Soviet government with over seventeen million long tons of supplies valued at over ten billion dollars.[13] Included were over 4.4 million tons of food, 468,000 tons of railroad transportation equipment, 2.2 million tons of trucks and other vehicles, 3.3 million tons of metals, 1.1 tons of chemicals and explosives, 2.1 million tons of petroleum, and 1.2 million tons of machine equipment.[14] The Soviet contribution to the war effort was in terms of property and men. According to John F. Kennedy, over the course of its war with Germany at least twenty million Soviet military and civilian personnel lost their lives. Countless millions of homes and farms were burned or sacked. A third of the nation's territory, including nearly two thirds of its industrial base, was turned into a wasteland.[15]

Besides having the very obvious virtue in Stalin's eyes of

preserving the Soviet state and his position, fighting off the Nazi invaders forced Hitler's armies to continue fighting a two-front war. Thus when the United States and Britain invaded Europe in June 1944 they faced not the army of a consolidated Germany with the resources of all Europe at its command but a fragmented German army faced with an advancing Soviet army to the east and a deteriorating situation at home.

After the Japanese defeat at Midway and the German defeats at Stalingrad and Moscow it was clear that the Axis powers were headed toward defeat. As a result the focus of the Allied leaders shifted, in part, toward the nature of the postwar world. As the German army was pushed farther and farther out of the Soviet Union and back toward Germany, the focus on postwar arrangements expanded accordingly. To begin dealing with the issues involved, the leaders of the United States, Britain, and the Soviet Union began a series of meetings that extended over the course of the European and Asian conflicts.

The first conference to bring together Franklin Roosevelt, Winston Churchill, and Joseph Stalin took place in Teheran, Iran, in late 1943. Code-named EUREKA, the conference began on November 28, 1943, and continued until December 1. In addition to discussing plans for a United Nations organization and the future of France, the Allies reached one of the major decisions of the war—that the invasion of Europe by the United States and Britain would take the form of a crosschannel onslaught against German-occupied France, rather than an invasion of the Balkans, as desired by Churchill.[16]

Also discussed were the fates of Germany and Eastern Europe. Stalin's objectives in this area were quite clear: the dismemberment of Germany, and an Eastern Europe subservient to the Soviet Union. This had become apparent at the Moscow Conference of Foreign Ministers of late October and early November 1943. Ambassador W. Averell Harriman informed Roosevelt that Stalin would insist not only on territorial gains in the case of Poland but also on having a "friendly" government installed in Warsaw. Roosevelt's response was to attempt to make the Russian grip as loose as possible while simultaneously trying to convince the East Europeans that their own best interests would be served by cooperating with the Soviet Union.[17]

While American officials worried about Soviet present and future actions in Eastern Europe, Winston Churchill began making plans to come to concrete agreement with Stalin over the Balkans. On May 6, 1944, Churchill instructed his foreign minister, Anthony Eden, to draft a paper for the British cabinet that would state "the brute issues between us and the Soviet Government which are developing in Italy, in Roumania, in Bulgaria, in Yugoslavia and above all in Greece."[18]

On October 9 Churchill and Stalin met in a private session. Churchill, according to his memoirs, said, "Let us settle our affairs in the Balkans" and wrote out on a half sheet of paper the percentages of influence the Allies were to command in the postwar Balkan states:

Romania	
Russia	90%
the others	10%
Greece	
Great Britain (in accord with U.S.A.)	90%
Russia	10%
Yugoslavia	50–50%
Hungary	50–50%
Bulgaria	
Russia	75%
the others	25%

Churchill further claimed that Stalin "took his blue pencil and made a large tick on it, and passed it back to us. . . . It was all settled in no more time than it takes to set down."[19] Thus by Churchill's account he and Stalin had settled the fate of millions in a matter of seconds—without the consent of those millions. In fact, Churchill's proposal represented only the first round in British-Soviet negotiations on the Balkans that were carried on by Eden and Soviet Foreign Minister Molotov. Those negotiations produced an implicit final agreement that left the British proposal unchanged with respect to Romania, Greece, and Yugoslavia but was more favorable to the Soviet Union with respect to Hungary and Bulgaria: In both cases the division was to be 80–20 percent in favor of the U.S.S.R.[20]

This agreement between Britain and the U.S.S.R. helped set the stage for the exclusion of the Balkans as a subject of serious discussion at the second tripartite meeting of Allied heads of state, at Yalta in February 1945. Code-named ARGONAUT, the conference began on February 4, 1945, and concluded on February 12. In addition to dealing with questions concerning Soviet entry into the war against Japan, Soviet territorial gains in the Far East (specifically, southern Sakhalin and the Kuril Islands), and reparations issues concerning Germany, a major focus was the fate of Poland. Two questions were involved: Poland's territorial boundaries and its political composition. The first of the questions was given only a small amount of attention. Roosevelt repeated to Stalin his opinion, previously stated at Teheran, that he was "in general" in favor of the Curzon line (which marked the beginning of the territory claimed by both Poland and the U.S.S.R. since 1921) as the eastern boundary of Poland.[21]

The composition of the government that would rule Poland was a much more difficult question to settle. Due to both political pressure at home and his own beliefs, Roosevelt stressed the need to create a Polish government that "would command the support of the three great powers and would include members of all Polish political groups." He emphasized the need to implement the Atlantic Charter principle that maintained "the right of all peoples to choose their own form of government." Churchill supported Roosevelt's position—specifically the suggestion that the formation of a provisional Polish government was to be only a temporary one. The actual postwar Polish government would be established by free elections—which Churchill and Stalin suggested would occur within one or two months after the end of the war.[22]

To Churchill's remark that the fate of Poland was a question of honor for Britain, Stalin replied that for the Soviet Union it was a question of both honor *and* security. Stalin suggested a "reorganization" of the Lublin government to include some Poles from the London government-in-exile, whom he regarded as hostile to the Soviet Union. After much discussion a "compromise" solution was reached—a final communiqué that supported the reorganization of the Lublin government into a "new" government. Thus the final communiqué called for: ". . . the establishment of a Polish Provisional Government . . . more broadly based than . . . before the . . . liberation of western Poland. The Provisional Government . . . should therefore be reorganized on a broader democratic basis with the inclusion of democratic leaders from Poland itself and from Poles abroad. This new Government should then be called the Polish Provisional Government of National Unity."[23]

The wording of the communiqué was such that Roosevelt could publicly represent it as an acceptance of his position while acknowledging the truth of an aide's observation that the agreement was "so elastic that the Russians can stretch it all the way from Yalta to Washington without ever technically breaking it."[24] Likewise, Stalin could leave Yalta "believing his allies had at least acquiesced to his domination over Eastern Europe."[25]

The rest of Eastern Europe was dealt with only briefly and only in the most general terms. Roosevelt persuaded Churchill and Stalin to sign a "Declaration on Liberated Europe" reaffirming the principles of the Atlantic Charter (a Roosevelt-Churchill pledge renouncing territorial aggrandizement, opposing territorial changes that did not agree with popular will, and promising respect for political self-determination of all nations) and calling for the formation of provisional governments in Eastern Europe "broadly representative of all democratic elements in the population and pledged to the earliest possible establishment through free elections of governments responsive to the will of the people."[26]

By the summer of 1945 two major events had occurred since the end of the Yalta conference. On April 12 Franklin Delano Roosevelt suffered a fatal stroke, making Harry S. Truman the thirty-third President of the United States. Eighteen days later Adolf Hitler, his Third Reich in ruins, committed suicide. Germany surrendered on May 8, ending the war in Europe. Thus when Truman, Churchill, and Stalin met at Potsdam, just outside Berlin, for the TERMINAL conference in July 1945, only two major questions remained. One was wrapping up the war against Japan; the other, determining the fates of Germany and Eastern Europe (including the Balkans).

Decisions made concerning Germany strengthened the control of the zonal commands established at Yalta, which "undermined the principle of a unified Germany for which proponents of rehabilitation had long fought."[27] It was agreed that the Soviet Union could take reparations out of their own occupation zone of Eastern Germany, but in the three Western occupation zones (controlled by the United States, the United Kingdom, and France) the Soviets could have only 25 percent of the reparations.[28] As expected, the primary source of conflict occurred over the former German satellites in Eastern Europe: Romania, Hungary, and Bulgaria. When Stalin and Molotov pressed for U.S. recognition of the governments then in place and under Soviet supervision, Truman and Secretary of State James Byrnes were emphatic that there would be no U.S. recognition until the governments had been reorganized and until American press and radio correspondents had been admitted to monitor the situation. Byrnes told Molotov that the United States "would frankly, always be suspicious of elections in countries where our representatives are not free to move about and where the press cannot report freely," while Truman promised Stalin that "when Hungary, Romania, and Bulgaria were set up on a basis where we could have free access to them, we could recognize them but not sooner."[29]

As a result of the impasse, the Potsdam conference communiqué skirted the Eastern Europe issue to the greatest degree possible. It did not mention the desirability of reorganizing the governments of Romania and Bulgaria, the necessity of joint Allied involvement in the holding of free elections, nor even include a reaffirmation of the principles of the Declaration on

Liberated Europe. The only reference to the establishment of democratic governments in Eastern Europe was the statement, "The conclusion of Peace Treaties with recognized democratic governments in these states will also enable the Three Governments to support applications from them for membership in the United Nations."[30]

While Potsdam represented the last time that the leaders of the Big Three would meet, their foreign ministers continued to meet over the next two years—in London, Paris, and Moscow. Such meetings were required to attempt to resolve outstanding issues and to deal with implementation of agreements reached during the war. The most notable of these foreign ministers' meetings occurred in June 1947 in London and December 1947 in Moscow. The June 1947 conference further widened the gap between the United States and the Soviet Union—with the wedge being Eastern Europe. The draft proposals the Soviet delegation submitted shocked the Eastern European experts of the U.S. delegation, who concluded that, if implemented, the proposals "would eliminate American participation in the reconstruction of the Balkans and guarantee to the U.S.S.R. even more important roles than her physical position and power would insure."[31] While the Soviet Foreign Minister stated that elections would quickly follow upon United States recognition of Romania and Bulgaria, he rejected Secretary of State James Byrnes's suggestion for some changes in their governments to "convince the world" that those governments were really representative.[32] Molotov emphasized that the Soviet Union would not tolerate hostile governments in Eastern Europe and that only after the holding of elections would the governments of Romania and Bulgaria be reorganized. Thus the London conference ended with the situation at an impasse: The Soviet Union demanded recognition (and presumably elections) before reorganization, while the United States demanded reorganization first.[33]

The Moscow conference represented the last serious (or semiserious) attempt to resolve the Eastern European deadlock. When his meetings with Molotov produced no agreement, Byrnes appealed to Stalin himself. Stalin reemphasized the Soviet Union's need to have only friendly governments along its borders. He suggested, however, that some members of the opposition could be included in the Bulgarian government and that some changes could be made in the case of Romania.[34] The concessions were purely cosmetic and did nothing to alter the reality of the situation in Bulgaria and Romania. In his memoirs George Kennan, previously U.S. ambassador to the Soviet Union, described them as "fig leaves of democratic procedure to hide the nakedness of Stalinist dictatorship."[35]

The breakdown in relations between the United States and the Soviet Union was not neatly divided, of course, between a breakdown of viewpoints and a breakdown due to actions. Part of the tensions and aggravations that came forth at the conferences stemmed from actions taken prior to and between conferences—actions that made it very clear that the superpowers had some major differences. As the war drew to a conclusion and the postwar world moved from the future to the present, actions taken by the Soviet Union became an even greater source of concern as they began to take on a permanent rather than an interim status.

For example, in January 1945 Romanian Communist Party leaders Ana Pauker and Gheorghe Gheorghiu-Dej traveled to Moscow to discuss strategy. On January 20, the United States military representative in Bucharest, General Cortlandt Schuyler, informed Washington of a secret party meeting at which Pauker and Gheorghiu-Dej informed their followers of a decision to bring the Communists to power. Thus, on February 24, Communist-sponsored demonstrators rioted in an attempt to bring down the government of General Nicolae Radescu. The Communists demanded formation of a new government under their control and several reforms and measures designed to injure their political opponents seriously: radical land reform, punishment of "war criminals," and "democratization" of the army.[36]

Three days later Deputy Foreign Minister Andrei Vyshinski "descended on Bucharest to teach Romania a lesson . . . he bullied a weaker neighbor into submission by an elaborate display of bad manners. Having lectured King Michael on the necessity of appointing the government the Communists wanted, Vyshinski is said to have slammed the door so hard when he left the plaster around it cracked badly."[37] Vyshinski's tactics worked: He obtained the subservient government that Moscow wanted.

But it was not only the situation in Eastern Europe that served to poison U.S.-Soviet relations. It was a combination of factors: Soviet actions in Iran; United States fear of communism in Western Europe; the U.S. response and Soviet counter-response; events concerning Turkey and Greece; and finally the crisis over Berlin. The confrontation over Iran stemmed from the Anglo-Soviet decision to occupy northern Iran jointly in 1941 as a result of the close relationship between the Shah and Nazi Germany. The objectives of the occupation were twofold: to protect the oil fields and refinery that were crucial to the Allied war effort and to safeguard an important supply route into the Soviet Union. In January 1942, Britain and the Soviet Union signed a treaty with Iran pledging to evacuate their troops six months after the end of the war.[38]

Before that deadline there already were U.S. concerns over the Soviet objectives in Iran. One concern was whether the Soviets would actually withdraw their troops by the deadline of March 2, 1946. The other was the existence of a separatist regime under Soviet protection in the North, in Azerbaijan. By the late December meeting of foreign ministers in Moscow there was apprehension in both the United States and Britain that the Soviets were intent on acquiring all of Iran. Concern was exacerbated when the March 2 deadline passed with the removal of British but not Soviet soldiers. According to TASS, the Soviet soldiers would remain "pending examination of the situation."[39]

Alarm grew when an American consul in northern Iran reported large-scale Soviet troop movements in the vicinity and then "full-scale combat deployment." President Truman told Averell Harriman that a very dangerous situation was developing in Iran: "The Russians are refusing to take their troops out . . . and this may lead to war." On March 19 the Iranian ambassador placed the matter before the United Nations Security Council. The Soviet representative, Andrei Gromyko, requested that consideration be delayed until April 10—promising that evacuation would be completed in five to six weeks. On April 4 the crisis ended. The Iranian and Soviet governments agreed to a settlement framed during the trip in February and March of the Iranian premier, Ahmad Qavam, to Moscow. The settlement included the withdrawal of Soviet troops, a joint agreement concerning the exploration of oil, and a new Soviet ambassador.[40]

In Western Europe the United States also saw a Soviet threat—not so much of an invasion but of "subversion." The war had left Western Europe in ruins and with few resources to stage a recovery, particularly in the face of especially harsh winter conditions. Further, the Communist parties and trade unions in France and Italy had significant support, in part due to their wartime opposition to fascist rule. U.S. policymakers were fearful of a peaceful takeover in Western Europe that would produce an entire continent under Soviet domination.

To try to forestall such an outcome, the United States adopted both overt and covert measures. Covert measures involved the funding of French non-Communist trade unions and the Italian Christian Democratic Party.[41] It was the overt measures, however, that led to a Soviet counterresponse in Eastern Europe that finalized the division of Europe.

On June 4, 1947, Secretary of State George Marshall proposed an economic recovery program that came to be known as the Marshall Plan. The objective of the plan was to prevent the catastrophic economic situation from being employed by Communist forces to their political advantage as well as to create an international economic environment favorable to capitalism. According to one State Department official speaking in 1947, "The failure to reach agreement on Germany at Moscow was due primarily to Soviet anticipation of continued deterioration in France, Italy, and Western Germany, plus hope for a U.S. depression. It is essential to improve the Western European situation in order to prevent further weakening in our bargaining power."[42]

The proposed economic recovery program was to be open to all of Europe, including the Soviet Union, although U.S. officials had no desire to see the Soviets participate. The extent of economic information that participants would be required to divulge was enough to ensure that the obsessively secretive Soviets would refuse to participate. Thus Molotov arrived in Paris on June 26, 1947, along with an entourage of eighty-nine economic experts and clerks, but left only six days later with a blast at American imperialism.[43]

Molotov's departure not only ended any chance of Soviet involvement but also any chance of the participation of any of the East European nations. Obviously the Soviet Union would not allow the United States to become the prime benefactors of those states nor pry into their economic records. Shortly after Molotov returned to the Soviet Union the Soviets announced their "Molotov Plan," and the Poles and the Czechs, who had indicated an interest in the Marshall Plan, informed the Paris meeting that they could not attend because to do so "might be construed as an action against the Soviet Union."[44]

In addition, the Soviets began to impose a greater degree of orthodoxy on all of Eastern Europe than they had insisted on previously. Bulgaria, Romania, and to a lesser degree Poland were already under Soviet domination. However, the Soviets had not exercised the same degree of control over Hungary and Czechoslovakia. Thus in the immediate postwar period a Soviet-supervised election in Hungary resulted in a non-Communist government.[45] Czechoslovakia, which unlike Bulgaria, Romania, and Hungary had not allied herself with Germany, also managed to maintain a certain degree of independence in its dealings with the Soviet Union.

However, the end of such liberal treatment was officially declared at the organizing conference of the Communist Information Bureau (Cominform) in September 1947—held in a manor house belonging to the Polish security service. Andrei Zhdanov, the chief Soviet representative and Stalin's cultural-ideological watchdog, denounced "national communism." In Berlin, East German Communists were informed that it was no longer acceptable to think or talk of a separate German road to socialism.[46]

The previous month Soviet actions in Hungary had terminated that nation's fragile independence. In August, after a purge of left-wing anti-Communist political leaders, the Soviets directly intervened by rigging elections to eliminate all opposition.[47] Even prior to June and the Marshall Plan there were danger signs. In February 1947 the former Secretary General of the Smallholders Party was arrested, allegedly confessed to espionage, and disappeared. In May Premier Ferenc Nagy was implicated in the "confession" and chose exile.[48]

The events that placed Czechoslovakia totally within the Soviet orbit were more complex. In late 1943 Czech leaders signed a treaty with the Soviet Union that, in effect, obligated Czechoslovakia to become part of the Soviet bloc. At the same time, however, President Edward Beneš and his foreign minister, Jan Masaryk, managed to keep doors to the West open—a particularly remarkable achievement since the Communist Party had emerged from the 1946 parliamentary elections with the largest percentage of the vote (38 percent) of any party.[49]

In late 1947 Klement Gottwald, the Czech Communist Party leader, demanded the elimination of independent political parties. The crisis culminated at the end of February, when twelve non-Communist Cabinet members, a minority of the governing coalition, submitted their resignations—believing that President Beneš would refuse to accept them. They expected, on the basis of previous consultation with Beneš, that he would use the occasion either to force a reorganization of the Cabinet on more favorable lines or advance the date of the planned May elections.[50]

From the day of the submissions, February 20, till February 25, five days of crisis ensued. Both sides sought to generate public support, with the Communists being more successful. Rumors spread throughout the country—the Soviet military was going to intervene, a general strike was imminent being just two. The Communists also used their control of the police to search, arrest, and intimidate their political opponents. The Social Democratic leadership then threw their support to the Communist Party. As a result, on February 25, Beneš allowed Communist leader Gottwald to form a new Communist-dominated government, one without pro-Western politicians.[51]

In the midst of the deteriorating situation in Eastern Europe in 1947 and 1948, U.S. attention also was drawn to the situations in Greece and Turkey. During the first months of 1945 Stalin sought, as had Soviet leaders for hundreds of years before him, to attain joint control of the Dardanelles straits along with Turkey. During the war he had been assured by Churchill and Roosevelt that the Soviet Union was "justified" in having access to the straits, particularly given Turkish collaboration with Germany. However, in light of growing suspicion of Soviet objectives, the U.S. and British attitudes had changed.[52] Diplomatic probing continued until August 7, 1946, when Stalin sent a note to Turkey that requested revision of the Montreux Convention to allow joint Russian-Turkish defense of the Dardanelles. The note was interpreted by Under Secretary of State Dean Acheson as a Soviet attempt to dominate Turkey, threaten Greece, and intimidate the remainder of the Middle East.[53] Acheson advised and Truman agreed to a "showdown." Truman informed Stalin that Turkey would retain primary responsibility for the straits and ordered a display of military muscle to back up his declaration. An American naval unit (including marines) that had been sailing in the Mediterranean since early spring was reinforced, while the most powerful American aircraft carrier, the *Franklin D. Roosevelt,* moved into the area. Soviet pressure ceased by the end of 1946.[54]

The situation in Greece was the most complicated of all. The most successful of the guerrilla groups resisting the German occupation had been the National Liberation Front (EAM) and its military arm, the National Popular Liberation Army (ELAS). Both had been created by the Greek Communist Party (KKE) but they were not simply extensions of the KKE—rather, they represented a diverse grouping of political viewpoints.[55] By the time of Greece's liberation in October 1944 most of the Greek mainland was under the control of EAM/ELAS.[56] Yet the government that assumed power after liberation was decidedly to the right of EAM/ELAS, much less the KKE.[57]

The composition of the Greek government resulted from a succession of changes in the Greek government-in-exile during the war. Some of the changes resulted from the attempt by EAM/ELAS to form a rival government in March 1944—the Political Committee of National Liberation (PEEA). A conference in Lebanon in May 1944 produced a call for unification of all resistance forces, a Government of National Unity, and an end to fighting among the resistance groups and other political factions. In August PEEA decided to accept the proposals and joined the government. The arrangement was formalized with the signing of the Caserta Agreement on September 26, in which all the guerrilla forces recognized the authority of the Government of National Unity.[58]

But the Caserta Agreement did not solve the problems brought on by the war—economic crisis, political divisions, and public disorder. Because each problem fed on the others and divided society along the same lines, the situation was particularly dangerous. Thus, outside of Athens the country still was in the hands of resistance groups, while inside the capital there were frequent shootings. To restore order the government of George Papandreou relied on British and Greek forces that either were opposed to the left or, worse, had a reputation as Nazi collaborators (e.g., the Athens police and gendarmerie).[59]

When police fired on an EAM demonstration in Athens in December 1944 the tenuous political understanding that had been reached between left and right fell apart, ushering in the "second round" of the Greek Civil War. By the middle of the next month an armistice had been arranged and a peace agreement, the Varkiza Agreement, was signed between the government and EAM on February 12, 1945. The agreement, however, did not prevent the arrest of the twenty thousand left and center supporters between February and July 1945. Many of the twenty thousand were put to death. By the end of the year as many as eighty thousand may have been under arrest. Under such circumstances the KKE turned to the Communist leaders of Yugoslavia and Bulgaria—Tito and Dimitrov. Both promised aid to the KKE in the event of an insurrection in Greece.[60]

The insurrection began on March 30, 1946, with a guerrilla attack on Litókhoron in Macedonia, northern Greece, signaling the opening of the "Third Round." Albania, Yugoslavia, and Bulgaria provided aid to the guerrillas, while on September 20 the Soviet Union vetoed a Security Council resolution to investigate incidents along Greece's frontiers.[61] To U.S. officials the Greek Civil War thus came to represent another in a series of attempts to expand Soviet control in the Balkans at the expense of the West. Thus a full-scale review of U.S. policy toward Greece, conducted in January 1947, resulted in the conclusion that EAM was a tool of Soviet policy.[62] The evidence on which the conclusion was based was circumstantial—the activities of Yugoslavia, Bulgaria, and Albania. Stalin, in fact, lived up to his 1944 accord with Churchill and remained aloof from the events in Greece. However, given the tenor of the times, the circumstantial evidence was enough.

By 1948 the suspicion and hostility between the United States and the Soviet Union were the major defining aspects of their relationship. In 1948 things were to go from bad to worse. Indeed, they almost went from bad to world war. The near-catalyst was Berlin.

On the night of June 23–24, 1948, the chief of the transportation department of the Soviet Military Administration ordered all rail traffic between Berlin and Helmstedt, on the border in Allied-occupied West Germany, suspended due to "technical disturbances" on that portion of the line. The suspension eliminated all forms of ground communication between Berlin and the U.S.-British zone of Germany. Simultaneously, all electric power flowing from areas under Soviet control to the Western sectors of Berlin was cut. In addition, the SMA advised the central food office of Berlin that from then on no food would be delivered from the Soviet sector to the other sectors of Berlin.[63] The Berlin blockade had been established.

The roots of the blockade can be traced to "those moments of 1945 and 1946 when the breakdown of the Four Power Allied Control Council made impossible the reunification of Germany.

The Soviets continued to hope they could create a unified but demilitarized Germany under their own aegis."[64] The more immediate origin was the breakup of the foreign ministers' conference of November 25 to December 15, 1947. Two and a half years after the defeat of Germany and after numerous meetings between national leaders and foreign ministers it still was impossible to resolve the questions concerning the future of West Germany. The United States was faced with a dilemma, one outlined by General Lucius Clay, the U.S. commander in Berlin: "Anything that we do to strengthen the Bizonal administration will create a hazard with respect to the U.S.S.R. in Berlin. On the other hand, appeasement of the U.S.S.R. will continue the present unsatisfactory administration of Bizonal Germany and make economic reconstruction difficult."[65]

The United States was faced with a choice of proceeding with the measures it felt necessary to reestablish the portions of Germany under Western control as a viable economic and political unit at the risk of antagonizing Stalin, maintaining the situation in limbo, or accepting the Soviet position. The first option was selected, and the Western powers began a series of actions to begin the transformation. A meeting of the United States, Britain, France, and the Benelux countries ended on March 7 with an agreement in principle concerning: (1) the establishment of a federal system of government for Germany, (2) German representation in the European Recovery Program, (3) international control of the Ruhr, and (4) closer economic integration of France with the Anglo-American zone.[66]

A walkout of the Soviet delegation from the Allied Control Council on March 20 was followed by French parliamentary approval of the March 7 agreement. The French approval occurred on June 17 and led almost immediately to a declaration of currency reform in the Western zone on June 18. The decision resolved an issue that had been the subject of discussion among all four occupying powers since 1946, when General Clay reported to Washington that currency reform in Germany was "essential and of immediate urgency" due to problems of hoarding, the black market, barter, and inflation.[67]

A Western currency reform to cover the Western-controlled portions of Germany as well as the Western sectors of Berlin was an anathema to the Soviets. In a meeting on June 22 the Soviet delegation demanded that there be only one currency for the Soviet zone and the area of greater Berlin. The head of the Soviet finance administration in Germany was emphatic about the possible consequences of the Allied decision: "We warn both you and the German population that we will use economic and administrative sanctions which will enforce the transition to a single currency in Berlin and the currency of the Soviet zone."[68]

The next day the Soviet Military Administration announced a currency reform for the Soviet zone and the area of Greater Berlin to begin on June 24. The acting mayor of Berlin was informed by the Soviet chief of staff that "these measures are necessary since Berlin lies in the Soviet zone and economically forms a part of it. In the future no other currency will circulate in Berlin except the currency of the Soviet occupation zone. Any breach of this order will entail suitable steps by the military authorities." The commandants of the three Western sectors responded by declaring the Soviet order null and void in the Western sector and made plans for the introduction of the deutsche mark into the Western sectors of Berlin.[69]

In light of the Soviet blockade, representatives of the State and Defense departments and the Joint Chiefs of Staff met on June 28. Three options were specified as the result of that meeting: withdrawal from Berlin; maintenance of the Western position by all possible means, "accepting the possibility of war as a consequence if necessary"; or "to maintain an unprovocative but firm stand . . . utilizing first every local means, and subsequently every diplomatic means." That same day President Truman chose the third option, saying that the United States "was going to stay. Period."[70]

The United States then began a series of measures to circumvent the blockade—the most important being a massive airlift of food and material into West Berlin. Within a month the airlift was providing twenty-five hundred tons a day of supplies. Eventually the figures reached thirteen thousand tons a day.[71] These supplies kept Berlin alive for the next ten months as the Western powers tried to reverse the Soviet blockade decision—a period during which the Cold War had a continual potential to become a hot war, given the Soviet threat to interfere with the airlift and Western determination to maintain its position. Finally, in May 1949, the Soviets lifted the blockade in return for minimum concessions on the part of the West—a cessation of the Western counterblockade and a reconvening of the Council of Foreign Ministers.[72]

The Berlin crisis was only the most concrete manifestation of a Cold War that began in 1946. By 1946 the perceptions of U.S. policymakers and the speeches of Churchill and Stalin had all reflected the belief that the "other side" was hopelessly hostile— although not necessarily eager for war. The events of 1947 and 1948 only solidified those beliefs and gave impetus to organizational and policy changes to deal with the perceived danger.

In an "election" speech on February 9, 1946, Stalin had proclaimed that "the unevenness of development of the capitalist countries" could lead to "violent disturbance" and "the consequent splitting of the capitalist world into two hostile camps, and war between them." War, according to Stalin, was inevitable as long as capitalism existed. Stalin's words had a devastating effect in Washington. Even a staunch liberal such as U.S. Supreme Court Justice William O. Douglas was alarmed. To Douglas Stalin's speech was "the Declaration of World War III."[73]

Less than a month later, Winston Churchill delivered a speech titled "The Sinews of Peace" to an audience in Fulton, Missouri. Churchill called for a "fraternal association of English-speaking peoples" to reorder the world. The association would operate apart from the United Nations but under its principles. Such a unilateral policy was necessary, according to Churchill, because "from Stettin in the Baltic to Trieste in the Adriatic, an Iron Curtain has descended across the Continent," allowing "police government to rule Eastern Europe." While the Soviets did not want war they did, in Churchill's view, desire "the fruits of war and the indefinite expansion of their power and doctrines."[74]

In the interim between Stalin's speech and Churchill's, Washington's highest foreign affairs officials had received the analysis of George Kennan from his post in Moscow. Taken ill in mid-February with a cold, fever, sinus infection, and tooth trouble, Kennan responded to a request for his views on U.S.-Soviet relations by dictating an eight-thousand-word telegram, in five parts, to his secretary.[75] The telegram arrived in Washington on February 22.

In his analysis Kennan stressed the internal motivations for Soviet policy—the Soviet need for external threats to legitimize its domestic authority and policies—as well as the role of ideology. Thus further concessions by the United States would be futile.[76] He described the Soviet Communist Party/government as a "political force committed fanatically to the belief that with the United States there can be no permanent modus vivendi, that it is desirable and necessary that the internal harmony of our society be disrupted, our traditional way of life be destroyed, the international authority of our state be broken, if Soviet power is to be secure."[77] In the final analysis Soviet diplomacy "moves along the prescribed path, like a persistent toy automobile wound up and headed in a given direction, stopping only when it meets some answerable force." Soviet aggression could be "contained by the adroit and vigilant application of counterforce at a series of constantly shifting geographical and political points."[78] Kennan's telegram probably was read by President Truman and certainly by Secretary of the Navy James Forrestal. Forrestal had it duplicated and, according to Kennan, "made it required reading for hundreds, if not thousands, of higher officers in the armed services."[79]

Kennan's views were reinforced throughout the higher echelons of the government in late 1946 by a special report prepared by Truman aide Clark Clifford. In addition to enumerating U.S. grievances concerning Soviet conduct in Eastern Europe, the report stated that "Soviet leaders believe that a conflict is inevitable between the U.S.S.R. and capitalist states, and their duty is to prepare the Soviet Union for this conflict" and that "[u]ntil Soviet leaders abandon their aggressive policies . . . the United States must assume the U.S.S.R. may at any time embark on a course of expansion effected by open warfare and therefore must maintain sufficient military strength to restrain the Soviet Union."[80]

Two years later, in the midst of the Berlin crisis, a CIA study echoed the same themes. According to the report, "[t]he Soviet regime . . . is essentially and implacably inimical toward the United States." Further, the report stated:

> Although the Kremlin is unlikely to resort deliberately to war to gain its ends within the next decade, it would do so if ever it came to consider such a course expedient particularly if convinced that time was on the side of the United States. In this respect the situation will remain critical pending the successful accomplishment of U.S. efforts to redress the balance of power. Moreover, there is constant danger of war through accident or miscalculation.[81]

Not only was the Soviet Union perceived as implacably hostile but also it was feared that she would, in the not too distant future, have the capability to deliver nuclear weapons against U.S. territory—the first time the U.S. could be seriously threatened by an enemy air force. Indeed, if one looked at the world through a polar projection map, as General James Doolittle emphasized in Congressional hearings, the situation was quite striking. The polar projection showed the "vast and ominous landmass of the Union of Soviet Socialist Republics" hovering over the United States, within easy flying distance.[82]

To deal with this threat, the United States needed, in the minds of its top officials, to be organized properly for national defense, to have a more than adequate level of conventional and nuclear forces, and to acquire detailed intelligence about the potential enemy. Many of the techniques and methods of collection used to help defeat the Axis were to be used now against the Soviet Union. Intelligence could aid the U.S. officials in three ways: by aiding day-to-day planning and policy formation concerning the U.S.S.R. and avoiding hysteria; by providing early warning of any possible Soviet aggression; and by providing information to target planners—to identify critical military and economic facilities and determine their vulnerability to attack.

The importance of intelligence in peacetime was noted by the Clifford report, which stated that "[s]uspicious misunderstanding of the Soviet Union must be replaced by an accurate knowledge of the motives and methods of the Soviet government. Only through knowledge will we be able to appraise and forecast the military and political moves of the Kremlin; without that knowledge we shall be at the mercy of rumors and half-truths."[83]

It was not thought that the Soviets were likely to launch an attack in the near future. But as noted in the Clifford and CIA reports, war could occur by miscalculation (including a Soviet belief that the United States was going to attack, which would lead the Soviets to launch a preemptive attack). And in any case, the Japanese attack on Pearl Harbor still was fresh in the minds of U.S. political and military officials; whatever likely Soviet behavior was, the United States could not afford to neglect early warning. Thus the United States needed to detect signs of increased military activity that might be symptomatic of a forthcoming Soviet attack—troop movements, increased bomber alert rates, and heightened levels of communication. The importance of early warning was clearly stated by General Curtis LeMay, a head of the Strategic Air Command in the 1950s: "When I led the Strategic Air Command I operated on the premise that we should have some warning of enemy preparations to attack us. . . . Toward this end we spent a great deal of our energies learning what the opposition was doing day to day. Believing I could foresee an attack, I was prepared to beat him to the draw and attack all of his bomber and his missile bases."[84]

Of course, to attack targets in the Soviet Union they had to be identified and precisely located—the third reason why intelligence was required. If the desire had been simply to attack cities, little effort would have been required. However, by 1950 there were three categories of targets—code-named BRAVO, ROMEO, and DELTA—for blunting, retardation, and disruption/ destruction of war-making capacity. These targets included facilities associated with the Soviet capability to deliver nuclear weapons—airfields and aircraft, weapons storage sites, and weapons production facilities. Electric power, atomic energy industry, submarine building yards, petroleum refineries, aircraft factories, steel mills, and chemical plants also were included in the target set.[85] Over the next thirty-five years the number of targets in U.S. war plans would grow along with the number of warheads and would come to include a wide range of political, strategic, and tactical nuclear targets, command, control, and communications (C^3) targets, conventional military forces, and industrial facilities. (Of course, even if U.S. nuclear war plans called exclusively for attacks against cities, intelligence concerning the facilities in the BRAVO, ROMEO, and DELTA categories would have been necessary to gauge the peacetime capabilities of the U.S.S.R. as well as to provide an order of battle of military forces in case of war.)

Beginning in the 1960s a fourth reason for intelligence collection directed against the Soviet target would appear—the monitoring of Soviet compliance with arms control agreements such as the Limited Test Ban Treaty (banning atmospheric nuclear testing), SALT, and the Threshold Test Ban Treaty (banning all tests over 150 kilotons). In some ways the monitoring process would be the most demanding burden on intelligence-collection activities, as it imposed strict criteria concerning the quantity and quality of the intelligence to be acquired.

The means for gathering the required intelligence also would be diverse—human agents, ground stations, aircraft, ships and submarines, and ultimately satellites. The agencies involved in the collection effort would be diverse as well—the Central Intelligence Agency (created in 1947), the Air Force Directorate of Intelligence and Air Force Security Service (and their descendants), the National Security Agency, various Navy and Army intelligence organizations, and the National Reconnaissance Office. The cost would be enormous—after all, the territory to be surveilled stretched five thousand miles from east to west and two thousand miles from north to south. That and the most secretive government on earth ensured that there still would be areas of mystery. The areas of mystery would shrink over the years, but the ones that remained would often be significant.

II.

HUMINT

The oldest method of collecting information about a foreign power is, of course, through human spies. Until the technical revolution of the mid- to late-twentieth century, human intelligence (HUMINT) was the prime source of clandestine intelligence for any government. Even with the explosion of technical collection capabilities, human intelligence still can be important in providing information that even the most proficient technical collectors cannot—for example, decision memoranda and weapons manuals.

U.S. human intelligence operations directed against the Soviet target have, as might be expected, produced only sporadic successes. The factors militating against success were and are numerous and formidable: the world's most extensive and efficient secret police network, sharp limitations on the areas where foreigners can travel and whom they can meet, and a system that indoctrinates Soviet citizens in the correctness of the Soviet path and the machinations of foreign intelligence services.

U.S. HUMINT operations against the Soviet target did not wait for the Cold War to commence before they were initiated. A supersecretive ally, with a radically different political system, receiving billions of dollars in U.S. aid was a logical (if subsidiary) intelligence target. The fact that the United States was a wartime ally did next to nothing to "open up" the Soviet Union. Thus Kemp Tolley, the assistant U.S. naval attaché at the Moscow embassy in the 1942–1944 period, found that frequent requests to visit military establishments and arms factories produced invitations to inspect a chocolate factory, a hospital, and the Novodevichij deirichie Monastery. Even the photo archives of TASS, the Soviet news agency, from which he had ordered dozens of copies of Soviet warship photographs, were belatedly closed off by the NKVD (the People's Commissariat of Internal Affairs). Tolley did manage to visit the Soviet destroyer *Razumny* and therefore was able to send back an intelligence report that covered the main battery guns, the absence of radar, the torpedo tubes, machine guns, cooking facilities, the sources of power, and living arrangements.[1]

Given the infrequency and limited value of such successes, the Office of Strategic Services and other agencies resorted to more surreptitious means of gathering information. The first attempt by the OSS to gather information covertly took place in the immediate aftermath of Pearl Harbor. It involved a plan to disguise OSS Secret Intelligence Branch operatives as State Department officials and obtain Soviet approval for them to travel through Siberia, the Caucasus, and central Asia. The Soviets rejected the request.[2] In January 1943 the chief of the OSS, William J. Donovan, began reexamining the possibility of clandestine intelligence collection in the U.S.S.R. He instructed his representative at the State Department, William A. Kimbel, to determine the State Department's views. On January 23, 1943, Kimbel reported:

1. Russia has reportedly the best counterespionage system in the world. Any undercover representative would probably be disclosed upon arrival.
2. The movements of any stranger would be so restricted as to make it impossible to obtain observations and results of value.

3. Our relations with Russia are such that if any undercover agent were disclosed, the repercussions could be serious both from a military point of view and politically. Such repercussions could have a serious effect on relations with Russia in this country, in that the State Department has taken a firm stand on prohibiting the activities of any agents of Russia or other Allied nations in the United States. Any indication that we were resorting to such methods in the territory of an allied nation could therefore be serious.

4. The State Department would therefore be opposed to our undertaking the undercover activity and would not provide necessary cooperation.

Kimbel also noted that "[E]ven if the OSS were to get an agent into Russia it would still be practically impossible to maintain communication with him."[3]

However, by September 1943 the OSS had made an informal arrangement with R. E. McCurdy of E. G. Badger and Sons, a large engineering firm. McCurdy was going to the Soviet Union to supervise the erection of six oil refineries the Soviets were to receive under the Lend-Lease program. McCurdy and a staff of three men were to depart shortly and would be followed by another thirty men. The organization was to be spread over six different locations and was to remain at least eighteen months. The information they were asked to provide included industrial, agricultural, and cultural as well as some political intelligence. McCurdy's subordinates were to provide him with information he would then pass on to the OSS. To facilitate communication with McCurdy, the OSS planned to establish personnel at Vladivostok, at Teheran, at Wusu in China's Sinkiang Province, and in Afghanistan.[4]

Additionally, with the assistance of W. Averell Harriman, the U.S. ambassador to the Soviet Union, the OSS was able to place a representative of the OSS Research and Analysis Branch, Thomas Porter Whitney, on the embassy staff. Whitney, a Russian specialist, was described on the embassy list as being a member of the Auxilliary Foreign Service with his mission being the "research, collection and forwarding of printed materials for the United States Government."[5]

The Office of Naval Intelligence was also able to produce some information. In June 1944, ONI personnel covertly managed to photograph the Molotovsk Naval Yard from a small motor launch in Nikolski Inlet, near Severodvinsk in the northern Soviet Union on the White Sea. Likewise, a naval attaché photographed a Leningrad Class destroyer.[6]

By 1945 U.S. officials were looking for additional ways to increase their intelligence coverage. When the question of expanding the number of consulates was raised it was argued that such an expansion would serve to increase the number of diplomatic observation posts. Likewise, in that same year Donovan attempted to obtain the aid of the U.S.-dominated United Nations Relief and Reconstruction Administration (UNRRA)—offering to provide men to fill UNRRA positions while simultaneously serving as OSS information gatherers. The offer was rejected by UNRRA administrator Herbert Lehman.[7]

As 1945 faded into 1946 and beyond, alliance turned to hostility, and the subsidiary intelligence target became the primary target, and an urgent primary target. It became a major objective to recruit individuals who could operate throughout the Soviet Union—in other words, people who could pass as Soviet citizens. Of course, the task of recruiting Soviet citizens living within the Soviet Union was monumentally difficult. The movements of diplomats were restricted, while Soviet citizens who dared to engage in so much as an unauthorized discussion with foreigners, much less official U.S. representatives, could find themselves in severe trouble.

There was, however, a large pool of individuals who had lived in the Soviet Union, spoke Russian, and would be quite at home there—the thousands of displaced persons created by the war and the thousands of émigrés who had escaped Stalinist Russia but who were willing to return as U.S. intelligence and covert action agents. These prospective agents, mainly Ukrainians and Byelorussians, were recruited from displaced-persons camps in Germany and from recent military defectors in Europe, Turkey, Iran, and South Korea as well as through émigré groups. CIA spotters in DP camps interviewed new refugees and notified the agency of likely candidates, while military defectors and individuals sponsored by émigré groups were scrutinized by their potential case officers.[8]

In the spring and summer of 1948, the CIA's secret operations division was assigned its intitial mission against the Soviet target: "to collect secret intelligence on the Soviet Union itself, its military intentions, atomic weapons and advanced missiles; on Soviet actions in Eastern Europe, North Korea and North Vietnam; on Moscow's connections with foreign communist parties and groups fighting for national liberation . . ." The demand placed on the CIA by the Pentagon was immense—information was requested on the location of Soviet military units and aircraft, the condition of Soviet airfields, and Soviet military plans. During one briefing an Army colonel pounded the table and demanded "an agent with a radio on every goddamn airfield between Berlin and the Urals."[9]

Operations began late in 1949 with the air-dropping of agents into the U.S.S.R., part of the infiltration operation codenamed REDSOX.[10] For the next five years agents were sent into the Soviet Union by a variety of means—land, sea, and air—from a variety of locations—Scandinavia, West Germany, Greece, Turkey, Iran, and Japan. According to Harry Rositzke, a member of the CIA's Soviet Russia Division at the time, the agents "covered intelligence targets from the Murmansk area to Sakhalin, mostly on the margins of the Soviet landmass, some deep within. Their task was to satisfy priority intelligence requirements from the Pentagon that could not be satisfied by any less expensive or dangerous means."[11]

The first missions were one- or two-man operations. Their purpose was to establish "legal residents" who would cover specific early-warning targets and report any indications of imminent Soviet military action. With Soviet development of the A-bomb, Soviet atomic energy installations were assigned equal priority with early-warning targets.[12]

Such agents had to be supported by a "legend" or fictional life history. This legend had to be made believable not only by an agent's ability to talk about his past, present, and future plans but also by valid documents. In particular the agent had to be able to display the internal passport required of every Soviet citizen. Production of passports that could pass as valid was made more difficult in the 1949 to 1953 period by a Soviet passport re-registration campaign intended to detect those Soviet citizens, of which there were quite a few, carrying false or altered documents. The main stock of internal passports for various Soviet republics came from captured German archives, all of them fabricated by the Germans. It was not until 1951 that the CIA learned the process by which Soviet documents were printed. Further complicating matters was the requirement that each citizen provide a live witness for identification before being re-registered—a difficult task for a recently infiltrated single agent.[13]

In one case infiltration was all too successful. Agent "Ivan" was dropped into the U.S.S.R. in September 1949 by a C-47 aircraft to observe an airfield. Over the next thirteen months Ivan sent five radio messages and three letters with secret writing to an address in West Germany. In that period he had gotten a job as an electrician in a canning factory and established himself as a legal resident. Since the airfield remained quiet he decided to sign off, and the CIA never heard from him again.[14]

In any event, by 1954 the air dispatch of such radio-equipped agents virtually ceased. The losses were high, the expenditures substantial, and the results minimal. Further, with the death of Joseph Stalin other means for gathering intelligence became available.[15]

In addition to agents infiltrated into the U.S.S.R. for long-term collection missions agents also were infiltrated to examine a particular installation and then exfiltrated. In 1952 agents were delivered by boat from Japan to Sakhalin Island to gather intelligence on several important military installations. The agents would be put ashore from PT boats and picked up later for return and debriefing.[16]

One particular mission took place in the spring of 1952 after the CIA received a priority request for intelligence from the Pentagon. An airfield with an unusually long runway had almost been completed at Provideniya Bay in the Soviet Far East. The Pentagon wanted to know whether the airfield's runway would be thick enough to bear the weight of the size of the bomber needed to carry atomic weapons. Additionally, the Pentagon wanted to know if there was a pit at either end of the runway—at that time, the only way of loading an atomic bomb onto an aircraft, given the size of such bombs, was to dig a pit, lower the bomb into it, roll the plane over the pit, and hoist the bomb up into the aircraft.[17]

Four Russians were selected from a pool of displaced-person agents to be infiltrated by submarine and boat. Selection was followed by an intense four-month training period. Much of the training took place in cold water near an island off the coast of Maine, some of it on a submarine based in Key West. Collapsible rubber boats were designed and fabricated, and silent-running outboard motors were perfected. (An air operation to infiltrate the agents was ruled out because of Soviet air defense effectiveness.)[18]

The team that landed was equipped with special equipment to allow the agents to measure the depth of concrete and to photograph the field as well as radio equipment to be used in short bursts to keep the base (in Alaska) informed of their activity. When the mission was completed the agents rigged a radar-reflective panel on the rubber boat that allowed the submarine to rendezvous with the team the following night.[19]

Attachés, especially in Stalinist Russia, were of little use in collecting information concerning the activities at military bases and atomic energy facilities far from Moscow. However, occasionally they could collect some very useful information from within the Moscow area—particularly since the Soviet leadership would bring some of their latest military hardware to Moscow for the yearly May Day and Revolution Day parades as well as for Soviet Air Day shows. These displays were of great significance to the military attachés and U.S. intelligence—particularly with respect to the bombers flown in the parade. In an era before ICBMs, SLBMs, and reconnaissance satellites, the bombers represented the nuclear threat to the United States and the parades one of the few ways of judging the quantity and quality of the fleet. By noting the number of bombers flown in a given year and making assumptions concerning production rates, an analyst could estimate the number of bombers the Soviet Union would have over the next several years. By comparing the number of bombers flown in two successive May Day (or Revolution Day) parades one could estimate the production rates.[20] Similarly, the Army Attaché and his assistants would be interested in viewing the parades of tanks that would roll into Red Square, particularly the latest-version tanks the Army might encounter rolling across Germany in the event of war.

The importance of the air shows in obtaining information about Soviet aircraft was very clearly stated in a November 1948 letter by Colonel H. M. McCoy, the chief of the Air Material Command's Intelligence Department, to the Air Force Chief of Staff. McCoy wrote:

> An estimated 95% of the qualitive intelligence on
> Russian aircraft, and usually first knowledge of
> the existence of new types of aircraft becomes
> known to our Air Attaché during the 1 May Air
> show and the earlier practice flights. Based on the
> past two years' experience from six to nine
> months elapse until other confirming and qual-
> itative data on these new aircrafts comes thru
> other sources.[21]

To collect the information, U.S. military attachés used the most sophisticated photographic and electronic equipment available that they could bring, overtly or covertly, within the vicinity of the parade. Included were a binocular camera and a variety of tripod arrangements with zoom lenses and telescopic sights capable of still photography and motion-picture photography.[22] The quality of such equipment could have a substantial impact on the value of the information acquired. Thus Colonel McCoy's letter also noted, ". . . the improved camera equipment furnished the air attachés a year ago resulted in improved photographic coverage of several hundred percent, permitting detailed and qualitative evaluation to be made for the first time of all the aircraft which it was possible to photograph, including the engine, armament, gun sighting, navigation and communication equipment."[23]

Some of this equipment (or possibly more advanced versions) was employed by Major Edison K. Walters, the Acting Air Attaché, when he attended the Soviet Air Day Show on July 17, 1949, and shot thirty photographs, primarily of YAK-15 fighters. Held at Tushino Airdrome in Moscow, the show included 348 military aircraft. In his report Walters described the twenty-one events that constituted the three-part show. Among the events he described was a mock battle between nine TU-2's and four fighters in which "all firing was observed to come only from the lower portion of the nose of the fighters. The battle consisted of only a few attacks from the sides by the fighters. A couple of the bombers and a couple of the fighters dropped away on either side trailing a long streamer of smoke for show effect, the fighters were firing blanks and were assisted for sound effect by the AA guns on the ground." Walters also noted Stalin's presence and that "he appeared to be in excellent health and had a suntan."[24]

Having produced reports, photographs, and films of an air show and rehearsals, the attachés might then be "tasked" to provide additional information and clear up ambiguities that might have arisen. Thus, in 1949, the Air Attaché at the Moscow embassy was asked to answer the following questions:

    1. MIG swept-back wing aircraft
        a. How many of this type were noted in the
           practice runs on 17, 19, and 25 April? . . .

c. What are the two black spots underneath the fuselage approximately two thirds of the distance back from the nose?
2. The Lavochkin swept-back-wing aircraft
   a. Were air inlet and exit any different on this design as compared with the MIG design?[25]

At times the attachés at these events had to use this equipment under "very difficult circumstances." In one case the U.S. Air Attaché had MVD (Ministry of Internal Affairs) men standing on both sides of him and very close. Additionally, three cameras were focused on him within distances of eight, twenty, and thirty feet. On one occasion he surrounded himself with attachés of nations such as Great Britain and Canada as well as his wife "to ward off the possibility of any undesirable person asking to use the equipment in question, for the ostensible purpose of watching the show."[26]

In addition to the parades and air shows, attachés also obtained photographs of Soviet aircraft during visits to Soviet airfields—such as the one at Ramenskoye, just outside of Moscow. On July 30, 1953, the U.S. Air Attaché, along with the Canadian and British assistant attachés, observed an aircraft similar to the U.S. B-47 at Ramenskoye. Photographs taken by the U.S. attaché showed the aircraft to be one and a half times larger than the main Soviet bomber, the TU-4, with a tail section and fuselage very similar to those of the B-47. The Air Attaché further reported observing thirty to thirty-five TU-4's; twenty-five to thirty IL-28's; fifteen to twenty MiG 15's; and numerous small, unidentified aircraft.[27]

Attachés also were able, on occasion, to photograph installations to which they had not been invited. Thus, on April 30, 1950, Major Walters photographed a portion of Tili Airfield in the vicinity of Moscow from the northern side of the road opposite the airfield. The photograph showed two radar systems, nine Army trucks, four dug-in huts for housing gun crews and radio operators, and eight antiaircraft guns.[28]

In addition to photographing installations and aircraft, attachés were also involved in collecting electronic intelligence. Thus, on March 3, 1953, Major George Van Laethan drove along the Kiev highway on the way to Vnukovo airport. Major Laethan was equipped with a vest-pocket radar detector to intercept radar emanations. The signals were then recorded on a wire recorder. Just thirteen miles south of the highway, Major Laethan's detector picked up the signals from a new temporary AAA (antiaircraft artillery) position that was in the process of being installed.[29]

Beginning in 1953, the United States sought to improve the collection of intelligence via official travel in the Soviet Union. In January, the U.S. Intelligence Advisory Committee approved the Travel Folder Program for the Soviet Bloc—"a coordinated U.S.-U.K. program for improving the collection of intelligence through official travel within the Soviet bloc countries. . . ." Travel folders were prepared that stated the need for information on different types of industrial, military, and scientific facilities based on travel routes between key cities in the Soviet Union. The CIA would collate the requirements from various Washington agencies and transmit them to Moscow, where the "Moscow coordinator" (the U.S. Naval Attaché) would make the travel folders available to other attachés and embassy staff members.[30]

By the end of 1954, 125 travel folders had been deployed covering large portions of the Soviet Union where travel restrictions, in the aftermath of Stalin's death, had been lifted. The travel folders would be available for consultation by those making one of the sixty trips during the May–November time period. It was anticipated that "by 1 May 1955, Travel Folders will be current and field collectors will be in a position to perform collection action with assurance that the most recent needs of . . . Washington intelligence agencies are reflected in the travel folder files."[31]

It is not clear whether Senator Richard Russell and his two traveling companions, Lieutenant Colonel E. U. Hathaway and Ruben Efron (both attached to Russell's Armed Services Committee), were given access to travel folder material before or during their late 1955 trip through portions of the Soviet Union. When the group arrived at Hlavni Station in Prague, Czechoslovakia—direct from Kiev—they were taken to the residency and dinner, after which Colonel Hathaway expressed a desire to report something to the U.S. Air Attaché Lieutenant Colonel Thomas Ryan. It was, he told Ryan, "something you may not believe, but something that we've been told by your people (USAF) doesn't exist." For security reasons Ryan suggested that any discussion should wait until the following morning in his office.[32]

On October 13, 1955, the meeting began in the larger office of the Army Attaché. Hathaway began the conversation by stating, "I doubt if you're going to believe this but we all saw it." The "it" was a flying saucer—in fact, two flying saucers, with the first seen initially by Senator Russell. The two sightings occurred at 6:10 P.M. on October 4, 1955, between Atjaty and Adzhijabul in the southwestern Soviet Union. According to the Air Attaché's report, the witnesses saw one disc ascend almost vertically at a relatively slow speed, with its outer surface revolving slowly to the right. At an altitude of about six thousand feet its speed increased sharply as it headed north. The second disc was seen performing the same actions about one minute later. According to the attaché, the "significance of this report re the USAF project 'Unidentified Flying Objects' is remarkable and lends credence to many 'saucer' reports."[33]

Of more practical value, the observers also visited Dnepropetrovsk Airfield in the Ukraine on the ninth of October. Colonel Hathaway counted forty-two very stubby jet fighters parked at the field. The jet fighters were described as "short, stubby, smaller and higher horizontal tailplane, wings more forward, canopy more forward." Additionally on a trip outside of Moscow, exactly at the forty-two-kilometer signpost from Moscow on the Moscow–Minsk highway, on the right side of the road a radar site was noticed. Sketches provided by Colonel Hathaway allowed the radars to be identified as one "moodgage or Gage and one square Pole Freya."[34]

A second program, run by the CIA and code-named REDSKIN, involved nonofficial travelers from the United States as well as European and Third World nations. These travelers included tourists, businessmen, journalists, scientists, academics, athletes, chess players, and church leaders who were recruited to gather information during their trips through the Soviet Union. The information they were asked to gather was obtainable without breaking the law—they were not requested to penetrate secret military installations nor to try to recruit Soviet citizens. Rather, the REDSKIN program sought to take advantage of ordinary travel itineraries to gather intelligence about facilities in main metropolitan areas and along the main transportation routes.[35]

To make efficient use of these observers, the CIA had to ascertain who was planning to visit the U.S.S.R. and their itineraries. Once the CIA had that information, it could then task the traveler—specifying points of interest for observation or photography. Points of interest might include a specific factory, a railroad yard, a port installation, a construction site, civil aircraft, or liquid-oxygen tank cars. In addition they might be requested to purchase samples of Soviet merchandise, including electronic devices. In addition to being tasked, the travelers were warned to avoid behavior that might result in their being arrested and charged with espionage. Beyond that, they were briefed on the types of physical surveillance, bugging, or provocative approaches they might encounter.[36]

A major effort was involved in providing the tasking for the travelers. Technical requirements concerning atomic energy, aircraft production, and missile installations had to be translated into simple requests for visual observation from trains, planes, or roads that could be performed by an individual with no particular technical background. A traveler might therefore be asked to identify the color of the smoke being emitted by a specific factory chimney or the color of a sand pile outside a specific plant.[37]

The information provided by the REDSKIN program helped close many information gaps concerning the Soviet Union. At the beginning of the program "analysts in Washington were ignorant across the whole range of Soviet industrial production—facilities, output, technology, bottlenecks." The travelers who purchased Soviet typewriters, who noted the serial numbers of

Soviet-made boxcars and civilian airplanes, and who photo-graphed and examined products of Soviet technology on display at trade fairs allowed analysts to deduce annual production fig-ures, the availability of machine tools, and the alloys employed in production.[38]

In the 1957–60 period legal travelers also provided much in-formation of value concerning Soviet offensive and defensive missile programs as well as useful intelligence concerning Soviet strategic bombers and submarines, nuclear propulsion systems, manned space programs, and bacteriological warfare capabilities. During this period much of the collection requirements were based on the products of U-2 reporting. In some cases one indi-vidual was dispatched to cover a single target, while in other cases a person was given a set of requirements generally suited to his professional competence.[39]

Tourists flying on civil nonjet aircraft managed to produce "small format" aerial photos of the SA-2 surface-to-air missile that had been detected earlier by U-2 overflights. Further, they discovered previously unknown SA-2 locations. Altogether they photographed more than twelve SAM missile tests. More impor-tantly, the travelers "provided an extraordinary amount of infor-mation on high-priority targets. They supplied thousands of photographs of facilities for the production of ICBMs, and of the sites at which ICBMs had been deployed."[40]

Travelers also provided a substantial amount of information concerning the early stages of the Soviet ABM program to go with the information provided by returning German technicians who had worked on the program and by clandestine sources. The information provided concerned construction of a new test range at Sary Shagan in the south-central Soviet Union, an insti-tute involved in a 1956 antimissile test, and activity in and around several ABM sites in the Leningrad area.[41]

The travelers also described one of the first Soviet nuclear submarines, a missile-launching destroyer, and scores of missile-support facilities and direction-finding antennas. Finally, their streams of reports on aircraft markings doubled the Pentagon's estimate of the production of one type of aircraft.[42]

*   *   *

Of course, as valuable as they might be, legal travelers cannot be compared to a well-placed agent in the Soviet military or foreign affairs establishment in terms of the quality and quantity of information that can be provided. The CIA has achieved at least four such penetrations in the past twenty-five years.

In the first case, that of Oleg Penkovskiy, the CIA at first dismissed their prospective agent's approach as that of an *agent provocateur*. Born on April 23, 1919, Oleg Vladimirovich Penkovskiy entered the 2nd Kiev Artillery School in 1937 and graduated in 1939. In 1939 and 1940 he saw combat duty first as commander of an artillery unit in the Ukraine and later in the war against Finland. Penkovskiy was wounded in action and decorated four times in that period. During the remainder of the war he split his time between Moscow and the 1st Ukrainian Front, serving as Assistant Chief of the Political Section for Komsomol (Young Communists) and with work at an artillery school in Moscow, as senior instructor of the Political Directorate for Komsomol activities in the Moscow Military District, and as special assignments officer of the Military Council of the Moscow Military District. At the 1st Ukrainian Front he served successively as chief of training camps and artillery battalion commander in the 27th Tank Destroyer regiment, as liaison officer for the commander of artillery, and as commanding officer of the 51st Guards Tank Destroyer Artillery Regiment.[43]

For the eight years after the end of the war, Penkovskiy attended first the Frunze Military Academy (1945–48) and then the GRU's Military Diplomatic Academy (1949–53). After graduation from the MDA he began his career as an officer in the GRU, the Chief Intelligence Directorate of the Soviet General Staff. In the 1953–55 period he was senior officer of the 4th Directorate (Near East desk). In 1955 he received his first foreign assignment—as assistant military attaché, senior assistant to the GRU resident in Ankara, Turkey. However, as a result of a dispute with his superior, Penkovskiy was recalled in November 1956. Inasmuch as he basically was vindicated in his complaints concerning the military attaché, he resumed his position in the 4th Directorate and was allowed to begin preparations for assignment to India as the GRU resident. Unfortunately for Penkovskiy, before the assignment ever came to pass, it was discovered that his father had been a White Army officer. Although it was ultimately decided that Penkovskiy's skills and experience overrode his impure heritage, he was not sent to India but rather kept at Moscow headquarters.[44]

In 1958 and 1959 he was simultaneously GRU officer (still in the 4th Directorate) and student. During those years he attended the higher academic artillery engineering courses of the Dzerzhinsky Military Artillery Engineering Academy in Moscow. In 1960 he became a member of the Mandate Commission of the MDA, which selected candidates for admission to the academy. He was also assigned to the Special Group of the 3rd Directorate—the GRU area directorate responsible for collecting intelligence in the United States, Canada, Great Britain, and South America. Then in November 1960 Penkovskiy was detailed to the State Committee for the Coordination of Scientific Research Work of the U.S.S.R.—the organization that would serve as a cover for both his GRU activities and his collaboration with British agent Greville Wynne.[45]

In addition to his successful position in the GRU, additional factors made Penkovskiy an unlikely agent of the United States and Britain. He made full colonel at age thirty in 1950 and married the daughter of a top general who was Chief of the Political Directorate of the Moscow Military District before his death in 1952. Additionally, Penkovskiy was on close terms with some of the top military officers in the Soviet armed forces. Included in this group was General Ivan Serov, Chief of the GRU, and Chief Marshal of Artillery Sergey S. Varentsov, who headed the Tactical Missile Forces.[46]

According to his and Wynne's accounts, Penkovskiy became completely disillusioned with the Soviet system; the disillusionment was greatest with respect to the motives and behavior of the Soviet leadership, fearing that their actions would result in a Third World War. It was a long road, however, from disillusionment to acting as an agent of a foreign intelligence service.

Penkovskiy came to the attention of the British Secret Intelligence Service (SIS), popularly known as MI6, while he was serving as assistant military attaché in Ankara. It was noted that his "antisocial" behavior (by Soviet standards)—sitting alone for long periods in sidewalk cafes—made him worth watching. However, no attempt was made to contact him.[47]

Indeed, it took three tries on Penkovskiy's part before he was "recruited" by the SIS and eventually the CIA. Penkovskiy first tried to signal his availability when a group of Canadians representing Canada's pulp and paper milling industry arrived in Moscow for talks with Penkovskiy's committee. Penkovskiy approached one of the younger representatives, requesting that he take an envelope out of the country. The Canadian refused, fearful of becoming embroiled in espionage activities, but reported the incident to the Canadian authorities upon his return. The Canadians, in turn, informed the SIS of Penkovskiy's approach.[48]

Penkovskiy next approached the United States. Two American students arriving for a reception at the American Club, located in a Moscow suburb, were confronted by Penkovskiy and asked to take an envelope inside and hand it to the U.S. military attaché. As the students hesitated, Penkovskiy thrust the envelope into their hands and walked away, ignoring their protest. The U.S. official who examined the contents of the envelope was not terribly impressed by its contents—a letter giving personal details and requesting rendezvous places, dates, and times for making contact—and the attaché dismissed it as a crude provocation.[49]

The Secret Intelligence Service, however, was prepared to take a limited risk and assigned two agents to the case. Both operated under business cover that took them to Moscow and put them in contact with Penkovskiy in his role as a member of the State Committee. The agent who made meaningful contact and became Penkovskiy's closest friend was Greville Wynne, whose cover was as an agent for an array of British companies. On December 8, 1960, Wynne went to the Moscow Airport with Penkovskiy and two other State Committee members to greet British delegates due to arrive on the 5:00 P.M. flight. In the process of waiting with Penkovskiy for what turned out to be a long-delayed flight, Wynne began to establish a personal relationship.[50]

Among the subjects discussed that evening was a planned visit to Britain of a delegation of Russian specialists, who would examine the products Wynne's clients had to offer the Soviets. Wynne had stressed the need for the delegates to be actual experts, qualified to judge the value of the goods Britain had to offer. Subsequently, when Penkovskiy presented Wynne with a listing of delegation members, Wynne strenuously objected on the grounds of their lack of expertise. When Wynne suggested canceling the visit, Penkovskiy grew agitated and told him, "But Greville, you don't understand. They've given me permission to go. It is I who must go to London. Not for pleasure; I . . . I have things to bring with me. Papers. Important papers. Your government must have them." That night Penkovskiy handed Wynne an envelope containing documents specifying the location of rocket installations and minutes of plenary meetings of the Central Committee. Penkovskiy was able to obtain such documents due to his role as twice-a-year lecturer on military and policy matters to officer cadets being trained for the GRU; as such he could go down into the ministry vaults and rummage around undisturbed.[51]

By April 1961, when Penkovskiy made his first visit to London at the head of a Soviet trade delegation consisting of six senior Russian officials, arrangements had been made to give him a thorough debriefing. Also, the CIA had been brought into the operation due to the importance of Penkovskiy's data and the agency's willingness to pay the bills. George Kisvalter, a Russian-speaking CIA officer with experience in a previous penetration of the GRU in Austria, was assigned as case officer, and Penkovskiy was assigned the code name ALEX.[52]

On April 20, 1961, Penkovskiy was ushered into a suite of rooms on the floor above those of the Soviet delegation at the Mount Royal Hotel. Waiting for him were four debriefers—two from the CIA and two from the SIS—although only Kisvalter and his agency colleague spoke Russian. Kisvalter chaired the meeting, and Penkovskiy proceeded to deliver a massive amount of information into the hands of the CIA and the SIS. Included were copies of Soviet training manuals, photographs of military documents, and details of the latest Soviet missiles. In addition, ALEX provided personal "biographies of every GRU officer he had come into contact with and dozens of others who were known to his family."[53]

Penkovskiy returned to Moscow on May 6 and began a new round of collection efforts. He photographed a wide variety of documents, some in their entirety. The documents included technical papers of highly classified instructions and tactical manuals in use by the ground (tactical) missile force, intelligence procedures manuals, and manuals concerning the operations of Penkovskiy's committee. When Wynne arrived in Moscow on May 27, Penkovskiy met him at Sheremetyevo Airport. While driving him back to the city he handed Wynne a packet of approximately twenty exposed films plus other materials. Later that evening Penkovskiy visited Wynne in his Metropol Hotel room and received thirty fresh rolls of film and additional instructions from the intelligence officers who had met him in London.[54]

During July, Penkovskiy made his second trip to London, this time to attend the Soviet Trade Exhibition, and stayed at the Kensington Close Hotel, which was only a short walk from his embassy. Debriefings took place nearby at a rented apartment in Coleherene Court on Old Brompton Road. In the midst of this trip Penkovskiy and Wynne made a side trip to Washington. Penkovskiy had stubbornly insisted on meeting the Queen—a request his British controllers tried to explain was out of the question. Penkovskiy settled for the proposed substitute: President John F. Kennedy. When Penkovskiy and Wynne entered the president's office, Kennedy was already there, with three others. Kennedy moved immediately to greet Penkovskiy and Wynne, shook their hands, and told them, "I've heard about the work you've done for us. I'd just like to add my personal thanks, and the thanks of the United States."[55] Naturally, the trip was kept extraordinarily secret—even the thickest Soviet counterintelligence officer could correctly interpret the meaning of an unauthorized trip by a GRU officer to see the President of the United States.

Penkovskiy returned to London, and then to Moscow on August 7. Prior to that date he was briefed on the use of a long-range transmitter and coding techniques so he could broadcast information without waiting to make contact or travel abroad. The following month, on September 20, Penkovskiy arrived in Paris for another trade fair. He arrived with several additional rolls of film, and his SIS debriefers met him on the top floor of a house in an expensive Paris neighborhood. He was given the names and telephone numbers of approximately a dozen members of the British and American diplomatic establishments. Previously he had been introduced to Janet Chisholm, the wife of an SIS agent attached to the Moscow embassy, who became his contact. He was "officially" introduced to her at an official reception and then met her while she was with her children in Gorky Park.[56]

In one instance one of the children served as a courier. On one day in September 1961 Penkovskiy approached Chisholm's three children while they were playing in a sandbox in the park. After talking to them briefly, he offered one a box of Drazhe candy drops. The child accepted the box and brought it over to his mother, who subsequently extracted the film hidden in the package. A month earlier, Wynne had been in Moscow to attend the French industrial fair. While there Penkovskiy visited him at his hotel and turned over several packets of information.[57]

In January 1962 Penkovskiy first noted signs that he might be under suspicion. It became apparent to him that his "casual" meeting with Janet Chisholm had been observed by the KGB. As a substitute for face-to-face meetings, Penkovskiy resorted to the use of dead drops in which he would leave his information and then inform his case officer to pick it up. The signal involved telephoning the home of his CIA contact twice and then hanging up after a specific number of rings. The case officer would empty the dead drop provided there was a telltale black mark on a particular lamppost on Kutozov Prospekt—the mark indicating that Penkovskiy had successfully completed his drop. For extra safety no dead drop was used more than once, and there was only a single drop and pickup operation each month.[58]

There was also a system for communicating with the SIS in

London. Penkovskiy would send apparently innocent tourist postcards to SIS cover addresses there. The system would allow him to give advance notice of any further Western visits, although the only use he was able to make of it was on January 12 to call off further direct contacts, excluding those at official receptions and other official occasions. Thus Penkovskiy passed more rolls of film to Janet Chisholm at a March 31, 1962, reception at the British embassy (in honor of the Queen's birthday) and at a July 4 American embassy party.[59]

KGB surveillance intensified between January and the summer of 1962. As a result Penkovskiy advised Wynne to leave Moscow a day earlier than he had planned during a visit that summer. It was later established that their last conversation at the Ukraina Hotel had been taped. Penkovskiy, despite the KGB surveillance, continued to place material in dead drops until a September 5 American embassy reception, where he could not find any of his CIA contacts and thus kept the films he had brought with him. Finally, on October 12, he was arrested. The arrest was kept secret, and Wynne was arrested in Budapest on November 2 after a cocktail party at his mobile trade exhibition. The exhibit contained a pair of specially constructed vehicles to be used to smuggle Penkovskiy out to the West by road. To further aid Penkovskiy's escape, a Soviet passport with all the correct authorizing stamps had been forged in the United States to permit him to visit Hungary after he had hopefully eluded the KGB in Moscow. After Wynne's arrest eight Americans and British "diplomats" were declared *persona non grata* and expelled from the Soviet Union.[60]

In May 1963 a four-day trial was held in Moscow, with the world press in attendance. Penkovskiy was described by Lieutenant General A. G. Gornyy, the military prosecutor, as ". . . an opportunist, a careerist, and a morally decayed person who took the road of treason and betrayal of his country and was employed by imperialist intelligence services. . . ." According to the prosecution, the search of Penkovskiy's apartment turned up:

> . . . the telephone numbers of . . . foreign intelligence officers, six message postcards with instruc-

tions for them . . . and . . . exposed rolls of film. . . . In addition, the following articles were discovered in a secret hiding place installed in his desk and were attached to the file as tangible evidence: a forged passport, six cipher pads, three Minox cameras and a description of them, two sheets of specially treated paper for writing secret text . . . fifteen unexposed rolls of film for the Minox camera, and various instruction manuals provided by the foreign intelligence services: on taking photographs with the Minox camera, on the encipherment and decipherment of radio communications, on the procedure for receiving radio transmissions from the intelligence headquarters, and on the selection and use of secret drops.[61]

To no one's surprise, Penkovskiy was convicted and sentenced to death and confiscation of all his property. Wynne was sentenced to eight years in jail. In April 1964 Wynne was exchanged for a Soviet agent, Konon Molody, who operated under the alias Gordon Lonsdale.[62] According to *Izvestiya*, Penkovskiy was executed by firing squad on the afternoon of May 16. Wynne, however, maintained that Penkovskiy was not executed but taken for further interrogation to a remote village, where he committed suicide in 1965.[63]

The most important question concerning Penkovskiy was: What was the value of the information he provided? According to Wynne, the material Penkovskiy provided the West included:

1. The names—among them Lonsdale's—and in many cases photographs of over 300 Soviet agents working in Western countries, in addition, several hundred agents under training in the Soviet Union, Czechoslovakia and other Eastern countries were made known to the West. . . .

2. Details of the Soviet rocket sites throughout the Soviet Union, together with statistical details of

       training manpower, weapon production, stock-
       piling and drawing board designs for future
       programmes.

3. . . . information that Khrushchev had allowed
       most important control equipment, which was
       in very short supply, to be sent with rockets to
       Cuba. . . .

4. Photographic copies of reports which Khrush-
       chev had given to the Soviet Praesidium, pur-
       porting to be an account of a meeting between
       Kennedy and himself, and the Italian Foreign
       Minister and himself.

5. Statistics of agricultural production throughout
       the Soviet Union. . . .

6. Production figures, location, lay-out and oper-
       ating procedures for all the main Soviet indus-
       tries, including the electronics industry, and
       the production of steel, aircraft and military
       equipment.

7. Considerable information dealing with the So-
       viet Union's relations with Eastern European
       countries; photostatic copies of secret agree-
       ments; details of future policy of the Soviet
       Government towards those countries.[64]

Despite the quality and quantity of material delivered by
Penkovskiy, some within and out of the U.S. and British intelligence communities have expressed doubts about the validity of
all or part of his tenure as a Western agent. Such doubts were
partially due to Penkovskiy's carelessness with regard to matters
of security as well as his propensity for reporting gossip and half-
understood remarks picked up in Soviet military bars and can-
teens.[65]

It has been observed that it took the KGB nine months between the point that Penkovskiy discovered what he believed to
be surveillance before arresting him. A possible explanation is
that due to Penkovskiy's seniority and political connections it

was necessary to develop an unimpeachable case before action could be taken. Another is that Penkovskiy's reaction in January 1962 was an overreaction to standard KGB surveillance of Westerners. Others, though, have questioned whether toward the end of his espionage activities Penkovskiy had been turned by the KGB and GRU to provide disinformation. Some have even suggested that the entire Penkovskiy episode was a monumental deception, that the material Penkovskiy passed was really of little value and that he still is alive and a Soviet hero. Among the advocates of that view were James Jesus Angleton, the perpetually suspicious chief of counterintelligence for the CIA, who would appeal to "secret knowledge" to support his view.[66] Such claims were not credible to CIA personnel who saw the five thousand frames of microfilmed documents provided by Penkovskiy and were dazzled by their quality.[67]

Yet another penetration of the GRU began in Algiers during the mid-1970s when a GRU colonel, Anatoli Nikolaevich Filatov, approached the CIA with a proposal to pass information to the United States. Over the next fourteen months Filatov provided the United States with a variety of Soviet intelligence and military secrets, including details of Soviet links with national liberation groups. After being reassigned to GRU headquarters in Moscow, Filatov continued to provide the CIA with information. This continued for about a year—at which time he was detected filling a dead drop, which they had probably located from routine surveillance on known CIA agents.[68]

After several months of interrogation, the Soviets sentenced Filatov to death. However, in exchange for the United States returning two KGB officers who were arrested for espionage and had no diplomatic immunity, the Soviets promised to commute Filatov's death sentence to fifteen years' imprisonment.[69]

Filatov's was only one of two CIA penetrations that shook the Soviet establishment in the 1970s. The second also began abroad—this time in Bogotá, Colombia, where Alexsandr Dmitrevich Ogorodnik was serving as a secretary in the Soviet embassy.[70] According to one account Ogorodnik was an official "who changed from an idealistic Communist into a passionate anti-Communist," while another described him as the victim of a "honey trap" operation.[71] The latter account states that Ogorodnik was set up with a woman working for the CIA. The CIA subsequently photographed them in bed together and presented Ogorodnik with photographs. Along with the photographs he was given two choices—pass information to the CIA, or have the pictures wind up on the desk of his superiors. Given Soviet policies concerning unauthorized contact, sexual or otherwise, with foreigners, the consequences would include disgrace, reassignment to the Soviet Union, and the end of his career.[72]

Whatever the motivation, Ogorodnik became a CIA agent in 1974 and was assigned the code name TRIGON. By the time his tour ended in 1975, he had been thoroughly trained in espionage tradecraft. Upon his return to Moscow he managed to get a position in the Ministry's Global Affairs Department, "one of the few MFA sections the KGB trusts with sensitive intelligence" and "the repository of other exceedingly secret and revealing data."[73] The department would receive the year-end comprehensive report of each Soviet ambassador—a report analyzing the political situation, likely developments, and the Soviet standing in the country where he is stationed. The KGB residency is required to assist by contributing information and judgments based on the reports of its agents. In cases where the chief resident and the ambassador are on good terms, the chief resident often will make available virtually all the information obtained from his agent network. Examination of such reports could reveal Soviet views of the world and Soviet strengths and weaknesses in specific countries, allow inferences about Soviet intentions, and in some cases permit an estimation of the nature and extent of KGB penetrations.[74]

According to Barron's account, over the next twenty months TRIGON provided the CIA with microfilm of hundreds of secret Soviet documents, including ambassadorial reports. The basic content of the reports was circulated to the White House, the NSC, and the State Department. By the summer of 1977 the KGB became aware that the Soviet Union was suffering a loss of secret information and eventually narrowed the potential sources to include Ogorodnik's department. The initial surveillance and analysis of its employees produced no clues, but KGB-installed television cameras captured Ogorodnik photographing documents with a tiny U.S.-made camera.[75]

Barron's account differs substantially from that of Soviet defector Arkady Shevchenko. According to Shevchenko, he was informed by a colleague that the KGB had begun to suspect the loyalty of a secretary in a Soviet embassy in Latin America. The KGB did nothing to alert TRIGON while keeping track of his contacts with the CIA. What appeared to be a routine transfer back to Moscow was arranged, and the suspect was assigned to the Policy Planning Department of the ministry—an office with wide access to coded cable traffic. Over the next several months, according to Shevchenko's account, he was closely watched until discovered passing documents to a CIA agent.[76]

According to a third account, which accords partially with Shevchenko's, not long after Ogorodnik's return to Moscow there were signs that the KGB may have turned Ogorodnik. The quality of his information began to decline and no longer agreed with that of other sources. Then in April 1977 TRIGON submitted a copy of a cable allegedly from the Soviet ambassador to the United States, Anatoly Dobrynin, to the Politburo. The cable described an alleged breakfast meeting between Dobrynin and Henry Kissinger in which Kissinger derided then President Jimmy Carter as a prisoner of his own human-rights illusions in dealing with the Soviet Union, and national security adviser Zbigniew Brzezinski as an "ideological dogmatist." Kissinger also is alleged to have told Dobrynin that he did not blame the Soviets for rejecting Carter's March 1977 SALT initiative that proposed drastic cuts in each side's nuclear arsenals and that the United States would not hold out for "equal aggregates" of strategic weapons. Further, the cable also said that Kissinger told Dobrynin that he still had some sources on the NSC and therefore expected to be kept up to date on developments that would be of interest to the Soviets.[77]

Not everyone in the intelligence community accepted that the cable indicated that TRIGON was under Soviet control. Indeed, it was the cause of a bitter dispute with some analysts, arguing that there was no Soviet motive for attempting to discredit Kissinger. Kissinger did meet with Dobrynin on that date; he denied saying any of the things quoted in the purported telegram but was vague about what actually was discussed, describing the talk as a "not very important conversation." "What could have been the point of going over Secretary Vance's proposals in Moscow, which had already been rejected a month before?" asked Kissinger.[78] Some intelligence officials were not convinced by Kissinger's denials. The CIA deputy chief of the Counterintelligence Staff prepared an operational analysis of the cable and concluded that "what Kissinger had done 'bordered on treason.'" As a result the Deputy Chief was transferred from his headquarters position and assigned overseas.[79]

It does seem likely, however, that by spring 1977 TRIGON was under some sort of suspicion. The "Kissinger cable" was his last contribution to the CIA. On July 15, 1977, the KGB arrested CIA officer Martha Peterson, who operated under embassy cover as a vice consul, at one of TRIGON's dead drops. Her cover position involved interviewing potential Soviet immigrants to the United States and helping American visitors with passport problems. According to the Soviet account she was caught in the act of stocking the dead drop "with cameras, gold Russian currency, instructions, and ampules of poison." In a significant departure from standard Soviet practice concerning the expulsion of those with diplomatic immunity, *Izvestiya* played up the case in a sensational manner.[80] The *Izvestiya* account stated that Peterson drove toward the center of Moscow on July 15, parked her car in a poorly lit area, and changed from her white dress into a black jumper and slacks. She then locked her car and got onto a city bus. Two stops later she transferred to a streetcar, then went down into a subway, and finally took a taxi. She left the taxi at a river embankment and, according to *Izvestiya*, "walked along an alley near a tennis court, waited until no one was around who could somehow be alerted to her, and hurried to the bridge."

There she put a cache into a chink in the stone of the bridge and was arrested.[81]

The TRIGON affair also touched Brzezinski's deputy David Aaron. Leaks to various newspapers suggested that TRIGON's identity had been blown by the indiscreet comments of a "senior official of the National Security Council" to a Romanian diplomat. It became clear in short order that the senior official was Aaron. However, an FBI investigation showed no wrongdoing by Aaron.[82]

TRIGON, of course, suffered most of all. All accounts suggest he committed suicide.[83] According to Barron's account, Ogorodnik upon being arrested admitted his guilt immediately and offered to cooperate completely. After undergoing preliminary questioning, TRIGON was led to a cell and given a desk, pen, and paper. Allegedly he then requested a particular pen from his apartment on the grounds that he had written with it for many years. Contained in the pen was a well-hidden pill that TRIGON swallowed, causing his death within ten seconds. Thus the KGB never determined how he communicated with the CIA in Moscow, all the information he passed on, or whether he had any co-conspirators.[84]

The most recent known penetration of the Soviet national security establishment involved a civilian involved in military research. Thus, *Pravda* reported on September 22, 1985, that

> The USSR State Security Committee has uncovered and arrested an agent of the U.S. secret service—A. G. Tolkachev, a staff member of one of Moscow's research institutes. The spy was caught in the act during an attempt to pass on secret defense materials to Paul M. Stombaugh, an officer of the U.S. CIA, who acted under the cover of the second secretary of the U.S. Embassy in Moscow.

> It has been established that the U.S. secret service
> provided Tolkachev with miniature cameras of a
> special design, by means of which he photo-
> graphed secret documents, as well as with means
> of cryptography, codes, ciphers, quick-acting two-
> way communication radio apparatus, and other
> equipment for espionage work. . . .[85]

Tolkachev was arrested in June 1985 (and subsequently executed) but announcement of his arrest was withheld until after
the CIA officer, Edward L. Howard, who apparently told the
KGB of Tolkachev's role as an American spy, had been exposed
and fled the United States. Howard had been trained to become
Tolkachev's case officer for a prospective assignment to Moscow
but had been discharged by the agency when a routine poly-
graph indicated drug use and petty theft.[86]

An electronics expert at a military-aviation institute in Moscow, Tolkachev was, according to one source, "one of our most
lucrative agents," who "saved us billions of dollars in development costs" by telling the United States about the nature of
Soviet military aviation efforts. The information made it signifi-
cantly easier for the United States to develop systems to counter
Soviet advances.[87]

Specifically, over a period of several years, Tolkachev passed
on information concerning Soviet research efforts in electronic
guidance and countermeasures, advanced radar, and "stealth" or
radar-avoidance technologies. In addition, Tolkachev may have
been the key to U.S. discovery of the large phased-array radar
being built at Krasnoyarsk in violation of the ABM Treaty.[88]
United States satellite photography of the radar was obtained,
according to one expert, only after "we were told where to look."

Other indications of U.S. human intelligence activity in the
Soviet Union have appeared from time to time, although it is difficult to determine the accuracy of the indications. Thus, it has
been reported that human sources provided information on the
deployment and/or storage of SS-16 missiles as well as the dam-

age done to the Soviet Northern Fleet from an enormous explosion in May 1984. Also, there are the intriguing comments made by Secretary of Defense Harold Brown and his deputy for research and engineering, William Perry, during the Carter administration that the United States had "other ways" of monitoring Soviet weapons programs besides technical collection systems. Perhaps one or more of the many Soviet students who come to the United States to take courses in the physical sciences and mathematics were recruited by the CIA and went on to work in the defense industry.[89]

And in 1982 four Soviet scientists were arrested on charges of spying for the CIA.[90] In addition, there have been several expulsions of U.S. diplomats—whether for actual espionage activities, for retaliatory purposes, or both is difficult to tell. Thus, Richard Osborne, a first secretary at the U.S. Embassy, was declared persona non grata for "actions incompatible with diplomatic status." *Izvestiya* reported the he had been caught with portable electronic equipment that was intended for "transmission of espionage information via the U.S. Marisat communications satellites." Subsequently, a U.S. vice consul in Leningrad was expelled for espionage activities. The vice consul had been accused of picking up a "spy container" outside Leningrad.[91]

The Ukrainian edition of *Pravda* of October 21, 1985, named several U.S. diplomats it alleged were involved in espionage activities. It charged that Lieutenant Colonel James Furleigh "attempted to photograph industrial works at Kiev while pretending to take a picture of his wife on a bridge." Then "deputy military attaché William Henry and his wife, Deborah, also tried without any more success to photograph the same installations." The same issue also accused Colonel William Halloran and his assistant, Roy Peterson, who were arrested at Rovno in the Ukraine, of photographing military installations and the assistant to the air force attaché of attempting to photograph the port area of Odessa in the guise of taking a family snapshot.[92]

Whatever the validity of the Soviet charges, it is certain that CIA representatives at the U.S. Embassy and consulates in the Soviet Union, as well as the military attachés, continue to seek to acquire intelligence of interest to Washington. The value of a major penetration, such as Penkovskiy, can be immense. U.S. inability to penetrate the inner workings of the Soviet government, particularly at the higher levels of political and military policy formulation, by technical means often leaves the United States in the dark concerning political battles and personnel changes. Thus, in December 1983 when Soviet General Secretary Yuri Andropov had dropped out of sight for health reasons, a CIA official said that there was no "inside dope, just a lot of speculation."[93] Likewise, Paul Henze, a former CIA official, commented that ". . . we know so little that it's like watching the water surge and roil without seeing the sharks fighting beneath the surface. . . . Only when a dead one floats to the surface do we learn something about what's happening."[94]

However, in the absence of a Penkovskiy or other major penetration, technical intelligence provides by far the major portion (in terms of value) of the information acquired, particularly concerning Soviet weapons systems. Given the difficulty of penetrating into secret Soviet military facilities with any consistency, human sources must, over the long term, take a backseat to collection from ground stations, from the air, from the sea, and from the final frontier—space.

III.

Ground Stations

*T*he development of Morse code, radio, and other forms of electronic communication allowed individuals and states to communicate across vast distances. It also allowed those interested in what was communicated to intercept the signals transmitted in the ether and use them to their advantage, as the United States and Great Britain did in World War II.

In the absence of hostilities between the United States and the U.S.S.R. there still was a vast array of communications that U.S. intelligence analysts would find most helpful in analyzing Soviet plans, policies, and capabilities. Included would be communications among the Soviet leadership and between and within: the Moscow headquarters of the Ministry of Defense and military districts, air and missile bases; ground controllers and aircraft; weapons design bureaus and higher authorities; weapons test centers and later, space launch centers; and the Ministry of Internal Affairs in Moscow and its regional offices.

In addition to communications signals there were the electronic emissions of operational radars and aircraft as well as of missiles undergoing testing. Such emissions could reveal the existence and operating frequencies of the radars (permitting them to be targeted, jammed, or avoided during war), as well as the capabilities of the aircraft and missiles. Additionally, the characteristics of Soviet nuclear weapons could be estimated based on the electromagnetic pulse, seismic, acoustic, and hydroacoustic signals generated by nuclear test explosions.

Further, the United States was able to use radar for monitoring Soviet air and naval activity in areas close to both the United States and the U.S.S.R. As noted earlier, radar, an acronym for *ra*dio *d*etection *a*nd *r*anging, involves transmitting a signal in a particular direction; if the signal bounces back, an object has been detected. The speed at which it bounces back indicates the distance of the object. The more advanced the radar the more detail can be determined about the object in question.

To gather the communication and noncommunication signals as well as to conduct radar surveillance the United States began, in the late 1940s, to establish a vast collection network using ground stations, aircraft, ships and submarines, and ultimately satellites. The ground stations have been located in the United States and around the periphery of the Soviet Union—in Europe, the Near East, the Middle East, and Asia. This network has changed its composition over the years, often reflecting U.S. political fortunes in a particular nation as well as the development of new technologies for intelligence collection, such as satellites.

One of the earliest postwar ground-based surveillance sites was at Gambell, St. Lawrence Island, just to the east of the U.S.-Russia 1867 Convention line and less than fifty miles from Soviet territory—specifically, the Chukotski Peninsula. The primary purpose of the site was radar surveillance of Soviet shipping in the Chaplina Narrows, with the detection of Soviet air activity as a secondary mission.[1]

In 1949 the first target, a ship, was not detected as moving beyond Chaplina until July 16, and for several periods during the year the radar had been inoperative due to a lack of spare parts. On May 11, 1950, the site was reactivated and resumed operations. It was believed by the Alaska Air Command that the surveillance of the Bering Strait would, over a period of years, help to determine the extent of North Sea shipping and permit an assessment of Soviet activities in northeastern Siberia and along the Arctic coast.[2]

On June 11, 1950, the first indication of shipping traffic through the Chaplina Narrows occurred when the radar detected two targets, probably cargo vessels, northbound in the vicinity of Cape Chaplina. The first radar targets showing positive signs of proceeding past Chaplina were blips on June 27, which faded well off to the east of the cape on northbound courses. All were classified as probables.[3]

Subsequently, a study of the project indicated that its potential value was great. At the same time the study noted that the lightweight radar in use was inadequate for effective coverage— the range was so limited that detection might easily be avoided both by sea and in the air. In addition, the station's proximity to northeastern Siberia subjected it to possible neutralization by countermeasures or by a raiding party. It was recommended that the project be continued, operated on a full-time basis, and the equipment upgraded or replaced by more powerful equipment.[4]

In addition to the radar at Gambell, Alaska also was the home of the Air Force's 3rd Radio Squadron Mobile—a field unit of the Air Force Security Service. Reactivated on November 12, 1949, the unit consisted of a headquarters (at Fort Richardson) with nine officers, fifty-eight airmen, and three detachments. Detachment A at Davis AFB, Adak, had a contingent of four officers and one hundred airmen as well as twelve antennas—nine Class B and three Class A rhombic-type antennas.[5] A rhombic antenna consists of a wire several feet off the ground and attached to four posts in the shape of a diamond. Each side is approximately ten feet long, and at one end the wire is connected to a coaxial cable that runs underground to a centrally located operations building.[6] The detachment's mission was the reception of skywave signals over moderate to long distances, with the signal strengths varying from very weak to very strong.[7]

England might not seem to be a particularly desirable location for monitoring the Soviet Union. However, the nature of radio signal propagation made England, particularly in the 1950s, a very desirable location. Radio waves transmitted at low frequency (LF) or very low frequency (VLF) (as opposed to those transmitted at UHF, SHF, or VHF) will travel past the curvature of the earth, bounce off the atmosphere, and return to earth, where they can be picked up. Hence, LF signals that began in the Soviet Union could easily wind up in England. In the 1950s before the use of UHF, SHF, and VHF, such radio signals constituted the bulk of signals employed by the Soviet government and military.

One of the earliest sites in Britain was the one established in May 1952 at Kirknewton, Scotland, a small farm village approximately thirteen miles southwest of Edinburgh. Originally it was a British base—built in 1939 to operate as a satellite station for RAF Turnhouse. It never became operational as an airfield due to the discovery of a severe downdraft at the end of the runway. When it became known to the commander of the 10th Radio Squadron Mobile at Chicksands, near Bedford, that the USAF Security Service desired to deploy an RSM (Radio Squadron Mobile) in the Scotland area, he sent a site survey team to Kirknewton in December 1951. The team tested reception characteristics and concluded that Kirknewton would be an excellent site.[8]

Thus on May 23, 1952, the 37th Radio Squadron Mobile became operational at Kirknewton, the station being designated USA-55, with two sloping "V" antennas to conduct intercept operations. The two antennas constituted merely an interim capability until a permanent antenna field could be constructed.[9] Of course, the stations interception mission was highly classified, and it was given a cover as a communications relay station. The cover did not deceive knowledgeable observers such as members of the local populace who had a background in such operations, since there were no transmission towers at the facility, only interception towers. (The products of USA-55's operations were sent by landline.)

Over the next year much experimentation took place—trying different antennas and gauging performance. Thus it was found that some of the rhombic antennas installed did not provide optimum performance, and a fan antenna installed in October 1952 provided only fair reception. A rhombic antenna installed on September 30, 1952, was found to be "very satisfactory."[10] By June 1953 the interim antenna field consisted of five antennas—

two fan-type, two sloping V, and one rhombic. All the antennas would eventually be dismantled and replaced by the eleven rhombic antennas that would constitute the antenna field.[11]

The personnel at Kirknewton operated under harsh conditions during that first year. The entire complex consisted of three or four buildings. There was neither heating nor showers at the barracks. Neither wood nor coal was available to burn in the stoves, and a major activity of the men stationed there was finding something to burn. Since Scotland in fall and winter could hardly be confused with the tropics, sleeping could be quite uncomfortable, as was the walk back from the officers' bathhouse after a wintertime shower.[12]

Toward the end of 1953 Kirknewton saw a major influx of personnel—thirty-five radio-interception operators in October and another forty-four in December, resulting in an overall contingent at the end of December of seventeen officers and 463 airmen.[13] Additionally, a new operations building and permanent antennas were being constructed by the end of the year.[14]

Interception operations originally focused solely on voice messages and messages transmitted in Morse code. Thus Kirknewton monitored naval traffic—both military and commercial—along the coast of the Kola Peninsula in the vicinity of Murmansk. USA-55 also intercepted communications concerning the construction of new Soviet radar systems and Soviet air movements. Information about the latter was designated by the classified code word FROTH. "Froth" was a word Kirknewton's cleared personnel were not to utter outside security-controlled areas. Employees of the 37th RSM might comment about the head on their beer but not the Froth. Indeed, when an uncleared cook told some cleared airmen that, as a result of a newly acquired blender, they could have froth on their orange juice, the reaction was stunned and embarrassed silence.[15]

USA-55 moved on to broaden its range of interception targets over the next few years. By 1955 it was monitoring the new Soviet radars that were coming on line to replace those the Soviets had obtained from the United States and Britain under Land-Lease. It also was conducting FAX (facsimile) interception operations, intercepting pictures and information transmitted on Soviet domestic news lines to outlying areas. Additionally, Kirknewton was heavily involved in the interception of multiplex radioteletype signals; to facilitate this, an all-Cyrillic-character teletype machine was employed.[16]

Over the years the size of the Kirknewton contingent decreased to three hundred and its mission shifted. Its major targets became commercial nonradio links between major European cities. The station also was partly responsible for the security of the Washington–Moscow "hot line" as the cable passed through Kirknewton en route to Moscow. On August 1, 1966, USA-55 was closed.[17]

Another early SIGINT (signals intelligence) station in Britain directed at the Soviet Union was Chicksands Priory—a medieval building and country estate near Bedford. Chicksands was first employed for interception in 1941, when it was taken over by hundreds of RAF wireless interceptors. The RAF proceeded to string dozens of aerials across the two-thousand-acre estate and discovered it to be a remarkably good site for intercepting German communications from Berlin, Poland, and the Eastern Front. It became the most productive interception site for top-level German High Command communications.[18]

When the U.S. Air Force sought its own base for the interception of strategic signals from the Soviet Bloc, Chicksands Priory was given to it. Thus by 1952 the 10th Radio Squadron Mobile (subsequently the 6950th Electronic Security Group) was installed at Chicksands under the supervision of the USAF Security Service (subsequently the USAF Electronic Security Command). This time the target was the Soviet Air Force. Specifically, the voice communications of Soviet pilots with each other and with ground controllers were plucked out of the air by the Chicksands antennas.[19]

Over the years Chicksands expanded both in capability and targets. In 1964 Chicksands, along with a similar installation at San Vito dei Normanni in Italy, received AN/FLR-9 "Elephant Cage" antennas.[20] The AN/FLR-9 consists of three arrays, each made up of a ring of antenna elements around a circular reflecting screen. In the middle of the triple array is a central building, which contains the electronic equipment for forming the directional beams for monitoring and direction-finding. The entire system is about nine hundred feet in diameter. An underground tunnel connects the antenna array to Building 600, the heavily guarded Chicksands operations center.[21]

Chicksands' expanded mission focused on the military and diplomatic signals of West European nations, particularly France. Inside the Chicksands facility are rooms and compartments with interception and direction-finding allocated to different mission targets. Signs hang above the heads of coordinating "mission supervisors," which included, in the early 1970s, "France," "Czechoslovakia," and "Civil Aircraft." On each of the three daily shifts, about two hundred operators staff interception positions. Their analysis operations are supported by a large IBM computer, which runs automatic Morse and telex receivers that require little human intervention. With over 1,750 military staff alone, Chicksands is the USAF's largest nonflying base in Britain.[22]

A facility at Edzell in eastern Scotland plays an important role in U.S. monitoring of Soviet naval movements in the North Sea area as well as of Warsaw Pact activities. An RAF airfield until 1958, it was host to a U.S. Air Force radio facility from 1951 to 1958 and became the site of a Naval Security Group activity in 1960.[23]

The number of personnel at Edzell has grown over the years, and by the end of September 1987 it is to have thirty-eight officers, 712 enlisted men, and 261 civilians.[24] The civilians may largely be NSA cryptanalysts who work in the 140-person operations center, with its more than forty million dollars' worth of equipment.[25]

The main interception equipment is an AN/FLR-12 circular antenna system 1,640 feet in diameter and sixty-six feet high. The official guide issued to new Edzell personnel states that the base's mission is to "operate an HF-DF facility and provide communications and related support, including communications security and communications manpower assistance to navy and other Department of Defense elements within the [northeast Atlantic] area."[26] In Congressional hearings it was said of Edzell that "radio receivers are operated here that can listen for American or foreign broadcasts from all directions."[27]

One target of the AN/FLR-12 antenna will be Soviet naval activity in the North Sea area—detecting the existence of those movements, characterizing the ships involved, and intercepting their communications. The other may well be land-based Warsaw Pact activity, including troop and armor movement in Eastern Europe and the U.S.S.R.

At present there appears to be plans to add a new surveillance facility, at Orford Ness in Suffolk, on Englands' North Sea coast. Orford Ness previously was the site of an over-the-horizon (OTH) radar called COBRA MIST, which operated between 1971 and 1973. COBRA MIST was run by the Air Force Security Service and was believed to monitor ICBM tests and launches. The radar to be developed under the name COLD WITNESS will have a 1,860-mile range and will "enable the United States to monitor military movements over a [three-million-square-mile] wide area of the North Atlantic Norwegian and Barents seas, and around such key Soviet centers as the Kola Peninsula. . . ." This surveillance of Soviet ports, military installations, and naval movements apparently is intended to aid, among other things, the targeting of ground- and sea-launched cruise missiles.[28]

To the west of the northern Soviet Union, Norway also provides a home for several interception and nuclear detection stations targeted on the Soviet Union and the surrounding ocean area. The stations are operated by personnel of the Norwegian Security Service but were erected by NSA and operated for them. Further, according to a former U.S. intelligence official, Victor Marchetti, CIA and NSA personnel were regularly on assignment at those stations, although no U.S. personnel are assigned there anymore.[29]

One of the stations is at Vadsø, a small fjord town in Norway's Arctic region and close to the Soviet border. Somewhere between several hundred and fifteen hundred of the town's five thousand residents are said to work at the interception station.[30] There are four interception locations at Vadsø. The principal high-frequency (HF) listening equipment is a 492-foot diameter array of monopole antennas, within which is a further array of monopoles. About two miles to the southeast is a smaller circular antenna array. There the outer ring is eighty-two feet in diameter and consists of twelve dipoles, while the inner ring consists of six dipoles. There is a hut in the center of the array. Its location apart from the main HF site may mean that it is used for transmission rather than for reception. The location of the antenna arrays on the northern shore of Varangerfjord gives them uninterrupted oversea propagation paths all the way to the Soviet Union.[31]

In addition to the circular arrays there are two VHF/UHF interception sites in the Vadsø area. The main site is at the summit of a 397-foot hill. The site is the home of a variety of VHF/UHF antennas known as Yagis, log-periodic arrays (LPAs), vertical wire dipoles, and broad-band dipoles, the latter backed by corner reflectors. Four of the antennas are pointed in the direction of Murmansk and the associated complex of naval and air facilities—one toward Wickel; two to the coast; and one northeast, toward the Barents Sea. The antennas at the smaller site also point toward the Soviet Union. It has been suggested that the Yagi antennas at the main site are intercepting emissions from a Soviet troposcatter communications system similar to the NATO Ace High system. It has also been reported that Vadsø has the capability to intercept voice communications from Soviet pilots down to their ground controllers.[32]

Also in the very north of Norway are Viksjøfjell and Vardø. At Viksjøfjell, on a 1,476-foot-high hill only three miles from the Soviet border, is a concrete tower with a geodesic radome. On the side of the tower facing toward the Soviet border is a semi-cylindrical extension apparently made of the same material as the radome and surmounted by a VHF log-periodic antenna. The dome itself is surmounted by a VHF Adcock direction-finding antenna. The Viksjøfjell facility appears to be a very sophisticated VHF installation, and it might be presumed that the dome con-

tains a movable dish antenna that can either be constantly rotated in a scanning mode or in a tracking mode. Installations of
this type are capable of monitoring all kinds of VHF-SHF frequencies, including ground-based and air-based radars, communications, and missile command and control links.[33]

At Vardø there is a tower identical to the one at Viksjøfjell
except that the external direction-finding and log-periodic antennas are absent. Vardø can intercept signals from Plesetsk, a major
Soviet missile testing and space center. It has also been suggested that another likely target is the telemetry from Soviet
SLBM tests in the Barents Sea. The Soviet Union tests the SS-
N-18 missile as well as the Typhoon-based SS-N-20 missile from
the White Sea and the Barents Sea. The Viksjøfjell station apparently was established in 1972, the Vardø one in 1971, at the same
time that an earlier submarine-launched missile, the SS-N-8, became operational.[34]

At Skage (in Namdalen) and at Randaberg (near Stavanger,
on Norway's western coast) there are arrays similar to the smaller
of the Vadsø arrays. These arrays probably are used mainly to
intercept HF communications from Soviet ships, submarines, and
long-range marine reconnaissance aircraft in the Norwegian Sea.
Probably the two stations are operated as pairwise units to allow
triangulation of emitter locations.[35]

Norway also serves as the home of nuclear explosion detection
stations. Until 1975 a detachment of the Air Force Technical Applications Center (AFTAC)—the organization responsible for operating the U.S. Atomic Energy Detection System—was in the Lappish
community of Karasjok. At the top of a defense station were two
large cylindrical tanklike structures, the upper halves of which
were made of transparent material. Apparently they housed optical
sensors—a fisheye lens and two plates of photosensitive material.
In addition, there was an arrangement of galvanized pipes that
appeared to be a manifold for a microbargraph—a sophisticated
barometer that records small short-term variations in air pressure,
variations that indicate the overhead passage of acoustic pressure
waves in the atmosphere, waves generated by nuclear explosions
within the atmosphere.[36]

There also was a vertical whip antenna that may well have helped detect atmospheric explosions by detecting the VLF signals that are sensitive to such explosions. In addition there were three sensors connected to the main site by overhead cables, which may have been microbargraphs capable of detecting the noise made by missile launches at distances on the order of 620 miles (approximately the distance of the Soviet launch site and test facility at Plesetsk) as well as detecting the reentry of largish bodies from space.[37]

A still-operational array, NORSAR (Norwegian Seismic Array), is run under a cooperative arrangement between the United States and Norway. The array is in southeastern Norway, north of Oslo and near the town of Hamar. NORSAR's location places it on the same continental plate as the Kazakh Soviet Socialist Republic, home of the Semipalatinsk nuclear weapons testing area. The result is an uncomplicated vibration travel path from Semipalatinsk, over twenty-five hundred miles away, to NORSAR—a prime requirement for producing high-confidence estimates of the yield of a nuclear explosion. NORSAR also is only fifteen hundred miles from Novaya Zemlya, a large island in the Barents Sea that also is used by the Soviets for nuclear weapons testing.

Since 1970, when it began operation, NORSAR has detected about a hundred thousand earthquakes and more than five hundred presumed nuclear explosions. A teleseismic array, its optimum performance occurs when the seismic event takes place 1,860 to sixty-two hundred miles away. Thus NORSAR also is able effectively to detect U.S. nuclear tests in Nevada. The array itself is made up of twenty-two subarrays, seven of which are operational. Each subarray is approximately six miles in diameter and consists of one long-period and six short-period seismometers, all placed in vaults or shallow boreholes with depths ranging from ten to forty-nine feet. The long-period seismometers measure ground motion in the vertical, horizontal north–south and horizontal east–west directions, while the short-period seismometer senses vertical ground motion. The recorded earth motions are transmitted via trenched cables to a central terminal vault at the subarray center and then to the NORSAR Data Processing Center at Kjeller, just north of Oslo, for analysis. The data also can be transmitted by satellite back to the United States.[38]

A newer facility, the Norwegian Regional Seismic Array (NORESS), opened in June 1985. Located about sixty miles northeast of Oslo, NORESS was designed and constructed on a cooperative basis by the U.S. and Norwegian governments. Data from each of the twenty-five sensors in the array's four concentric rings are sent via fiber optics to a hub. The data are collected at the hub and then retransmitted to four receiving stations. The hub is connected by telephone link to the Norwegian analysis center in Kjeller. The same information is sent via satellite to U.S. sites in Virginia, California, and New Mexico. NORESS's capabilities were demonstrated in July 1985, when the array detected a Soviet test of a 0.25-kiloton nuclear device at Semipalatinsk.[39]

One U.S. ally whose territory offered an almost ideal location for monitoring stations was Turkey. On October 2, 1951, the U.S. Air Forces Europe (USAFE) first proposed the establishment of signals intelligence ground stations in Turkey. Ten days later, Air Force headquarters in Washington gave USAFE permission to examine the possibility further.[40] Fourteen months later, on January 13, 1953, a Department of Defense Site Survey Team headed by Colonel Arthur C. Cox of the Air Force Security Service arrived in Ankara "to locate a site conducive to the creation of Radio Squadron Mobile in Turkey."[41]

By the mid-1950s the USAFSS effort to establish ground-based sites in Turkey, code-named Project PENN, had resulted in the establishment of sites at Karamursel, on the southeast shore of the Sea of Marmara, and Samsun, on the Black Sea coast. The unit assigned to Turkey, the 75th Radio Squadron Mobile, had its main operating headquarters at a site adjacent to the Karamursel airstrip and by 1956 had a contingent of twenty-seven officers and 597 airmen.[42]

Karamursel was a peasant farming village with a population of between five thousand and ten thousand. It was extremely rural, with muddy streets—a throwback to the nineteenth century and a dreadful shock to those Americans who had been stationed in Ankara or more modern Turkish towns. It was also, according to a former naval officer who had been stationed there, "not a place for dependents." Pregnant wives were sent to Ankara for the final three months of their pregnancy.[43]

Despite its location in the backwoods, Karamursel was a station of major importance in the 1960s. By 1965 it was under the command of the Naval Security Group Command and possessed a full antenna field. Included were rhombic antennas and a AN/FLR-9, the latter installed in about 1964. The targets of those antennas included the voice and Morse communications of the Soviet Black Sea air and naval elements—the Black Sea Air Force, the Black Sea Naval Aviation, the Black Sea Navy (surface and subsurface). Encrypted messages were sent back to NSA headquarters at Fort Meade for analysis.[44]

Information from Karamursel could provide the first data on new Soviet naval systems and tactics, since the Black Sea was the Soviet training ground where new equipment and operational doctrines were tested. In addition to its monitoring of naval activity, Karamursel also monitored various Soviet missile and space launches. Its atomic clock allowed Karamursel to monitor missile telemetry. Karamursel also monitored the conversation between Soviet Premier Aleksei Kosygin and Cosmonaut Vladimir M. Komarov in which Kosygin tried to console the soon-to-die Komarov—who had been informed by Soviet ground controllers that the braking parachutes designed to return his spacecraft safely back to earth were malfunctioning and he was doomed.[45]

By the early 1970s the facility's main function was to track Soviet naval traffic in the western Black Sea and the area surrounding the Dardanelles. In 1975 Karamursel was shut down by Turkey, along with all other U.S. sites in Turkey, in response to a Congressional embargo of arms sales to Turkey. In 1977 it was decided not to continue operating Karamursel but to transfer command of its four officers and fifty-seven enlisted men to Sinop, on the Black Sea coast seventy-eight miles northeast of Samsun. Thus, whereas the other bases resumed operations in 1978 the Karamursel facility never was reopened.[46]

Samsun, on the Black Sea coast, was another site opened in the mid-1950s. By mid-1955 an AN/FPS-17 radar built by General Electric had begun operating at Samsun. Almost at the same time Soviet ICBM tests commenced at Kapustin Yar. The radar was the result of the lobbying of Trevor Gardner, the Air Force Assistant Secretary for Research and Development, who believed that the United States had to exploit every conceivable intelligence method to track Soviet missile programs and who fought back opposition from the military over such projects. Once Gardner persuaded the Air Force of the potential value of the project, it was quickly approved by President Eisenhower.[47]

With its initial range of about a thousand miles, the AN/FPS-17 could detect and track the intermediate-range missiles fired to the southeast toward the Afghan border and intercontinental-range missiles fired eastward on a heading of about seventy degrees to the Pacific Ocean in the area around Vladivostok in Siberia. The data provided by the radar about the Soviet IRBM program was fairly complete and included the missiles' speed, attitude, track, and approximate range. As a result of this collection activity the United States detected a significant shift from the irregular pattern of experimental test firings to a regular five-month pattern—indicating a switch to production.[48]

Detection of tests of the longer-range multistage ICBM along the seventy-degree track toward the Pacific began in late 1956. A variety of shots were recorded, including stage-separation tests, maximum-altitude attempts, and finally long-range firings impacting about a thousand miles from the launch site. Tests that began in the summer of 1957 extended beyond the thousand-mile range of the AN/FPS-17 and included eight tests during June, July, and August along the Siberian track. As a result the radar was modified to increase its range to three thousand miles at the extreme altitudes.[49] The present status of the Samsun site is uncertain, as it was not mentioned in a 1980 U.S.-Turkish agreement concerning the bases. It is possible that it has been deactivated, with its collection activities taken over by other sites in Turkey or by space-based collection systems.

Sinop (or, more accurately, Diogenes Station) also began operating in the mid-1950s. Sinop is a fishing port and farm center with a population of just over eighteen thousand people. The station is two miles west of the town and is a three-hundred-acre facility on a bleak seven-hundred-foot hill at the end of a peninsula. Its huge white radar domes and microwave antennas are clearly visible from sea and air. On November 3, 1978, the station officially became a joint U.S.-Turkish installation, and Turkish and American flags fly over the station. The Turkish Army commander at the base in 1978 described its function as "observation and control of the opposite bloc" and stressed that the observations were directed at technical and economic as well as military developments.[50]

The 450 Americans, 125 military personnel, and 340 Turkish civilians at the base are involved in HF and VHF monitoring of Soviet air and naval activity in the Black Sea area and Soviet missile testing activities.[51] The monitoring of Soviet air and naval activity can be a rather "boring job. . . . A morse operator, for instance, just sits there in front of a radio receiver with headphones, and a typewriter copying morse signals."[52]

The single most important U.S. intelligence facility in Turkey is the one at Pirinclik Air Base—a satellite operation of Diyarbakir Air Station. Located on a rocky plateau in southeastern Turkey, Pirinclik had its operations suspended from 1974 to 1978. During that time U.S. housekeeping personnel rotated one radar dish to prevent roller bearing damage while the Turks locked up a key piece of radar equipment to make sure the radar was inoperative.[53]

The base resumed operations on November 3, 1979, with its two radar antennas fixed permanently toward the northeast, where the Soviet border lies 180 miles away. The electronic beams of the radar operate through a natural "duct" in the mountains around the plateau, picking up Soviet missiles and space launches as they rise above the horizon. The radar can detect an object one meter in diameter up to five thousand miles away. The AN/FPS-17 detection radar operates in tandem with an AN/FPS-79 tracking radar. After the detection radars indicate that a missile launch or space shot has taken place, the AN/FPS-79 "swings its white, round face in a noiseless arc in the same direction, ready to track the missiles along their course."[54] In addition to detecting and tracking launches from Tyuratam and Kapustin Yar via radar, the presence of associated

VHF and UHF antennas allows the interception of communications associated with missile tests. The antennas also can be used to intercept other communications, such as those of a Soviet tank commander. The equipment underwent upgrading in 1979—both because it had been neglected since 1973 and because Turkey then represented the only nation close to the U.S.S.R. from which the United States could monitor Soviet missile tests.[55]

The radars are operated largely by civilian technicians from the contractor, General Electric. In addition to the seventy contractor personnel there are about 145 Air Force personnel, mostly enlisted people. Few of them are permitted in the top-secret radar control rooms. Rather, they are more likely to operate the communications facilities that transmit the data via the Defense Satellite Communications System (DSCS) back to Washington.[56]

Also of importance is a seismic monitoring facility at Belbasi run by Detachment 301 of AFTAC. Located near Ankara at the Anatolian Plateau in central Turkey, the station monitors Soviet underground nuclear tests at the Semipalatinsk testing facility over two thousand miles away.[57]

The U.S. installations on Turkish soil have provided a basis for the Turkish government to extract concessions from the United States or to punish the United States for its policies with regard to Turkey, Greece, and Cyprus or military rule in Turkey. In late July 1975, when the U.S. Congress chose not to resume military assistance and sales to Turkey, the Turkish government declared the 1969 Defense Cooperation Agreement and related agreements invalid. It further declared that all U.S. installations were now under the "full control and custody of the Turkish armed forces." As we indicated earlier, Turkey proceeded to suspend intelligence collection operations at Karamursel, Sinop, Diyarbakir, and Belbasi.[58]

With the exception of Karamursel, the stations were reopened on October 8, 1978, after the lifting of the arms embargo, based on a one-year interim agreement. During the year a new Defense Cooperation Agreement was to be negotiated.[59] In fact, an agreement was not signed until 1980, but the facilities continued to operate under extensions of the interim agreement—extensions granted certainly because of U.S. willingness to offer a variety of military assistance.[60] Thus in November 1979 the United States agreed to provide Turkey with $450 million in direct military assistance, about $350 million in debt rescheduling and other financial credits, plus at least $30 million in equipment to enable Turkey to set up its own production line for 90mm "neat" artillery shells and 2.75-inch rockets.[61]

The willingness of the United States to provide such aid was a clear reflection of the practical, political, and psychological utility of the bases—with the latter two possibly being the crucial factors. In 1977 it was estimated that 25 percent of the hard information the United States had obtained regarding Soviet missile launches had come from the Turkish facilities and that some of that data could not be totally replaced by relocation or other means.[62] Some experts, however, said that much of the data only provided confirmation of information obtained from other sources. According to one expert, the information "would have been nice to have but, let's put it this way the peace of the world did not depend on it."[63] But the Turkish bases represented, after the fall of the Shah of Iran, the only bases near Soviet missile test centers—thus representing the only "visible" verification capability that could be pointed to by U.S. officials.

In the early 1950s Iran served as the location of several U.S. seismic monitoring devices. The operation, known as B/65, was conducted by AFOAT-1-section 1 of the Office of the Air Force Assistant for Atomic Energy (the predecessor organization to AFTAC). At the peak of the Iran operation the staff consisted of three officers and thirteen enlisted personnel, above and beyond those assigned to the Air Attaché's Office, which was employed as a cover by the AFOAT-1 personnel.[64]

However, by the end of 1952 the Shah's continuation in power seemed problematical. Thus the Air Force's Directorate of Intelligence expressed concern to the Air Attaché, Iran, over the security of the AFOAT-1 operation. As a result plans were made and implemented for the removal of seismic and acoustic instrumentation covertly located at four sites on a hunting preserve. However, to avoid the "impression of lack of confidence in the shah," the instruments were replaced by dummy boxes and the removal was made to appear as a routine overhaul.[65]

By the mid-1960s the United States, specifically the CIA, had established sites in Iran that were even more advantageous than the Turkish sites for monitoring the progress of the Soviet ICBM program. Whereas the Turkish bases would pick up the missile after it had climbed above 250 miles, the Iranian sites could pick up the missile after sixty miles. Thus the Iranian stations were capable of direct line-of-sight monitoring of the Soviet test site in Tyuratam and could pick up the telemetry from the last moments of the firing of the first missile stage. By contrast the Turkish sites could provide line-of-sight monitoring of the firing of the last moments of the second stage. This difference translated into a greater degree of confidence in the information gathered concerning missile dimensions and throw weight, although alternative means could be used to produce approximately the same results—specifically by watching the speed and trajectory of the missile at other points and by counting and "weighing" the objects that fell to earth.[66] In addition, the Iranian sites enjoyed a better "duct" for listening to ground and air communications.[67]

Altogether the United States maintained seven intelligence sites in Iran, probably including a facility for monitoring Soviet nuclear weapons tests. Two sites were near the western shore of the Caspian Sea, two near Klarabad in the middle of the Caspian's southern shore, two in the northeast, and one at Beshahr.[68] The two major Iranian posts—known as Tacksman I and Tacksman II—were at Kabkan, forty miles east of Meshed in northeastern Iran, and at Behshahr, on the southeastern corner of the Caspian Sea. The Kabkan facility was described by a CIA staff member as a twenty-first-century facility, with advanced electronic equipment. The facility itself was in stark contrast to the surrounding area—a remote mountainous locale inhabited by nomads. However, it was not the local environment that interested the CIA but rather the fact that Kabkan was only 650 miles south of the Tyuratam space center and ICBM test facility.[69]

The Behshahr facility consisted, by 1978, of four major units—a command center built into a hilltop, a radar antenna inside a thirty-foot-high dome, a radio monitoring device atop a steel tower, and a relay station pointed upward for communication with U.S. satellites. The radio monitoring device, built by Scientific Atlanta

Inc., was a Pedestal Model 310—a device with four eight-foot-long arms studded with quill-like protrusions. The arms were almost joined at the front and pointed toward the Caspian Sea. Nearby was Scientific Atlanta's "power with Pedestal Model 300-L," a dish-shaped device fifteen feet high that pointed upward. At the beginning of 1979 there were one hundred U.S. technicians who operated the equipment.[70] They wore no uniforms and probably were a combination of CIA and contractor personnel.

The Iranian outposts were considered important enough by President Carter that he told his ambassador to Iran, William Sullivan, that intelligence cooperation between the CIA and SAVAK should continue, despite the Shah's poor human rights record.[71] When the Shah did fall from power in 1979, the United States lost its Iranian outposts. Kabkan was besieged by militiamen, and twenty-two U.S. technicians were captured. Subsequently they were returned to the United States. On January 31 the U.S. technicians abandoned the post at Behshahr. The equipment was left running by the technicians—perhaps because the intelligence collected was automatically transmitted via satellite to the United States.[72]

While losing the stations was a serious blow, U.S. officials hoped to avoid compounding the disaster by loss of the equipment to "unfriendly" powers. Certainly the GRU would have paid a handsome amount to acquire the equipment. Indeed, one reason the Iranians did not shut off the electricity when they took over was fear of damaging the equipment and therefore their ability to sell it. An Iranian logistics supervisor at the facility stated, "We don't know who will get the equipment. Maybe Iran will sell it to someone. Maybe we will use it. It might hurt the machinery if we turned off the electricity."[73] Thus the U.S. ambassador to Iran was informed on February 12 that "preventing sensitive military and intelligence equipment from falling into unfriendly hands" was one of two immediate U.S. concerns.[74] According to one recent report the Soviet Union did get to examine the equipment.[75]

The loss of the stations was damaging in both an intelligence and a political sense. The Iranian sites had unique capabilities. A worst-case view was given by one official who said in 1979 that "Kabkan is not replaceable. No tricks are going to overcome that in the short run, and the short run could be three or four years. It is going to affect our capability on verification. I don't think people realize how important that base was, not just for SALT, but generally for keeping up with the Soviet missile program. It provided basic information on Soviet missile testing and development. You're talking about a pretty big loss. It's serious."[76] Additionally, coming after the public exposure of the loss of information concerning a satellite reconnaissance system, RHYOLITE, employed for intercepting Soviet telemetry, the loss further exacerbated concern over U.S. ability to verify the new SALT II Treaty. Thus the Secretary of State at the time, Cyrus Vance, has written, "The loss of the collection stations in Iran . . . was a serious setback, both in the sense of temporarily impairing our ability to check Soviet compliance with certain SALT limitations and in its impact on key senators, such as John Glenn, who had become the Senate's leading expert on monitoring."[77]

Among the most important present-day ground stations run by or for the United States are those at Qitai and Korla in China's northwestern Xinjiang Uighur Autonomous Region, which borders the Soviet Union. The United States first suggested setting up such posts in 1978, prior to the establishment of diplomatic relations. At first the Chinese were reluctant to agree, apparently concerned about cooperating too closely with the United States. The issue was raised again after the overthrow of the Shah in January 1979.[78] In an April 1979 meeting with a visiting U.S. Senate delegation, Peking PRC Vice Premier Deng Xiaoping indicated that China was willing to use U.S. equipment to "monitor Soviet compliance with a proposed new arms limitation treaty." Deng also indicated that the monitoring stations would have to be run by the Chinese and that the data would have to be shared with the PRC.[79]

The United States and the PRC reached a basic agreement in January 1980. According to a TASS report the selection of the Qitai and Korla sites resulted from an exercise called Karakoram-80. Actual operations began in the fall of 1980. The stations were constructed by the CIA's Office of SIGINT Operations (part of the agency's Directorate of Science and Technology), whose personnel trained the Chinese technicians and who periodically visit the stations to advise them as well as to service the equipment if required.[80]

The initial set of equipment allows interception of telemetry from Soviet missile test and space shots conducted from two major Soviet launch sites—at Tyuratam near the Aral Sea and at Sary Shagan near Lake Balkhash.[81] While somewhat farther from Tyuratam than the Iranian sites, the Chinese sites are closer to the Sary Shagan ABM test site. In the latter part of 1985 the United States began negotiations with the PRC to establish a seismic facility for monitoring nuclear tests. Chinese territory lies only 350 miles from the Semipalatinsk test site.[82]

Until the United States began to operate via China with intelligence facilities in Xinjiang, Japan clearly was the most important country in the Far East to the United States for purposes of monitoring the Soviet Union. Even with the establishment of the sites in China and the closing down or transfer to Japan of several sites, Japan still remains an important part of the U.S. ground-based collection program.

Many of the U.S. intelligence sites in Japan (e.g., Atsugi, Torri Station on Okinawa) are involved in ocean surveillance activities—either functioning as part of the land-based BULLSEYE DF network or serving as a base for the airborne activities of EA-3B, EP-3, and P-3 naval reconnaissance aircraft. Likewise, Kadena AB serves as a base for SR-71, P-3, and EP-3 aircraft.

Four miles northwest of Misawa AB is the "Hill"—a major U.S. signals intelligence collection site. On the Hill is a hundred-foot AN/FLR-9 antenna system, the largest in the world. The base and its antenna lie at the northern tip of Honshu Island, about five-hundred miles west of Vladivostok and four-hundred miles south of Sakhalin Island. Their importance is testified to by the presence of representatives of all four service cryptological authorities—the branches of the four military services that conduct signals intelligence and communications security operations for their parent services and the NSA. Thus there is a nine-hundred-person detachment from the Electronic Security Command (the 6920th Electronic Security Group) and a seven-hundred-person detachment from the Naval Security Group. And in addition to the two hundred representatives of the Army's Intelligence and Security Command there are eighty representatives of Company E, Marine Support Battalion.[83]

According to one account Misawa's AN/FLR-9 "can pick up a Russian television broadcast in Sakhalin or an exchange of insults between Chinese and Soviet soldiers on the Sino-Soviet border."[84] Of course, the various intelligence units stationed at Misawa are concerned with more than an exchange of insults. The INSCOM contingent focuses its attention on Soviet Army and General Staff activity, as well as on Afghanistan. The Navy contingent monitors Soviet shipping and the Soviet Navy. The Air Force detachment monitors, among other targets, the internal communications of the Soviet Air Defense Forces. Among the more sensitive signals monitored from Misawa are diplomatic communications, communications involving Soviet or Chinese strategic nuclear forces, and Soviet satellite communications.[85] In addition to the interception activities at Misawa, the base also is the home of AFTAC's Detachment 422.[86]

By the latter part of the 1970s radar surveillance from Gambell on St. Lawrence Island had ceased. However, a whole series of signals intelligence, ocean surveillance, and nuclear detection stations have emerged and have continued to operate, run by the Air Force Electronic Security Command, AFTAC, and the Naval Security Group Command. These sites include Adak, Attu, Burnt Mountain AFS, Elmendorf, and Eielson. In most cases the stations operate a variety of antennas for HF/DF, signals interception, or seismic monitoring equipment.

An exception to this is a base at Shemya Island. The island, described as a two-by-four "speck of desolation," is near the western tip of the Aleutian Islands chain, approximately four hundred miles across the Bering Sea from the Russian Eastern

Seaboard. Only 4¼ miles long and 2¼ miles across at its widest point, Shemya rises to only 280 feet, far less than similar islands in the area. Sometimes referred to as the "Black Pearl of the Pacific," Shemya is more commonly referred to as the "Land of Horizontal Snow." The island is a meteorological disaster area that receives an abnormally large amount of rain and snow, with three of every five days marked by one or the other.[87]

Despite its climate, Shemya was a perfect place to locate an intelligence radar to monitor Soviet ICBM tests. The island is only 480 nautical miles from Kamchatka Peninsula and the surrounding ocean area—the primary impact area for practically all Soviet ICBM tests. From Shemya such a radar would be able to gather information on missile trajectories, separation velocities, payload maneuvers, and signature data on reentry vehicles from missiles fired from both the Russian landmass and the primary SLBM launch at Nenonska.[88]

Thus, on February 1, 1972, USAF headquarters issued a directive defining the functions of the AN/FPS-108 radar to be located at Shemya and code-named COBRA DANE. The directive stated that COBRA DANE's primary purpose would be to acquire "precise radar metric and signature data on developing Soviet ballistic missile weapons systems for weapons system characteristic determination. The Soviet developmental test to Kamchatka and the Pacific Ocean provided the United States with the primary source for collection of these data early in the Soviet developmental programs." Secondary missions were to be early warning and tracking of space objects.[89]

When constructed, the COBRA DANE system would replace the radars then in operation—AN/FPS-17 detection and AN/FPS-80 tracking radars. The Air Force directive of February 1 stated that those systems were "not adequate to collect the required data on the current Soviet multiple R/V reentry vehicle systems and can be expected to be more inadequate when the test of the new Soviet systems (currently under preparation) commence."[90]

The COBRA DANE system consists of the new AN/FPS-108 radar facility, measuring eighty-seven by 107 feet at its base and approximately six stories or one hundred feet in height, plus an attached one-story Precision Measurement Equipment Laboratory (PMEL) measuring eighty-seven square feet. Both structures were built on a 230-foot-high bluff in the northwestern section of Shemya, where it overlooks the Bering Sea.[91]

The most important characteristic of COBRA DANE is that it is a phased array radar. To an observer depending only on his eyes or using binoculars, a phased array radar is simply a dormant structure—sort of an electronic pyramid. This is in sharp contrast to the older, more traditional radar dish "sweeping its beam of microwave radiation along the horizon in the search of distant objects." Rather, COBRA DANE consists of 15,360 radiating elements that occupy ninety-five feet in diameter on the radar's face, each of which emits a signal that travels in all directions. When the signals are all emitted at the same time, only targets in the immediate vicinity of the array's perpendicular axis are detectable. However, by successively delaying by a fraction of a wavelength one can "steer" the beam to detect objects away from the perpendicular axis.[92]

COBRA DANE achieved initial operating capability on July 13, 1977, when it was turned over to the U.S. Aerospace Defense Command. Previous to that time, when it was in its test phase it first detected and tracked a Soviet missile on July 28, 1976, and a second on August 26, 1976.[93] COBRA DANE can detect (with 99 percent probability) and track a basketball-size object at a range of two thousand miles with a 120-degree field of view extending from the northern half of Sakhalin Island to just short of the easternmost tip of the Soviet Union near the Bering Strait—although its ability to provide information on the size and shape is available only over a forty-four-degree range centered on the upper portion of Kamchatka.[94] (See Figure 1, page 98.) Whereas its predecessors, the AN/FPS-17 and AN/FPS-80, could detect and track only one object at a time, COBRA DANE can simultaneously track up to a hundred warheads when operating in an intelligence collection mode. COBRA DANE also can be employed in early warning and space surveillance; in these modes it can track up to three hundred incoming warheads and up to two hundred satellites, respectively.[95]

The major limitation of COBRA DANE is that the final near-earth trajectory of Soviet reentry vehicles is not visible to it due to line-of-sight constraints imposed by the curvature of the earth.[96] An associated sea-based radar named COBRA JUDY (discussed in Chapter VI) is used to collect those data.

Finally, there is the "Moscow ground station." It is well known that the Soviet Union makes extensive use of its diplomatic establishments in foreign countries for communications intelligence—particularly in the West and most especially in the United States. While the United States does not use its diplomatic establishments to the same extent, relying more on satellites, it does make use of its Moscow embassy for COMINT purposes.

At what point use of the Moscow embassy for COMINT purposes began is not apparent, but at least one operation had begun by August 1952. By that time the Army had located two miniature electronic search receivers in the Moscow embassy. Initial results of the part-time operation of these receivers was negligible. Further, a crucial piece of equipment in the AN/PPR-4 became inoperative and had to be returned to the United States for extensive maintenance.

A more recent operation, conducted in the late 1960s through 1971, involved the use of an antenna on the embassy to intercept the microwave radio/telephone conversations of Soviet Politburo members—including General Secretary Leonid Brezhnev, President Nikolai Podgorny and Premier Alexei Kosygin—as they drove around Moscow. The operation, code-named GAMMA GUPPY, was conducted by Army Security Agency unit USM-2 under the direction of the National Security Agency.[97]

The interception and reading of the messages was feasible because the phone messages were insufficiently "scrambled"—a means for preventing an interceptor of the signals from translating them into spoken words. Traffic from the interception operation was transmitted back to a special CIA facility a few miles from the agency's Langley, Virginia, headquarters.[98]

What the CIA personnel in that facility read were not the political and military secrets of the Soviet Union. According to a former intelligence official involved in GAMMA GUPPY, the CIA "didn't find out about, say, the invasion of Czechoslovakia. It was very gossipy—Brezhnev's health and maybe Podgorny's sex life." At the same time the official said that the operation "gave us extremely valuable information on the personalities and health of top Soviet leaders."[99]

The operation was terminated in late 1971 after a Jack Anderson column that stated that the United States was eavesdropping on the Soviet leaders and that the United States therefore was privy to a great deal of gossip concerning the ailments and habits of the Soviet leadership. According to Anderson, his source for the story told him that the Russians were already aware than their phone traffic was being monitored.[100]

Figure 1. Range of COBRA DANE radar

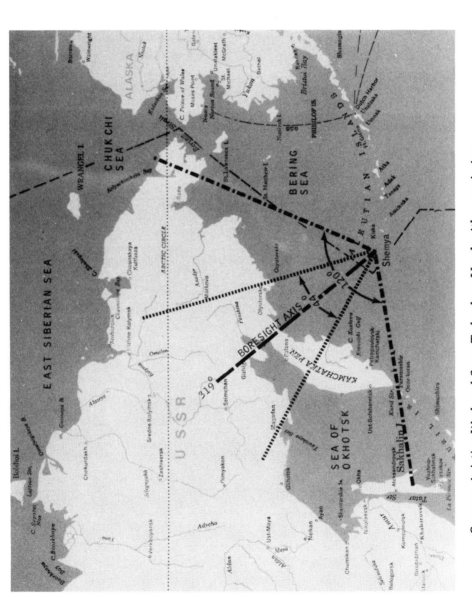

Source: *Aviation Week and Space Technology* Used with permission.

IV.

Patrolling the Periphery

Despite the value of ground stations, they provide only a portion of the information required by the United States. They cannot produce photographs of Soviet military installations, nor can they produce all the forms of signals intelligence required. As a complement and supplement to ground stations, specially equipped aircraft have been used by U.S. intelligence agencies since the late 1940s.

These aircraft mainly provided a peripheral reconnaissance capability. An aircraft would patrol the Soviet periphery, staying outside Soviet territorial waters, but would be able to "reach" inside Soviet territory for a limited distance to acquire photographs or intercepts. Thus the United States would acquire photographs of Soviet military installations, such as airfields, along the coastlines as well as intercepts from similarly located early-warning and air defense radar systems.

On April 5, 1948, the Secretary of the Air Force, Stuart Symington, addressed a short note to General Carl Spaatz, Air Force Chief of Staff. Symington informed Spaatz:

A pretty queer looking map was sent me along
with a memorandum I was sending Secretary
Marshall on what we know is across from the
Bering Straits.

I asked that the map be looked into, found it was
wrong in some places, and attach it.

In addition, however, I also found out that there
are no pictures of any kind of these airfields. Isn't
there some way we could take pictures?[1]

What was across from the Bering Straits was Chukotski Peninsula. What particularly concerned Air Force officials was the possible existence of airfields, for Soviet aircraft based at such airfields could, according to Air Force Intelligence:

a. . . . reach the largest number of strategic installations in North America with least effort and greatest effect

b. . . . carry out tactical operations against our force in Alaska[2]

In fact, photography of certain coastal portions of Chukotski Peninsula had been taken on December 22, 1947, by a U.S. aircraft involved in electronic reconnaissance activities as part of Project 23. The primary object of the project was the acquisition of information concerning Soviet radar installations. Photography was a second function to be attempted only if conditions—e.g., weather—were opportune. Due to the short focal length of the cameras, no significant intelligence resulted.

At approximately the same time, early spring, that Secretary Symington was expressing his concern, several intelligence sources indicated unusual Soviet activity in the northern, northeastern, and eastern areas of Siberia—including the construction of airfields, launching sites, and military bases. For example, one source reported bomber and fighter bases at Provideniya Bukhta and Veikal, a jet fighter base at Anador, and an expanding over-water reconnaissance base at Anadyr. Such information required substantiation by photographic reconnaissance.[3] With that requirement and Secretary Symington's note in mind, it was recommended by Air Force Intelligence that specially fitted aircraft with long-focal-length cameras be assigned the mission of conducting oblique photography against Chukotski Peninsula and ultimately other targets.[4] What was being proposed was a program of peripheral photographic reconnaissance; U.S. planes would fly outside Soviet territory but by using oblique photographic techniques would be able to photograph installations inside Soviet territory.

However, Air Force plans ran into a roadblock in the form of the State Department. A crucial question in determining the feasibility of the proposed reconnaissance was the distance from which the photographs would be taken. For any given camera system the further the distance the less the clarity of the photograph. International law specified that national sovereignty extended three miles past the end of a nation's landmass. However, since 1909 Russian and Soviet governments alike had claimed a twelve-mile limit, and that was the limit it was suggested such flights observe. The Joint Chiefs of Staff believed that the limit should be three miles. However, discussions between General Lauris Norstad, Deputy Chief of Staff, Operations, and State Department officials resulted in a decision to increase the limit to twenty-four miles and then to forty miles to avoid undue provocation.[5]

At such distance Air Force cameras, even those with the greatest focal length, could not hope to produce photography of value. Hence it became an Air Force objective to persuade the State Department to reverse itself and concur in reconnaissance missions conducted just outside the twelve-mile limit. The Air Force's case was stated in a draft letter prepared for Secretary Symington to send to the Secretary of State:

> Chukotski Peninsula, U.S.S.R. faces across Bering Strait upon Seward Peninsula, Alaska. Airfields sited on this easternmost tip of Siberia constitute

an airhead for potentially hostile air action against North America.

A most urgent intelligence requirement exists within the Department of Air Force to photograph the Chukotski airfields.

Overflying sovereign Soviet territory to procure vertical photographic coverage is certain to be construed by the U.S.S.R. as a warlike act. Oblique coverage made to now by *short* focal length cameras in aircraft flying some twelve miles off the Chukotski shore line has not resulted in significant intelligence.

The Department of Air Force proposes to photograph the Chukotski airfields with long focal length cameras from outside the three mile limit. It is not intended that our aircraft penetrate the general landmass where it is indented on the littoral by large bays or gulfs, even if this be possible with respect to the three mile line.

It is believed that hazard to life and property will not be seriously increased by photographing from three rather than twelve miles. The shorter distance increases the probability of getting photos having intelligence value.[6]

The letter was, apparently, never sent. But by mid-August 1948 the State Department had approved an Air Force proposal to reduce the limit in the Pacific to twenty miles. Because even at twenty miles the standard-focal-length cameras would not produce useful photography, it was requested that a long-focal-length (100-inch) camera be placed at the disposal of the Alaskan Air Command to obtain oblique photography of the Chukotski airfields.[7]

The missions that followed were conducted by the 72nd Photo Reconnaissance Squadron, and apparently code-named

LEOPARD, produced excellent and reassuring results. Oblique photography of the Uelin, Lavrentiya, Mys Chaplina, and Provideniya areas of the Chukotski Peninsula revealed "very little activity in those areas at the time of the missions, and no visible bases at these particular sites from which any long range bombing attack could be launched." At the same time it was noted, in a comment that presaged the overflight programs of the 1950s that "there well might be elaborate inland bases on which no information is available or which no photo coverage exists."[8]

At the same time it was still felt that the twenty-mile limit was too stringent and that a large amount of intelligence would be gained by reduction of the limit to three or at least twelve miles. Further, it was believed that photographic reconnaissance needed to be a continuous operation for a variety of reasons—including the greater detail revealed by comparing contrasting prints of the same installation taken at different seasons as well as the weather conditions that prevented a high percentage of successful photographic missions. The most important reason, according to Colonel H. M. Monroe of the Alaskan Air Command, was that "the Soviets are believed to be expending considerable effort and material toward developing the Far East, and KAMCHATKA and the CHUKOTSKI area particularly, so that a detailed picture of a base installation needs to be taken at least every three months to indicate developments."[9]

This theme was repeated in a November letter from the chief of the AAC to the Air Force Chief of Staff. In addition to noting the reasons why northeastern Siberia was so important a target and the value of "repeat reconnaissance," it requested:

> a. . . . photography of approximately twenty (20) key Soviet coastline targets, ranging from Ambarchik . . . to Petropavlovsk . . . and including Ostrov Vrangelya, to Komandorski Islands and the Northern Kuriles, be accomplished each spring and fall with a K-30, 100 inch focal length camera, or an improved version thereof.[10]

By October 1949, in addition to the LEOPARD missions, other sets of missions with code names such as RICKRACK, STONEWORK, and OVERCALLS had been flown and had produced over eighteen hundred photographs. The STONEWORK missions, conducted prior to November 1948, focused on the Kuril Islands—a series of islands extending seven hundred miles from northern Japan to southern Kamchatka—and Kamchatka. The OVERCALLS missions, also known as AAC Project 35, began on October 30, 1948, and continued through July 27, 1949. They were directed at twenty-eight targets ranging from the Kurils up Kamchatka, around the Chukotski Peninsula, and along the East Siberian Sea. To cover the targets sixteen sorties were flown along three routes.[11]

The OVERCALLS missions revealed no indication of a reported bomber and fighter base in the Provideniya Bukhta area, but the existence of airfields at Velkel, Anadyr, and Lavrentia and the existence of several well-dispersed storage and barracks areas in the vicinity of Provideniya. Additionally, the OVERCALLS missions also showed the growth of activities at Provideniya, Petropavlovsk, and Anadyr as well as the utilization of Petropavlovsk and the Tarinski Bay Naval Base as submarine bases.[12]

In addition to the AAC, both Far Eastern Air Forces (FEAF) and U.S. Air Forces Europe (USAFE) also were involved in the photographic reconnaissance program. Thus, in 1951, following reports of an extensive underground installation or missile-launching site on the southern tip of Karafuto—an island previously controlled by the Japanese but controlled by the U.S.S.R. as a result of World War II—the FEAF conducted a peripheral mission to photograph the area. That and further missions failed to support the reports but did indicate a 40 percent increase in aircraft between January and April 1951.[13] By March 1953 the USAFE was engaged in Project PIEFACE—flights along the Turkish-Soviet Caucasus border to obtain photography.[14]

Planes employed for the photographic reconnaissance missions were remodeled versions of World War II and early post–World War II bombers—the B-29, B-36, and B-45; hence the designations RB-29, RB-36, and RB-45. The most important piece of equipment on the RB-29 was the K-30 hundred-inch-focal-length camera, which was mounted on the port side of the forward bomb bay at a fifteen-degree angle. Taking a picture required the coordination of four people—the pilot, the navigator, and the first and second photomen. The airplane commander had an optical gunsight mounted on the port window alongside the seat. The navigator would identify the target to the airplane commander who would, in turn, attempt to keep the target in optimum position in the sight. The airplane commander would notify the first photoman, located in the rear pressurized section with a viewfinder with a twenty-four-inch lens mounted on the port side at an angle. When the target entered the viewfinder the camera would be put into action.[15]

Thus it was a RB-29 that took off on May 3, 1951, from Japan at 6:07 A.M. on Mission R 30-17. The entire mission was planned so as to reach the target area during critical sun time—from nine to eleven in the morning or from two to three-thirty in the afternoon. Such timing was necessary so that enough shadow would appear on the negatives to allow photo interpreters to interpret the photos correctly.[16]

The general instructions for the mission were to take continuous photographs along the entire eastern coast from the very southern tip of Sakhalin Island up to the Yuzhno-Sakalinsk area. All photography was to be taken from a twenty-five-thousand-foot altitude. The specific targets assigned were: Ikotsuki Airfield, Yuzhno-Sakhalin Airfield, Komuna Airfield, the city of Otamari (specifically its oil storage area, port facilities, and airfield), and Nagahoma Airfield. The mission was accomplished without incident, although a second run had to be made to obtain the photographs of Otamari. The plane left the target at ten-forty and arrived at Yokota AB a little less than four hours later. No flak had been encountered nor any enemy fighters, although some were seen taking off from Ikotsuki Airfield on the second run.[17]

Similarly, on October 14 of that same year Captain Clifford took off with his crew from Misawa Air Base at 4:30 A.M. to cover the Sakhalin Island area. The main targets were the Katanyk oil storage area; a seaplane base; the Okha target complex at the very northern tip of the island; and the Moakaliva complex at the Nikolayevsk complex, which was on the Soviet mainland directly across from northern Sakhalin. After initial photography of southern targets, the RB-29 proceeded up the Sakhalin coast, encountering bad weather at Okha, which prevented photography. Around the northern tip of Sakhalin, however, photography of targets in the Moskalvoaren and Nikolvayesk areas was accomplished. The plane then returned to the Okha area and twice attempted to photograph the area but broken clouds made successful runs impossible. A third attempt was successful as the clouds dissipated.[18]

On some occasions the weather—particularly cloud cover—made visible light photography impossible, as had occurred on the previous mission flown by Captain Clifford. In such situations the crew did not have to return to base empty-handed. Rather they could resort to radarscope photography—the photographing of the plane's radarscope to record the presence and location of objects below.

When the airborne photo reconnaissance program was in its earliest stages, the idea of overflying Soviet territory was rejected. The risks involved were considered to be so great as to preclude such overflights. By 1951, however, overflights of portions of Soviet-controlled islands had begun. Thus on October 9, 1951, an RB-45 took off from Yokota Air Base at 10:30 A.M. Designated Project 51, the RB-45's mission was to conduct reconnaissance over the southern end of Sakhalin Island. At an altitude of eighteen thousand feet, employing both regular and radar cameras, all the targets were photographed. Neither flak nor Soviet fighters was encountered, and the aircraft returned to Yokota Air Base by the preplanned route and landed at 2:40 P.M. after four hours, ten minutes of flying time.[19]

Other portions of Soviet territory that the Air Force was requested to overfly were islands north of the Soviet mainland—Franz Josef Land, Wrangel Island—as well as the Kola Peninsula, where several naval bases were located. In March 1952 the Air

Force refused to overfly Franz Josef Land "due to international complications."[20] In September 1953 the Air Force Directorate of Intelligence sought to obtain Joint Chiefs of Staff approval for a photographic overflight of the Kola Peninsula. The requirement was justified on these grounds:

> In order to assess properly a portion of the Soviet Air Force capability to launch strategic attacks against the continental United States, a critical requirement exists to obtain aerial photographs of certain specific areas on the Kola Peninsula. This photographic reconnaissance will assist in determining the ground and naval threat from the same area. Since the Kola Peninsula is one of the most favorably situated forward base areas in the U.S.S.R. for launching long range air attacks against the United States, accurate information on air base status and military and logistical activities for support of such operations represents one of the highest intelligence priorities.[21]

Whatever hesitancy the Air Force felt about overflights appeared to be selective. In May 1954 the Director of Naval Intelligence, in a letter to Major General John A. Samford, Air Force Director of Intelligence, wrote:

> 1. Information has been received that the U.S. Air Force, in accordance with Joint Chiefs of Staff authority, have completed the following reconnaissance overflights:
>   a. Murmansk-Kola Inlet area—two missions completed with radar scope photography being obtained on the first missions and visual photography obtained on the second mission;
>   b. Siberian area—four flights over Siberia, including coverage of Wrangel Island and

Vol; three of these flights obtained radar scope photography and the fourth obtained partial photographic coverage.[22]

At the same time as the United States was conducting peripheral and overhead photographic reconnaissance flights, it was also heavily involved in similar electronic reconnaissance flights known as ferret flights. The basic objectives of the program were to establish the location of radar systems and their physical characteristics. With such information electronic countermeasures could be designed to jam or negate those systems in wartime (indeed, the flights often were referred to as electronic countermeasure [ECM] flights), or knowing their location, simply destroy them.

As with photographic reconnaissance the Alaskan Air Command was heavily involved in the ferret program. As of July 1948 the AAC had two B-29 aircraft available that were equipped for ferret operations.[23] The AAC program had the objective of collecting raw information with respect to two general areas—radar emissions and the electronic emissions of guided missiles or pilotless aircraft. The first priority with respect to radars was to establish the location of the radars, after which attention turned to identifying the function of the radar—early warning, aircraft control, gun-laying antiaircraft, or active countermeasures. Similarly, after identifying the location of an electronic emission related to a guided missile or pilotless aircraft, the next subject of concern was whether the signal was for ground-to-air control, air-to-air control, or some other purpose. Additionally, a communications intercept program was being conducted on an experimental basis and each aircraft had one position allocated to the COMINT function.[24]

The value of the collection of radar intelligence was spelled out in a letter to the Commanding General of the Strategic Air Command that stated that the objective of the program was a

complete and detailed picture of the operational electronic capabilities of the target country. This would include the accurate mapping of early warning nets of target nations and capabilities of the defensive installations clustered around the vital industrial and strategic centers of such a nation. In addition by continuing an exhaustive analysis of the raw information, a progressive picture of the electronic capabilities of the target country can be deductively constructed.[25]

The specific types of information desired included the radio frequency employed by the radar system, its pulse recurrence frequency, and its pulse width, as well as items such as antenna rotation rate, antenna polarization, and horizontal and vertical antenna pattern. The radio frequency would provide the first clue to the type of equipment—for example, signals with low PRF's usually indicated a long-range early-warning radar, while those with high PRF's generally indicated ground-controlled interception or gun-laying radar. Pulse width would provide an indication of minimum range and equipment design while the other characteristics would be important "to the Research and Development personnel who use the characteristic information in designing equipment to counter the emission."[26]

By July 1948 the AAC program had located nine Soviet radar installations in the Far East—at Wrangel Island, Diomede Island, Velkal, Anadyr, Cape Kronotski, Petropavlovsk, a location south of Petropavlovsk, Cape Pervenets, and Vladivostok.[27]

Officially the AAC flights were to remain forty and later twenty miles offshore in conducting their missions. However, a major purpose of the program was to get the Soviets to turn on all their radars—the entire set that would be used in a wartime situation—to provide United States with a complete order of battle. Thus in some instances planes would penetrate briefly into Soviet air space to get the Soviet air defense radars to begin full-scale operation.

On other occasions, at least in 1948, flights actually penetrated deep into Soviet territory. First Lieutenant Richard Meyer was at the time a copilot assigned to the 46th Reconnaissance

Squadron at Ladd Field, Fairbanks, Alaska. Meyer recalls that in the summer of 1948 "we were given a new project requiring an all-volunteer crew to fly a highly modified, stripped-down B-29 on special missions. The aft compartment of the aircraft was jammed with electronic receivers and consoles for about five to eight operators. These operators had not been a part of the squadron before; they were temporary for these special missions only." The first mission departed from Ladd Field on August 5, leaving Alaskan air space near Point Barrow, then flying deep into Siberia and exiting into the Sea of Japan. After nineteen hours, forty-five minutes, the plane landed at Yokota AB near Tokyo. Three further missions into the Soviet Union were conducted that summer—on August 8, September 1, and September 6. The August 8 mission reversed the flight path—going from Yokota AB to Ladd Field in seventeen hours, forty-five minutes. Mission three consumed a little under twenty hours from Ladd to Yokota, with the fourth and final flight returning the plane to Ladd in exactly seventeen hours.[28]

Obviously the penetration flights risked being shot down or forced to land by Soviet air-defense forces. Even though the peripheral missions were supposed to maintain a substantial distance from the Soviet coast, it was recognized that there still was a possibility of a flight going off course or suffering from weather or mechanical problems that would result in a forced landing in the U.S.S.R. As a result, crew members on such missions were provided with a cover story. Initially they were on a "weather reconnaissance mission." This story was subsequently amended when it was pointed out that "a good interrogator could readily determine that the crews are not qualified for weather reconnaissance." As a result the crews are instructed in the fall of 1949 to claim that they were on a long-range navigation training mission.[29]

As with the photographic reconnaissance program, the AAC was only one of several commands conducting ferret flights. The Far East Air Forces conducted similar missions under the code name OVERSALT, while the USAFE conducted ECM missions under the code name BIOGRAPH.[30] In the European theater,

USAFE shared the ferret mission with the Navy. USAFE primarily covered the Baltic, Gulf of Bothnia, Murmansk, and Caucasus area, while the Navy was primarily responsible for the Mediterranean and Black seas.[31]

These lines were not rigid, however. Thus during the late night of January 23 and early morning of January 24, 1952, a Naval P4M aircraft conducted a ferret flight into the Baltic Sea that determined that the Soviet early-warning and air-defense systems in the region were in an alert state.[32]

During the early years of the program USAFE employed RB-29, RB-45, RB-36, and RB-50's, while the Navy relied on Privateers and Mercators to conduct ferret flights.[33]

A major base for ferret planes in the European theater was Great Britain, two units being established there between May and July 1950. The 72nd Strategic Reconnaissance Squadron, with RB-50's (based on the four-engined and heavily armed wartime Superfortress), arrived at Burtoonwood after initially having been set up in Sculthorpe, Norfolk. A detachment of the 91st Strategic Reconnaissance Squadron, with RB-45 Tornados, arrived at Manston Air Base in Kent, while a RB-29 squadron was temporarily stationed at Lakenheath. In addition, Brize Norton served as a base for RB-36 reconnaissance bombers on detachment from the United States (subsequently, SAC operated RB-47's from Brize Norton). The Navy planes, although their main base was at Port Lyautey, Morocco, also made use of a U.S. air facility at Blackbashe Airfield, Surrey.[34]

According to Duncan Campbell, the RB-45's from Sculthorpe engaged in penetration missions—although the extent of any penetration is not clear. Just before entering Soviet territory the Tornado would refuel from an accompanying KB-29 tanker over Germany or Greece. Altogether, flight time approximated twelve hours, which would have allowed the planes to penetrate up to thirteen hundred to sixteen hundred miles inside Soviet territory. Additionally, RB-36 Convairs were used in penetration missions. The RB-36's, which mixed jet and propeller engines, with an optimal altitude of greater than forty thousand feet, were impossible to shoot down and difficult to intercept.[35]

Penetrations also were conducted by the aircraft based at Brize Norton. Such flights were scheduled when it was believed that there had been a significant change in the Soviet air order of battle. When a penetration was planned, the Kirknewton ground station would be informed in advance so as to be sure that the full complement of personnel and equipment were on duty at the appropriate times. Such penetrations, in addition to collecting intelligence on radar systems, allowed the United States to determine if new Soviet aircraft weapons were used and how effective they might be. In part this was accomplished by Kirknewton's eavesdropping on the chatter between the Soviet pilots employed in trying to intercept the ferret.[36]

By December 1953 USAFE had established a requirement for nineteen RB-50 BIOGRAPH missions over each three-month period. Four routes were established:

Route Victor (Frank Josef Land)	1 each, 90 days
Route Whiskey (Barents Sea, Murmansk Area)	6 each, 90 days
Route Extra (Baltic Sea)	6 each, 90 days
Route Yankee (Black Sea)	6 each, 90 days[37]

One of the major products of USAFE's peripheral and penetration operations was the frequent publication of the *USAFE Radar Order of Battle: European Soviet and Satellite Areas*. The document would provide a sketch of each type of radar system and information on its function, the type of installation, frequencies, performance, and accuracy as well as the distribution of radars in the Western Soviet Union.

The missions conducted by AAC, FEAF, and USAFE were, by late July 1949, under the supervision of the Strategic Air Command. SAC had been designated by the JCS to supervise the ferret program in accord with the JCS determination that "an aggressive program to obtain the maximum amount of intelligence concerning foreign electronic developments shall be carried out as a safeguard to the national defense."[38]

One manifestation of SAC control was the activities of the

91st Strategic Reconnaissance Squadron at Yokota Air Base, Japan, from which numerous ferret missions were flown. In August 1951 alone the 91st SRS carried out seven ferret flights—four employing RB-29's and three with RB-50's. The first mission of the month, Mission 19 of August 1, was intended to provide information on radar installations on Karafuto Island and the Maritime provinces of the U.S.S.R. Thus at 9:50 A.M. the RB-29 took off, after which the ECM operators checked their equipment against friendly radar. During the passage by Soviet territory the operators monitored frequencies from 36 to 6230 megacycles and intercepted the signals of several early-warning stations. The aircraft's direction-finding equipment indicated the presence of radar installations at the southwestern tip and western coast of Karafuto and in the vicinity of Sovetskaya Gavan on the Soviet mainland. No gun-laying, ground-controlled interception, or airborne interception radar was observed during the flight, but audio recordings and photographs of the early-warning signals were obtained—the photographs by using a Warrick Hi-speed 35mm camera to photograph the signal as it appeared on the oscilloscope.[39]

Mission 209CZ of September 7 involved the flight of a RB-50 from Alaska, where it had landed after an earlier mission, back to Yokota. The aircraft closely paralleled the East Siberian and Kamchatkan coasts and the Kuril Islands chain. Lasting nineteen hours, fifty-five minutes, the mission resulted in four signals being detected—one with ground-control interception characteristics, an early-warning signal in the vicinity of Shipunsky, above Petropavlovsk on the Kamchatka Peninsula, and a shipborne signal north of the aircraft as well as near the center of the Kuriles.[40]

On September 25 an RB-50 took off on Mission 213 GZ. The plane made a long circuit from Yokota to a point off the shore of the far northeastern corner of Korea, up along the Vladivostok area, and still over water, up the Soviet coast to just above Sovetskaya Gavan, then down along the western coast of Sakhalin Island, and across the Japanese islands of Hokkaido and Honshu to Yokota Air Base. The mission produced seven signals—five early-warning-type signals (near Vladivostok, Statsenko, Selembe, Kuznetsovo, and Akhole), one of the gun-laying or GCI type (near Sovetskaya Gavan), and one with gun-laying characteristics (some fifty miles northeast of Sovetskaya Gavan).[41]

In addition to electronic reconnaissance missions, the 91st SRS at Yokota also, by 1953, was home for an RB-29A, whose mission was to conduct communications interceptions of Soviet VHF networks in support of FEAF intelligence requirements— the aircraft actually being operated by the Air Force Security Service's 6920th Security Group.[42] The RB-29A was (at least in the latter part of 1953) the only such craft allowed to conduct its missions during daytime. As a result of an incident in July 1953, electronic reconnaissance flights were restricted to operation under nighttime or instrument weather conditions and at no closer than twenty miles from Soviet territory. However, because communications facilities were most active during daylight hours and because of the atmospheric interference associated with instrument flight conditions, the communications interception flights were allowed to proceed during daylight while maintaining a distance of fifty miles from Soviet shores.[43]

A third, equally secretive aspect of the early airborne reconnaissance program involved the monitoring of Soviet nuclear test explosions and production. Eventually a variety of means were employed to monitor above- and below-ground nuclear explosions. But initially the Air Force's Long Range Detection Program—also known as Project CENTERING (and later Project COTTONSEED)—relied almost exclusively on airborne collection.

That there was any systematic technical collection program in place for monitoring possible Soviet nuclear tests in the late 1940s was due largely to the endeavors of Atomic Energy Commission member Lewis Strauss. Strauss first raised the question in April 1947, pointing out that there was no evidence that the military services had set up a system for the continuous monitoring of radioactivity in the atmosphere—which constituted the best means of determining whether the Soviets had tested a nuclear weapon.[44]

There appeared to be two reasons for the failure—one bureaucratic, the other perceptual. Bureaucratically, a monitoring system seemed to fall through the organizational cracks—many government offices had an interest in the subject but none had a primary responsibility.[45] Beyond that, many in the military and some in the AEC considered any such program premature and therefore a waste of funds and personnel. They considered it premature because they did not believe—on the basis of intelligence reports or their own judgment—that the Soviets were even close to constructing a bomb. Thus a Central Intelligence Group study in the fall of 1946 predicted that the Soviets would not test an atomic bomb until sometime between 1950 and 1953.[46] According to Strauss:

> The experts for the most part believed the construction of an atomic bomb was simply beyond the immediate competence of Russian science or the capability of existing industrial organization in the Soviet Union. The earliest date any of us had seen estimated for Russian achievement of nuclear weapons capability was five years. Intelligence reports to President Truman varied in estimates of the date when Russian achievement of an atomic weapon could occur, but in general none expected the Soviets to detonate any atomic device before 1952.[47]

In June a formal request was made by Strauss in the name of the AEC to the Military Liaison Committee. Strauss followed up with personal appeals to Secretary of the Navy James Forrestal, Secretary of the Army Kenneth Royal, and then, in September, to Eisenhower. The result was the establishment of the Long Range Detection Program under the direction of the Air Force.[48] The directive establishing the program called for establishing and operating a system to have as its objective "the determination of the time and place of all large explosions which might occur anywhere in the world and to ascertain in a manner which would leave no question, whether or not they were of nuclear origin."[49]

The system, relying primarily on airborne collection of air samples, was established in short order and tested during the U.S. Sandstone nuclear tests that took place in the Marshall Islands in early 1948.[50] The beginnings of the airborne program were evident at Lagens, Azores, where Flight C of the 373rd Reconnaissance Squadron, Very Long Range Weather, was stationed. In late April 1948 all the 373rd's B-29 aircraft were sent to Warner-Robins AFB, Georgia, to have a large boxlike can installed on top of the aircraft. The cans were filter holders, and filters about the size of photographic plates (approximately eight by ten inches) were installed in the holders.[51]

On May 12 a B-29A arrived at Lagens. Arnold Ross, the chief radio operator of Flight C, was selected to participate in the top-secret Operation Blueboy. Ross, who kept a personal logbook on flying time, recalls:

> We left Lagens on the 14th of May and proceeded to Wheelus Field, Tripoli, Libya. Using Wheelus . . . we flew high altitude (35,000 feet) missions through Egyptian airspace, up to the Turkish border, through the Mediterranean area, and on one occasion, on 30 May we flew a 15 hour mission from Wheelus to the Cape Verde Islands. On all of these missions, the filter box was used, with filters being changed every hour on the hour. When removed from the filter box they were placed in a lead lined container, and upon completion of Operation Blueboy on 6 June 1948, the containers were returned to Washington.[52]

Between the beginning of the program and September 3, 1949, the radiation count on a filter paper exceeded fifty counts per minute 111 times. Any count greater than fifty resulted in an Atomic Detection System Alert. All 111 alerts had been determined to be the result of natural occurrences—volcanic explosions, earthquakes, or normal fluctuations in background radioactivity.[53]

Alert No. 112 was to prove to be the real thing. On September 3 a WB-29 weather reconnaissance plane flew a routine patrol from Japan to Alaska. Flying at an altitude of eighteen thousand feet, a filter paper exposed for three hours had a radioactivity measurement of eighty-five counts per minute. The second filter paper was checked and found to show 153 counts per minute. As a result, other planes were dispatched and picked up even higher measurements of radioactivity. A filter paper exposed at an altitude of ten thousand feet on a weather flight from Guam to Japan produced a measurement of more than a thousand counts per minute.[54]

The samples collected by the airborne platforms and ground stations were distributed to labs such as Los Alamos and the Naval Research Laboratory, which concluded that the samples were the product of nuclear fission—a nuclear explosion.[55] Based on these reports and their own expertise, a study panel, which included Dr. J. Robert Oppenheimer, concluded that the phenomena "are consistent with the view that the origin of the fission products was the explosion of an atomic bomb whose nuclear composition was similar to the Alamogordo bomb and that the explosion occurred between the 26th and 29th of August at some point between the east 35th meridian and 170th meridian over the Asiatic land mass."[56] (Subsequently it was determined that the blast took place at Semipalatinsk on August 29.[57]) As a result of the scientific opinions, the Air Force Chief of Staff proceeded to inform the Secretary of Defense, "I believe that an atomic bomb has been detonated over the Asiatic land mass during the period 26 August to 29 August 1949."[58]

The implications of the Soviet bomb were significant. The Joint Intelligence Committee, under the JCS, revised upward its estimate of the Soviet atomic bomb stockpile. It was now projected that the Soviets would possess ten to twenty bombs by mid-1950, twenty-five to forty-five by mid-1951, forty-five to ninety by mid-1952, seventy to 135 by mid-1953, and 120 to two hundred by mid-1954. Additionally, with the question of Soviet capability to construct an A-bomb conclusively settled, renewed attention was given to the Long Range Detection Program. Thus the Director of Central Intelligence wrote the JCS on October 28, recommending a program of technical surveillance that would acquire information on the type of weapons tested, time and place of nuclear explosion, and the location of nuclear processing plants.[59]

The expansion meant further development of experimental methods—acoustic, seismic, electromagnetic pulse, rainwater sampling—as well as turning experimental stations into permanent stations. But the major collection technique remained airborne, and the major airborne collector remained the WB-29. On the top of the WB-29 was the aperture that allowed air to get in and pass through the filter paper, which would slow down and stop the particles while letting the air through. The filters might be changed as often as every hour, as they were in Operation Blueboy. The particles caught on the filter papers were used to reveal the composition of a bomb, while the location of the blast could be determined by tracing the wind tracks backward.[60]

By May 1951 the United States was sampling the air masses moving out of the U.S.S.R. and over the Middle East. Flights were conducted once every seventy-two hours over a limited flight path from Dhahran, Saudi Arabia, to Lahore, Pakistan—a frequency that was not sufficient to intercept all the clouds moving out of the area.[61]

The use of WB-29's in such activities continued throughout the early 1950s, supplemented in some cases by fighter planes employed after the initial detection, the smaller fighters being more efficient.[62]

In 1953 a modified B-57A flew into the cloud from a detonation at an altitude of fifty-four thousand feet. This marked the beginning of modified B-57's in a reconnaissance role. Under a classified program named BLACK KNIGHT, the Air Force directed the Air Materiel Command to procure six Martin Model 294 aircraft, which became the RB-57D Intruder.[63]

Ultimately the plane was produced in three versions—one for photographic reconnaissance, one for radar mapping, and one for signals intelligence operations. All the planes had a wingspan of 106 feet, a length of over sixty-seven feet, and a ceiling of between fifty-five thousand and sixty thousand feet. In the fall of

1957, under Operation SEA LION, RB-57D's were based at Yokota AB, Japan, for one year. The operations flown under SEA LION consisted of SIGINT and sampling missions.[64]

The aerial sampling mission of the RB-57D involved atmospheric sampling and tracking the progress of the resulting clouds of radioactive materials scattered over wide areas by winds. During the most intensive period of atmospheric testing two aircraft would be employed. One plane would actually enter the areas of radioactive contamination. The second would remain clear of the contaminated area, serving as a monitor and aborting the mission before completion if radiation levels—being recorded by the machine actively involved in sampling and simultaneously being transmitted to the control aircraft—exceeded previously established limits for safe exposure.[65]

By 1954 the aerial sampling program had yielded important information on more than simply the Soviet nuclear weapons testing program. The highest priority was to estimate, with a reasonable degree of accuracy, the Soviet nuclear weapons output. U.S. scientists were able to do so on the basis of determining the plutonium production rate in the U.S.S.R.—a rate that could be determined by the Krypton 85 being emitted into the atmosphere from Soviet production facilities. That the Krypton 85 level was the key to U.S. ability to estimate Soviet nuclear weapons production was *the* deepest secret of AFOAT-1 as of late 1954.[66]

Even without planned penetrations of Soviet territory it was inevitable that reconnaissance fights would result in Soviet protest and ultimately encounter Soviet fighter planes that sought to harass them or shoot them down. One of the earliest protests was communicated by the Soviet embassy in Washington to the State Department on January 5, 1948. The embassy's note stated:

> On December 23, 1947 at 14 hours and 15 minutes an American airplane violated the Soviet frontier in the region of Cape Chukotsk, flying for about seven miles along the coast of the Chukotsk Peninsula at a distance of two miles from shore.

> In communicating the foregoing, the Embassy upon instructions of the Soviet Government, requests that the case of violation of the Soviet frontier by an American airplane be investigated and that measures be taken not to permit such violations in the future.[67]

In addition, the U.S. embassy in Moscow received a protest from the Soviet Foreign Office, charging than an American aircraft overflew Big Diomede Island on December 25, 1947.[68]

An investigation by the Air Force of the January 5 charge established that the plane was involved in electronic reconnaissance as part of Project 23 and "that the Department of State limitation (of conducting such flights at least twelve miles from Soviet territory) has been violated but it is impossible to determine that the Soviet frontier has been violated as alleged."[69]

The first recorded attack by Soviet air defense forces, in this case fighters, on a U.S. reconnaissance plane occurred on October 22, 1949. In that case a RB-29 was attacked over the Sea of Japan, but the plane avoided being shot down, and no injuries resulted.[70] The crew of the next reconnaissance plane attacked was not so lucky. On April 8, 1950, a U.S. Navy Privateer—a Consolidated Vultee PB4-Y2 patrol bomber (whose mission may have been reconnaissance of new Soviet missile bases along the Baltic coast)—was attacked by Soviet fighters.[71] According to the Soviet account the plane was mistaken for a B-29 flying fourteen miles inland near Leyaya in Soviet Latvia.[72] Another account suggests the plane was shot down some eighty nautical miles southeast of Gotland, a Swedish island in the Baltic Sea about a hundred miles east of Latvia.[73] All ten members of the crew were lost—life rafts and aircraft parts were found with bullet holes. It was reported in 1955 that eight of the crewman may have survived and been sent to prison camps.[74]

The Baltic incident resulted in a "high level" decision on April 17 to suspend further electronic reconnaissance flights for thirty days. In fact, the suspension lasted much longer. On June 6, presidential authority was received for the resumption of the flights, and the Air Force planned to begin operating two weekly missions over the Baltic route with fully armed and partially ECM-equipped B-29's, starting on July 16. However, on July 8, 1950, the Air Force was requested by a State Department representative to conduct no such flights for approximately two weeks "in view of current tension in WE [Western Europe]." The Air Force, in turn, directed USAFE to suspend further Baltic flights until further instructions were received from Washington.[75]

At least one additional incident involving the U.S.S.R. took place in 1950 but without loss of aircraft or crew. A B-29 ferret was intercepted by Soviet fighters on the night of July 15, approximately forty miles off the Soviet East Coast, near Permskoye Airfield. Four aircraft took off from the airfield at about one-minute intervals, with the first takeoff approximately nine minutes prior to the interception, which occurred at twelve minutes before midnight local time. One fighter approached the B-29 at five o'clock high, while another approached at seven o'clock high—with a landing light or searchlight on each plane. Evasive action by the B-29 was successful in shaking the fighters.[76]

November 6, 1951, saw the second fatal encounter between U.S. reconnaissance planes and Soviet fighters. Once again the victim was a U.S. Navy plane—a P2V Neptune. The incident occurred over the Sea of Japan some twenty miles outside Soviet territory in the vicinity of Vladivostok. Another crew of ten was lost and two Soviet fighter pilots were decorated.[77]

Over the next four years (1952–55) there were at least seven more incidents, with over thirty crewmen dead or missing as a result. On October 7, 1952, a RB-29 took off from Hokkaido Island in the vicinity of Nemura—just south of the Soviet-controlled Kuril Islands—and disappeared after tracking indicated that the craft "merged" with two Soviet fighters. The aircraft and crew of eight were lost. Japanese eyewitnesses indicated that the RB-29 crashed on the Soviet side of the international demarcation line.[78]

A March 1953 MiG attack on an RB-50 east of Kamchatka resulted in no damage, but four months later, on July 29, 1953, another RB-50 was attacked by Soviet MiG's. This time the attack took place over the Sea of Japan, about seventy nautical miles southeast of Vladivostok, and was successful—one crewman was rescued but sixteen were lost.[79] As a result of the latter incident it was reaffirmed that USAF "electronic reconnaissance aircraft will not approach closer than twenty (20) nautical miles to any shore of U.S.S.R." It was also decreed that no electronic reconnaissance flights would be conducted during daylight hours.[80]

Two further incidents occurred in September and November 1954. The September incident involved a Navy P2V Neptune that was attacked on September 4, forty-four miles from the Siberian coast and a hundred miles east of Vladivostok, over the Sea of Japan. The attacking force apparently consisted, according to the State Department, of two MiG-15's. The first attacker made one pass, causing no damage, but bullets from the second hit the patrol bomber in the wings. A fire broke out immediately, and the Neptune had to be ditched. Nine crewmen were rescued unharmed, but a tenth was believed trapped in the navigator's compartment and assumed dead.[81]

After the November 1954 shooting down of an RB-29 photographic reconnaissance plane in the vicinity of Hokkaido, Japan, that resulted in one death, there was only one certain incident over the next three years. On April 18, 1955, southeast of Kamchatka, an RB-47 *may* have been shot down, possibly by two fighters from Petropavlovsk, with the aircraft being lost. According to a 1956 Air Force Security Service study, "all that is definitely known is that the aircraft departed Eielson Air Force Base . . . carrying 13 hours of fuel [and] failed to return."[82]

Approximately two months later, on June 22, a U.S. Navy P2V-5 was attacked a little after ten o'clock local time by a MiG-15. The attack happened off the southeastern coast of the Chukotski Peninsula. Firing did not begin until the P2V-5 made the turn toward the coast. The plane crash-landed on St. Lawrence Island, just on the U.S. side of the 1867 Convention line. Of the eleven-man crew, four were unhurt, four were injured in the landing, and three were hurt by gunfire.[83]

By June 22, 1958, it might have seemed that U.S.-Soviet clashes over reconnaissance flights were things of the past—it had been exactly three years since the last incident. Yet one week later, on July 29, a twelve-month period began in which no less than five incidents in widely separated areas of the world occurred. Further, some of the incidents propelled the secret war into public consciousness.

The June 29 incident apparently involved a transport aircraft with no reconnaissance functions, which perhaps explains why the Soviets returned the entire crew within days of the time they landed in Soviet territory. If there was any evidence of reconnaissance activity on board the plane it was soon destroyed, as the crew blew up the plane shortly after landing. Just over two months later, a far more serious incident occurred—indeed, the most serious to that date. On September 2, a RC-130 Lockheed Hercules four-engine turboprop with a crew of seventeen took off from Adana Air Base in Turkey to intercept and record signals from the southern Soviet Union, possibly including the missile range at Kapustin Yar. It was to fly a hook-shaped path northwest to Trabzon on the Black Sea, then proceed southeast to Iran and back to Adana. The plane had a range of 3,350 miles, cruised at 260 miles per hour, and had an operational ceiling of thirty-four thousand feet. Its flight plan called for it to fly no closer than eighty-five miles to the Soviet border.[84]

According to the Soviet account the plane "penetrated for a significant distance into Soviet air space and had fallen within Soviet territory and has thus intentionally violated the Soviet border."[85] It was suspected that the Soviets may have been meaconing the plane across the Soviet border—meaconing being the sending of false navigational signals to a plane to direct it off course.[86]

According to one account, the Soviet navigational beacons at Poti and Batumi on the eastern shore of the Black Sea operated on the same frequency as the Trabson beacon used by the C-130. Likewise, the Turkish beacon at Van, also to be used by the C-130, and the Soviet beacon at Erivan operated on similar frequencies. Thus the C-130 might have been lured over the border by altering the power of beam configurations of the beacons, confusing the Air Force navigator.[87]

The plane crossed the Soviet border between Trabzon and Van and was approached by five MiG-19 fighters which, at first, signaled for the plane to land at a Soviet airfield.[88] They then, however, cut loose with a burst of cannon fire. The conversation of the Soviet fighter pilots was monitored:

> 582 I see the target to right . . .
> Its altitude is 100 [hectometers—about 32,800 feet] as you said.
> I am 201, I see the target. Attack!
> I am 201, I am attacking the target . . .
> Attack, attack, 218, attack.
> The target is a transport, four-engined. I am attacking the target . . .
> Target speed is 300 [kilometers]. I am going along with it. It is turning toward the fence . . .
> The target is burning . . .
> There's a hit . . .
> The target is banking . . .
> Open fire . . .
> 218, are you attacking?
> Yes, yes . . .
> The target is burning . . .
> The tail is falling off the target . . .
> I am in front of the target.
> Look at him. He will not get away. He is already falling.
> Yes, he is falling. I will finish him off, boys, I will finish him off on the run.
> The target has lost control, it is going down.
> The target has turned over.
> Aha, you see, it is falling.
> Yes . . . form up, go home.[89]

At least six of the seventeen-man crew died, and their bodies were returned on September 24. The fate of the eleven other crew members has never been conclusively established, but on

February 24, 1959, the parents of one crew member announced that they had been informed that their son was imprisoned in a Soviet camp. In 1961 a Soviet magazine reported that eleven crew members parachuted and were caught on the outskirts of Yeveran.[90]

The final two months of 1958 saw several incidents, including several firsts. Until October 31, 1958, there had been no attempts to shoot down aircraft flying along the Turkish border and over the Black Sea. On that day a Soviet fighter closed in on a RB-47 ferret mission over the central and eastern Black Sea. The ferret departed the area without further delay. Then on November 7, another RB-47 ferret was attacked east of Sweden's Gotland Island in the Baltic Sea. Soviet fighters made two firing passes when the reconnaissance aircraft was approximately fifty nautical miles from the Soviet coast.[91]

On November 17, two attacks occurred—both on RB-47's, both by MiG's—in very different parts of the world. One attack was over the Baltic Sea, while another took place over the Sea of Japan. In both cases no casualties or damages resulted. Then on June 16, 1959, a U.S. Navy patrol craft was attacked by two MiGs, and the tail gunner was hurt.[92]

Two further incidents were to occur involving U.S. reconnaissance planes and the Soviet Union. One, the U-2 incident (discussed in the next chapter), led to the breakup of the 1960 Paris summit. The second provided a way for Soviet Premier Nikita Khrushchev to involve himself in the American presidential election contest between John Kennedy and Richard Nixon by refusing to release the fliers captured as a result of that incident until after the election despite the repeated requests of the Eisenhower administration—thus depriving Nixon of a political coup.

V.

Overflights

While peripheral reconnaissance flights managed to produce valuable photographic and electronic reconnaissance data, there were certain obvious limitations. Oblique photography, whether conducted from three, twelve, or forty miles outside Soviet territory, could reach only a very limited distance into the U.S.S.R. Similarly, it was noted by an officer in the Air Force's Directorate of Intelligence that "efforts of the Air Force to secure information concerning Soviet electronic installations is generally limited to the perimeter areas where reconnaissance may be conducted by ferret aircraft. Practically, no information is available concerning electronic installations within the interior of Russia."[1]

Penetrations that might be undertaken by reconnaissance bombers were dangerous and could cover only small areas of Soviet territory for brief periods. Hence it was apparent to those concerned with collecting information about the Soviet Union that some means of obtaining regular coverage, both photographic and electronic, of the Soviet interior was needed. The idea of satellite reconnaissance was suggested as early as 1946 in RAND Corporation studies. However, it also was recognized that the late 1950s was the earliest that a satellite reconnaissance vehicle could be expected to be operational. In the interim two other means were developed: balloons and aircraft.

Before actually resorting to an overflight program, the United States tried to open up the Soviet Union to airborne inspection via a diplomatic initiative. On July 21, 1955, at a summit conference in Switzerland, President Eisenhower proposed that the United States and the U.S.S.R.

> give to each other a complete blueprint of our military establishment from beginning to end, from one end of our countries to the other; lay out the establishments and provide the blueprints to each other
> . . . to provide within our countries facilities for aerial photography to the other country, ample facilities for aerial reconnaissance, where you can make all the pictures you choose and take them to your own country to study; you to provide exactly the same facilities for us and we to make these examinations, and by this step to convince the world that we are providing as between ourselves against the possibility of great surprise attack, thus lessening danger and relaxing tensions.[2]

Of course, in addition to helping to prevent surprise attack such an arrangement would provide an intelligence bonanza to the West. Naturally, Eisenhower's proposal was spoken of favorably by the Prime Minister of Britain (Anthony Eden) and the Premier of France (Edgar Faure). Surprisingly, the fourth participant at the summit—Soviet Premier Nikolai Bulganin—also reacted favorably.[3] According to Eisenhower, Bulganin declared that the proposal appeared to have real merit and the Soviets would give it thorough and sympathetic consideration. However, Eisenhower soon discovered that the real power in the Soviet delegation, General Secretary Nikita Khrushchev, did not share Bulganin's view, claiming that the "Open Skies" proposal was nothing more than a flagrant espionage plot against the U.S.S.R.[4] While there would have been some Soviet advantage to be gained from participation—particularly in the collection of precise targeting data—other factors served to produce a negative response. Included was a Soviet sensitivity to espionage and penchant for secrecy as well as the Soviet ability to gather much data on the United States from open sources. More fundamentally, the very nature of the Soviet state mitigated against acceptance of the proposal. The leadership of a closed society such as the Soviet Union could hardly justify the secrecy, hardship, and repression it imposed on the average Soviet citizen on the grounds of the "imperialist threat" and at the same time open up the country to overflights by the chief imperialist power.

The idea of using balloons for photographic reconnaissance was by no means an original or even a twentieth-century idea. In 1794, eleven years after the first successful hot-air balloon flight, the French used the balloon for reconnaissance.[5] A hundred fifty-six years later, in October 1950, the U.S. Air Force took its first positive steps toward developing a balloon reconnaissance capability for use against the Soviet target. A memorandum for the record, dated October 3, noted:

> the present AF holdings of USSR photography are both out of date and extremely incomplete. The major coverage is the Turban material limited to that part of the USSR west of the Urals.
>
> Since it is captured German photography it does not show post-war developments in the USSR. Except for recent coastal coverage . . . Asiatic USSR is virtually without photocoverage. This Directorate lacks prints to aid in the confirmation or denial of such reports as those of atomic production centers, of new industrial developments of new rail yards, and airfields

It also noted that there were four possible solutions, most of which had "serious diplomatic or developmental difficulties."[6]

The potential solutions were:

a. Use of airplanes to perform day photographic reconnaissance. This must be ruled out since the use of manned airplanes over USSR prior to hostilities is considered an act of aggression.
b. Use of guided missile SNARK will not be available until 1953.
c. Use of satellite vehicle. This will probably not be practical for several years.
d. Use of balloons. All of the "hardware" needed is available. Some meteorological problems must be solved but if program is properly phased these problems appear soluble. It is believed that balloon surveillance can be in operation in 1951.[7]

As a result the Air Force Directorate of Intelligence established Project GOPHER on October 9.[8]

On November 6, a 1-A priority was established for the construction of several test vehicles for pilot experimentation within the United States. It was decreed that the test vehicles should have automatic camera equipment sufficient to produce photography of a scale of approximately one to one hundred thousand, to be able to operate at between sixty thousand and eighty thousand feet and, if feasible, a system to determine the time of day, altitude, and direction within the area photographed. Another problem requiring examination was how the balloons were to be recovered—in the air, on land, or at sea—with homing beacons/interrogation equipment, and gas valves to lower balloons for pickup offered as initial suggestions.[9]

The original schedule for GOPHER envisioned five phases: The balloon vehicle was to be developed by January 18, 1951, an upper-air-trajectory test was to be completed by February, the gondola design was to be completed by March, test flights across the United States were to be conducted in April, and the balloon pickup was to take place in July. However, by April neither the first nor the second phase had been completed.[10] Indeed, by December of that year it was judged that "little progress had been made on GOPHER" due to the delivery of faulty polyethylene to General Mills (the balloon fabricator), competition between the Air Force and Navy for General Mills' limited capabilities, and the failure of the Air Research Development Command consistently to push vigorously and to coordinate properly GOPHER development.[11]

Almost a year and a half later, the GOPHER system was at a point where a decision had to be made: Was there going to be a commitment by the Air Force to complete the project, and could approval be obtained from higher authorities actually to conduct overflights of Soviet territory? Although there had been no tests of the entire system, all of the individual components had performed satisfactorily, and it was believed that an operational system could be ready in about one to two years. The cost of further development would be about $2.5 million, and the cost of the actual operation would be between $31 million and $51 million.[12]

With the decision-makers confronted with a choice of either going ahead with the project and obtaining the necessary high level approval or canceling the project, it began to be pushed ahead. On June 17, 1953, Brigadier General John Ackerman of the Air Force Directorate of Intelligence informed the Director of Research and Development that the Director of Intelligence concurred in the recommendation that GOPHER be brought to the production stage.[13] On September 11 the Air Force Chief of Staff submitted, on an informal basis, to the Joint Chiefs of Staff an outline concept of the balloon project, which was by then code-named GRANDSON. At that time the Air Staff envisioned a three-thousand-balloon campaign over a four-month period beginning in November 1955. The JCS approved the outline but recommended that State Department approval be obtained via the Secretary of the Air Force and the Secretary of Defense.[14]

Although the necessary approvals were obtained, there still were four technical problems that had to be solved before operations could commence: production of very high quality film, development of a gondola that would stay warm enough to protect the electronics and camera despite flying in the stratosphere for more than the usual three days, development of a parachute capable of floating a six-hundred-pound load safely from altitudes of seventy-five thousand to ninety thousand feet, and determining a recovery technique for airplane recovery at twelve thousand to fourteen thousand feet in the air.[15]

Each of the problems was solved experimentally by August 1954.[16] By March 1955 the program was ready to enter its operational phase. Responsibility for all further development, coordination, and implementation was assigned to the Strategic Air Command on March 21, 1955.[17] The project also had a new code name, GENETRIX, and a weapons system designation, WS-119L.[18]

SAC, in turn, established the 1st Air Division at Offutt Air Force Base (SAC headquarters) on April 15 and defined its mission on June 15: It was to be responsible for launching the balloons from Western Europe. The balloons were to move to the target area in seven days and then be tracked and recovered within the Far East and in Alaskan areas.[19]

The most favorable launch period was determined to be from November 1 to May 1. During that time the prevailing winds were predicted to be west to east at all altitudes. Therefore it was planned to use the period May through September for testing and training within the United States and the September to November period for deployment to and preparation of forward bases. However, delays in July and equipment problems resulted in pushing the conclusion of the training period to October 16 and the beginning of operations to December 1.[20]

The training exercise, known as Moby Dick Hi, involved the launch of 162 balloons, tracking, and recovery from Charleston AFB, South Carolina. Recovery involved both air and surface operations. Air recovery was achieved in twelve of the thirty-nine cases where such recovery was possible. As a result of the testing the launch device was altered from a forklift launch vehicle (which was determined to be inadequate and unsafe due to size, weight, limited visibility, and limited mobility) to a truck with a superimposed structure from which the gondola was suspended and released. Finally, vulnerability tests were conducted in which the Air Defense Command was advised of launch times and expected trajectories. It was determined that the balloon system could be detected visually and by radar but was not "unacceptably vulnerable."[21]

To conduct the actual operation the 1st Air Division was assigned operational control of several Air Force units. The 456th Troop Carrier Wing, Tactical Air Command, equipped with C-119 aircraft, was responsible for air recovery operations; the 1110th Air Support Group at Lowry AFB, Colorado, was assigned the responsibility of launching the balloons; and the 6926th Radio Squadron (Mobile) of the Air Force Security Service was to track the balloons.[22] In addition, the 1st Air Division established Detachment 1 at Adana, Turkey, on June 9. Its initial assignment was to coordinate launch, support, and public information requirements and perform liaison duties with supporting agencies. Subsequently its mission was expanded to include operational control of all European area launches.[23]

Selection of the launch sites was based, in part, on the study of meteorological data—which indicated that more complete coverage could be obtained if sites were widely dispersed in Western Europe. After general areas were selected, determination of specific sites was left to the commander in chief of U.S. Air Forces in Europe. Five launch sites were selected: Adana, Evanton (Scotland), and three in West Germany. Additionally, as indicated in Figure 2 there were six recovery sites in the Pacific region and ten tracking sites.[24]

Deployment began with the 6926th Radio Squadron (Mobile) in June. By August, 725 personnel and 1,780,000 pounds of equipment had been deployed. The 1110th Air Support Group deployed a similar number of personnel and 477,500 pounds of equipment between October 10 and November 1. The most massive deployment of all occurred between October 5 and November 20, when the 456th Troop Carrier Wing deployed a total of 1,763 personnel and over 2,750,000 pounds of equipment. On December 1 all units were in place and ready to begin operations. Until the go order arrived they conducted command post exercises and various training missions. Included in the training missions was the continuation of Moby Dick Far East, in which 211

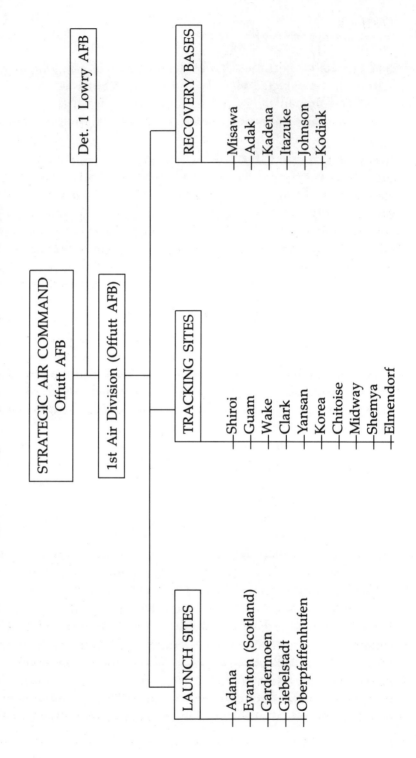

Figure 2. Organization for Project GENETRIX

STRATEGIC AIR COMMAND
Offutt AFB

Det. 1 Lowry AFB

1st Air Division (Offutt AFB)

LAUNCH SITES
Adana
Evanton (Scotland)
Gardermoen
Giebelstadt
Oberpfaffenhufen

TRACKING SITES
Shiroi
Guam
Wake
Clark
Yansan
Korea
Chitoise
Midway
Shemya
Elmendorf

RECOVERY BASES
Misawa
Adak
Kadena
Itazuke
Johnson
Kodiak

balloons were launched to test the tracking capabilities of the 6926th.[25]

On January 9, 1956, one day before the GENETRIX launches were to commence, balloons were launched from Okinawa, Hawaii, and Alaska—the first of 124 such to be launched between that day and July 1956. The launches were part of an actual meteorological program called Moby Dick. An official statement declared Moby Dick to be "a project which aims at exploring the meteorological problems including high-altitude circulation and the jet stream."[26] The objective was to cover the GENETRIX program with Moby Dick, for the United States could neither keep the GENETRIX balloon launchings secret nor admit their true purpose. The plan to cover GENETRIX with Moby Dick had a separate code name—White Cloud.[27]

On January 10 GENETRIX began with the launch of eight balloons—two under the limit of ten balloons a day penetrating to the target area set by Air Force headquarters for the first seven days of the operation. The Air Force also restricted the ceiling to fifty-five thousand feet. The limit on the number of balloons was raised to twenty on January 17, to thirty on January 25, and to forty on January 28.[28]

Two types of balloons were involved. The original plan had called for operating Model 128TT balloons at eighty thousand feet, but during Moby Dick it was decided that Model 66CT balloons, which flew at lower altitudes and promised twice the rate of arrivals in the recovery area, were preferred. At the same time, since the lower-altitude balloons would travel through the recovery area at a speed that would outrun that of the C-119 recovery planes, it was necessary to develop means to terminate balloons from the ground.[29]

The Model 66CT balloons, when launched from two bases in West Germany, were launched at times that ensured border crossings during darkness. The Model 128TT balloons were not restricted as to border crossings, nor were the Model 66CT balloons when launched from the other three sites. To obtain the planned seven- to eight-day lifetime, the 66CT balloons were prepared for an initial altitude of approximately 46,500 feet and a ballasting altitude of forty thousand feet. The 128TT balloons were prepared for an initial altitude of fifty thousand feet and a ballasting altitude of forty-five thousand feet.[30]

The types of information to be gathered by the GENETRIX project were spelled out in an October 23, 1953, memorandum that stated:

> To support the USAF combat mission, intelligence has a requirement of the highest priority for information to measure the Soviet capability for taking direct military action against the continental U.S. and its possessions, our allies and their possessions. In addition, information is required to determine Soviet capability to interfere with U.S. strategic air attacks. Specific intelligence is required on the following:
>
> 1. Bomber bases, fighter airfields and missile launching sites, especially where stockpiling of Atomic and Hydrogen weapons is indicated.
> 2. Military installations as indications of enemy intentions.
> 3. Industries, transportation systems and other economic development in sufficient detail to indicate current status and potential growth.
> 4. Anti-aircraft artillery and radar sites.[31]

The balloon launchings were of course noted by the Soviet Union, which did not believe that nothing more than meteorological investigations were involved. In early February the Soviet Union accused the United States and Turkey of sending radio-equipped photographic balloons over Soviet territory and in diplomatic notes to both nations termed the activity "inadmissible." In its note it accused the United States of having committed a "gross violation of Soviet air space." The State Department responded that the Soviet note evidently referred to large weather balloons carrying radio and other equipment to record meteorological and cosmic ray data that "may" have floated over the Soviet Union.[32]

On February 7 the American embassy in Moscow delivered to the Soviet Foreign Ministry a reply to the Soviet note of February 4. It claimed that the balloons were "equipped with instruments to measure and record meteorological phenomena such as jet streams, and with photographic apparatus to provide pictures of cloud formations which bear on air movements at various velocities." The note further claimed that "much valuable scientific information is being accumulated" and stated that "in the interest of scientific research, it would be much appreciated if the Soviet Government would return the instruments which have come into its possession."[33]

Two days later the Soviets held a press conference outside Spridonovka Palace. Disassembled balloons and the radio equipment they carried were presented in carefully prepared exhibits, with the driveway containing about fifty balloons and instrument containers while the entire scene was floodlit from trucks carrying portable generators. Colonel A. V. Taranstov of the Soviet Army explained how the radio-controlled balloons were able to traverse the Soviet Union in seven to ten days and release their apparatus by parachute into "friendly" hands. In addition, he displayed a role of exposed film that he claimed to have taken from one of the photo containers. He exhibited photographs of mountainous areas and of an airfield that he said Soviet photographic interpreters had identified as being in Turkey.[34]

Soviet protests had their desired effect. In a February 6 meeting between Eisenhower and Secretary of State John Foster Dulles, Eisenhower recalled that he and Dulles "had been rather allergic to the project and doubted the results would justify the inconvenience involved." Eisenhower then suggested that the operation should be suspended, a recommendation that Dulles seconded but with the proviso that "we should handle it so it would not look as though we had been caught with jam on our fingers."[35] Hence the immediate suspension of operations was ordered and the February 7 message to the Soviet Foreign Office concluded with the pledge that "in view of the Soviet Government's objection, the U.S. Government will seek to avoid the launching of additional balloons which, on the basis of known data, might transit the USSR."[36]

On March 1, 1956, the Air Force directed that the operational phase of GENETRIX be terminated except that the search for and recovery of unaccounted for gondolas would continue. During the operational period a total of 516 balloons had been launched, 399 of which became operational, while 117 were failures. All carried photographic equipment. Early termination of the project prevented the planned use of the balloons for electronic reconnaissance.[37]

Twelve of the 399 operational balloons failed to enter Soviet territory. Of the remaining 387, a total of 243 never were heard from after launch. Of the 144 later heard to transmit, twenty-one transmitted termination signals immediately and 123 were tracked. Sixty-seven of those 123 entered the recovery area, fifty-seven terminated in the recovery area, and forty-four were recovered by March 5.[38]

There were at least two reasons for the failure of many balloons to reach the recovery area. The lifetimes of the balloons tended to be four to five days rather than the planned seven to eight days, bringing them down in Soviet territory rather than in the recovery area. The other was the apparent Soviet success in developing effective countermeasures. Of the balloons launched after January 26, only twenty-eight were heard to transmit, and only two were recovered.[39]

Altogether, forty missions produced photographs—a total of 13,813 visible exposures. Those exposures produced charting photography of 1,116,449 net square statute miles of Sino-Soviet territory—about 8 percent of their entire landmass—at a cost of $48.49 per square mile.[40]

The exact value of the photographs is a matter of dispute. The Secretary of Defense at the time of the operation, Donald Quarles, thought the operation was "useful, but not of a vital importance," whereas the Air Force Chief of Staff; General Nathan Twining, thought the information acquired would "be very valuable for the future."[41] The final project report stated that "the type of photography obtained affords an excellent source for pioneer reconnaissance . . . but due to limiting factors, detailed interpretation of the new intelligence is difficult."[42] A historical study notes that while "much of the photography . . . was of clouds, there were also some worthwhile results. Dodonovo, the vast nuclear refining facility in Soviet Siberia, was discovered in GENETRIX photography."[43] Two former CIA officials heavily involved in reconnaissance activities remember the photography as basically useless. The late Herbert Scoville, one of those officials, referred to the program as a "disaster."[44]

Many in the CIA were opposed to GENETRIX. Aside from whatever doubts they had about the utility of the operation, they were afraid it would muddy the water for a much more valuable project that was in the development stage—a project known to a smaller number of officials and code-named AQUATONE.

In one sense Project AQUATONE was a product of Soviet construction of a missile testing center at Kapustin Yar on the Volga. Late in 1954, a number of apparent telemetry signals from Soviet missile launches had been intercepted from the vicinity of the Kapustin Yar area. Certain characteristics of the signals revealed a similarity to the telemetry system designed by German scientists for the Soviets, but the data were not unambiguous. Further intercepts obtained by Army Security Agency personnel in Turkey conclusively established that the signals were indeed telemetry.

Obtaining photographs of the center became a top priority for the CIA. According to Robert Amory, a former CIA Deputy Director for Intelligence, General Nathan Twining said that it could not be done. The CIA turned to the British, who flew a Canberra all the way from Germany to the Volga and down into Persia—obtaining "some fair pictures."[45] But one such fate-tempting mission was enough for the British, whose plane arrived in Iran full of bullet holes. The CIA appealed to Twining to have the Air Force develop a plane that could fly high enough so that it could fly over Soviet radar. However, the Air Force insisted that every plane be an all-purpose plane—with some fighter capability, some maneuverability, and so on. Thus the CIA contacted airplane designer Kelly Johnson at Lockheed.[46]

The conclusive or final impetus to the project was provided by a 1954 presidential commission headed by James Killian, President of the Massachusetts Institute of Technology. The commission, formally known as the Technological Capabilities Panel, was set up to deal with the threat of surprise attack on the United States. A subcommittee headed by Edwin H. Land of Polaroid recommended development of a very high altitude aircraft equipped with special photographic equipment that repeatedly could overfly the Soviet Union with impunity.[47]

On November 24, 1954, at a meeting with the Secretary of State, Secretary of Defense, CIA Chief Allen Dulles, and several high-ranking military officers, Eisenhower gave his approval for a program to build thirty special high-performance aircraft at a total cost of about $35 million. It was further agreed that while the CIA would be placed in charge of the operation, the Defense Department would provide a substantial amount of the funding. Further, after the aircraft had been developed, plans for its use would be examined again.[48]

The CIA's Directorate of Plans established a Development Project Staff to manage the program, and Richard Bissell, a special assistant to Dulles, was given responsibility for running the program.[49] According to Bissell,

> I was summoned one afternoon into Allen's office; and I was told with absolutely no prior warning or knowledge that one day previously President Eisenhower approved a project involving the development of an extremely high-altitude aircraft to be used for surveillance and intelligence collection over "denied areas" in Europe, Russia and elsewhere. I was to go over to the Pentagon, present myself in Trevor Gardner's office and there with Gardner, General Donald Putt of the Air Force, General Clarence Irvine and others, we were to decide how the project was to be organized and run.[50]

It was agreed that the Strategic Air Command would provide a detachment to do pilot training, and tests pilots would be recruited from SAC but would be given civilian status because Eisenhower wanted the operation conducted as a civilian intelligence project.[51] Bissell thus found himself "running an organization in which, broadly there was about one third Air Force personnel on active duty, about one third agency personnel (including people in the field of finance, procurement, and also security and communications), and in field units one third contractor employees."[52]

With bureaucratic problems settled, full attention could be focused on the construction of the aircraft. The task was assigned to Kelly Johnson. Johnson, in fact, had previously responded to an Air Force request for proposals from four airframe builders, including Lockheed, for a very-high-altitude reconnaissance aircraft. The four proposals, submitted simply in sketch form, included those for a plane that became the RB-57D, as well as Johnson's idea for an austere plane with only two functions—to fly high enough to be immune to Soviet air defenses and to take pictures of the secret installations the Soviets were at such pains to hide from the West. The Air Force had rejected Johnson's proposal.[53]

In December 1954 Johnson began work and set a date of August 1955 for the first flight.[54] On August 4, 1955, the first plane was flown from a secret CIA facility at Watertown/Groom Lake in Nevada. On August 8 it made its first official flight.[55] The plane was given the unclassified designation U-2, for Utility-2, to hide, at least on paper, that it was a reconnaissance plane. It was given the classified code name IDEALIST. The plane was a single-seater with a wingspan of eighty feet and a length of fifty feet. The plane could be flown with slipper tanks on the wings to give it an extra 190 gallons of fuel and thus additional range. With the additional fuel and allowing for a one-hundred-gallon reserve, the plane could fly twenty-six hundred statute miles, its cruising speed was 460 miles per hour, and it could photograph 120-mile-wide swaths while flying at about sixty-eight thousand feet—an altitude that it was believed was out of range of Soviet air-defense missiles and fighters.[56]

The U-2's were tested for speed, altitude, range, and photographic capability. The plane's photographic capability was demonstrated to Eisenhower by presenting him with U-2 photographs of San Diego as well as ones of his favorite golf courses.[57] In addition the planes were tested for their ability to evade Soviet radar. Tests were conducted in which radar operators were warned that strange planes would be flying over U.S. territory. Despite the advance notice the U-2 flights were either unseen or imperfectly tracked. These tests, according to Eisenhower, "gave us confidence that, in the then existing state of radar efficiency and the inability of fighter planes to operate at altitudes above some fifty thousand feet, U-2 reconnaissance could be undertaken with reasonable safety."[58]

By the first half of 1956 the CIA had begun deployments to the overseas bases from which the U-2's would fly. The first two U-2's were sent to RAF Lakenheath, England, where the first agency U-2 detachment was to operate under the cover of the fictional 1st Weather Reconnaissance Squadron, Provisional (WRSP-1). However, due to an espionage fiasco later that year known as the Crabbe affair, the British government decided that it preferred the flights not originate from British soil. Thus the WRSP-1 was moved to Wiesbaden, West Germany.[59]

In late May the second group of U-2 pilots entered training at the secret Groom Lake facility. From there they were shipped to Incrilik Air Base near Adana, Turkey, and became part of WRSP-2, operating as Detachment 10-10. The detachment comprised about a hundred personnel. At times there were as many as seven pilots and five aircraft.[60]

While the CIA was preparing to begin the overflight program, the civilian-run National Advisory Committee on Aeronautics (NACA) was providing a cover story for the operation. In the spring of 1956 the committee announced the development of a new airplane for use in high-altitude meteorological studies. The plane was the U-2 and it would to be flown, according to NACA, by civilian pilots on loan from Lockheed. NACA also sought to provide a cover story for WRSP-1, announcing that it was extending its weather program to Europe, where the

WRSP-1 would collect data on weather conditions in the vicinity of the Baltic Sea.[61]

At the end of June Bissell, along with CIA Director Allen Dulles, went to Eisenhower to seek permission to begin the overflight program. After making his presentation Bissell was excused and asked to wait outside while Eisenhower, Allen Dulles, Secretary of State John Foster Dulles, and military aide Andrew Goodpaster discussed the proposed mission. Goodpaster brought Bissell news of the decision—that overflights were authorized for ten days. The ten days referred not to ten days of good flying weather, as Bissell had hoped, but ten calendar days. If ten days of bad weather made flights impossible, new approval would have to be obtained. Fortunately, three days later the weather man reported that conditions were good over central Russia. Bissell sent a signal to Wiesbaden authorizing the first flight.[62]

Thus, on July 4, 1956, the first U-2 flight to overfly the Soviet Union took off from Wiesbaden and headed northeast, overflying Moscow, Leningrad, and the Soviet Baltic Sea coast and then back. It was a route that Allen Dulles, Bissell's boss, didn't find out about until the plane was already in the air. Upon hearing the specifics he was shocked and suggested it might be a rather big risk for a first mission, but Bissell countered that it probably was safest the first time around.[63]

The mission was completed without incident and four more missions followed in short order: two on July 5 and two on July 9. The five missions produced a large quantity of data of interest to intelligence analysts—photographs of the heavily defended areas of Moscow and Leningrad as well as the industrial activity around those cities. The photographs also delineated atomic plants, launching pads, and aircraft caches. The missions revealed that the feared Soviet jet bomber threat—represented by the MYA-4 Bison and the TU-95 Bear—was relatively small. They also revealed that Soviet activity in the ICBM field was accelerating.[64]

While the missions escaped Soviet territory unscathed, they did not escape undetected. Thus, on July 11, 1956, the Soviets protested the intrusions to the State Department. The note specified, for the first two missions, the route flown, the depth into Soviet territory the plane penetrated, and the time spent overflying Soviet air space. According to the Soviet note the July 4 route was Minsk, Vilngas, Kaunas, and Kaliningrad; the depth was 320 kilometers; and the time was one hour, thirty-two minutes. One of the July 5 routes was given as Brest, Pinsk, Baranovichi, Kaunas, and Kaliningrad. The depth was said to be 150 kilometers; the time, one hour, twenty minutes. The Soviet note concluded that the "violation of the air frontiers of the Soviet Union by American aircraft cannot be interpreted as other than intentional and conducted for the purposes of reconnaissance."[65]

By the time the note was delivered the Soviets knew the speed, altitude, and range of the U-2 but not the capabilities of the camera systems.[66] Most importantly of all, they did not know how physically to stop the plane from flying over the Soviet Union. Their fighters could not come within twenty-five thousand feet of the spy plane. Their air-defense missiles were optimized for sixty thousand feet, after which they began to run out of control in the thinner air. While the CIA believed the missiles had a potential to reach seventy thousand to eighty thousand feet, it never happened.[67]

But as with GENETRIX, their political protests did have an effect. As a result of the diplomatic note of July 11 no flights were undertaken for several months.[68] The program resumed in late 1956, and in 1957 the third class of U-2 pilots completed training at Watertown, and WRSP-3 opened at Atsugi, Japan, fifteen miles west of Yokohama. Additionally, the U-2's at Wiesbaden were moved to Giebelstadt, later to be merged with the WRSP unit at Incrilik. Furthermore, operating locations were set up in Pakistan—at Lahore and Peshawar. The Pakistani bases had the virtue of being close to their targets and along the least defended area of the U.S.S.R. These bases were tasked with the mission of searching for atomic energy installations along the Trans-Siberian Railway; locating and photographing a large radar near the terminal site for missile launchings from Kapustin Yar; and overflying missile test activities at Tyuratam, where the SS-3, SS-4 IRBM's, and SS-6 were being tested. It was the U-2 that led to the discovery of Tyuratam facility in 1957.[69]

Richard Bissell recalls that the discovery of Tyuratam occurred when a pilot "used his authorization to deflect from his course. He was flying over Turkistan, and off in the distance he saw something that looked quite interesting and turned out to be the Tyuratam launch site—and unlike almost every other target we went after, not even the existence of that had been suspected . . . and he came back with the most beautiful photographs of this place, and within about five days the photo-interpreters had built a cardboard model of the whole Tyuratam site—roads, railway sidings, feeder roads, everything."[70]

The purpose of the flights in 1957 remained the same as before—collecting information via photography of the Soviet bomber force, the Soviet missile program, the Soviet air-defense system, the Soviet atomic energy program, and the Soviet submarine program.[71] The specific facilities or areas to be photographed on a mission would be decided through a complicated process. Richard Bissell recalled that

> when for some reason or other we were particularly anxious to be given permission to fly, and there had been some lapse of time, this matter would be raised, and if the President was willing to entertain the petition, we would then first of all go through the Intelligence Board, and a requirements committee to set off specific targets. We would draw up on a map an illustrative mission plan actually covering those targets with times and other details. There would then be a briefing of the President, and as a general rule—it became, I think, an almost invariable rule—I would go with Allen Dulles and Cabell for the Agency. Foster Dulles would usually be there, occasionally the Undersecretary, the Secretary of Defense would usually be there, failing him the Deputy, and the Chairman or acting Chairman of the Joint Chiefs

of Staff would be there. He would run through this. At the end the President would ask a lot of questions and as a "general rule," it came more and more to be his habit that he would let us go and give us his decision through Goodpaster a day or so later.

However, he would always get the map on his desk and look at it, and always ask me to come around and explain this or that feature of it, and there were occasions, more than once, when he would say, "Well, you can go there, but I want you to leave out that leg and go straight that way. I want you to go from B to D because it looks like you might be getting a little exposed over here," or something of the kind.[72]

The exact flight plan that was presented to Eisenhower and the ones employed after his revisions resulted from taking the array of high-priority targets and determining which of those targets could be reached from a particular base. Once the set of targets and the general area was decided on the specific routing would be turned over to the operations people, who would determine the order in which the targets would be covered, where the plane would turn, and other aspects. The exact details of the flight plan would be known only to about a dozen people in Washington—the President, the Secretaries of State and Defense, the Chairman of the JCS, Director of Central Intelligence Dulles, Bissell, and three to five members of his staff.[73]

The number of times that overflight plans were developed and implemented were, in absolute terms, small. Over the life of the program a total of perhaps twenty overflights were conducted—fifteen in western Russia and five in the eastern part of the country, with three of the eastern flights being over Kamchatka, the target area for long-range missile tests.[74] The flights over Kamchatka were flown from Alaska, apparently the only overflights originating from U.S. territory.[75] Thus after the initial burst of overflights in 1956, the programs involved rare periods of activity and long, dormant periods.

While overflights were only sporadic, peripheral electronic reconnaissance and photographic reconnaissance were undertaken more frequently. In his memoirs Francis Gary Powers recalled, "I flew my first electronic surveillance mission along the borders outside Russia, the specialized equipment monitoring and recording Soviet radar and radio frequencies. Routes on such flights varied. We usually flew from Turkey eastward along the Southern border of the Soviet Union over Iran and Afghanistan as far as Pakistan, and back. We also flew along the Black Sea and, on occasion, as far west as Albania, but never penetrating, staying off the coast, over international waters . . . our territory was the southern portion of Russia's perimeter."[76]

Often such missions involved monitoring rocket launches, launches the United States apparently knew about several days in advance, probably because the prolonged countdown was being detected at the Turkish ground stations. The U-2's flying peripheral missions during these events were armed with highly sophisticated interception equipment. One unit came on automatically the moment the launch frequency was used and intercepted all signals sent out to control the rocket.[77]

In only one instance was an overflight used for signals interception rather than photographic reconnaissance—an either/or situation because the size of the plane did not allow it to carry both photographic and signals interception packages. About eighteen months after the inception of the program, a U-2 equipped with a Ramo-Woolridge signals interception package left Bodø, Norway, flew down the Russo-Finnish border, along the Russian Baltic coast, the Russian border with Bulgaria and Hungary, and finally down to Turkey, where it landed at Adana.[78]

In 1958 a U-2 also was sent to Bodø, to gather nuclear debris from the Soviet nuclear tests being conducted on the Arctic islands of Novaya Zemlya and Franz Joseph Land. Such nuclear monitoring missions were to become the major task of WRSP-3 at Atsugi—a location that the wind patterns and upper atmospheric currents made ideal for the interception of nuclear debris from tests at Semipalatinsk in southern Russia.[79]

Overflights began tapering off in 1958 as high officials, particularly Eisenhower, were growing more and more anxious concerning the possibility of an incident and its potential consequences. The intelligence community had predicted that it would take the Soviets about two years to develop effective countermeasures. It was expected from the beginning that a plane would be shot down or that a near-miss would demonstrate that the operation was no longer viable.[80]

By 1958 Eisenhower was greatly concerned with avoiding such an incident. Thus on March 7, 1958—shortly after a March 1 mission over the Soviet Far East—Eisenhower's military aide Brigadier General Andrew Goodpaster informed Allen Dulles that "further operations contemplated in the plan for special reconnaissance activities should be discontinued, effective at once."[81] While the discontinuance was not permanent, the anxiety persisted. At a December 16 meeting with his Board of Consultants on Foreign Intelligence Activities, Eisenhower questioned the continuation of the overflight program, suggesting that the United States had located adequate targets and that the intelligence being gathered might not be worth the resulting exacerbation of international tension.[82]

In the early months of 1959 Eisenhower continued to question the desirability of continuing the operation. At a February 12 meeting of the National Security Council, he was "reserved on the request to continue reconnaissance flights on the basis that it is undue provocation. Nothing . . . would make him request authority to declare war more quickly than violation of our air space by Soviet aircraft." While one or two flights might be permissible, he would oppose any extensive program.[83] The following month, Eisenhower "decided to disapprove any additional special flights by the U-2 unit in the present abnormally tense circumstances." On April 6 he approved a mission but the very next day he called in Richard Bissell and Secretary of Defense Neil McElroy to tell them that he had decided not to go ahead with the flight.[84]

In early 1960 Allen Dulles and Richard Bissell requested a resumption of overflights. Apparently there had been no deep overflights since the Camp David meeting between Eisenhower and Khrushchev in September 1959.[85] With a summit conference coming up in Paris in May, Eisenhower was as concerned as ever. In a prescient comment Eisenhower, according to General Goodpaster, said on February 8 that "he has one tremendous asset in a summit meeting, as regards effect in the free world. That is his reputation for honesty. If one of these aircraft were lost when we are engaged in apparently sincere deliberations, it would be put on display in Moscow and ruin the President's effectiveness."[86]

Dulles and Bissell wanted to photograph ICBM launch sites in the northern Urals and westward near the White Sea as well as bomber fields, factories, and other installations.[87] Eisenhower was persuaded, and on April 9 an overflight produced photography showing that work on the ICBM program was progressing at a far faster rate than had been expected. But the photography produced was not the quality that would have been preferred, and another mission was requested. The main target would be the ICBM facility at Plesetsk, where the April 9 flight found evidence of an operational ICBM capability.[88]

The mission, argued Dulles and Bissell, would be of considerably above average importance and could not afford to be delayed. Delay might mean missing the opportunity to see the missiles under construction. Afterward, the missiles might be camouflaged. Additionally, climatic conditions imposed severe constraints on when a successful mission could be flown. Missions over Plesetsk could be flown effectively from April through July, it was argued. If the mission was postponed until July and weather was poor, no photography could be obtained until April of the following year.[89] Another mission was approved on April 25. Bissell was informed by General Goodpaster that one additional mission could be flown prior to May 1, and no operation was to be carried out after May 1.[90]

As a result, on May 1 Francis Gary Powers left Peshawar for a flight that was scheduled to conclude at Bodø. His route would take him through the heart of the Soviet Union—over the Tyuratam Cosmodrome to monitor any space-launching activity that might have been scheduled to coincide with the May Day celebration; an industrial complex at Sverdlovsk; the ICBM site at Plesetsk; and finally on to Archangel and Murmansk to collect information on activities at the long-range bomber, submarine, and other military bases in the area.[91]

Powers never made it to Norway. At five o'clock on the morning of May 1, Nikita Khrushchev received a phone call from his Minister of Defense, Rodion Malinovsky, who informed him that a U-2 had entered Soviet air space from Afghanistan and was headed toward Sverdlovsk. Khrushchev ordered the plane to be shot down by whatever means were necessary.[92]

Somewhere over Sverdlovsk, Powers' plane was shot down. At first the United States, believing Powers dead, claimed the plane was on a weather mission and had strayed off course. The National Aeronautics and Space Administration, which had replaced NACA, issued a press release that stated:

> A NASA U-2 research airplane being flown over Turkey on a joint NASA-USAF Air Weather Service mission apparently went down in the Lake Van Turkey area at about 9:00 A.M. (3:00 A.M. EDT), Sunday, May 1.
>
> During the flight in eastern Turkey, the pilot reported over the emergency frequency that he was experiencing oxygen difficulties. The flight originated in Adana with a mission to obtain data on clear air turbulence.
>
> A search is now under way in the Lake Van area. The pilot is an employee of Lockheed aircraft under contract to NASA. The U-2 program was initiated by NASA in 1956 as a method of making high-altitude weather studies.[93]

When Khrushchev produced not only the plane's cameras but also its pilot—alive and well—Eisenhower admitted the U-2's mission and accepted personal responsibility. As he feared, the plane was put on display and the summit was wrecked.

Despite the consequence of the May 1 flight, the U-2 program had been a major breakthrough in attaining information on the Soviet Union and particularly on its military activities. In testifying before an executive session of the Senate Foreign Relations Committee in the aftermath of the incident, Allen Dulles stated:

> The U-2 program has helped confirm that only a greatly reduced long-range bomber production program is continuing in the Soviet Union. It has established, however, that the Soviet Union has recently developed a new medium range bomber with supersonic capabilities. The U-2 program has covered many long-range bomber airfields, confirming estimates of the location of bases and the disposition of Soviet long-range bombers. It has also acquired data on the nuclear weapons storage facilities associated with them.
>
> Our overflights have enabled us to look periodically at the actual ground facilities involved with respect to the Soviet missile system programs. . . .
>
> Our photography has also provided us valuable insight into the problem of Soviet doctrine regarding ICBM deployment. It has taught us much about the use to which the Soviet Union is making of these sites for training troops and the operational use of the short- and intermediate-range ballistic missiles.
>
> The program has provided valuable information on the Soviet atomic energy program. . . . This coverage has included the production of fissionable materials, weapons development and test activities, and the location, type, and size of many

stockpile sites. . . . The Soviet nuclear testing ground has been photographed with extremely interesting results more than once.

The photography also has given us our first firm information on the magnitude and location of the U.S.S.R.'s domestic uranium ore and uranium processing facilities vital in estimating the Soviet fissionable material production. We have located national and regional nuclear storage sites and forward storage facilities.[94]

VI.

Reconnaissance at Sea

*J*ust as ships and submarines were outfitted during World War II with electronic equipment to intercept enemy signals, so such missions continued throughout the Cold War period. Part of the purpose was to collect information on developments within the U.S.S.R.—to intercept communications and missile telemetry and to photograph port areas and coastlines from sea level.

A second aspect of sea-based intelligence collection was the monitoring of Soviet naval movements. All Soviet naval movements—military or commercial—were considered targets for U.S. intelligence-collection ships. Additionally, when the Soviet Union finally developed, in the 1960s, a submarine ballistic missile force whose missiles could reach United States territory, that submarine force became the most closely monitored component of Soviet naval forces. A major role in that monitoring was played by a set of passive listening devices installed at selected locations on the ocean's floor.

In the summer of 1948, naval submarine reconnaissance "revealed a 7,000-ton vessel heading for Providence Bay with several military trucks on top deck."[1] By 1952, the Navy was conducting such submarine reconnaissance operations on a regular basis from outside the twelve-mile limit. A ship was maintained to watch maritime traffic between the northern shores of the Soviet Union and Vladivostok. Each submarine would be on duty for one month and was then replaced by another.[2]

The use of surface ships for intelligence collection was reflected in a 1953 memo from the Commander in Chief of the Atlantic Fleet (CINCLANTFLT) announcing that a cruise by a U.S. vessel would occur during the summer of 1953. The vessel would cruise in the Barents Sea, taking it near the Kola Peninsula and Murmansk Naval Base as well as the Soviet nuclear test site at Novaya Zemlya. In his memo he requested the submission of intelligence requirements. While Air Force Intelligence did not have any specific requirements, it declared its interest in "any data on specific locations of port and communication facilities, navigation aids and other fixed installations and activities with particular emphasis on specific operation and activity data that may be directly linked with such facilities."[3]

Two new programs for the use of surface vessels and submarines for intelligence collection began in the last years of the Eisenhower administration. By 1960, the National Security Agency had overcome opposition within the Pentagon to operating its own set of intelligence-collection ships. NSA wanted to emulate the Soviet practice of deploying spy trawlers or AGI's along the coast of intelligence targets. What was wanted was a ship that, according to former NSA official Frank Raven, "could mosey along a coast relatively slowly, take its time, and spend time at sea."[4] The slow speed was optimal for intercepting the maximum amount of traffic without it appearing that the ship was purposely loitering.

The first ship selected was the U.S.N.S. *Private José F. Valdez*, "a rusting veteran salvaged from the mothball fleet of the U.S. Maritime Administration."[5] The *Valdez* had been constructed at the Riverside Yard in Duluth, Minnesota, in 1944 and had served as a coastal transport with the Military Sea Transportation Service.[6] The *Valdez* began operations from its home port of Cape Town, South Africa. From there it had the option of traveling up either coast of Africa. Its primary mission was intercepting the communications of the new African nations and the remaining colonies. However, to give it a "cover," a small amount of travel time was spent in the South Atlantic off Namibia monitoring the impact of Soviet missile warheads that had been launched from the Kapustin Yar test range.[7]

By July 1961, the Navy had gained operational control of the program, although it still had to satisfy NSA's tasking requirements. Hence a second set of intelligence-collection ships was commissioned. Given the general designation AGTR (for Auxiliary General—Technical Research), the ships were converted World War II Liberty ships. Liberty ships were longer (at 458 feet), heavier (at 10,680 tons), and faster than their predecessors. The latter characteristic had the drawback of making it obvious that such ships were hovering.[8] Ultimately seven AGTR's were commissioned: *Oxford, Jamestown, Georgetown, Belmont, Liberty, Muller,* and *Valdez.* The ships also differed from their predecessors in one of the means used to transmit the data they gathered. The system was known as TRESSCOMM (for Technical Research Ship Communications). It involved a sixteen-foot dish antenna that tracked the moon. When both an AGTR and the listening station—the Naval Communications Station at Cheltenham, Maryland—were in line of sight of the moon, the antenna would transmit its data via microwave signals to the moon. The signals would bounce off it and be received at Cheltenham—or at least they would in theory. However, problems with the complex hydraulic system and the need to keep the antenna pointed directly at the moon despite the movement of the ship made successful communication problematical. The hydraulic mechanisms were not adequate to adjust the massive dish to the required angle.[9]

By 1965 it was concluded that the United States needed to engage in a substantial ship-based intelligence-collection effort against the Soviet fleet. Using intelligence ships to mingle with the Soviet fleet and intercept the signals being transmitted (as the

Soviets used their AGI's to mingle with the U.S. fleet) would provide valuable information on the expanding Soviet Navy.[10]

Building more AGTRs to produce a fleet large enough to satisfy both NSA's and the Navy's requirements was ruled out because of the expense involved. Nor was using destroyers in an even greater intelligence-collection role considered feasible. The option of building a trawler fleet and equipping it with electronic interception equipment in direct emulation of the Soviet Union also was ruled out; given that the Navy did not have the funds to build all the combat ships it felt were needed, it would be impossible to justify spending money on trawlers. The solution was to pull some ships out of mothballs and convert them for intelligence collection. The ships then would be assigned to collecting intelligence against purely naval targets and monitoring the activities of the Soviet fleet.[11]

The Naval Security Group Command was put in charge of the operation, and an officer was assigned to find the appropriate ships. He considered tuna boats, fleet tugs, and old destroyer escorts but eventually (if somewhat reluctantly) settled on the old cargo ships known as AKL's. The first ship to qualify for the program was in the process of heading toward the United States and retirement in the mothball fleet, having spent its career in the vicinity of the Marianas. Thus the U.S.S. *Banner* was subjected to an extensive conversion process costing over $1.5 million, including the installation of the electronic equipment by Ling-Temco-Vought's Electro Systems Division, a part of the project first designated Project FIELD MOUSE and then Project SOD HUT.[12]

The conversion process that took place at the Puget Sound Naval Shipyard in Bremerton, Washington, turned the old cargo ship into an AGER ship (AGER stood for Auxiliary General—Environmental Research). Of course, it was not specified that the environment to be researched was the electronic environment. The ship itself was only 935 tons and 176 feet long—making it only a fraction of the size of the AGTR's.[13]

According to U.S. government official statements, the "primary mission of each AGER was to conduct surveillance of and collect intelligence against naval forces and coastal installations in support of naval and National Intelligence Collection requirements. These multi-sensor platforms were tasked with the gathering of [deleted] visual (photographic), acoustic and oceanographic intelligence data. . . ."14

After a seventeen-day trip from Bremerton, the U.S.S. *Banner* (AGER-1) arrived at Yokosuka Harbor on October 18, 1965, to begin operations designated as CLICKBEETLE. They were to involve a series of four- to six-week patrols in the Sea of Japan to conduct "tactical surveillance and intelligence collection against Soviet naval units and other targets of opportunity." The *Banner* was to be free to depart from its assigned patrol areas to monitor Soviet naval deployments or exercises. Surveillance was to be conducted outside Soviet-bloc claimed territorial waters (twelve miles) and not normally closer than five hundred yards from any Soviet ship except "for briefly closing to two hundred yards as necessary for visual-photo coverage of unusual interest items."15 The orders also specified that "upon sailing for patrol station, *Banner* will check out of the movement report system and will proceed to her assigned patrol areas in strict electronic silence. Silence will be maintained until *Banner* is detected and comes under surveillance by Soviet bloc forces, at which time *Banner* will break silence and submit periodic reports. When surveillance of *Banner* by Soviet bloc forces ceases, *Banner* will resume electronic silence."16

The *Banner* departed Yokosuka on her first mission almost immediately after arrival. According to Trevor Armbrister, this mission involved an exception to the twelve-mile limit, much in the way that ferret flights occasionally were directed to penetrate Soviet air space in violation of general policy. The mission would take the *Banner* to within four miles of Siberia's Povorothy Bay in an attempt to test whether the Soviets took serious their twelve-mile limit, which was nine miles greater than was standard in international law.17

In addition to being confronted with a storm as it headed toward Siberia, it then was confronted by Soviet destroyers and patrol boats when it got closer. The boats began harassing the *Banner*—"darting in and out toward the bobbing travelers, some-

times closing to within twenty-five yards before veering away."
Confronted with the storm, the fear of capsizing due to the quantity of ice that had formed on the ship, and the harassment, the
Banner's commander, Lieutenant Robert P. Bishop, informed
Yokosuka that he was turning back. Hours later he was instructed not to be intimidated and ordered to turn around. Following orders, he headed back into the storms, but then gave up
after losing two miles in the next twenty-four hours.[18]

In the following three years, the *Banner* conducted a total of
fifteen similar missions—seven in the Sea of Japan followed by
three off the coast of mainland China and then the final five off
the Sea of Japan again. When in the Sea of Japan its primary
mission was the monitoring of the major Soviet naval base at
Vladivostok.[19]

In December 1967, the *Banner* received a companion when
the U.S.S. *Pueblo* (AGER-2) had arrived in Yokosuka Harbor. By
that time the PINKROOT schedule had been drawn up—a
schedule of missions for the *Banner* and the *Pueblo* extending
from January 1968 to June 1968. The *Banner's* missions
(PINKROOT Operations 1, 3, 5, and 7) were to involve a January
5–February 4 patrol in the vicinity of North Korea and the
Tsushima Strait, a February 19–March 21 patrol in the Sea of
Japan, an April 3–May 3 patrol near Petropavlovsk, and a May
17–June 26 patrol in the Sea of Japan.[20]

Like the *Banner,* the *Pueblo* was small—177½ feet long, thirty-
three feet wide, and only 935 tons. Also like the *Banner,* she was
over twenty years old. On her decks and superstructure were a
variety of antennas of different shapes and sizes. From her forward
mast hung domelike direction finders and triangulators. The
eighty-three-man crew included two civilian oceanographers, two
Marine linguists, and twenty-eight communications technicians
who worked inside secret "research spaces." The twenty-eight
technicians were separated into six branches, including an "I" or
interpreter branch with Russian and Korean linguists, a "T" or
technical analyst branch, and an "R" or Morse code branch.[21]

In its initial mission the *Pueblo* was to "sample the electronic
environment of east coast North Korea" to "determine the nature

and extent of naval activity off North Korean ports." In monitoring North Korean ports such as Wonsan it might also get a chance to eavesdrop on Soviet nuclear submarines, since they often operated from Wonsan during the winter months when their activities at Vladivostok were endangered by massive ice floes. She also was to "intercept and conduct surveillance of Soviet naval units operating Tsushima Straits."[22] The mission was approved by the Joint Reconnaissance Center of the Joint Chiefs of Staff and then by the 303 Committee of the National Security Council. Unfortunately for the crew of the *Pueblo*, the North Koreans did not approve and expressed their disapproval not through a strongly worded diplomatic note but by force. On January 23, 1968, fifteen days after departing Yokosuka, one crewman of the *Pueblo* was dead and the rest were in North Korean custody. It was to be a year before they were freed.

The *Pueblo* incident, coming less than a year after the Israeli bombing of an AGTR (the U.S.S. *Liberty*), led to the decision to decommission the entire AGTR and AGER fleets. In six months the fleet was no longer operational and was ready to be sold for scrap.[23]

A program that also had its genesis in the later years of the Eisenhower administration but still is operational today involves not surface ships but submarines. Known by a variety of code names, the best known of which is HOLYSTONE, the program is one of the most sensitive intelligence operations of the U.S. government. The program is managed by a special committee, probably called the National Executive Committee for Special Navy Activities, chaired by the Director of Central Intelligence and reporting to the Secretary of Defense.

HOLYSTONE, which also has been known as PINNACLE, BOLLARD, and most recently as BARNACLE, began in 1959 and has involved the use of specially equipped electronic submarines to collect electronic communications and photographic intelligence. The primary target always has been the Soviet Union, but at times countries such as Vietnam and China have been targets of the operations, which sometimes involved penetration of the

Soviet, Chinese, and Vietnamese three-mile territorial limits.[24]

The missions lasted about ninety days. Crews were given cover stories—such as being on an undersea geodetic survey project that was using sonar to study ocean water temperatures to support data collected by satellites. The crews also were forbidden to use any active electronic or sonar gear while on a HOLYSTONE mission so as to avoid detection by Soviet antisubmarine devices. In addition, hatches were required to be tied down to prevent rattling.[25]

By 1975 the program apparently had provided vital information on the Soviet submarine fleet—its configuration, capabilities, noise patterns, missiles, and missile-firing capabilities. One mission involved obtaining the "voice autograph" of Soviet submarines. Using detailed tape recordings of noise made by submarine engines and other equipment, analysts of the Naval Scientific and Technical Intelligence Center (now the Naval Intelligence Support Center) were able to develop a methodology for the identification of individual Soviet submarines, even those tracked at long range under the ocean. The analysts then could follow the submarine from its initial operations to its decommissioning.[26]

HOLYSTONE operations also provided information about theater and strategic sea-based missiles. Some Soviet sea-based missiles were tested against inland targets to reduce U.S. observation. On occasion, HOLYSTONE submarines would penetrate close enough to Soviet territory to observe the missile launchings, providing important information on the early stages of the flight. Thus, according to one government official, the most significant information provided by the HOLYSTONE missions was a readout of the computer calculations and signals put into effect by Soviet technicians before launching the missiles. Beyond that the U.S. subs also provided intelligence by tracking the flight and eventual landing of the missiles, providing continuous information on guidance and electronic systems.[27]

In addition to providing acoustic intelligence and telemetry intelligence, the HOLYSTONE submarines also tapped into Soviet land communications cables on the ocean floor. The tapping operation allowed the United States to intercept higher-level military messages and other communications considered too sensitive to be entrusted to insecure means of communication, such as radio and microwave transmissions.[28]

Beyond signals intelligence, the submarines also were to bring back valuable photographs, many of which were taken through the submarine's periscope. In the early 1970s the weekly Thursday morning regular intelligence briefing session in the Chief of Naval Operations' briefing theater was followed by a discussion of HOLYSTONE missions. The lights would be dimmed and slides employed to indicate where the missions were on station. One participant recalled seeing close-up photographs of Soviet submarines that had been taken by a HOLYSTONE vessel. On an earlier occasion, in the mid-1960s, photographs were shown of the underside of an E Class Soviet submarine that appeared to be taken inside Vladivostok Harbor.[29]

The operations were not unknown to the Soviet government nor without risk. Thus, on August 28, 1961, Radio Moscow broadcast a TASS statement charging that foreign submarines had committed "a number of violations of the state seacoast of the Soviet Union" and that submarines had been "making observations for intelligence purposes." As a result, the Soviet government, according to TASS, instructed the Ministry of Defense "to take measures to destroy the violators."[30]

While no U.S. submarines were attacked, the potential for an international incident was there—and several close calls resulted. The same submarine that photographed the underside of the E Class submarine also scraped the bottom of the submarine, damaging its own conning tower. Despite a search by Soviet vessels, the submarine escaped.[31] Another incident is reported to have occurred in May 1974 involving a collision between a HOLYSTONE submarine and a Soviet submarine in Soviet waters off Petropavlovsk on the Kamchatka Peninsula. Both submarines were armed with nuclear weapons, according to the report.[32] In a third incident a HOLYSTONE submarine was beached for about two hours off the Soviet coast, according to a former government aide. The incident was the cause of concern in the National Security Council that a major international incident would result if the submarine was discovered.[33]

In one instance a collision involving a HOLYSTONE ship, the U.S.S. *Gato,* led to the filing of a series of falsified reports. The incident occurred late in 1969, when the *Gato* collided with a Soviet submarine fifteen to twenty-five miles off the entrance to the White Sea—in the Barents Sea off the northern Soviet Union. At one point the *Gato* had been only one mile off the Soviet coast due to drifting beyond its prescribed four-mile limit.[34]

According to crew members, the *Gato* was armed with nuclear weapons. Included was at least one SUBROC torpedo missile, capable of destroying a submerged submarine up to thirty miles away. The ship also had been specially modified before leaving New London, Connecticut, with a special compartment for eight members of the NSA, who spent much of their time monitoring Soviet communications.[35]

The *Gato* was assigned to sail to the entrance of the White Sea and track vessels leaving the Archangel submarine base. Further, once on station it was to detect and identify Soviet submarines in an attempt to pick up their sonar patterns as well as to take photographs if possible. To accomplish the mission the *Gato* would secretly trail the Soviet submarine, staying in an area behind the ship's propellers so that Soviet sonar technicians would be unable to hear the trailing submarine.[36]

At approximately nine in the evening of either November 14 or 17, 1969, the *Gato* made initial contact with a Soviet submarine that was transiting from the White Sea to the Barents Sea. After determining the course and speed of the Soviet submarine, the *Gato's* sonar operators were responsible for charting her course. Unfortunately, due either to errors or poor data, the sonarmen estimated that the Soviet vessel was moving at eight knots. On the basis of that conclusion, her position was fixed. In reality, the Soviet submarine was traveling at seven knots, and the *Gato* began overtaking her on the left. At the same time, the sonar operators reported that the Soviet vessel appeared to be turning to the right.[37]

In response the *Gato* turned right, and as a result of overtaking, the Soviet submarine crossed her bow. The result was a collision, with the Soviet sub hitting the *Gato* at about a ninety-degree angle. The *Gato* was struck in the heavy plating that served as the protective shield around the vessel's nuclear reactor and sustained no serious damage. The *Gato*'s weapons officer immediately took steps to prepare for a confrontation—running down two decks and preparing for orders to arm the SUBROC nuclear torpedo and three smaller nuclear-topped torpedos. All that was needed for him to begin to prepare the torpedos for launching was a single authentication—from either the ship's captain or her executive officer. The captain of the Soviet ship appeared to believe it struck a sea mount or similar underwater object, and surfaced moments later. Subsequently, Soviet ships and planes searched the area. The *Gato* sailed two days underwater to reach an area in the Atlantic where radio silence could be broken. Rather than being permitted to file a true report, the captain was instructed to file a false report stating that the *Gato* had broken off operations early due to mechanical problems.[38]

As was the case when the *Gato* operated, today's BARNACLE missions employ the thirty-eight nuclear-powered Sturgeon Class submarines such as the *SSN-637* (Sturgeon). The submarines have dimensions of 292 by 31.7 by twenty-six feet and carry SUBROC and antisubmarine torpedos as well as Harpoon and Tomahawk missiles. With their 107-person complement (twelve officers and ninety-five enlisted personnel), the ships can travel at speeds of over twenty knots when surfaced and at over thirty knots underwater and can reach a depth of 1,320 feet. Their standard electronic equipment includes a search radar and both active and passive sonar systems.[39]

The special equipment placed on such submarines for HOLYSTONE/BARNACLE operations has included the WLR-6 Waterboy Signals Intelligence Systems. The WLR-6 is in the process of being replaced by a more advanced system known as SEA NYMPH (AN/WLQ-4[V]), described in one document as "an advanced, automatic, modular signals exploitation system designed for continuous acquisition, identification, recording, analysis and exploitation of electromagnetic signals." All the Sturgeon submarines will carry a basic skeleton system that can be upgraded to full capacity when authorized.[40]

Another reconnaissance project involving submarines that was conducted after 1975 was code-named IVY BELLS. The project involved implanting a device to intercept the signals transmitted along a Soviet underwater cable in the Sea of Okhotsk between the Kamchatka Peninsula and the eastern Soviet coastline. The information being transmitted along the cables included the trip reports sent by Soviet submarines to military command posts once they had returned to port. The reports provided information on the whereabouts (at given points in time) and activities of the submarines. Such information could be exploited by the United States not only to enhance her picture of the Soviet submarine fleet but also to fine-tune the detection capability of the SOSUS arrays (see following material) that are employed to track Soviet submarines.[41] Other information transmitted on the cable apparently included information concerning Soviet military movements, planning, and weapons capabilities.[42]

Emplacement of the device could be done by two means. The Navy has reconfigured some nuclear-powered submarines into APSSN's—submarines outfitted with one- or two-person minisubs known as SEAL Delivery Vehicles. These minisubs can be employed to transport the naval commandos known as SEALs (for sea-air-land) to areas within the territorial waters of another nation, to its coastline, or to the ocean bottom. The SEALs could emplace the device and return to the minisubmarine.[43]

Another possible means of emplacement would involve using one of the vehicles that constitute the deep submergence vehicle fleet. The fleet consists of three deep submergence vehicles (DSVs), two deep submergence rescue vehicles (DSRVs), and the nuclear-powered *NR-1*. These minisubs are all manned and can operate at extreme depths. One of the DSVs, the *Sea Cliff*, can reach twenty thousand feet, giving it the ability to reach 98 percent of the ocean depths. It can remain at twenty thousand feet for four hours before it must return to the surface.[44]

The approximate location of the device used to intercept the cable traffic was revealed to the Soviet Union by Ronald Pelton, an NSA employee. Although Pelton's designation was several hundred miles off, the Soviet Union still was able to recover the device.[45] However, other devices in other locations may still be operating.

While the United States terminated the AGER and AGTR programs in the wake of the *Pueblo* fiasco, the United States has not foregone the use of surface ships to collect intelligence, although the details of some operations are obscure. One target of these surface operations apparently is missile telemetry and other missile-test-related signals. Thus it was reported in 1979 that "American ships equipped with sensitive listening gear similar to the Iranian sites patrol the North Atlantic, where they collect telemetry broadcast by the new Soviet submarine-launched missiles tested in the White Sea, northeast of Finland."[46] Likewise, on the night of August 31, 1983, when the United States was expecting the Soviet Union to test an SS-X-24 missile, the frigate *Badger* was stationed in the Sea of Okhotsk.[47]

The *Badger* and the rest of the forty-six Knox Class frigates have dimensions of 438 by 46.8 by 24.8 feet, can travel at twenty-seven knots, and carry 275 personnel. In addition to ASROC antisubmarine weapons, search radar, and sonar, they are fitted with satellite communications antennas for both transmission and reception.[48] As a result, they can transmit any data collected back to organizations such as NSA virtually immediately.

In 1981 the United States began to employ Spruance Class destroyers in a signals intelligence role. Primarily antisubmarine ships, the destroyers can be augmented with SIGINT antennas to conduct offshore collection operations. Thus the seventy-eight-hundred-ton destroyer *Deyo*, with its search radar, sonar, gunnery, and missiles, cruised the northern Baltic in August 1980.[49] During the birth of Solidarity in Poland in August 1980, the *Caron* cruised fourteen miles off the coast of Gdansk.[50] Simultaneous to being fourteen miles off Gdansk, the *Caron* also was about fifty miles from Kaliningrad, of the Soviet Baltic Military District. Kaliningrad serves as a home port of Golf II submarines armed with SS-N-5 submarine-launched ballistic missiles and is home of the headquarters of Soviet Naval Aviation Baltic as well as of a VLF/LF transmitter operating to the Baltic and North seas. It also is possibly an SS-4 and SS-20 IRBM base.[51] During another North Atlantic cruise the *Caron* came within miles of major Soviet naval bases at Severomorsk, Iekanga, and Polyarnyy.[52]

The *Caron* was again employed in an intelligence-collection mission against the Soviet target in 1986. Along with another warship, the U.S.S. *Yorktown*, the *Caron* entered Soviet territorial waters in the Black Sea on March 10 and remained there a week, coming as close as six miles to the Soviet coast. While a Pentagon official claimed that intelligence collection was not the primary rationale of the exercise—which had been ordered by the Joint Chiefs of Staff in the name of Secretary of Defense Weinberger— it was at the very least an important secondary mission.[53]

Among the equipment carried by the *Yorktown* is an Aegis fire-control system that can track hostile planes, ships, and submarines. The system can also select, aim, and fire the weapons best suited to destroying a target. In addition to helicopters to gather information, the *Yorktown* also is outfitted with electronic equipment that can monitor voice communications and radar signals. It has been normal procedure to use such systems to determine if new radars have been deployed onshore and to check the readiness of Soviet forces. Additionally, with the headquarters of the Soviet Union's Black Sea Fleet at Sevastopol, nearby communications monitoring would be certain.[54] In a previous expedition, the *Yorktown*'s equipment was used in part to monitor aircraft movements within the Soviet Union.[55]

The Soviets responded to the *Yorktown/Caron* mission both militarily and diplomatically. A destroyer was used to trail both ships, while military aircraft overflew them. In addition, a Soviet protest note said the episode "was of a demonstrative, defiant nature and pursued clearly provocative aims."[56]

The most important ship-based system for monitoring Soviet missile tests is a phased array radar designated COBRA JUDY, which resides upon the U.S.N.S. *Observation Island*. Until 1983 the United States employed Advanced Range Instrumentation Ships, under the code name COBRA JEAN, for forty-five-day periods to collect intelligence in the warhead impact area on Kamchatka. The primary function of the ships was to provide support for U.S. missile and space launches: Each ship would be laden with satellite dishes, radar, and various antenna and communications equipment. Thus a ship such as the *Redstone* was converted into an advanced-range instrumentation ship by being cut in half and having a seventy-two-foot midsection inserted. With its 595-foot length, the *Redstone* supported approximately 450 tons of electronic equipment.[57]

The retirement of the *Redstone* and other advanced-range instrumentation ships from the spy role was due to the conversion of an ARIS, the *Observation Island*, to provide a platform for a phased array radar to be called COBRA JUDY. Emplaced on the 563-foot-long ship is a four-story-high turret on the aft deck that houses the major components of COBRA JUDY. The turret is essentially a thirty-foot cube with one face tilted slightly inward. An antenna array 22½ feet in diameter occupies an octagonal raised area on the slanting face. In addition, on top of the superstructure there are two thirty-two-foot-diameter geodesic radomes containing a complex of passive receiving antennas funded by NSA.[58]

The deployment of COBRA JUDY was designed to allow the monitoring of the final near-earth trajectories of Soviet reentry test vehicles during the portion of their flight not "visible" to COBRA DANE because of the line-of-sight constraints imposed by the curvature of the earth. In particular the sensors provide information on the radar signatures of reentry vehicles and warheads.[59] To enhance that capability, an X-band radar with parabolic dish antenna was added in 1985 to improve COBRA JUDY's capability further. Because of the higher degree of resolution and target separation, the radar may be able to distinguish between multiple warheads and penetration aids such as decoys and chaff.[60]

In addition to active reconnaissance missions at sea, a set of ocean-bottom arrays has been employed since the early 1950s to monitor the movements of Soviet submarines. Since the 1950s the Soviet submarine force has grown markedly both in size and capabilities. Soviet attack and ballistic-missile-carrying submarines now represent a significant component of Soviet strategic capabilities.

The set of arrays is known as SOSUS—Sound Surveillance System. Development of the SOSUS system began in 1950 under the code name CAESAR. Bell Telephone was approached by the Navy with a new concept of sonar—a combination of transducers in long string configurations stretching along the seabeds, tops of sea mountains, and continental shelves. The research and development part of the program was assigned to Bell Laboratories, while Bell's Long Lines Department—which operated the C.S. *Long Lines*, the largest cable-laying ship in the world—was assigned the cable-laying and deep-sea operations. The first array was placed on the continental shelf off the East Coast of the United States in 1954.[61]

SOSUS was described by the Stockholm International Peace Research Institute (SIPRI) in 1979 as follows:

> Each SOSUS installation consists of an array of hundreds of hydrophones laid out on the sea floor, or moored at depths most conducive to sound propagation, and connected by submarine cables for transmission of telemetry. In such an array a sound wave arriving from a distant submarine will be successively detected by different hydrophones according to their geometric relationship to the direction from which the wave arrives. This direction can be determined by noting the order in which the wave is detected at the different hydrophones. In practice the sensitivity of the array is enhanced many times by adding the signals from several individual hydrophones after introducing appropriate time delays between them. The result is a listening "beam" that can be "steered" in various directions towards various

sectors of the ocean by varying the pattern of time delays. The distance from the array to the sound source can be calculated by measuring the divergence of the sound rays within the array or by triangulating from adjacent arrays.[62]

Over the years the SOSUS network has grown, with new arrays being established throughout the world and the data collection and processing capabilities being frequently upgraded. After the initial CAESAR array proved successful, arrays were installed elsewhere off the East Coast of the United States and covering the Greenland-Iceland-United Kingdom (GIUK) Gap— the latter being the portion of the Atlantic through which Soviet submarines stationed at the Polyarnyy submarine base in the northwestern Soviet Union must pass to head toward the United States. Even earlier warning is provided by an array strung between Andoya, Norway, and Bear Island.[63]

By the late 1960s several more arrays had been established. An upgraded variant of CAESAR, COLOSSUS, was deployed along the Pacific coast of the United States and extends from the top of Alaska to the Baja Peninsula. COLOSSUS employed a more advanced form of sonar than CAESAR. Farther out in the Pacific a circular array thirteen hundred miles long and code-named SEA SPIDER surrounds the Hawaiian Islands. Another Pacific array extends from Alaska and runs parallel to the Aleutian Islands. An array that runs down the western side of the Kuril Islands allows detection of Soviet submarines exiting the naval base at Petropavlovsk or the Sea of Okhotsk.[64]

Construction began on the array, known as the Azores Fixed Acoustic Range (AFAR), in September 1968 off the island of Santa Maria, the southernmost of the Azores group. In May 1972 the system was commissioned by NATO with a dual mission—to track Soviet submarines approaching the Strait of Gibraltar or on passage around the Cape of Good Hope.[65] An array in the Bosphorous between Yugoslavia and Turkey can detect submarines exiting the Soviet Black Sea Navy port of Sevastopol. Yet another array is placed next to the coast of Taiwan and the Philippines, while there is an Indian Ocean array in the vicinity of Diego Garcia.[66] Altogether there are fifty such arrays.

The hydrophones are sealed in tanks—approximately twenty-four to a tank—with cables transmitting the data to shore facilities. The first step in converting the data collected by the hydrophones to finished intelligence are the Naval Facilities (NAVFACs) and Naval Regional Processing Facilities (NRPCs), which are the initial recipients of the data. There were, in 1983, seventeen Naval Facilities (down from twenty-two a few years before)—eight Pacific Fleet and nine Atlantic Fleet facilities. Among the NAVFACs still operating are those at Adak, Alaska; Brawdy, Wales; Keflavik, Iceland; Point Sur, Big Sur; Naval Air Station, Barbers Point, Oahu; and Ritidian Point, Guam.[67] From the NAVFACs and NRPCs the data are sent by landline or by FLTSATCOM (Fleet Satellite Communications) satellite to Main Evaluation Centers, which are responsible for centralized reporting, correlation, localization, and tracking of submarine targets. The FLTSATCOM System has a variety of missions in addition to transmitting SOSUS data—especially providing a communications link between command and communication centers and ships and submarines at sea.[68]

The data collected about each submarine detected—its sonar echo and the noises made by its engine, cooling system, and the movement of its propellers—can be translated into a recognition signal. A distinctive pattern can be determined that indicates not only a particular type of submarine—an Alfa Class attack submarine versus a Typhoon Class ballistic-missile-carrying submarine—but also the individual submarine. Thus the data, when analyzed, operate much as fingerprints or voiceprints do in identifying different individuals.

In addition to its identification capabilities the SOSUS can localize a submarine to within a radius of fifty miles at ranges of several thousands of miles. A Massachusetts Institute of Technology study concluded that location of older and noisier Soviet submarines to within ten miles of their actual position from a distance of ten thousand miles was possible under the best circumstances, while a localization to within twenty-five miles from several thousand miles was feasible in most cases.[69]

The capabilities of the SOSUS system were demonstrated in the Cuban missile crisis of 1962, when every Soviet submarine in the area was detected and closely trailed. In April 1978 two Soviet Yankee Class submarines moved exceptionally close to the East Coast of the United States. The submarines were detected and tracked by SOSUS. The U.S. response—a raised alert level at several Strategic Air Command bomber bases, one of the prime targets of Soviet submarine-launched ballistic missiles—apparently resulted in Soviet withdrawal of the subs to their more standard patrol areas.[70]

While SOSUS capabilities are excellent in many regards, the system can be vulnerable and fallible. The cables laid by the Navy's underwater construction teams can be—and have been—cut by Soviet ships. Soviet trawlers have attempted to hook the cables, while undersea midget submarines patrol to locate and identify the location of the hydrophone arrays. According to one account, when it can be made to appear accidental, the cables are cut and recovered for examination.[71] To deal with damage to the cables, the United States has a fleet of cable repair ships, designated T-ARC, operated by the Military Sealift Command.[72]

Of particular concern has been the fact that in 1980 a Soviet Alfa attack submarine slipped past SOSUS in the North Atlantic and would have gone undetected had it not broken radio silence.[73] The Alfa Class achieved initial operational capability in 1978 and is the second smallest of the Soviet attack submarines at seventy-nine meters in length, with the nine other classes ranging in size from seventy to 150 meters long.[74] As Soviet submarine quieting programs progress, more such incidents may occur. To attempt to prevent such incidents, a SOSUS update was planned early in 1984.[75]

However, irrespective of the race between Soviet quieting programs and SOSUS enhancement programs, a fundamental change in Soviet submarine capabilities over the years has reduced the value of SOSUS. The first three generations of Soviet sea-based ballistic missiles—the SS-N-4 Sark, the SS-N-5 Serb, and the SS-N-6 Sawfly—had ranges between 350 and sixteen hundred nautical miles. Beginning in 1973 with the operation of the SS-N-8, with a range of forty-two hundred nautical miles,

Soviet subs did not have to exit Soviet home waters to hit targets in the United States. Soviet capability in this regard has grown over the years with deployment of the SS-N-8 Mod 2, with a forty-nine-hundred-nautical-mile range, and the SS-N-18 and SS-N-20, with ranges from thirty-five hundred to forty-five hundred nautical miles.[76] As a result, Soviet submarines do not need to cross SOSUS barriers to hit vital targets in the United States.

VII.

Keyholes and Ferrets

*T*he single most revolutionary development in the intelligence offensive against the Soviet target has been the move into space. Space reconnaissance produced a quantum leap in the access to targets that could be obtained as well as the frequency of coverage. Whereas U-2 missions were conducted only over small portions of the U.S.S.R., at infrequent intervals and involving a great deal of risk, a satellite could overfly the entire Soviet Union in the course of a day and do so day after day. Interior targets could be covered as easily as peripheral targets.

Operations from space also helped remove the stigma of "espionage" from such reconnaissance activities. It was no longer necessary to penetrate Soviet air space to gather such intelligence. While the Soviet Union first protested the overflights as space espionage, their opposition faded in a few years as they developed similar capabilities. By the 1970s both the United States and the Soviet Union based their participation in arms control agreements on their ability to "verify compliance" using "national technical means" of verification.

                              *   *   *

The concept of employing a space satellite for reconnaissance purposes originated in 1946 at the RAND Corporation in Santa Monica, California. In 1946 RAND produced the study *Preliminary Design for an Experimental World-Circling Spaceship*, which noted that reconnaissance was feasible from such a vehicle.[1] On February 17, 1948, RAND was requested by its sponsor—the Air Force—to establish a satellite project to foster the development of the components and techniques required for the successful construction and operation of a reconnaissance satellite. Among its responsibilities, RAND was to "prepare a detailed specification for the optimum satellite in the light of present knowledge," to revise continually and alter the specification to stay current with advancements in relevant areas, and to advise the Air Force regarding the level of effort and timing for different phases of the project.[2]

In addition to RAND, a variety of other institutions became involved in the project. North American Aviation was assigned to study the altitude control system, while RCA researched a television transmission and presentation system. The Ohio University Research Foundation was to study the impact of altitude and resolution errors on the accuracy of target location, while Boston University was to be involved in minor flight tests relative to television equipment. Television station KWBH in Hollywood was to conduct television experiments. In addition, experts on trajectory, atmosphere, altitude control, and solar heating engines were consulted.[3]

In 1950 RAND received further support for research into the potential utility of satellite reconnaissance. Two RAND reports issued in April 1951—*Utility of a Satellite Vehicle for Reconnaissance* and *Inquiry into the Feasibility of Weather Reconnaissance from a Satellite Vehicle*—discussed "pioneer reconnaissance" with extensive earth coverage at resolutions (employing television) of between forty and two hundred feet.[4]

A December 1952 summary of RAND studies on satellite vehicles noted that the subjects examined included the proposed specification, cost estimates, launching sites, communication and observation problems, power plant, structure and weight, stability and control, propellant systems, the analysis of atmospheric properties to extreme altitudes, dynamics and heat transfer problems, flight mechanics, political and psychological problems, and the utility for reconnaissance.[5]

The studies indicated that engineering of an unmanned rocket vehicle for use as a satellite could be accomplished with only a minor improvement in then current technology, that the payload would have to be two thousand pounds or less in the earliest version, and that returning the entire satellite vehicle to earth would be difficult and unwise to attempt in the early version. Further, it was found that the various components of a reconnaissance satellite vehicle were "individually feasible in various degrees" but "to combine the parts into a reliable operating whole will require considerable basic scientific and engineering effort."[6]

Specifically, it was concluded that a two-stage rocket vehicle weighing about seventy-four thousand pounds and carrying a one-thousand-pound payload of television, power plant, and control equipment would be capable, at the very least, of conducting weather and terrestrial reconnaissance with a resolution of two hundred feet. The effective life of the satellite could range from a few days up to one year, depending on the reliability of the electronic equipment. Further, it was believed that "should the operational television equipment be improved to a state now attained under laboratory conditions it is believed that minimum resolvable surface dimensions on the order of 100 feet can be provided with continuous coverage over most of the U.S.S.R. every day. At the expense of daily coverage these dimensions can probably be further reduced to values as low as 40 feet, complete coverage being attained after no more than one month's operation."[7]

The need for such a satellite was emphasized by the Air Force in 1952. The projected near-term Soviet development of an H-bomb required, in the view of the Air Force, that all possible means of obtaining reconnaissance and surveillance data concerning Soviet capabilities and intentions be explored.[8] A further push resulted in 1954, with reports by the Technological Capabilities Panel and RAND, with the RAND Project FEEDBACK report recommending that the "Air Force undertake at the earliest possible date completion and use of an efficient satellite reconnaissance vehicle as a matter of vital strategic interest to the United States."[9]

On March 16, 1955, the Air Force issued "General Operational Requirement No. 80," a formal requirements document calling for the development of a photographic reconnaissance satellite.[10] Martin, RCA, and Lockheed participated in the competition that followed. On October 29, 1956, the Air Force awarded Lockheed a contract to develop Weapon System 117L, the Advance Reconnaissance System, or Pied Piper.[11] In its initial form WS/117L included development of recoverable and nonrecoverable photographic techniques as well as electronic reconnaissance subsystems.[12]

The Pied Piper project was revealed in an article in *Aviation Week* on October 14, 1957.[13] This revelation created concern over the secrecy of the reconnaissance satellite program. Combined with the fear that the Pied Piper technology could not produce a near-term satellite to match the Soviet Sputnik, this concern led to consideration of alternative courses of action.

One alternative was to accept an Army proposal for development of a reconnaissance satellite. On October 26, 1957, the Army submitted to the Department of Defense a proposal for a military reconnaissance satellite capable of providing complete photographic coverage of the U.S.S.R. every three days, cloud cover permitting. A November 10, 1957, briefing on the proposal specified a development program progressing from twenty- to one-hundred- to five-hundred-pound payloads. Initial photographic coverage was to be attained with the first five-hundred-pound-payload launch of January 1959, with monthly launches commencing in May of that year. The satellites were to be placed in a three-hundred-mile circular orbit with an eighty-three-degree inclination so that the sun always would be overhead. The briefing also specified use of television-type cameras and that photo prints would be available for intelligence processing approximately thirty minutes after the pictures were taken.[14]

A more attractive proposal was made by the CIA, which had experience in the secret development of an overhead collection system (the U-2) and could provide funding directly from the DCI's contingency fund. Thus in February 1958 President Eisenhower approved Project CORONA, with the expectation that it would result in an operational photographic reconnaissance satellite employing a recoverable capsule system by the spring of 1959.[15]

Richard Bissell, who had managed the U-2 program as chairman of a USAF/CIA joint task force, was appointed a cochairman of Project CORONA as was an Air Force officer. Within two months a joint technical review led to a change of conception: rather than a spinning satellite with a fixed camera, the satellite would be stabilized while the camera scanned.[16]

Eisenhower's February decision followed shortly after NSC Action No. 1846 of January 22, 1958, assigned highest-priority status to development of an operational reconnaissance satellite. This was reaffirmed on June 20, 1958, in NSC 5814, "U.S. Policy on Outer Space," which stated that the United States should "at the earliest technologically practicable date use reconnaissance satellites to enhance to the maximum extent the U.S. intelligence effort."[17]

In November 1958 the Department of Defense revealed that its WS 117L program consisted of three elements: Discoverer, Sentry (the new name given to Pied Piper), and MIDAS.[18] Officially, Discoverer was to be a "research and development" satellite. The project objectives were described, in classified documents, as consisting of:

a) flight-test of the satellite vehicle airframe; propulsion; guidance and control systems; auxiliary power supply; and telemetry, tracking, and command equipment
b) attaining satellite stabilization in orbit
c) obtaining satellite internal thermal environment data
d) *testing of techniques for recovery of a capsule ejected from an orbiting satellite* [emphasis added]

   e) testing of ground-support equipment and development of personal proficiency
   f) conducting biomedical experiments with mice and small primates, including injection into orbit, reentry, and recovery[19]

While the Discoverer program did involve biomedical experiments and other nonreconnaissance-related activities, its primary function was to serve as a cover for Project CORONA. Thus the central concern was the "testing of techniques for recovery of a capsule ejected from an orbiting satellite" and other techniques related to reconnaissance satellite development.[20]

MIDAS was the acronym for Missile Defense Alarm System. The project was aimed at establishing a series of satellites carrying infrared detection scanners capable of detecting missile launches.[21]

While the CIA went ahead with CORONA, the Air Force proceeded with Sentry in the belief that a recoverable film system was not a near-term possibility. Other options considered were a television camera system and a conventional camera system. The television option was rejected in August 1957 after a study by RCA had shown that resolution would be extremely poor.[22] Instead, the decision was made to develop a film-scanning technique using a conventional camera to photograph the target. The film would be developed on board and scanned by a fine light beam with the resulting signal being transmitted to a receiving station on the ground, where it would be used to build up a picture.[23] While the scanning process would degrade picture quality to some extent, it was expected to be far better than television.[24]

The launch of *Discoverer 1* on February 28, 1959, preceded the first Sentry launch by twenty months (by which time it was called SAMOS). The February 28 launch marked the beginning of a year and a half of problems that prevented an entirely successful mission from being completed. Problems included failure to orbit, improper functioning in orbit, failure to respond, and human error. The *Discoverer 2* mission of April 13, 1959, appeared to be successful until a human error caused the reentry sequence to be initiated too early and the descent of the capsule in northern Norway. Despite several reported sightings of the descending capsule, a search party was unable to locate it.[25]

As of a year later there still had not been a successful flight. According to Bissell:

> . . . one after another was a failure, it was a most heartbreaking business. If an airplane goes on a test flight and something malfunctions, and it gets back, the pilot can tell you about the malfunction, or you can look it over and find out. But in the case of a recce satellite you fire the damn thing off and you've got some telemetry, and you never get it back. There is no pilot, of course, and you've got no hardware, you never see it again, so you have to infer from telemetry what went wrong. Then you make a fix, and if it fails again, you know you've inferred wrong. In the case of CORONA, it went on and on. By April of 1960 there had been eleven flights, none successful.[26]

It was not until the *Discoverer 13* mission of August 1960 that a successful recovery was achieved, by frogmen near Hawaii. Cloud cover made the primary method of capsule recovery (that is, interception of the capsule at the last stage of its descent by a C-119 Flying Boxcar) infeasible.[27]

Apparently the mission of *Discoverer 14* was the first to involve attempted photography. It also was the first mission during which aircraft recovery of the descending capsule was achieved. The eighty-four-pound instrument capsule had been ejected from *Discoverer 14* over Alaska while on its seventeenth pass around the earth, a day after its launching on August 18. A timing device triggered the operation of gas jets to pitch the vehicle sixty degrees down from its horizontal plane, after which a series of explosive bolts and springs were fired to achieve separation. A retrorocket within the capsule then was fired to slow the vehicle to reentry velocity, which permitted it to assume the proper trajectory for reentry into the earth's atmosphere. Before it had descended to sixty thousand feet, a switch was activated by deceleration forces that released a parachute. A C-119 operating as part of the recovery team—which included five additional C-119's, a C-130, and several other aircraft and ships—plucked the capsule out of the air.[28]

Discoverer 14's camera had taken pictures of the suspected ICBM base at Plesetsk. The pictures showed railway lines required to transport ICBM's to a base; these lines were absent from World War II maps, thus confirming suspicions. However, in general the pictures were dark and of poor quality. Nor did the two further film recoveries of 1960 provide good-quality film, possibly due to cloud cover.[29]

However, from mid-June 1961 (with the launch of *Discoverer 25* on the sixteenth) to mid-September (*Discoverer 31*), good photographs were recovered from the satellites. The pictures from *Discoverer 29*, launched on August 30, provided enough detail of the Plesetsk site to confirm it as the first Soviet ICBM site and to establish what a Soviet ICBM site looked like. The photographs showed the SS-6 in launching sites identical to the configuration for the missile that existed at Tyuratam. On this basis numerous "suspect" sites could be eliminated, and by September 1961 the intelligence community had reduced their estimate of deployed SS-6's to just over ten.[30] (The actual number turned out to be four.)

Thus, despite the extensive initial problems of the Discoverer/CORONA program, by its termination with the launch of *Discoverer 38* on February 27, 1962, it had proven the feasibility of both satellite photographic reconnaissance and capsule recovery. Based on the initial recovery of the *Discoverer 14* capsule, contracts were awarded to General Electric for the capsule and to Eastman Kodak for the camera system.[31]

At the same time as the CIA was fine-tuning its CORONA program, the Air Force was attempting to develop SAMOS—the Satellite and Missile Observation System—into a worthwhile photographic reconnaissance satellite. The launch of *SAMOS 1* on October 11, 1960, represented the first attempt to place a fully operational photo reconnaissance satellite into orbit. However, the umbilical cord that attached the Agena upper stage did not separate until after the missile became airborne, pulling off part of the Agena second stage and causing it to malfunction. As a result, orbit was not attained.[32]

SAMOS 2, launched on January 31, 1961, did orbit—at an inclination of 97.4 degrees and for a period of ninety-five minutes. Its orbital inclination ensured that it successively passed over virtually all of the Soviet Union and China, while its period meant that it made one revolution around the earth every ninety-five minutes.[33]

SAMOS 2 was launched from the Naval Missile Facility at Point Arguello, California. The length of the satellite was twenty-two feet, with a diameter of five feet and a weight at launch time of eleven thousand pounds, approximately seven thousand pounds of which constituted the fuel supply. Its perigee (its closest distance to earth) was 296 miles; its apogee (its farthest distance from earth), 348 miles.[34]

While *SAMOS 3* and *SAMOS 4* (launched on September 9, 1961, and November 22, 1961, respectively) failed to orbit, there were only two similar failures over the next twenty-six launches, with *SAMOS 30* of November 27, 1963, concluding the program on a successful orbital note.[35] Whether the SAMOS program was successful in terms of its primary objective—the provision of useful imagery—is another question.

According to Philip Klass, *SAMOS 2*'s resolution was in the neighborhood of twenty feet, while *SAMOS 5* to *SAMOS 30* had resolutions in the area of five to ten feet.[36] Both resolutions would provide valuable military intelligence. Thus Klass states that SAMOS photography provided the first positive signs that the Soviet Union was hardening its ICBM sites and led to sharp decreases in estimates of Soviet ICBM strength.[37] Likewise, Howard Simons made similar assertions and also links SAMOS to the discovery of ballistic missile defense emplacements around Leningrad as well as the possible discovery of Chinese construction of a gaseous diffusion plant for the production of nuclear weapons material.[38] On the other hand, Freedman suggests that SAMOS pictures were of very poor quality and that the entire program was generally a failure.[39] This view is supported by several former CIA officials involved in the early reconnaissance programs, one of whom stated that as of 1963 SAMOS "had not produced a single useful photograph."[40]

In any event, the SAMOS and Discoverer/CORONA programs established the basis of the U.S. photo reconnaissance satellite program until the end of 1976. In the midst of the SAMOS launches the Discoverer/CORONA program made the transition from "research and development" program to operational program with launches of the General Electric/Eastman Kodak satellite on March 7, 1962, using an Atlas-Agena B launch vehicle.[41] The satellite was orbited with an inclination of 90.89 degrees and a period of 93.9 minutes. Its perigee was 157 miles; its apogee, 423 miles. Five further launches of the satellite occurred (all in 1962): April 26, June 17, July 18, August 5, and November 11.[42]

The film brought back by one of the last three CORONA launches was affected by a series of high-altitude nuclear tests conducted by the United States. Known as the FISHBOWL series, the tests involved the detonation of a 1.4-megaton and three submegaton devices at high altitudes in the vicinity of Johnston Island, seven hundred miles southwest of Hawaii. The first explosion in the series was the detonation of the 1.4-megaton STARFISH PRIME device on July 9, 1962, at an altitude of approximately 248 miles. The three submegaton devices were detonated at altitudes of tens of miles on October 20 and November 1, 1962.[43] One satellite passed through a high concentration of radioactive material over the South Atlantic, irradiating the film and degrading the quality of the pictures obtained. Precautions then were taken to avoid a recurrence.[44]

The March 7 launch represented the formal beginning of the Keyhole program. In addition to being distinguished by their BYEMAN code names (such as CORONA), each satellite was assigned a Keyhole or KH number. CORONA was designated KH-4, while SAMOS was retroactively designated KH-1.

*   *   *

In preparation for the placing of reconnaissance and other military spacecraft into orbit, a "satellite control facility" was established. Consisting of a headquarters at Sunnyvale, California, and several remote tracking facilities, the Air Force Satellite Control Facility (AFSCF) was set up to perform four basic functions: tracking, telemetry, commands, and recovery.

These functions are particularly important with respect to reconnaissance satellites in low earth orbit. While satellites will not fall from the sky without ground control, they will drift out of proper orbit. A satellite control network serves to track the satellites to ensure that they are in the proper orbit at a given moment and also to guarantee that the exact location over which a picture is taken will be known. It also receives telemetry data from a satellite that allows controllers to be updated on the status of the spacecraft and its payload (such as its camera system) as well as to receive data collected by the spacecraft. While satellites can be provided in advance with commands that guide its behavior once in space, it also is necessary to be able to issue commands to the satellite after it has reached orbit—orders that keep it in the proper orbit, that instruct it to provide information or maneuver into a different orbit. Photographic reconnaissance satellites, which are subject to atmospheric drag and may be urgently required to photograph a particular locale on short notice, require frequent commands. Such satellites require support from an average of 1.5 tracking stations for each earth revolution. Since they are over a given station for only a short time—2.5 to ten minutes—this sends ground controllers scrambling.

A recovery function was established, since satellites such as CORONA ejected their film in capsules rather than transmit their data via radio. As a result, a recovery organization consisting of pilots, aircraft, and frogmen was established allowing the capsules to be recovered in the air or from the ocean.

The headquarters of the AFSCF at Sunnyvale was designated as the Satellite Test Center but became known as the "Big Blue Cube" for the shape and color of the headquarters building—"a nine story, windowless, pale-blue block, with an attached administrative building and several massive white radar and communications dishes in the parking lot."[45] By the end of October 1961 U.S. Remote Tracking Stations (RTS) had been established, all but one in the United States. The U.S. stations were at Vandenberg Air Force Station, California; New Boston, New Hampshire; Annette Island, Alaska; Kaena Point, Hawaii; Kodiak, Alaska; Fort Dix, New Jersey; Camp Roberts, California; and Donnelly Flats/Fort Greely, Alaska.[46]

The crucial role a remote tracking station can play was illustrated in 1960 by the Kodiak station during a test of the satellite ejection system for Discoverer/CORONA. Ejection of the capsule required a timer in the satellite. To start the capsule separation and reentry sequence it was necessary for the timer to be set by radio command during the few seconds the satellite was within range of the controlling station. An operator pressing a series of buttons in the correct sequence would automatically start the procedure.[47]

During the *Discoverer 2* test of April 1960, the Kodiak station was responsible for setting the timer. The buttons were pressed in the correct sequence, but a monitor showed that an incorrect command had been transmitted—a possibility foreseen by the equipment designers, who provided a way to reset the timer. Unfortunately, under pressure the operator neglected to push the reset button before sending the command signal. The new code pulses were added to the earlier ones, the results being that the capsule was ejected over Spitsbergen on Svalbard (a Norwegian island near the far north eightieth parallel and the Soviet-held Franz Josef Land) rather than over Hawaii.[48]

The single station outside the United States was at Thule, Greenland. Unlike the U.S. stations, the existence of the Thule station was classified. Indeed, as late as 1973 the Thule site was deleted from the list of AFSCF stations appearing in the public version of the Defense Department congressional hearings.[49]

Over the years the AFSCF has shifted and reduced the number of sites in the United States while expanding the number of sites overseas. At the beginning of 1978 there were six sites— with the Vandenberg (now an Air Force base), Thule, New

Boston, and Kaena Point sites remaining as part of the network.[50] The Thule station, because of its proximity to the North Pole, has been the last station to view the Keyhole satellites before their passes over Soviet territory. The Vandenberg station is a dual station that can simultaneously support two satellites, as are the Kaena Point and New Boston stations.

In August 1963, Mahe in the Seychelles became host to the Indian Ocean station. In September 1965, on Guam, a station was established that still is in operation.[51] The Guam tracking station is the busiest of all the remote tracking stations since it provides support to satellites in both polar and geosynchronous orbit.

The final addition to the AFSCF, in 1978, was the Oakhanger tracking station at Bordean Hauts near London, England. Unlike the other stations, Oakhanger is not a complete station and can provide full support only when "plugged in" to the Satellite Test Center at Sunnyvale.

Part of the AFSCF from its inception was the 6594th Test Group at Hickam AFB, Hawaii. The 6594th has been responsible for managing the effort to recover film capsules parachuted back to earth from film-return satellites. A newer part of the AFSCF network was the Satellite Data System (SDS) spacecraft, first launched in 1975. Among its functions (another of which is discussed later) SDS provides a communications link between Sunnyvale and the remote tracking stations around the globe.

The years 1958–62 produced significant organizational and policy changes in the handling of the satellite reconnaissance program. Organizational changes within the Department of Defense involved the shifting of responsibility for military space programs, including the reconnaissance program, from the Air Force to the Advanced Research Projects Agency (ARPA) and back to the Air Force. Thus, while the Air Force was in the process of creating a Directorate of Advanced Technology to manage its space programs, they were transferred to the Advanced Research Projects Agency (ARPA) on June 30, 1958.[52] ARPA continued to employ Air Force units for provision of support to its space activities.[53]

Thus when the Directorate of Advanced Technology was established under the Deputy Chief of Staff/Development in July 1958, it had little to do other than supervise a variety of studies, including the global surveillance studies and the twenty-four-hour reconnaissance satellite study. Subsequently, on April 13, 1959, the Directorate was issued a charter that gave it authority to coordinate within the Air Staff all Air Force space activities.[54]

More importantly, during the summer of 1959 Secretary of Defense Neil McElroy transferred the military space projects from ARPA to the military services, with MIDAS and SAMOS transferred back to the Air Force.[55] Total Air Force control, within the Department of Defense, of satellite reconnaissance was formalized on March 28, 1961, by Department of Defense Directive 5160.34 on "Reconnaissance, Mapping, and Geodetic Programs," which stated that the Air Force was to be responsible for:

1. research, development, and operation, including payload design, launch, guidance, control and recovery of all DOD reconnaissance satellite systems
2. research and development of all instrumentation and equipment for processing reconnaissance data from satellite sources[56]

The most significant organizational change was the creation of the National Reconnaissance Office (NRO) to act as a central management office for the reconnaissance program. The impetus for its creation included the same problems that led to the organizational changes within the Department of Defense plus the decision to accelerate the program in the wake of the U-2 incident. Thus on June 10, 1960, Eisenhower asked Secretary of Defense Thomas Gates, Jr., to reevaluate the program and brief the National Security Council on intelligence requirements and the technical feasibility of meeting the requirements with SAMOS and DOD's plans for the system. Gates, in turn, appointed a team of three individuals: Under Secretary of the Air Force Joseph

Charyk, Deputy Director of Defense Research and Engineering John H. Rubel, and George Kistiakowsky, the president's science adviser.[57]

The result of the briefing was, according to an official Air Force history, "a key decision by NSC and the President which, eliminating previous uncertainties, signalled the start of a highest priority project reminiscent of the wartime Manhattan effort. . . ."[58] The key decision was the creation of the National Reconnaissance Office, a national-level organization to be responsive to supradepartmental authority. The national-level character of the organization was a major point of importance to those involved in its formation. Thus George Kistiakowsky noted it was important "that the organization have a clear line of authority and that the top-level direction be of a national character, including OSD and CIA and not the Air Force alone."[59] One reason why such a framework was desired was to be certain that the utilization of the photographic "take" not be left solely in the hands of the Air Force.[60]

While NRO was created as a national organization—with Air Force, CIA, and Navy participation—the Air Force role was substantial, providing the organization with a director (Joseph Charyk). Charyk's appointment, while he maintained his position as Under Secretary of the Air Force, resulted partly from his experience in the development of high-altitude reconnaissance planes.[61] Charyk had suggested to Richard Bissell that Bissell would be the appropriate choice to head NRO. Bissell, who conceived of the organization more as a central repository and coordinating unit, was interested in becoming director of NRO while remaining as the CIA's Deputy Director for Plans. However, Director of Central Intelligence Allen Dulles told Bissell that he could not have a CIA official who would have "line control" over Department of Defense personnel. Hence Charyk became the first of a continuing series of Air Force officials who wore the "black hat."[62]

Within the Office of the Secretary of the Air Force an Office of Missile and Satellite Systems was created with primary responsibility for "assisting the Secretary in discharging his responsibility for the direction, supervision, and control of the SAMOS

Project."[63] Simultaneously, Brigadier General Robert E. Greer was named Director of the SAMOS Project, with offices at the Air Force Ballistic Missile Division, El Segundo, California. The SAMOS Project Office was designated a field extension of the Office of the Secretary of the Air Force, and its director was made directly responsible to the Secretary.[64]

NRO was classified secret at birth. At the same time, SAMOS and Discoverer launches still were announced and the reconnaissance function of SAMOS was discussed by Air Force officials in congressional testimony.[65] This dichotomy resulted from the split within the Eisenhower administration concerning the degree of secrecy that should be attached to the reconnaissance program. Thus Dr. James Killian, George Kistiakowsky's predecessor, was concerned that the visibility of the SAMOS and Discoverer programs would increase the priority the Soviets placed on interfering with U.S. reconnaissance satellites. Others, however, stressed the value of public knowledge concerning successful U.S. space programs.[66]

The fears expressed by Killian and other Eisenhower assistants to the incoming administration as well as the findings of the Weisner Ad Hoc Panel's *Report to the President-Elect of the Ad Hoc Committee on Space* led to a rapid change in policy. Protection of U.S. reconnaissance satellites by terminating official publicity became a priority concern, particularly in light of Soviet statements on the "illegality" of such activities and increasingly credible threats to shoot such satellites down.[67]

Such threats were taken seriously given the Soviet downing of the U-2 less than a year before. Many of those responsible for the CORONA and SAMOS programs had been involved with the U-2 program and therefore were inclined to take such threats as more than mere propaganda.[68] Further, the implications of the loss of the U-2 were clear to Kennedy. A major means of collecting intelligence about the Soviet Union was lost, and the international standing of the United States was damaged, as was Eisenhower's personal prestige and image. The domestic political costs also were significant.[69] Thus in January 1961 McGeorge Bundy, the Assistant to the President for National Security Affairs, and Defense Secretary Robert.McNamara initiated a review of public information policies concerning SAMOS launches.[70] The results were immediate and eventually drastic.

On January 26, 1961, Arthur Sylvester, Assistant Secretary of Defense for Public Affairs, in a memo to the President indicated the extent of the "gradual reduction of volunteering information on our intelligence acquisitions systems which . . . is your desire."[71] The changes in information policy included the elimination of four pages of questions and answers (twenty-two in all) concerning SAMOS, reduced advanced notice to correspondents (from five to one days) and made provision of photographs of SAMOS upon request only. Sylvester further noted, "Dr. Charyk has reviewed these changes and is satisfied that they meet all his security requirements and those of his SAMOS Project Director. . . ."[72]

Further restriction barred military officers, particularly Air Force officers, from mentioning the SAMOS program by name or mission. They were further prevented from making public statements dealing with the subject without obtaining prior approval.[73] As a result, General Bernard Schriever, who previously had discussed the SAMOS program in congressional testimony and public forums, removed all references to SAMOS in his public statements.[74] And on November 22, 1961, *SAMOS 4* was launched without any press release or publicity. Finally, after the launch of *SAMOS 5* exactly one month later, officials would no longer admit the existence of the SAMOS project.[75]

While the policy of complete secrecy was strongly supported by the highest officials in the White House (the President and McGeorge Bundy), the Department of Defense (McNamara), the NRO (Charyk), the CIA (Bissell), and subsequently the new DCI (John McCone), it was a policy that was not without its critics both in and out of government. *Missiles and Rockets* noted that the Soviet Union could track reconnaissance satellites and determine their orbital parameters. One governmental critic noted that the launches "could be observed by our press and the Russians. We knew the Russians were observing them and could observe them. . . . We were not fooling anybody except our own people."[76]

The main source of opposition within the Executive Branch

resided in the State Department, where Dean Rusk, Adlai Stevenson, and others argued that the blackout could produce the outcome it was intended to avoid. In the State Department view the United States was in a potentially vulnerable position legally with regard to satellite reconnaissance activities—as it had been with the U-2—and needed to establish the legitimacy of overhead satellite reconnaissance. This could best be done, it was felt, by a policy of openness and by not creating a distinction between military and civilian space programs. As a result, the State Department did not base its argument on Soviet tracking capabilities, a point conceded by the advocates of secrecy but considered irrelevant. Rather, it shared with the advocates of secrecy a diplomatic concern—an interpretation of the cessation of the U-2 program as being, in large part, the result of public and diplomatic pressure. However, the proposed solution was completely different.

The State Department view did not prevail in 1961, and 1962 saw a further extension of the blackout—probably partially in response to Soviet actions. That year the Soviets launched an international offensive in the United Nations and in publications, denouncing U.S. reconnaissance satellites as illegal and defending their right to take action against them. Placed in the context of what appeared to be increasing Soviet capabilities to conduct space operations, it was feared that the ultimate Soviet goal was to attain international acceptance of any attempt it might make to shoot down or intercept U.S. reconnaissance satellites.[77]

The U.S. response was twofold. A DOD directive written by NRO Director Charyk and signed by Defense Secretary McNamara on March 23, 1962, directed that all DOD space activities be classified secret. No individual projects were to be identified, nor was there to be any identification of any individual—civilian or military—with any specific project. All military launches were classified and identified only by registry letter and dates.[78] It was hoped that by making the entire program secret the reconnaissance portion would become undetectable.

In preparation for a diplomatic response, President Kennedy signed National Security Action Memorandum 156, "Negotiation on Disarmament and Peaceful Uses of Outer Space," on May 26, 1962.[79] The memorandum instructed Secretary of State Rusk to form an interagency committee to study the political aspects of U.S. policy concerning reconnaissance satellites. The "NSAM 156 Committee," as it came to be called, was formally the Interdepartmental Committee on Space and was chaired by U. Alexis Johnson. It rapidly agreed on eighteen recommendations.[80] On July 1, 1962, it delivered to Rusk its *Report on Political and Informational Aspects of Satellite Reconnaissance Programs*, which, while accepting the blackout policy, also stressed the need to attain legitimacy for such programs. This was to be done by the discussion in public and international forums of the benefits of observation satellites, by blurring the distinction between military and civilian space photography, and by briefings of foreign leaders. By the end of 1963 the U.S. policy on satellite reconnaissance that has continued to the present day was firmly established.

The year 1962 also was notable for the introduction of the first U.S. electronic reconnaissance satellite. Known as ferrets in the popular literature but as "balls" to the U.S. intelligence community, this class of electronic reconnaissance satellite has had the mission of intercepting the signals emitted by Soviet, Chinese, and other nations' air defense, ABM, and early-warning radar systems—the same basic mission as that of the early peripheral reconnaissance missions. And just like that of those early missions, the objective was to determine the characteristics of the radars so that appropriate countermeasures could be prepared in the event of war.

The first ferret was launched by a Thor-Agena B on May 15, 1962, into an orbit with a 190-mile perigee and a 392-mile apogee. Between the first launch and July 16, 1971, seventeen satellites of the initial type were launched, with between one and three such satellites launched each year. The inclination of the earlier satellites was approximately eighty-two degrees, while the inclination of the later satellites was approximately seventy-five degrees. Likewise, the orbit changed after the first several launches to a more circular orbit, with about three hundred miles separating the satellite from the earth. Switches to new boosters in June 1963 and October 1968 may have indicated new generations of satellites coming into operation.[81]

A second class of ferret satellites was put into operation beginning in August 1963. Unlike the first class, which were launched as the only payload on a rocket, the new class served as the second payload to photograph reconnaissance satellites. As for the first class, elliptical orbits of 180 by 250 miles gave way to more circular orbits, in the vicinity of three hundred miles above the earth. A break in the pattern occurred on December 12, 1968, and on February 5, 1969, when subsatellites were placed in 840-mile circular orbits.[82] It has been suggested that these two flights might have been specifically designed to probe Soviet ABM radars, which reached operational status in the summer of 1969.[83] Three subsequent launches of subsatellites into similar orbits all occurred during important periods in Soviet ABM development—a week after the ABM Treaty came into force (October 3, 1972); six months afterward; and on June 8, 1975, when there was a flurry of activity at the Soviets' Sary Shagan ABM test center. The activity included two new radar systems undergoing testing.[84]

By 1972 there were no longer launches solely to place ferret satellites in orbit. Rather, from 1972 to the present, only ferret subsatellites have been launched. In general, the satellites have been the secondary payload on launches of the KH-9 imaging satellite (discussed in Chapter X).[85]

The exact number of ferret types within each class is not known publicly. What is known is that code names for the satellites have had a common theme—they all were named after female sex symbols. Two of the satellites operating in the late 1970s were code-named RAQUEL and FARRAH while earlier satellites had been code-named BRIDGETTE and MARILYN.[86]

The year 1963 saw the introduction of the successors to SAMOS and CORONA—the second-generation area surveillance (KH-5) and close-look (KH-6) satellites. The first of the SAMOS successors—the KH-5—was launched on February 28, 1963, using a Thrust-Augmented Thor-Agena D (TAT-Agena D). Use of the TAT-Agena D allowed an increase in payload sufficient to permit the spacecraft to carry more film and consumables for a longer stay in orbit.[87]

Both the February 28 launch and the second launch—on March 18—failed to produce an orbiting spacecraft. However, with the exception of the March 24, 1964, and May 3, 1966, launches, all subsequent TAT-Agena D launches were successful. Altogether, forty-six KH-5 spacecraft were placed in orbit between February 28, 1963, and March 30, 1967. The average inclination was 78.7 degrees, while the mean lifetime was twenty-three days. KH-5's orbited at slightly lower perigees and apogees than SAMOS did, with average orbits of 114 by 243 miles as compared to figures of 134 by 261 for SAMOS.[88]

CORONA's successor, the KH-6, was launched on July 12, 1963, using an Atlas-Agena D booster. Between that date and June 4, 1967, a total of thirty-eight launches succeeded in placing thirty-six of the close-look satellites in orbit. Throughout its lifetime the KH-6 series satellites employed inclinations in the ninety to ninety-six- and 101 to 110-degree categories. Lifetimes were short (on average, 5.3 days), while perigees were, in the vast majority of cases, under one hundred miles (93.2 miles on average). In one case—a July 6, 1964, launch—the perigee was as low as seventy-six miles.[89]

Within a two-week period in the summer of 1966, third-generation U.S. area surveillance and close-look spacecraft were introduced. The first launch of the third-generation area surveillance craft—the KH-7—on August 9, 1966, represented the first of thirty such launches over approximately six years.

The twenty-nine KH-7 craft successfully orbited had an average inclination of eighty-two degrees—identical with that of SAMOS—and average lifetime of twenty-four days, only one day greater than that for the KH-5. Its orbit also was somewhat lower than that of its predecessor, with mean perigees and apogees of 107 and 196 miles, respectively.[90]

According to Klass the KH-7, which was launched on a Long Tank Thrust Augmented Thor-Agena D (LTTAT-Agena D), was equipped with infrared scanners in addition to its conventional cameras in an attempt to acquire imagery during night passes. However, the most that would have been produced by infrared equipment was the identification of heat sources rather than actual imagery. Additionally, it reportedly was equipped with a space-ground link system that employed a 1.5-meter unfurlable antenna, allowing pictures to be transmitted to the ground at a much higher rate.[91]

In one case a third-generation area surveillance satellite operated at a much lower inclination than other third-generation satellites. The satellite launched on July 23, 1970, had a sixty-degree inclination as opposed to the standard eighty- to eighty-four-degree inclination. It was noted by some observers that the resulting orbit would take it over Syria, Israel, and the northern part of the Suez Canal region, and thus it could have transmitted pictures showing the disposition of Soviet antiaircraft missiles for the two weeks prior to the August 7 cease-fire in the "war of attrition." Other observers suggested that the preplanning required for the launch indicated an intention to observe an event more predictable a month prior to the launch—specifically, Chinese missile tests.[92]

On at least one occasion the KH-7 was instrumental in providing reassurance concerning Soviet ICBM developments during SALT I negotiations. Thus on February 9, 1971, a KH-8 close-look satellite returned a film pack that was analyzed by the start of March. The pictures revealed ten new Soviet missiles in SS-9 fields in central Russia. The holes were larger than those normally associated with SS-9 deployments, and the Soviets were employing a digging technique that did not allow for the determination of the likely dimension of the missiles intended for the hole. These data were passed to Senator Henry Jackson, who claimed that the data presaged the deployment of "monster missiles"—a claim that did not help the SALT I negotiating atmosphere. These concerns apparently were raised by Henry Kissinger in discussion with Soviet Ambassador Anatoly Dobrynin, who offered verbal assurances that no "monster missiles" were being deployed. However, the Soviets offered more than mere verbal assurances. The pictures that came back from a KH-7 satellite on April 12 showed in great detail the contents of the new "holes." The photographs revealed next to several holes the entire set of liners for the silos, laid out in rank order of emplacement and face upward so they could be properly photographed. Even missile canisters were provided so the diameter of the new missiles could be assessed. Thus the Soviets had gone out of their way to allow reconnaissance satellites to gather photographic assurance.[93]

The first of the third-generation close-look satellites, the KH-8 (code-named GAMBIT), was launched on July 29, 1966, by a Titan-3B-Agena D rocket. Unlike the KH-7, which was phased out in 1972, the KH-8 was operational until 1984.

KH-8 satellites apparently were cylindrically shaped, twenty-four feet long, with a diameter of 4.5 feet and a weight of sixty-six hundred pounds. Between July 20, 1966, and June 15, 1971, there were thirty successful launches in thirty-one attempts—with an orbit that allowed the satellite at its perigee (about 80 miles) to take pictures with a resolution estimated to be (by 1980) six inches.[94] At the same time, the high apogee reduced the drag on the spacecraft and delayed the onset of orbital decay. Even with a high apogee the lifetime of the early KH-8's was in the neighborhood of a few weeks. The average lifetime for all launches between the KH-8's initial launch and the launch of April 22, 1971, was only thirteen days. The first KH-8 to stay in orbit for over twenty days (twenty-one days) was launched on April 22, 1971.[95]

The KH-8 operated at an inclination of 110 degrees for many years after it achieved initial operational capability rather than in a sun-synchronous north–south polar orbit that guarantees that each daylight pass over an area is made at an identical sun angle, avoiding differences in pictures of the same area that result from different sun angles. Film was returned in at least two reentry vehicles, which were recovered in midair by the Lockheed C-130's stationed at Hickam Air Force Base, Hawaii.[96]

The large battleship building dock at Molotovsk Navy Yard (now Severodvinsk Shipyard No. 402), U.S.S.R. Photographed during June 1944 by personnel of the U.S. Naval Attaché office, Moscow, from on board a motor launch in Nikolske Inlet.

Soviet Leningrad class destroyer photographed at Leningrad by a naval attaché, June 1944

COBRA DANE phased Array radar, Shemya Island

U.S. Ocean Surveillance facility at Edzell, Scotland

Chicksands listening post

DUNCAN CAMPBELL

U-2 reconnaissance plane

LOCKHEED

U-2 photograph
of Soviet space
vehicle platform
at Tyuratam

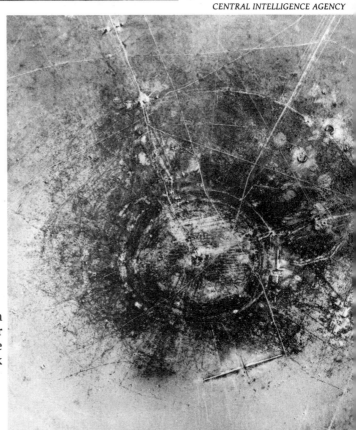

U-2 photograph
of Soviet nuclear
weapons test site
at Semipalatinsk

Kola Peninsula
naval base

637 Sturgeon class submarine

COBRA JUDY phased Array radar on USNS observation island

SR-71 reconnaissance plane

P-3C antisubmarine-warfare plane

Joint Defense Space Research Facility at Alice Springs, Australia
(Pine Gap), the ground control station for RHYOLITE and MAGNUM

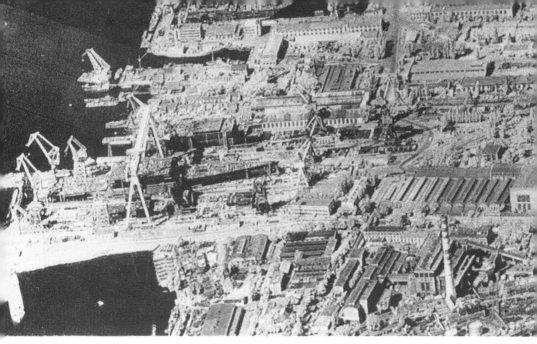

KH-11 photo of Soviet nuclear-powered aircraft carrier under construction

Fort Belvoir, Virginia, receiving station for KH-11 imagery

VIII.

PARPRO and the Soviet Target

The SAM that shot down Francis Gary Powers and his U-2 also shot down the entire program of overflying the Soviet Union. While the CIA initially suspended operations for seven months only and adopted a wait-and-see attitude concerning possible future overflights, there was no great expectation that another U-2 would ever be permitted to overfly the Soviet Union.[1]

There was one inadvertent overflight of Soviet territory. On October 27, 1962, in the midst of the Cuban missile crisis, a U-2 took off from Eielson Air Force Base in Alaska on what was said to be a "routine air sampling mission"—presumably in response to two Soviet nuclear tests on October 22—and strayed into Soviet air space over the Chukotski Peninsula. Soviet MiG's were scrambled from a base near Wrangel Island to intercept the plane, while the U-2 pilot called for help over clear channels. U.S. Air Force fighter aircraft in Alaska were immediately scrambled, and headed into the Bering Sea to attempt to rendezvous with the U-2. Fortunately, the U-2 found its way out of Soviet territory without an exchange of shots.[2] But that was the only overflight, and with the emergence of an operational satellite reconnaissance program in 1961 there was no longer any real need for such a program.

While aerial overflights of Soviet territory have ceased, the United States—and specifically the Strategic Air Command's 9th Strategic Reconnaissance Wing at Beale AFB, California—still does a brisk business in aerial reconnaissance. With U-2's, SR-71's, and RC-135's and other airplanes, the 9th SRW operates what is known as the Peacetime Aerial Reconnaissance Program, or PARPRO for short. Actual tasking is the responsibility of SAC's Strategic Reconnaissance Center at Offutt AFB in Nebraska. PARPRO involves overflights of North Korea, Cuba, Nicaragua, and other "troublesome" countries in the Middle East and Asia. Until 1971 it also included SR-71 and U-2 overflights of the Chinese mainland.

In addition, PARPRO includes peripheral flights of SR-71's, RC-135's, and other aircraft along Soviet borders—along the Baltic and White seas in the North, along the Kamchatka Peninsula and the entire Soviet Far East. The flights produce visible light, infrared, and radar imagery of Soviet installations, electronic intelligence on the emissions of Soviet radars, telemetry intercepts from Soviet missile tests, and photographs of the reentry vehicles.

The best known of the aircraft involved in these latter-day peripheral missions is the SR-71A. Even while the U-2 was operating with impunity in Soviet air space, plans were being developed for a successor aircraft. Thus, in 1958, Allen Dulles and Richard Bissell sought and received President Eisenhower's approval to develop a follow-on aircraft to the U-2.[3] The SR-71 concept originated in that year, when Kelly Johnson's Advanced Development Projects Office at Lockheed began submitting what were to be a dozen design proposals for a new reconnaissance aircraft, numbered A-1 through A-12.[4]

Proposal A-12, submitted on September 1, 1959, went into competition with a General Dynamics design and an in-house Navy design. Among the earlier General Dynamics proposals was one for a ramjet-powered Mach 4 aircraft to be carried aloft by a B-58 and launched at supersonic speeds. Two fatal flaws plagued the proposal. The B-58 could not achieve supersonic speed with a Mach 4 aircraft in place. And even if it could have achieved the required speed, the survivability of the piloted vehicle was problematic due to the likelihood of ramjet blowout in maneuvers. The final General Dynamics proposal for a plane to be known as the Kingfisher was eliminated by Air Force and Department of Defense technical experts in charge of evaluating the designs.[5]

The Navy had proposed a ramjet-powered rubber inflatable machine to be carried to a given altitude by a balloon. It would then be boosted to a speed where the ramjets could produce thrust. However, according to Lockheed Corporation studies, the balloon would have to be a mile in diameter to lift the vehicle, which had a proposed wing area of one-seventh acre.[6]

On January 30, 1960, the winner was announced: Kelly Johnson and Lockheed.[7] By December 1961, the speedy Johnson and his designers had completed design work on the aircraft. In mid-January 1962 the "Article," as it was referred to by those involved, was delivered almost completely assembled by two trucks and a special trailer to "The Ranch"—the Air Force's classified Groom Lake test facility in south-central Nevada. Over the next several months the plane, which then bore A-12 as its only designation, was reassembled over a period of weeks in one of the large Groom Lake hangars and prepared for its first test flight.[8]

On April 26, 1962, the A-12 flew for the first time. While the CIA began to receive the first of the initial batch of twelve A-12s in late 1962, it was not until 1964 that they had truly emerged from the test stage. In the two years from the first test flight there were a series of problems to overcome relating to construction materials, fuels, lubricants, new environment, sensor systems, structure, landing gear, and "virtually every other major or minor aspect of the aircraft."[9]

Another problem confronted those involved in developing the SR-71. On April 26, 1962, the very same day the A-12 first flew, the Soviets launched *Cosmos 4*, their first photographic reconnaissance satellite. Over the next two years another eleven such satellites were launched and spent a total of eighty-four days in orbit. To avoid the Soviets' prying eyes it would have been necessary to keep the plane in the hangar during satellite passes over the test flight.

During this two-year period the A-12 was simply one of many "black" (i.e., secret) projects hidden from public view. Its designation and purpose were classified. However, whatever secrecy had been maintained during its development was stripped away by President Lyndon Johnson on July 24, 1964. On that day he announced that Lockheed was developing an advanced strategic reconnaissance plane to be known as the SR-71.[10] In fact, the intention had been to name the plane the RS-71 for Reconnaissance Strike 71. However, in light of the presidential miscue the Air Force decided that it was better to alter its plans rather than contradict the unforgiving and temperamental Johnson.[11]

The first order of A-12's were single-seaters capable of traveling at a speed of Mach 3.6 (twenty-four hundred miles per hour) and at an altitude of 92,500 feet. Substantial modifications were introduced into the A-12 design to produce the SR-71A. The first SR-71A flight took place at Palmdale, California, on December 22, 1964, and the first SR-71A entered the operational Air Force inventory on January 7, 1966. After June 1968, all missions were performed by SR-71A's.[12]

The SR-71A has been nicknamed Blackbird for its black epoxy surface and code-named OXCART in its days as a classified project. Both names are deceptive to varying degrees. The color of the SR-71A, which was chosen after tests for heat emissions from the plane, becomes blue as temperatures increase at high speed and altitude. OXCART, the name of a slow-moving body, was selected from a list of deliberately deceptive names.[13]

The SR-71A is 107.4 feet long with a wingspan of 55.6 feet and a fuselage five feet, four inches in diameter. The height at the twin vertical stabilizers is 18.5 feet.[14] What an SR-71A looks like depends on the vantage point, since to "look at a three-view drawing of the SR-71 is to see three totally different aircraft—one like an arrow, another like a flying saucer, and a third like an enormous bat."[15]

As with the plane, both the engines and fuel employed are

different. The engines are huge Pratt & Whitney J-58 turbojets. Rather than pointing straight ahead, the jets' intake spikes point down and in at an acute angle instead of straight ahead. When the plane is operating at extreme speed and altitude, the airframe distortion that is created pulls them straight. The JT-7 fuel is unique to the SR-71. It is especially nonvolatile—so much so that the engines have to be started chemically with a substance known as polyethyl bromide (PEB).[16]

The shape, engines, and fuel of the SR-71A are what make it a viable strategic reconnaissance aircraft—one that can fly at over Mach 3 (twenty-one hundred miles per hour) and at an altitude of at least eighty thousand feet, putting it out of range of both the SAM's and MiG fighters possessed by countries such as North Korea. With aerial refueling the SR-71 has a global range.[17]

The exact speed limit and operational ceiling of the SR-71A have been matters of speculation for years. In a public demonstration on July 27, 1976, Captain Robert Holt and Major Larry Elliott established records of 85,069 feet in height and 2,193.17 miles per hour in a straight line.[18] It is thought, however, that the plane can do much better than that. While even secret documents specify the SR-71A's speed at over Mach 3 and its operational ceiling at over eighty thousand feet, it may in fact be able to travel faster and higher than those figures would seem to imply. Its speed may be Mach 4. Kelly Johnson has stated that its altitude exceeds one hundred thousand feet.[19] In any case, its combination of height and speed allow the SR-71A to photograph one hundred thousand square miles of territory in a single hour.[20]

The plane is not flown manually when on a reconnaissance mission. A human operator could not fly it with the precision necessary to allow its sensors to perform effectively. The plane's inertial navigation system is up to the task. According to Kelly Johnson, "The inertial navigation system is so good that you can take off, put in sixteen different checkpoints, and on autopilot fly at speed, altitude, and direction desired."[21]

The sensors that are placed in the nose or underbelly of an SR-71 can vary from mission to mission. Included is a variety of imaging and SIGINT equipment. Thus SR-71's can be equipped with a Technical Objective Framing Camera capable of producing high-resolution imagery of the terrain below and to each side of the flight path. These cameras are, in general, operated automatically and respond in flight to instructions from the on-board navigation system to image specific preselected geographic coordinates. Likewise, an Optical Bar Camera can be fitted in the nose and is capable of providing either high-resolution stereo or monaural coverage of the terrain below and to each side of the flight path. A third option is the High Resolution Radar System, which can produce imagery day or night under all weather conditions. The resolution magnitude is, however, less than that of the camera systems, so it is considered most valuable when used to supplement satellite and aircraft systems that have been neutralized by cloud cover or darkness. Finally, an ELINT system that has a collection radius of several hundred nautical miles is available for the SR-71. The signals collected are analyzed using special equipment at the Mobile Processing Centers at Kadena AB, Japan, and Mildenhall RAF, United Kingdom, as well as at the Central Processing Center at Beale AFB, California.[22]

There are at present nine SR-71A's remaining from the thirty-one originally produced.[23] In addition to those at Beale AFB, California, there are two SR-71 detachments—one at Kadena AB on Okinawa and the other at RAF Mildenhall in the United Kingdom. Each detachment has up to two SR-71A's. The first such plane arrived at Mildenhall in early 1982 and was augmented by a second during the last week of December that year to operate in support of both USAFE and national intelligence requirements. The second plane was painted with the U.S. Air Force's new low-visibility markings, with all national insignia removed. By this time all SR-71A's probably are painted in this fashion.[24]

SR-71's represent a quick-reaction capability as well as an alternative and cheaper means of producing imagery and electronic reconnaissance than the satellite systems that cost hundreds of millions of dollars, are limited in capacity, and have as their primary mission surveillance of the Soviet Union and China. From

Beale, SR-71A's may be used, as they were, to provide intelligence to Britain during the Falklands war. Or they can be employed to overfly Nicaragua, creating a sonic boom in the process to reemphasize U.S. government displeasure with the Sandinistas. From its Kadena base SR-71's have been used to overfly China—indeed, an SR-71 photographed the entire first Chinese nuclear test.[25] Other prominent Asian targets have included North Korea, Vietnam, and Laos. Thus the SR-71 was used to gather photographic intelligence concerning the Sontay POW camp in preparation for the raid that was designed to rescue the POWs.[26]

The Middle East also is a major SR-71 target area. It probably was an SR-71 that overflew the Negev Desert during the 1973 Arab-Israeli war on the basis of information that Israel was preparing to arm its Jericho missiles with nuclear warheads.[27] Today's SR-71's fly over the Middle East from Akrotiri Air Base in Cyprus on Middle East missions. Included are missions to monitor the disengagement lines resulting from the 1973 Yom Kippur War, and probably Libya.

To avoid detection and destruction, the SR-71 is equipped with a radar detector and infrared sensor. Not only the presence but also the intensity of the tracking can be detected. Further, the radar detector and infrared sensor are linked so that when a SAM is launched it can be detected and then tracked by following the missile's heat trail as it moves up the radar track. Together they can pick up approaching planes or missiles that are one hundred miles or more away.[28] Such a detector warned an SR-71 pilot of a North Korean SAM launched on August 26, 1981.[29] That launch represented only one of about a thousand attempts to shoot down an SR-71—all unsuccessful. Other countermeasures included "a range gate system that literally projects the plane's image several miles away when viewed on enemy radar," a means of electronically deflecting approaching missiles, and a powerful radar jammer.[30]

Another aid to its survivability are the SR-71A's stealth characteristics. Indeed, the SR-71A was the first stealth aircraft—with a shape that gives a very small radar cross section. Additionally, its black epoxy paint both absorbs hostile radar emissions and limits the heat given off that could be picked up by an infrared tracking system.[31]

Despite the radar detector, its stealth characteristics, and its operational ceiling of over eighty thousand feet, the SR-71 does not overfly the Soviet Union in peacetime. In the event of a nuclear exchange, however, the SR-71 would be employed for "postattack strategic reconnaissance missions," according to an Air Force fact sheet.[32] In peacetime it does fly along the Soviet periphery in both the Far East and Europe for ELINT and imagery-collection purposes.

From bases at Mildenhall and Kadena, SR-71A's fly a variety of different "tracks"—North Norway/Kola Peninsula, Baltic, Mediterranean/Black Sea, and Sea of Japan/Kamchatka. The Baltic track apparently involves runs made from Mildenhall over Denmark and then over the Baltic parallel to the borders of East Germany, Poland, and the U.S.S.R., turning back when the plane reaches the southern tip of Finland.[33]

In its imagery role it can photograph installations on the Soviet periphery such as airfields, ports, naval bases, and radar installations. In particular, its high-resolution radar is employed to obtain imagery of Soviet submarine port facilities. In its ELINT role the SR-71 is used to fly "peripheral intelligence missions . . . to pinpoint locations and characteristics of potentially hostile signal emitters."[34] Thus the SR-71 ELINT role continues the peripheral electronic reconnaissance that has been part of U.S. intelligence activities since the late 1940s. The SR-71 apparently also continues the tradition of inducing the Soviet air defenses to "turn on" critical radar systems. The commander of the Strategic Air Command in 1978, speaking of the SR-71 and the RC-135, stated, "It is possible to operate these systems in a way that tells us things we want to know. This can't be done with satellites."[35]

In conducting their peripheral missions on the Siberian coast, the SR-71's often have visitors—MiG-25's. In his debriefing, Soviet defector Viktor Belenko explained that the MiG-25's were ineffective in intercepting the SR-71's:

> First of all, the SR-71 flies too high and too fast.
> The MiG-25 cannot reach at or catch it. Secondly
> . . . the missiles are useless above about 27,000
> meters (88,582 feet), and as you know, the SR-71
> cruises much higher. But even if we could reach,
> our missiles lack the velocity to overtake the SR-71
> if they are fired in a tail chase. And if they are
> fired head-on, their guidance systems cannot ad-
> just quickly enough to the high closing speed.[36]

On April 14, 1969, an EC-121 carrying a crew of thirty-one, large enough to allow personnel to operate in shifts, took off from Atsugi Naval Air Station near Tokyo. Seven hours later, when about ninety miles outside North Korea—according to the official U.S. account—they were shot down by a North Korean-piloted MiG.[37]

The plane was a variant of the Lockheed C-121 Super Constellation, which became operational in 1949. Four years later, the EC-121C and the RC-121C joined the Air Defense Command's 552nd Airborne Early Warning and Control (AEWC) Wing at McClellan AFB, California. The plane had large dorsal (back) and ventral (belly) radomes and added about twelve thousand pounds of advanced electronic interception equipment.[38]

The EC-121 that was shot down was on its way to conduct electronic surveillance of North Korean targets—specifically to intercept radio communications and monitor radio activity. Such daylight missions were more hazardous in the event of hostile action. During nighttime an interceptor had to be vectored to the target via radar. Thus, after an incident on April 28, 1965, in which a RB-47 was damaged, only night missions were flown for two years. Daytime flying missions there resumed in 1967 after two incident-free years.[39]

Whether that specific mission was to involve any Soviet targets such as the very southern portion of the Soviet Far East, only a hundred miles away, is not known. However, just as the ill-fated *Pueblo* and its sister ships monitored both North Korea and the Soviet Union, so the EC-121 program included both sets of targets.[40]

In patrolling the Soviet as well as North Korean periphery the EC-121 would fly at twenty-five thousand feet, an altitude from which its radar could sweep a forty-thousand-square-mile area. The plane's equipment would first pinpoint a radar site and then its analysts would determine whether the signal was associated with early warning, SAM guidance, or other activity. The EC-121's antennas would be focused on a wide range of military communications and could overhear conversations between major command posts two hundred miles away, allowing analysts to plot troop movements and assess combat-readiness. The EC-121 also apparently had the capability of "exercising"—feeding a false signal back to the opponent's tracking radar at precisely timed intervals to simulate an intrusion into his air space and thus getting him to activate his entire radar network, the activation being monitored by the EC-121.[41]

Even without exercising, the EC-121's would gather significant amounts of intelligence as they passed along the Soviet coasts forty or fifty miles from Soviet territory. In addition to information about Soviet radar systems the communications monitored would have included those from air bases and naval bases to planes in the air and ships at sea, and between theater headquarters and bases with regard to supplies, procedures, and activities.

The present single most important airborne platform involved in the collection of signals intelligence is the RC-135, of which there have been twelve versions. The first RC-135 plane, a RC-135B, entered the SAC reconnaissance inventory in December 1965—beginning the replacement of thirty obsolescent RB-47H's and ERB-47H's that were then "performing the ELINT portion of the Global Peacetime Airborne Reconnaissance Program."[42]

At present there are eighteen RC-135's in the U.S. inventory.[43] The vast majority of these are the fourteen modernized RC-135V and RC-135M (RIVET CARD) models nicknamed RIVET JOINT (Block III). These and the other models of the RC-135 have an overall length of 129 feet, a wingspan of 131 feet, and an overall height of forty-two feet. At its operational altitude, 34,990 feet, it cruises at 560 miles per hour.[44]

RIVET JOINT planes fly from bases in Alaska (Eielson AFB), Panama (Howard Air Base), England (RAF Mildenhall), Greece (Hellenikon), and Japan (Kadena AB, Okinawa). RIVET JOINT missions average about seventy flights a month in Western Europe and the Far East and about twelve a month in Central America.[45]

The RC-135V carries a crew of seventeen and flies at thirty-five thousand feet for up to ten hours before it requires refueling. The COMINT capability can be expanded from a minimum of six positions to thirteen depending on the requirements of the mission. The RIVET JOINT ELINT System is comprised of three collection positions—an Automatic ELINT Emitter Location System position supplemented by two manual operator positions. From Alaska they can patrol along the Kamchatka and Chukotski peninsulas, intercepting signals from intelligence targets such as the VLF transmitter at Petropavlovsk employed for submarine communications. The Japanese-based RC-135's can cover targets on Sakhalin such as the Pulsed Phase Radio Navigation System installation as well as targets on the Sea of Okhotsk such as the submarine base at Magadan.[46]

British-based RIVET JOINT planes can fly along the Baltic Sea, and over the Barents Sea just off the Kola Peninsula, intercepting signals from the three naval bases in the Murmansk area or the Severodvinsk submarine construction yard. The pilots are under orders not to get within forty nautical miles of the Soviet coastline and generally loiter one hundred miles or more out over the Barents Sea until they intercept something of interest. The planes based at Hellenikon can be targeted against the Soviet Southwest. Flying over the Black Sea, the planes can intercept signals from the Pulse Phase Radio Navigation system at Simferopol and the headquarters of the Black Sea Fleet at Sevastopol.[47]

From Eielson AFB RIVET JOINT missions target the Soviet Far East. The missions proceed around the southern tip of Kamchatka and into the Sea of Okhotsk, a projected deployment area for Soviet missile submarines. If not assigned to patrol over the Sea of Okhotsk, they slide down the coast toward Sakhalin Island. The missions monitor the alert status of Soviet air squadrons on Sakhalin as well as Soviet Air Force exercises. In the latter case the planes track Soviet fighters in flight.[48]

The remaining four RC-135 aircraft are evenly divided between the RC-135U and RC-135S models. The RC-135U's, modified RC-135C's, bear the nickname COMBAT SENT. COMBAT SENT missions are flown along the periphery of the Soviet Union and other Warsaw Pact countries, with specific routes, tactics, and even aircraft configurations varying with the tasking requirements.[49]

As with the RIVET JOINT planes, the COMBAT SENT aircraft fly at thirty-five thousand feet and can fly for ten hours without refueling if necessary. The primary sensor is the Precision Power Measurement System, which determines the absolute power, power pattern, and polarization of selected target emitters. In addition there is a high-resolution camera and television and radar sensors in the tail that are used when the occasion permits. One of the COMBAT SENT planes is equipped with a system known as COMPASS ERA—a system containing infrared thermal imaging, interferometer-spectrometer, and spectral radiometer sensors.[50]

The RC-135S planes, based at Eielson AFB, Alaska, and operating on occasion from Shemya, are nicknamed COBRA BALL and are the result of a late 1960s modification of two C-135B's.[51] Their mission is the monitoring of the reentry phase of Soviet and Chinese ICBM, SLBM, and IRBM research and development tests. The reentry phase of Soviet ICBM tests from Plesetsk and Tyuratam takes place either at Kamchatka Peninsula or into the expanses of the Pacific. For example, in 1974 three Soviet ICBM test reentry phases occurred in the Pacific.

Because COBRA BALL missions are dictated by Soviet decisions to conduct missile tests, missions cannot be planned on any regular basis. Only some of these tests—specifically, multiple tests or tests that have their reentry phase outside Soviet territory—need be announced to the United States in advance. Thus the COBRA BALL aircraft must be ready to fly on a moment's notice—in response to notification by the Defense Special

Missile and Astronautics Center (DEFSMAC) that a Soviet test is about to occur. Immediate launches are "announced" by the sounding of a Klaxon horn at Eielson.[52]

The planes operate at thirty-five thousand feet and for up to ten hours unrefueled and eighteen hours when refueled. Each COBRA BALL carries three sensor systems—one ELINT system and two photographic systems. The ELINT system is the Advanced Telemetry System (ATS), which automatically searches a portion of the frequency band and makes a digital record of all signals present. The operator of the ATS system allocates its collection resources to Soviet reentry vehicle links and records all telemetry detected.[53]

The Ballistic Framing Camera System images all the objects of interest in the reentry phase, while the Medium Resolution Camera System photographs individual reentry vehicles.[54] The images produced by the MRC System are used to determine the reentry vehicle size. Size estimates are used in turn to produce estimates of the explosive yield of the warheads.

In addition to its sensors for intelligence collection, the RC135's also contain an advanced ultrasecure communications system as well as equipment that can be used to "jam" radar and radio transmissions in addition to some electronics systems in other aircraft. It also contains an internal warning system that is manned by personnel who are specially trained to monitor the tactical air activity and air defenses of the target nation. According to two former RC-135 crewmen, "the targeted nation's military aircraft and air defense radars [must] be monitored continuously for the earliest possible indication of any hostile activity that potentially could be directed against the intercept platform."[55]

During its orbit the RC-135S records and cross-checks its position coordinates at least every twenty minutes. It is also called on to provide a variety of information—including airspeed, altitude, estimated time of arrival, orbit point, adjustments in timing or track, track length in minutes, the status of the equipment, wind direction, and time remaining on the track.[56]

*   *   *

As a supplement to the COBRA BALL aircraft, NSA and SAC have employed another version of the C-135 to collect intelligence during Soviet missile tests. This variant is the EC-135N, a plane with a ten-foot radome built into its nose. The "droop snoot" radome would carry an antenna seven feet in diameter that allows the eight-person crew to intercept voice communications, and telemetered or radioed data on speed, temperature, and other characteristics of the objects being tracked. The plane also has a probe antenna on each wingtip for high-frequency radio transmission and reception, and a high-frequency trailing wire beneath the fuselage.[57]

The EC-135N has had as its primary mission tracking U.S. missiles during flight tests as well as keeping tabs on unmanned satellites. They performed these missions, according to the Air Force, "over land where tracking stations are limited by geographical constraints and over water where ships cannot move quickly enough to cover different portions during a launch."[58] However, as a secondary mission, the EC-135N known as ARIA's would be used to monitor the end phase of Soviet missile tests flying opposite Siberia or over the Pacific.

The EC-135N's have been augmented by a new set of ARIA aircraft, which resulted in an increase in 1985 flying time of 300 percent.[59] Three EC-135N's are being equipped with Pratt & Whitney TF 33-POW-102 engines. These aircraft will become EC-135E's and continue to be part of the ARIA program through the late 1990s.[60] The replacement craft are EC-18B—American Airlines 707-313—modified into the ARIA configuration by the Air Force System Command's Aeronautics Systems Division. The first two EC-18B's became operational in 1985, and by 1988 all four will be in operation.[61]

Much of the equipment on the EC-18B airplanes will be recycled from the retired EC-135N's. The recycled equipment includes radomes, antennas, and on-board mission equipment such as receivers, data processors, and recorders. Additions to the internal portion of the craft include a navigation station, a new flight director, a modified electrical system, and an improved environmental control system.[62]

Additions to the external portion of the aircraft include a large dropped radome housing the seven-foot steerable antenna, high-frequency (HF) probe antennas on each wingtip, and a trailing wire HF antenna on the bottom of the fuselage. Antennas for postmission data transmission and satellite transmission also have been added. As with the EC-135N's, the EC-18B's will have as their primary mission monitoring U.S. space and missile launches, including unmanned space launches, cruise and ballistic missile tests, and Space Shuttle launches.[63]

Another major component of the present U.S. aerial reconnaissance program is the P-3C Orion, named after the Greek god of the hunt. The P-3C is the third generation of the P-3 antisubmarine warfare aircraft that succeeded the Neptune P2V in the late 1950s. A typical P-3C mission, which can last up to fourteen hours, has three main objectives: selecting the area in which to search for a submarine, finding the submarine, and determining its identity.[64]

The first generation, the P-3A, was produced by converting an Electra airliner—shortening its airframe by twelve feet, equipping it with weapons, and giving it an increased fuel capacity.[65] The P-3A originally was fitted with most P2V avionics and sensor systems and subsequently retrofitted with advanced equipment. The P-3B version had a fourfold increase in acoustic processing capability, and in 1981 infrared detection and HARPOON missile systems were added. The P-3C placed into operation advanced avionics and sensor equipment and linked the systems together with an on-board general-purpose digital computer that integrates all ASW System components and provides an accessible memory. The computer system served to multiply the speed and accuracy of information display, transmission, and retrieval.[66] Operators on the previous P-3 versions tended to be overwhelmed by the quantity of sensor data, much of which was unusable.[67]

The P-3C itself has undergone three updates and is scheduled to undergo a fourth in 1989. In its present configuration it stands 33.7 feet higher, has a 1,168-foot length, and has a 99.7-foot wingspan. Its maximum speed is 410 knots an hour, while it has a service ceiling of 28,300 feet. Its sixteen hours' endurance capability and speed give it a range of forty-five hundred nautical miles. It can search up to ninety-five thousand square nautical miles in a hour.[68]

The P-3C can carry up to eighty-four sonobuoys (devices designed to send out a signal to bounce off a submarine hull and disclose its location). Forty-eight of the sonobuoys are preset and are loaded in external launch chutes prior to takeoff. The remaining thirty-six are carried internally and their operating channels can be chosen during the mission. For many of the sonobuoys, it is possible to select their operating depth and length of transmission time.[69] The acoustic operators on the P-3C can monitor up to sixteen sonobuoys simultaneously (compared to eight for the P-3B and four for the P-3A).[70] A sonar-type recorder stores all acoustic data for reference to reconstruct the missions in detail.[71]

In addition to the sonobuoys, there are several nonacoustic detection systems on the P-3C. Its Magnetic Anomaly Detector is used in concert with the Submarine Anomaly Detector to determine if known submarine magnetic profiles are present. To get a good MAD reading, the plane must fly two hundred to three hundred feet above the water. Under the base of the plane are automatic cameras. The Infrared Detection System converts infrared energy into visible light and provides an image of the target. An airborne search radar, designated AN/APS-115, is used to detect radar returns from ships or submarines on the surface and pick out periscopes at the waterline.[72]

P-3C's are based at sixteen locations around the world: Clark AFB in the Philippines; Misawa and Kadena in Japan; Adak, Alaska; Iceland; Hawaii; Guam; Spain; Italy; Ascension Island; Diego Garcia; Lejes air base on Terciera Island in the Azores; California; Canada; Bermuda; and Puerto Rico.[73]

Every P-3C mission begins at the ASW operations center with a briefing during which crew members are informed of the tactical situation, whether a Soviet submarine is believed to be in the area, and if so, the type of submarine it is believed to be and what the operations center believes it is doing.[74]

A training mission flown from Adak, where regular missions

involve flights along the edges of the Soviet Union, consisted of a two-hour flight. About thirty minutes into the flight the radar picked up a surface blip, and the plane closed in to check the sighted ship's name against a maritime register while taking pictures with the automatic cameras under the nose of the plane. The spotted ship turned out to be the *Dairin Maru*, a Japanese cargo vessel. The plane was then taken down for a practice search. A petty officer slipped sonobuoys through a tube in the floor. The buoys floated to the water on small parachutes and proceeded to send out their signals.[75]

Two modifications of the P-3 are used for intelligence. Five P-3C airframes have been specifically configured for the collection, analysis, and recording of high-quality acoustic data on Soviet submarines, sonars, and underwater communications. These aircraft, known by the code name BEARTRAP, have a four-thousand-nautical-mile range, an operational altitude of two hundred to ten thousand feet, and twelve hours' endurance.[76]

The EP-3E is a modification of the P-3A that has been specifically altered for signals intelligence collection. The plane is distinguished from the Orion by a flat circular radome under the fuselage and lacks the long, thin MAD boom at the tail. The twelve EP-3E's are assigned to the Atlantic and Pacific fleets' Fleet Air Reconnaissance squadrons VQ-1 PR and VQ-2JQ and are headquartered at Rota, Spain, and Agaña, Guam. The Rota-headquartered planes operate over the Mediterranean and Baltic seas and the Atlantic Ocean, while the planes subordinate to the Guam headquarters operate over all of the Pacific (especially the Sea of Japan and the South China Sea) and the Indian Ocean. Often detachments from the Guam headquarters are to be found at Atsugi, Japan, and Cubi Point in the Philippines.[77]

The plane is a four-engined land-based aircraft with a thirty-four-hundred-nautical-mile range, an operational altitude of eighteen thousand to twenty-five thousand feet, and an endurance capability of twelve hours. The targets of the EP-3E may be land-based radars and UHF/VHF communications systems as well as ship-based radars and communications systems. Thus a Soviet ship leaving its construction site for a trial in the open ocean may be visited by an EP-3E. For example, the new Soviet nuclear-powered cruiser *Kirov* is weighted down with a variety of radar systems—Top Pair and Top Steer 360-degree search radars, Palm Frond navigational radars, Top Dome missile-guidance systems for the SA-N-6 antiaircraft missiles, Pop Group radars for SA-N-4 aircraft missiles, Eye Bowl guidance radars for SS-N-14 antisubmarine missiles, a Kite search fire-control radar for the two 110mm cannon, Bass Tilt fire-control radars for the eight 30mm rotating machine guns, and two Round House and one Fly Screen navigational aids for the helicopters carried on board.[78]

IX.

RHYOLITE, KENNAN, and Beyond

The move of reconnaissance activities into space in the 1960s represented a quantum leap forward for the U.S. intelligence community. But there was more to come. The 1970s and 1980s saw new capabilities, represented by the deployment of a variety of follow-on and new satellite reconnaissance systems. Some systems operated from low earth orbit to obtain even more detailed images and relayed them to earth more rapidly. Some operated from a somewhat higher orbit and kept watch on the Soviet Navy on the high seas. Others—representing a major leap forward in signals intelligence capabilities—operated in geosynchronous orbit from 22,300 miles above the planet.

The proliferation of space reconnaissance systems gave the still-secret National Reconnaissance Office a yearly budget of several billion dollars—many times that of the CIA—and put it at the center of the intelligence process. It also made the committees that decided on reconnaissance tasking—such as the DCI's Committee on Imagery Requirements and Exploitation (COMIREX) and SIGINT Committee—arenas where major decisions concerning the data that would be available to intelligence analysts would be made.

While Deputy Director of Science and Technology at the CIA, Albert "Bud" Wheelon took on both the NRO and the NSA. Wheelon and Brockway MacMillan, Under Secretary of the Air Force and Director of NRO, engaged in a prolonged and acrimonious series of arguments concerning the division of satellite research and development projects between the CIA and the Air Force. Wheelon felt that MacMillan was favoring the Air Force in the assignment of projects. Wheelon's predecessor at DDS&T, Herbert Scoville, also found MacMillan difficult to deal with, referring to him many years later as an incompetent whose only talent was fighting organizational battles.[1]

The debate between Wheelon and MacMillan became so intense that the DCI, John McCone and Secretary of Defense Robert S. McNamara agreed in 1965 to create a National Reconnaissance Executive Committee, chaired by the DCI and reporting to the Secretary of Defense, to oversee NRO's budget, structure, and research and development activities.[2]

Wheelon's dispute with NSA was of a more technical nature and concerned the possibility of intercepting telemetry signals and microwave communications. The speed of a satellite in geosynchronous orbit, 22,300 miles above the earth, matches the speed of the earth's rotation. Thus the satellite essentially hovers above a single point on earth.[3] Such a satellite will be useless for photographic purposes because the resolution would make the resulting photography valueless for military intelligence purposes. However, the communications interception and telemetry interception tasks require just such a satellite. A satellite that operates in an orbit similar to a photographic reconnaissance, ferret, or other low-orbiting satellite would be able to intercept only portions of a conversation, since its speed soon would take it out of range of one set of conversations and move it into range of another set. A geosynchronous satellite, however, could continuously focus on a particular area, pointing its interception antenna toward targets of interest such as naval bases, missile fields, and C[3] facilities.

In the case of telemetry interception, a geosynchronous orbit guarantees that the satellite will be in position when a missile test takes place. Between 1972 and 1975 the U.S.S.R. conducted a total of 181 research and development missile tests, with flight times of twenty-five to thirty minutes.[4] Thus at most there were ninety-one hours of missile telemetry to be monitored for those four years. A satellite that could be out of position because its orbit took it over South Africa at the time of a test would be of little use. On the other hand, a geosynchronous satellite would be on duty at all times, "waiting" for the test to occur.

According to ex-CIA official Victor Marchetti, it was believed by NSA that millimeter and microwave signals could not be intercepted from anywhere outside a relatively short and narrow area. Thus the CIA's Office of SIGINT Operations, part of Wheelon's Directorate of Science and Technology, undertook the task in conjunction with TRW.[5] The effort produced the RHYOLITE series of satellites, each satellite being capable of intercepting signals across the VHF, UHF, and microwave frequency bands. RHYOLITE was described in an official TRW briefing as a "multipurpose covert electronic surveillance system."[6]

The first RHYOLITE satellite apparently was launched on June 18, 1970. One account stated that only four satellites were launched—on March 6, 1973; May 25, 1977; December 11, 1977; and April 7–8, 1978. All were launched from Cape Canaveral using a General Dynamics/Lockheed Atlas-Agena D booster.[7] However, an Australian computer operator involved in the program and who began work at Pine Gap in November 1970 has stated that the first RHYOLITE satellite became operational just at the time of his arrival—which would coincide with a June 18 launch and a four-month period for check-out.[8] Likewise, Christopher Boyce, who later sold information on RHYOLITE to the KGB, was told at a briefing on RHYOLITE in late 1974 that the first RHYOLITE satellite had been operational "for almost four years."[9] And a satellite was launched from Cape Canaveral on June 18, 1970, boosted into geosynchronous orbit by an Atlas-Agena D.

When the second satellite was launched on March 6, 1973, the satellite referred to as *BIRD 2* took over the task of monitoring Soviet signals for *BIRD 1*, which was redirected toward China and Vietnam.[10] By the time *BIRD 4* was in orbit, a two-station arrangement had emerged. Two of the satellites apparently were stationed near the Horn of Africa at 45 degrees east to receive telemetry signals transmitted from liquid-fuel ICBM's launched from Tyuratam in a northeasterly direction toward the Kamchatka Peninsula impact zone. Another two spacecraft were stationed farther east, over Borneo, at 115 degrees east, to monitor Soviet solid-propellant missiles such as the SS-16 and the SS-20 IRBM, launched from the Soviet Union's northern space-launch facility at Plesetsk.[11] Their respective ranges provided coverage of almost all the U.S.S.R. and Africa, Europe, Asia, and the Middle East. By now all the RHYOLITEs are probably inoperative.

Little is known about the physical characteristics of the RHYOLITE spacecraft. One source lists it at 1,540 pounds; five feet, seven inches in length; four feet, seven inches in diameter; and cylindrical.[12] The main antenna is a concave dish more than seventy feet in diameter, backed and supported by a framework to which also are attached a number of other appendages, including large panels of solar cells and several lesser antennas.[13]

In addition to the telemetry signals from Soviet and Chinese missile tests, RHYOLITE satellites have had the previously mentioned COMINT task. As noted, the satellites can intercept Soviet and Chinese telephone and radio communications across the VHF, UHF, and microwave frequency bands. Robert Lindsey has written that the satellites "could monitor Communist microwave radio and long-distance telephone traffic over much of the European landmass, eavesdropping on a Soviet commissar in Moscow talking to his mistress in Yalta or on a general talking to his lieutenants across the great continent."[14]

Among the radio/telephonic traffic intercepted by RHYO-

LITE are early-morning stock exchange and other business calls. A former member of the project has asserted, "We could pick up the dial tones. We listened to many business conversations and transactions. We could have made millions."[15]

Walkie-talkie traffic generated by Soviet military exercises, which fall in the VHF/UHF range, also were regularly monitored by RHYOLITE satellites. Among the other communications intercepted were cries for assistance from wounded or endangered U.S. troops during the Vietnam War. Beyond the Soviet Union, RHYOLITE satellites over China and Vietnam have intercepted signals emanating from Indonesia, Pakistan, and Lebanon.[16]

The RHYOLITE project was described by former CIA official Victor Marchetti as "a very interesting project, a very much advanced project in terms of technology, and a very desirable project because getting information of the type that we wanted and needed on Soviet ICBM testing, antiballistic missile programs, antisatellite programs, and the like, much of this activity of course takes place in eastern Siberia and central Asia, getting information on the Chinese ICBM program."[17]

The RHYOLITE program suffered a setback in 1975 when a TRW employee, Christopher Boyce, and his boyhood friend Andrew Daulton Lee sold the KGB technical details about RHYOLITE. In accordance with standard security practice, NRO changed the code name of the satellite once it had been compromised. The new code name assigned was AQUACADE.[18]

It has been asserted that as a result the Soviet Union began encrypting its missile telemetry to deny the U.S. intelligence that would be produced from its analysis.[19] However, encryption began prior to the disclosures and is a routine security practice. It seems likely that the motivation for Soviet encryption of their missile telemetry was not discovery of RHYOLITE but the beginnings of the Soviet multiple independently targetable warhead (MIRV) testing program. When Soviet ballistic missile testing involved only single-warhead missiles, the United States was able to obtain the information it required via radar—hence, Soviet encryption would not have denied the United States any information of value. With multiple warheads, telemetry interception played an important role in producing intelligence about numbers of warheads, their design, and their accuracy.[20]

RHYOLITE satellites have been controlled since the beginning of the program from a facility in Australia commonly known as Pine Gap. Officially the facility is the Joint Defense Space Research Facility and is code-named MERINO. Reference to it as Pine Gap is the result of its location, about twelve miles southwest of Alice Springs at Laura Creek in a valley called Pine Gap. The Pine Gap valley itself is a natural basin formed by rocky outcrops of the MacDonnell Ranges.[21]

The facility itself consists of seven large radomes, a huge computer room, and about twenty other support buildings. The radomes, which resemble golf balls with one end sliced off and then mounted on a pedestal, are made of Perspex and mounted on a concrete structure. The radomes are intended to protect the enclosed antennas against dust, wind, and rain and to hide some of the operational elements of the antennas from unfriendly observation—such as that by Soviet photographic reconnaissance satellites.[22]

The first two radomes were installed in 1968 and remain the facility's largest. The first appears to be about a hundred feet in diameter and the second about seventy feet in diameter. They now form the western line of the antenna complex. The third and fourth radomes were fully installed by mid-1969. The third radome is about fifty-five feet in diameter and some 196 feet east of the largest radome, while the fourth is under twenty feet in diameter and just north of the second radome. In 1973 the antenna, which originally was installed inside the third radome, was dismantled and replaced by a thirty-three-foot communications terminal designated SCT-35. The fifth radome is less than forty feet in diameter and was installed in 1971. The sixth dish is about the same size as the fifth and was installed in 1977. The seventh radome, which was built in 1980, houses a second communications terminal, designated SCT-8.[23]

On the northern edge of the complex is a high-frequency antenna that provides a direct communications link with Clark AFB in the Philippines. It is the only nonsatellite communications system linking Pine Gap with terminals outside Australia, and before the installation of the SCT-35 antenna in 1973 it was the primary communications link between Pine Gap and the United States.[24]

Originally the main computer room was about 210 feet square, but it was expanded twice in the 1970s to its present size—about sixty thousand square feet. Its immense size requires that operators at each end of the room communicate with each other using headphones. The room is divided into three principal sections. The Station-Keeping Section is responsible for maintaining the satellites in geosynchronous orbit and for correctly aligning them toward targets of interest. The Signals Processing Office receives the signals transmitted down from the satellite and transforms them into a form that can be used by the analysts. The Signals Analysis Section is staffed solely by CIA and NSA personnel—no Australian citizens or contractor personnel are included. Many of the individuals in the SAS are linguists who monitor the voice intercepts.[25]

As of January 1981 there were 445 people employed at Pine Gap—228 Australians and 217 Americans—with another thirty-five to forty, mostly Americans, projected to staff the new extension to the computer complex.[26] While in theory Pine Gap is a joint facility, the fifty-fifty relationship holds only with respect to the gross numbers of personnel. As indicated previously, there are no Australians in the sensitive Signals Analysis Section of the computer room. Indeed, of the 228 Australians, only sixteen are involved in performing technical functions.[27] The fifty-fifty relationship is achieved by counting Australian housemaids, cooks, and gardeners who work at the base as "equal" to the CIA and NSA personnel who conduct the actual operations. Thus one Australian computer operator has stated, "The Americans run that place . . . it is not a place where Australians can feel comfortable."[28]

The early 1970s also saw a leap forward in photographic satellite reconnaissance capabilities with the launch of the KH-9 satellite, also known by the code name HEXAGON. As were its predecessors SAMOS, the KH-5 and the KH-7, the KH-9 was an area surveillance satellite. Its value would lie in being able to produce photographs of entire military complexes—large bases, testing facilities—or border areas. Initially the KH-9 was developed as a backup to the Air Force's Manned Orbiting Laboratory (MOL).

The MOL's primary mission was to be strategic reconnaissance, employing a ninety-inch telescope. A potential secondary application was as a satellite inspector. That the primary mission of the MOL was to be strategic reconnaissance was demonstrated by the classified designation it was assigned: Keyhole-10 (KH-10).[29]

On August 25, 1965, President Lyndon Johnson announced that he had approved the start of development of the MOL—an announcement that apparently had been delayed by a bureaucratic struggle between the CIA and the Air Force over the MOL. The concept of employing a manned platform for photographic reconnaissance had been tested during NASA's *Gemini 4* and *5* missions of June and August 1965 and on subsequent missions. The results were clearly positive: One photograph taken when *Gemini 4* passed over Cape Canaveral showed roads, buildings, and launch pads—even when viewed with the unaided eye.[30]

At that time it was felt that a manned reconnaissance vehicle offered some significant advantages over unmanned satellites, particularly with regard to target selection. Astronauts equipped with moderately powerful binoculars could easily pick out objects of potential interest and photograph them immediately. As a result, objects or areas unworthy of being photographed might be ignored, while previously unknown targets might be photographed earlier than otherwise.[31]

It was planned to put the MOL in orbits with eighty-five- to ninety-two-degree inclinations. The MOL would circle the earth every ninety minutes at an altitude of between 150 and 160 miles. Data were to be returned either via digital data transmission or television transmission. The MOL orbiting vehicle was to consist of a Gemini capsule for returning astronauts from the laboratory as well as for shuttling new astronauts to the MOL, and a further two sections. At the very end of the vehicle would be the living section for the astronauts. In front of the astronauts' quarters would be the section that housed the telescope. The vehicle would be launched using a Titan 3C rocket and solid-propellant boosters.[32]

At the same time, a contract was awarded to Lockheed's Missile and Space Division to develop the backup system, which was numbered 612. By summer 1966 the projected weight of the MOL had grown to more than thirty thousand pounds. By the spring of 1967 the initial launch date had slipped from 1968 to late 1969 or early 1970. The estimated cost for Project MOL had grown from $1.5 billion to $2.2 billion. At the same time, the design for the backup vehicle had progressed to the point where the Air Force was able to contract for a launch vehicle—the Titan 3D. In 1968 the code number was changed from 612 to 467.[33]

By the end of 1967 the initial launch date for the MOL had slipped to late 1970 or early 1971. By June 1969 the projected cost of the first five MOL's reached $3 billion—twice the original esti-mate. The huge price tag was one reason why MOL was can-celed.[34] In addition, there was significant opposition within the CIA. It was argued that the Soviet Union might consider manned reconnaissance to be a violation of sovereignty and attempt to shoot down the MOL with an ABM interceptor when the MOL passed over Moscow. But aside from Soviet intentions it was felt by many that a manned program could too easily be grounded. The same objections were to be made several years later when the Space Shuttle was being considered as the sole system for placing military satellites into orbit.[35]

Thus it was a KH-9 that lifted off the launch pad at Vanden-berg AFB on June 15, 1971. From that point on, both the KH-7 and the KH-9 were employed until the supply of KH-7 craft was exhausted. As with the transition from second- to third-genera-tion close-look spacecraft, the new spacecraft was first deployed while several older-generation spacecraft remained, thus provid-ing a fallback if the new-generation spacecraft was found to be flawed. Once the new generation proved successful, it was alternated with the older generation until the supply of the latter was exhausted.

The KH-9 was reported to weigh approximately thirty thousand pounds and to be fifty feet long and ten feet in diameter—having dimensions twice that of the KH-8 and a weight almost five times as much. In addition to a conventional photographic camera, it has been reported also to carry infrared and multispectral scanners. Film was returned to earth in four film canisters, which are ejected from the spacecraft when a spool is exhausted.[36]

As with the KH-8, the KH-9 satellites were launched into a north–south polar orbit with an inclination of approximately ninety-six degrees. However, given its area surveillance role, it had a higher perigee and apogee. For the nineteen launches between June 15, 1971, and June 20, 1984, the average perigee and apogee were 103 and 165 miles, respectively.[37]

The most notable change in the operation of the KH-9 since its first launch has been the increase in its lifetime. The first satellite had a lifetime of fifty-two days, while the lifetimes associated with the next four launches were forty, sixty-eight, ninety, and seventy-one days, respectively. By 1974–75, lifetimes were in the area of 180 days, while the KH-9's launched on June 18, 1980, and May 11, 1982, had a lifetime of 261 and 208 days, respectively.[38]

The maximum lifetime was achieved by the KH-9 launched on June 20, 1983. That spacecraft operated for 275 days before it burned up during reentry on March 21, 1984. The KH-9 program apparently terminated on October 18, 1984, when the twentieth "Big Bird" was commanded into destructive reentry after a stay of only 115 days in space.[39] The shortened lifetime may have been due to a malfunction or because photographs were taken at double the normal rate.

The termination of the KH-9 program followed by only three months the termination of the KH-8 program. The last KH-8 launch occurred on April 17, 1984, with the craft being deorbited on August 13 after 118 days in orbit. Among the targets of its cameras may have been the early-warning radar at Krasnoyarsk in central Siberia that has been labeled a Soviet violation of the ABM Treaty.[40] Like the KH-9, the KH-8 showed a steady increase in its lifetime. In 1971 a KH-8 would be expected to stay in orbit for less than a month. By 1979 the satellite was exhibiting a ninety-day lifetime, and by 1981 it began attaining lifetimes of over 110 days.[41]

The mid to late 1970s saw the further deployment of space-based signals intelligence satellites. Thus on March 10, 1975, the first satellite belonging to a class of elliptically orbiting satellites was orbited from Vandenberg AFB using a Titan 3B-Agena D booster—the same booster used by the KH-8 and Satellite Data System spacecraft. The satellite, code-named JUMPSEAT, also traveled in the same orbit as the SDS spacecraft—a peculiar elliptical orbit that brought it to within 240 miles of earth when over the Southern Hemisphere and at twenty-four thousand miles above the earth when over the Arctic. Subsequently, similar satellites have been launched—on August 5, 1978, and on several later dates.[42]

SDS spacecraft have four functions: to transmit messages to bombers flying over the North Pole, to provide early warning of Soviet SLBMs fired from the North Sea, to relay messages between various elements of the Air Force's Satellite Control Facility, and to serve as the relay for imagery produced by the KH-11 satellite (discussed later). It was with these missions in mind that the elliptical orbit was designed—in effect, an SDS satellite hovers over the northern Arctic for eight hours or so—allowing it to perform its missions until replaced by another SDS satellite.[43] An elliptically orbiting SIGINT satellite can focus its collection antennas on a wide variety of targets in the northern Soviet Union, including Arctic staging bases and the naval bases around the Murmansk area.

In 1975, another SIGINT satellite was launched into geosynchronous orbit from Cape Canaveral, on a Titan 3C booster. The identity of the satellite, launched on June 18, 1975, has not been established beyond doubt. One possibility is that the system launched was a test version of a satellite known as ARGUS. Originally ARGUS was planned as a follow-on to RHYOLITE. ARGUS was to have a main antenna twice the size of RHYOLITE's—140 feet in diameter—and additional capabilities. The choice of the code word was appropriate because in "Greek mythology, Argus was a giant with one hundred eyes . . . a vigilant guardian."[44]

However, ARGUS ran into two roadblocks, the first being Secretary of Defense James Schlesinger. Schlesinger vetoed a recommendation by the National Reconnaissance Executive Committee, chaired by DCI William Colby, to proceed with ARGUS. Apparently Schlesinger wanted more relative emphasis on imaging activities. Colby, as was his option under the procedures set up by McCone and McNamara ten years earlier, appealed to President Gerald Ford. The council's report supported Colby, and Ford did so in turn. Congress, however, had gotten word of Schlesinger's opposition and decided to remove the funding.[45] Hence, if the satellite launching on June 18, 1975, was that of an ARGUS, it was a one-time event.

The other possibility is that the June 18, 1975, launch represented the first of the CHALET series of signals intelligence satellites. As with RHYOLITE, CHALET is a geosynchronous satellite. Unlike RHYOLITE, it had no telemetry interception role when first designed. However, in the wake of the loss of the Iranian tracking station as well as the discovery that Christopher Boyce and Andrew Daulton Lee had sold the KGB information concerning RHYOLITE, it was decided to modify future CHALETs to conduct telemetry interception.[46]

CHALETs were launched on June 10, 1978; October 1, 1979; October 31, 1981; and probably December 22, 1984. It appears that the October 1, 1979, launch was the first of the modified CHALETs.[47]

On April 30, 1976, the U.S. Navy acquired its first operational ocean surveillance satellite system. The entire system—space and ground segments—is known as CLASSIC WIZARD. The satellite portion of the system is known as WHITE CLOUD and apparently is equipped with a passive infrared scanner and millimeter-wave radiometers as well as radiofrequency antennas capable of monitoring radio communications and radar emissions from Soviet submarines and ships. A vessel's location then can be determined from data provided by several antennas that measure the direction from which a vessel's radar or radio signals arrive.[48]

A WHITE CLOUD launch places four objects in orbit—a mother ship and three subsatellites—possibly with the three subsatellites being tethered to the mother ship. The basic techniques involved in using multiple spacecraft to eavesdrop and direction-find on Soviet surface vessels and submarines were first demonstrated using three Naval Research Laboratory spacecraft launched on December 14, 1971.[49]

The present satellites are launched from the Western Test Range—Vandenberg Air Force Base—into a near-circular sixty-three-degree inclined orbit at an altitude of approximately seven hundred miles, employing a General Dynamics Atlas F booster. At the seven-hundred-mile altitude the spacecraft can receive signals from surface vessels more than two thousand miles away, providing overlapping coverage on successive passes. Each successive pass places the satellite approximately 1,866 miles away from its position on the previous pass.[50]

The subsatellites, illustrated in Figure 3, are relatively small—measuring approximately three feet by eight feet by one foot. The largest surface area on one side is covered by solar cells; four spherical objects that are deployed on the end of metal booms are believed to be sensors.[51]

The ground segment of the CLASSIC WIZARD system includes five ground stations—at the Naval Security Group facilities at Diego Garcia; Guam; Adak, Alaska; Winter Harbor, Maine; and Edzell, Scotland. Several tracking domes have been built at Edzell to control and receive information from the satellites. Information received at these stations can be transmitted quickly to regional ocean surveillance centers and via satellite to a main down link at Blossom Point, Maryland.[52]

The first WHITE CLOUD quartet was launched on April 30, 1976, while the second and third quartets were launched on December 8, 1977, and March 3, 1980. In 1983 there were two launches—on February 9, 1983, and on June 10, 1983. As a result of the increased frequency of launches, funding has been sought and received for antenna upgrades at all CLASSIC WIZARD sites.[53]

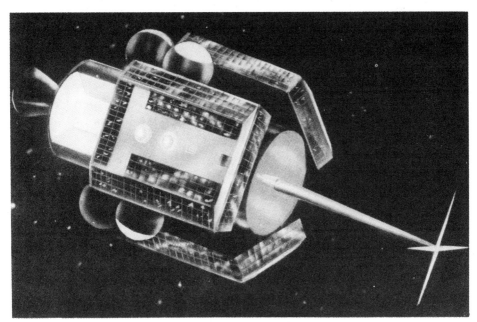

Figure 3. White Cloud Satellite

Perhaps the most significant advance in U.S. space reconnaissance capabilities was the KH-11 satellite, also known by the classified code name KENNAN.[54] This satellite revolutionized U.S. collection capabilities in a variety of ways. It brought reconnaissance imagery to earth in near real time.

The origins of the KH-11 go back to the 1967 Six-Day War. As a result of that conflict the CIA convened a panel to study the question of what kind of an imaging system was needed in such circumstances. The KH-11 system that emerged was less capable than a system designated the KH-X, which would have involved enough orbiting spacecraft to permit daily coverage of every point on earth. When the immensity of the data to be collected, processed, and analyzed became clear, plans for the KH-X were dropped.[55] On the other hand, the KH-11 was more complex than another system proposed by the Air Force. Richard Helms, then DCI, fought for the system designed by his Directorate of Science and Technology over the less complex system, taking his case to the President and emerging victorious. As a result, the KH-11 was born.[56]

On December 19, 1976, a single KH-11 was launched on a Titan 3D rocket from Vandenberg AFB into an orbit of 164 by 329 miles. The craft itself is sixty-four feet long and weighs thirty thousand pounds.[57] The satellites fly lengthwise, with the axis of the camera parallel to the earth. In front of the camera is a downward-looking mirror that can be rotated to look from side to side. Thus a periscope effect is obtained in which the direction in which the camera looks can change from moment to moment. Two benefits result from that capability: The same location can be viewed more frequently than if the camera could only look straight down, and the satellite can generate a stereoscopic image.

Only a very select set of government officials was permitted to know of the KH-11's existence or even see its product. The KH-11 was treated with even a greater degree of secrecy than usual in the black world of reconnaissance satellites—the photographs and data derived from those photographs were not incorporated with those of the KH-8 and KH-9. The decision to restrict the data to a very small group of individuals was taken at the urging of senior CIA officials, but opposed by military officers who wanted information to be more widely distributed throughout the armed forces. It was only when it was discovered that a disgruntled former CIA employee, William Kampiles, had sold the KH-11 technical manual to the KGB that the restrictive policy was changed.

The KH-11, in contrast to the KH-8 and KH-9, does not return imagery via film. Instead, to permit instantaneous transmission, its optical system employs an array of light-sensitive silicone diodes, and the array's charge is read off by an amplifier and converted from analog to digital signals for transmission.[58] The signals then are transmitted to Satellite Data System spacecraft while hovering over the Soviet Union. The SDS satellite then transmits them for initial processing to a ground station at Fort Belvoir, Virginia, about twenty miles south of Washington. The Mission Ground Site—a large, windowless, two-story concrete building—is officially the Defense Communications Electronics Evaluation and Testing Activity.[59]

Because of its return in digital form, the KH-11's data can be manipulated and enhanced in a variety of ways. Computers can disassemble a picture into millions of electronic Morse code pulses, then use mathematical formulas to manipulate the color contrast and intensity of each spot. Each image can be reassembled in various ways to highlight special features and objects hidden in the original image. A third technique is optical subtraction, whereby electronic optical subtraction of earlier pictures from later ones makes unchanged buildings or landscapes in a scene disappear and new objects, such as missile silos under construction, stand out.

Partially as a result of its electronic method of transmitting data, a KH-11 satellite can stay in orbit for a much longer period than either a KH-8 or a KH-9, could since a KH-11 cannot run out of film. An additional factor is the KH-11's higher orbit, approximately 150 by 250 miles, which reduces atmospheric drag on the spacecraft. Thus the lifetime of the first KH-11 was 770 days—over five hundred days longer than the lifetime of the longest-lived KH-9. The lifetimes of the subsequent KH-11's, shown in Table 1, give it an average lifetime of 1,018 days—almost three years.

Between the time the second KH-11 was deorbited on August 23, 1981, and August 28, 1985 (when an attempted KH-11 launch failed), a particular pattern had been established in which two KH-11's were kept in orbit at all times, and when one was deorbited it was replaced shortly thereafter by a new satellite.

Table 1. KH-11 Lifetimes

Launch Date	Deorbited On	Lifetime (Days)
December 19, 1976	January 28, 1979	770
June 14, 1978	August 23, 1981	1,166
February 7, 1980	October 30, 1982	993
September 3, 1981	November 23, 1984	1,175
November 17, 1982	August 13, 1985	987
December 4, 1984	—	—

Source: RAE Table of Earth Satellites, various issues

Thus the KH-11 deorbited on August 23, 1981, was replaced by one put into orbit on September 3, 1981, while the satellite launched on February 7, 1980, and deorbited on October 30, 1982, was replaced by a satellite launched on November 17, 1982. By the time one satellite was ready to be deorbited, both were circling the earth at a faster speed—every ninety minutes—than usual. After one satellite was removed from orbit the other made a major maneuver several days later, which increased its period to 92.5 minutes. The satellite replacing the deorbited satellite then was launched and made a few maneuvers to get the same period and desired plane spacing with the other, after which joint operations began. As shown in Figure 4, the satellite pairs divided up the work of providing late-morning and early-afternoon coverage. The combination of viewing angles produced is a substantial aid in interpreting the images produced.[60]

Beyond its longer lifetime, the KH-11 has an even more significant advantage over the film-return satellites. Its ability to provide data instantaneously allows it to be used in a crisis-monitoring role and an early-warning role. Whereas a film-return satellite could take days or even months to provide data, the KH-11 can return the data instantaneously—there is only a matter of an

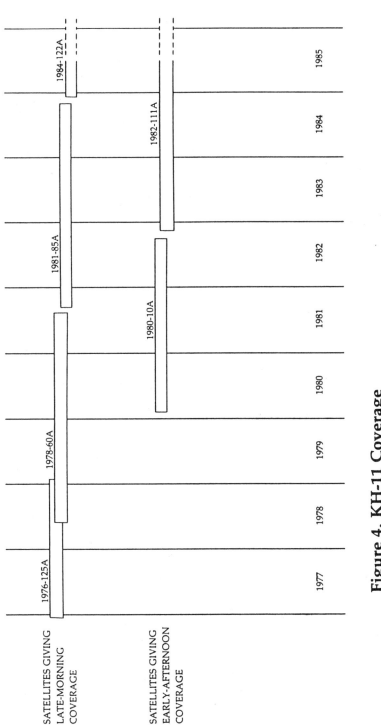

Figure 4. KH-11 Coverage

KH-11 satellites use sun-synchronous orbits so that their observational passes always occur at the same local time. The pattern for KH-11 is to have two satellites in orbit at any time, one making its passes in the late morning and the other in the early afternoon. The combination of viewing angles is a great aid in interpreting the images produced.

Source: Anthony Kenden

hour before the data can be processed at Mission Ground Site, analyzed at the CIA's National Photographic Interpretation Center, and then put in the hands of decisionmakers. According to one person familiar with the system, "You can call up the KH-11 and when it comes up on its geometry to the target area, you can get a photo and have it back down here, printed out, in an hour, and have it over to the White House."[61] Thus in 1985 CIA Deputy Director for Science and Technology Richard Evan Hineman testified that the KH-11 is used "against active military targets for early-warning purposes."[62]

Classes of targets that would be covered for early-warning purposes would be strategic bomber airfields (particularly Arctic staging bases), ports, submarine bases, airfields from which troop transport planes would fly, and border areas where troop concentrations might signal an impending invasion. Specific examples would include Anodyr Air Base in the Far East Military District; an Arctic staging base; the Baltic Fleet submarine base at Kaliningrad in the Baltic Military District; and, in the Far East Military District, Sovetskaya Gavan, a home port for surface ships up to destroyer size. In particular, the Soviet Union will on occasion move some of their TU-22M Backfire bombers to Arctic bases at Olengorsk and Severomorsk, putting them within striking distance of the United States. Such moves, made twice in 1983 and once in 1984, are, according to a National Security Council report, a "cause for concern and careful monitoring."[63]

In addition to its photographic capability, the KH-11 also may have some ELINT capability—possibly to collect the emissions of Soviet radars.

Several examples of the KH-11's photographic production have been exposed to public view. Among the data carried to the Desert One site in Iran during the hostage rescue mission was KH-11 photography left behind when a EC-130 and a helicopter crashed in the process of aborting the mission. Photographs left behind included overhead views of a sports stadium and the embassy compound. Among other uses, the data were employed to determine the location of the personnel in the compound and to scout the route the rescue team would take.[64]

In December 1981 a KH-11-produced photograph of a future Soviet bomber—the Blackjack—appeared in *Aviation Week and Space Technology*.[65] The photograph was taken on November 25, 1981, while the plane sat on the tarmac at Ramenskoye Airfield, a strategic test center. The photograph also showed two TU-144 Charger transports, similar to the Concorde. Distinguishable features included the passenger windows on the side of the aircraft. The picture was taken by the KH-11 satellite launched on September 3, 1981, on a southbound pass across the Soviet Union during the late morning, local time. The picture, which was taken at quite a steep slant or oblique angle, indicated a KH-11 capability to obtain a resolution between 5.46 and 17.7 inches, depending on apogee and perigee positioning.[66]

Most recently three KH-11 photos appeared in *Jane's Defence Weekly* of a Kiev Class carrier under construction, the carrier being code-named *Black Com II* (for *Black Sea Combatant II*) by the United States and *Kremlin* by the Soviet Navy.[67] The photos were taken at an oblique angle, although not as oblique as the angle at which the Blackjack photo was taken. In one case the slant angle was such that the photo was taken from 504 miles away.[68]

One computer-enhanced photograph, taken at an oblique angle, shows the general layout of the Nikolaiev 444 yard in the Black Sea, with what would appear to be a foundry in the foreground and assembly shops behind. Buildings housing the technical staff are shown to lie alongside the dry dock where the seventy-five-thousand-ton nuclear carrier was under construction. The photograph also shows the stern section of the *Kharkov*, the fourth Kiev Class carrier, in the process of being fitted out. Nearby, an amphibious landing ship, apparently of the thirteen-thousand-ton Ivan Roger Class, is shown under construction. The photography is distinct enough to identify objects such as ladders and windows. A second photo gives a more detailed view of the CVN dry dock. It also indicates the position of vertical silo-launched SAMs forward of the superstructure.[69]

More recently, in the summer of 1985, the KH-11 showed that Soviet personnel had cut off the tail sections of fifteen Bison bombers as part of its SALT II obligation to destroy old bombers to compensate for the deployment of new Bear H bombers. The bombers were placed in plain view at an airfield to facilitate monitoring by the KH-11.[70]

In April and May 1986 the KH-11 monitored the situation at the Chernobyl nuclear power plant, where a disastrous nuclear accident took place on April 26. Before the accident the last KH-11 photograph had been taken on April 16. After the April 28 TASS announcement of the accident, the KH-11 was instructed to take a photograph that very afternoon on its closest pass. However, the photography was taken at a considerable distance, and even computer enhancement did not produce a photograph that provided much information. The following morning another photograph was obtained, also from a considerable distance. However, by that afternoon the satellite was in a good position and obtained the first high-quality photograph.[71]

In addition, KH-11 imagery is reported to have revealed that the Soviets were constructing a new supersubmarine and a new miniaircraft carrier and disproved reports of a new Soviet CBW center by showing it actually to be a reserve arms storage facility. KH-11 imagery also apparently led to the discovery of a SS-20 ballistic missile in its canister alongside an encapsulated ICBM. It has been suggested that the Soviets were seeking to have Soviet reconnaissance spacecraft compare the two so that steps could be taken to increase the similarity and hence increase the chances for successful disguise.[72] The KH-11 also has been used to monitor directed-energy-related construction activities at Sary Shagan. According to one report, a number of experts knowledgeable on Soviet charged-particle-beam physics were convinced by KH-11 photographs that a particle-beam weapon was being constructed at Sary Shagan.[73]

In 1985 the KH-11 suffered its worst setback since the sale of the KH-11 Technical Manual to the KGB. On August 13, 1985, the KH-11 launched on November 17, 1982, was deorbited after a lifetime of 987 days. On August 28, the sixth KH-11 was to be placed in orbit, using a Titan 34D booster. However, a launch failure occurred when one of the Titan's core vehicle's two Aerojet engines shut down, resulting in the booster and payloads splashing down in the Pacific.[74]

The problem was compounded by two factors. There were no remaining KH-11s on the ground intended for launch, as the first KH-12 was expected to be launched in September 1986. All that was left was a KH-11 ground demonstration or "floor model" that had been used for flight qualification trials and other tests but never was meant to be placed in orbit. When the Space Shuttle *Challenger* exploded on January 28, 1986, the Space Shuttle program was dealt a major setback, the exact nature of which is not yet clear. However, it was clear that the first KH-12 launch will be delayed by a substantial number of months, since the KH-12 could be placed into orbit only by the Space Shuttle or by a new class of expendable launch vehicles that would not be available until 1988. As a result, plans were made to refurbish the ground demonstration model for launch around May 1986.[75]

Unfortunately, disaster struck again, on April 18, 1986, when a Titan 34D booster exploded shortly after launch just 250 to three hundred feet above the launch pad at Vandenberg AFB, creating an orange mushroom cloud. It appeared that the most likely payload aboard was the refurbished ground-demonstration model of the KH-11, as the only payloads that had been orbited from Vandenberg AFB on a Titan 34D were the KH-11 and the now terminated KH-9's.[76] However, other sources indicated that the payload was a signals intelligence satellite, possibly a follow-on to the JUMPSEAT Class.[77] Even if the payload was not the KH-11 ground-demonstration model, the United States will have only one operating photographic reconnaissance satellite in orbit until the Titan 34D is considered ready for launch or until the Space Shuttle places the KH-12 in orbit. Until then, if the KH-11 stops working prematurely, the United States will face a reconnaissance gap in which no coverage of the Soviet interior is possible.

To nurse the surviving KH-11 along, satellite coverage of areas that could be overflown by SR-71's and U-2's—such as Nicaragua, Cuba, and the Middle East—may be decreased. While SR-71's and U-2's cannot match satellites for repeat coverage, they can provide an intermittent look while preserving the KH-11 for use against the Soviet Union, Eastern Europe, and China.

To accelerate the first launching of the KH-12 it was decided to launch Space Shuttle mission 62-B (the mission carrying the KH-12) from Cape Canaveral rather than from Vandenberg AFB. While the optimal polar orbit can be achieved only from Vandenberg, the Space Shuttle launch complex there will not be ready until 1988. A KH-12 launched from Cape Canaveral could be placed in a medium-inclination orbit overflying much of the Soviet Union, even though a polar orbit could not be directly achieved from Cape Canaveral because of flight-path limitations.[78]

When the Space Shuttle *Discovery* lifted off from its Cape Canaveral launch pad on January 23, 1985, its cargo was a five-thousand-pound satellite code-named MAGNUM.[79] The launch, for the first all-military Space Shuttle mission, took place under an unprecedented blanket of security. Conversations between the astronauts and mission controllers were kept secret, being scrambled by a computer aboard NASA's Space Shuttle communications satellite before transmission to earth. MAGNUM's launch was two years overdue. Originally, 1983 was to be the year that MAGNUM—the follow-on to RHYOLITE—was to be placed in orbit from the Space Shuttle.[80] The dismantling of the Atlas-Agena D facility at Cape Canaveral stemmed from the reliability of the initial RHYOLITE satellites, the belief being that the Space Shuttle-launched successor would be ready before the RHYOLITE satellites became ineffective.[81] However, getting MAGNUM into geosynchronous orbit required firing a rocket from the Space Shuttle to carry the satellite to 22,300 miles. The rocket, known as the IUS (for Inertial Upper Stage), experienced problems in the first half of 1983 when it failed to deliver civilian communications satellites into geosynchronous orbit. As a result, Space Shuttle Mission 10, the first scheduled all-military flight, was postponed—first until late 1984, then until early 1985.[82]

The satellite is reported to have two huge parabolic antennas. One is intended to intercept radio, radar, and other electronic signals from the western Soviet Union. The other is designed to relay the signals to another communications satellite, which will in turn transmit them to a ground station (Pine

Gap).[83] Among the signals it will receive are those from implaced transmitters—such as those in a conference room or on a military facility. The Pine Gap facility has been undergoing additions for the past several years, with new antennas and radomes being installed, presumably in anticipation of the MAGNUM launch.

Exactly how much of an improvement MAGNUM will be over RHYOLITE is not known publicly. One possibility is that MAGNUM will be able to pick up lower-powered signals than RHYOLITE—such as "turned down" telemetry. MAGNUM's increased power might come from bigger antennas—on the order of those originally planned for ARGUS. The potential is suggested by a project being undertaken for NASA by Lockheed's Missile and Space Company. The project involves unfurling an antenna in space from the Space Shuttle's cargo bay. The antenna will resemble an umbrella, be nearly twice the size of a football field, and be so sensitive to low-powered signals from earth that it would pick up broadcasts from radios the size of a wristwatch.[84]

Another possibility is that it may have some stealth or spoofing capabilities that make it harder for the Soviet Union to find and more difficult to jam—as it has been alleged they have been doing to RHYOLITE in recent years. Assistant Secretary of Defense for International Security Policy Richard Perle charged in 1984 testimony before the House Foreign Affairs Committee that the U.S.S.R. had begun jamming telemetry-monitoring satellites to prevent the collection of even encrypted data for possible future decryption. The jamming was alleged to be electronically precise, to have begun sometime after the Soviets shot down the Korean 007 airliner in 1983, and to take place only during missile tests.[85] The distinctive visual and radar image of the satellite will ordinarily allow the Soviets to know where it is and its mission.[86] Hence some sort of stealth technology would be required to hide it from Soviet detection.

At the end of 1985 the U.S. space reconnaissance effort involved six types of satellites—the KH-11 for photographic reconnaissance, the WHITE CLOUD ocean surveillance satellites, ferret satellites to provide information on Soviet and other radar systems; and the MAGNUM, CHALET, and JUMPSEAT satellites to provide a variety of signals intelligence. To augment these capabilities there appear to be three new reconnaissance satellites under various stages of development.

The satellite that is farthest along—and that was scheduled to be launched in September 1986 on the second Space Shuttle launch from Vandenberg AFB—is the KH-12. The KH-12 is expected to be a forty-thousand-pound satellite with greater capabilities than the KH-11. As with the KH-11, it will transmit its data in real time—via SDS and via the elliptically orbiting MILSTAR satellites that will replace SDS. One significant improvement will be the KH-12's thermal imaging capability, significant at night—particularly valuable at a time when the Soviets are shifting more to night movements and night testing of new missiles.[87]

Additionally, the KH-12 will be equipped with a greater fuel supply—totaling about ten thousand to fifteen thousand pounds—allowing for a greater ability to maneuver. Thus it will be able to move from a high altitude of 560 miles to a low of eighty miles, although generally it will operate in a 150-nautical-mile circular orbit. It will be able to provide both high-resolution imagery of small areas and lower-resolution imagery of wider areas. Further, its maneuvering capability could be employed in attempts to evade Soviet ASAT weapons or to defeat Soviet cover, concealment, and deception activities.[88] For further protection the satellite also will be hardened against nuclear effects and contain a variety of protection devices to prevent damage from Soviet laser weapons.[89]

The availability of the Space Shuttle also will revolutionize the reconnaissance operation. The Shuttle will be able to retrieve KH-12's whose fuel supply has been depleted or that need to be repaired or refurbished. After being refueled, repaired, or refurbished on earth by the contractor, the KH-12 can be returned to orbit by the Shuttle.[90] Thus it is expected that KH-12's will have an eight-year lifetime.

Sometime after the KH-12 becomes part of the U.S. space

reconnaissance fleet another satellite system, a radar imagery satellite, will be added. That satellite will close a major gap in U.S. satellite imagery capabilities. While the KH-11 has worked wonders on clear days and the KH-12 will work wonders on clear days and clear nights, neither was provided with a capability to penetrate cloud cover.

Cloud cover is a serious impediment in monitoring the U.S.S.R., where some areas are covered by clouds about 70 percent or more of the year. In some cases, a particular installation—for example, the Kharkov tank factory—may be under cloud cover for the entire year.[91] In other cases the cloud cover is such that imaging a particular area or target may take several years. Possibly a complete picture will be formed only by constructing a photographic montage of the area made up of pictures taken on a number of orbital passes.[92] Thus in 1983 the United States was "surprised" at the discovery of a Pechora Class large phased array radar in central Siberia at Krasnoyarsk.[93] The early-warning radar, which had not yet been completed but was substantially under construction, represented an apparent violation of the ABM Treaty due to its inland location—a location banned by the treaty to prevent use of such radars for ABM "battle management."

The radar satellite apparently is a CIA project, with an intended late 1980s launch date. Its prime target will be Soviet and Warsaw Pact armor.[94] Data acquired by such a satellite would be relayed back to a ground station at White Sands, New Mexico, by the new Tracking and Data Relay Satellite.[95] In the event of a European crisis either within Eastern Europe or between East and West, the satellite will be able to keep watch regardless of weather conditions.

A third reconnaissance satellite program will be designed solely to monitor Soviet laser activites—especially those relating to strategic defense programs. A particular target will be the directed-energy R&D site at Sary Shagan. It has been reported that $1 billion in funding has been approved by Congress to develop the satellite, which would operate in low-earth orbit and pick up powerful or even very short bursts of laser light.[96]

X.

The Soviet Target Abroad

Gathering intelligence concerning Soviet military, political, and economic developments has been by no means restricted to operations on, over, or immediately nearby Soviet territory. It has been an effort with no geographical limits.

Soviet embassies and consulates are spread all over the world, and operating against Soviet personnel in a West European or Third World nation is far easier than in the police state atmosphere of the Soviet Union. Additionally, Soviet military equipment is to be found outside the Soviet Union—as the result of Soviet weapons sales to third countries as well as accidents that have resulted in crashed planes and sunken ships. Recovery of such equipment has provided U.S. analysts with significant information on construction, vulnerabilities, and capabilities of Soviet weapons systems.

Less obviously, information was to be searched for in the United States itself. The information was believed to be in the Library of Congress, on the beaches of Alaska, and in the letters of a wide variety of private citizens. Nor did the U.S. intelligence services ignore the information that might be obtained from dis-placed persons and ex-POWs who had spent the war years in the Soviet Union.

As with human intelligence, operations directed against the Soviet target abroad began even before the end of World War II. The first operation began on August 29, 1944, six days after Ro-mania withdrew from its alliance with Germany. On that day the United States Air Crew Rescue Unit, consisting of twenty-one members, landed at Popecti Airport in Bucharest.[1]

Romania was in chaos. The government was not function-ing, the Germans were evacuating as fast as possible, and the Soviet Army had not yet appeared. The U.S. rescue team, with the consent of what was left of the Romanian government, landed and proceeded to evacuate U.S. prisoners as quickly as possible. With that task completed, the unit, all of whose mem-bers also were members of the OSS, began their real mission. Lead by Frank Wisner, a future CIA Deputy Director for Plans, the unit's main function was to recover any documents and rec-ords concerning the Soviet Union that the Germans had left be-hind. The operation was code-named Operation BUGHOUSE.[2]

The unit thus began a search of the German and Romanian military and intelligence offices. They found stacks of intelligence files that the Germans had failed to evacuate. The files provided two types of information. The first concerned the Soviet Union that the Germans had collected from Romania. The second was the dossiers of German intelligence agents who had operated against the Soviet Union—agents who might be persuaded to stay in operation but simply switch masters.[3]

One aftermath of World War II was the personal chaos it created. Soldiers who had gone to war and been captured re-turned to Germany to find many of their relatives, friends, and often their own homes lost due to the war. Many spent time in resettlement camps, just as thousands of displaced persons lived for varying periods of time in DP camps.

In the midst of the Berlin Blockade it was decided to attempt to exploit the ex-POWs as an intelligence source. In a five-year period, in over a hundred refugee camps or urban interrogation centers throughout Germany, over three hundred thousand former Wehrmacht POWs repatriated from Russia after the war voluntarily submitted to interrogation. The result was over one million intelligence information reports relevant to topics such as the military capabilities and intentions of the Soviet Union, its military and industrial power, and Soviet control of Eastern Europe.[4]

In the spring of 1949 the nickname WRINGER was adopted to designate the POW interrogation effort. In June the European Command established the 7001st Air Intelligence Service Squadron and specified that its primary mission was "to collect positive Air Intelligence Information from open sources." The unit comprised forty officers, 101 airmen, and 103 foreign nationals. Operating from its Wiesbaden headquarters, the squadron selected small teams of officers and airmen to be deployed throughout the large and easily reached main cities of central and southern Germany. The teams took the form of "USAF Historical Research" units located in Ulm, Hof, Hersfeld, Frankfurt, Munich, Nuremberg, Stuttgart, Mannheim, Konigstein, and Oberusel.[5]

The teams located in the city centers then sent three- to four-man detachments into the German reception centers for POWs and refugees, to screen new arrivals. They were screened for current intelligence information and to identify any individuals who might subsequently be interviewed. Officers also were stationed in the main camps for returnees and refugees as well as being sent to small camps maintained by the individual German states for individuals awaiting resettlement whenever the size and composition of the camp population indicated that worthwhile intelligence might be obtained. The screening officers would record the ex-prisoner's name, his probable future location in Germany, his education, and his military training. A code letter then was assigned to indicate the likely relative value of his potential information.[6]

The city center prepared a similar index. The two eventually were combined to form a register of almost four hundred thousand sources. Based on those data, invitations would be issued to the most promising individuals to "talk about the real circumstances surrounding their lives in recent years."[7]

The POWs proved to be, within obvious limits, valuable sources of information. They had been in labor camps, which were distributed over the entire Soviet Union. Further, they had not simply been locked behind fences for the duration but put to work—repairing the installations damaged by German bombs as well as constructing new facilities. Additionally, many of the ex-POWs had received technical training in the Wehrmacht, allowing them to report accurately and in great detail about steel mills, chemical plants, power and communications facilities, and military installations.[8]

WRINGER reports focused on both urban areas and military facilities. The reports on urban areas were important in developing radar-target simulators. POWs were able to specify the Soviet terrain with sufficient detail to permit the development of three-dimensional models of key Soviet cities. The models then were photographed on radar-prediction film. Strategic Air Command crews on a simulated bombing run could see the terrain and the target configuration exactly as they would appear during an actual mission.[9]

A particular instance in which WRINGER information was crucial in developing an up-to-date simulator occurred with respect to the city of Magnitogorsk, the third-largest steel-producing city in the Soviet Union. Previous information indicated a large steel factory next to a lake west of the city. The lake, formed by an earthen dam across the Ural River, provided water for the city and the steel plant. Because it had high radar-reflective characteristics, the lake's center was considered a good aim point. However, the product of WRINGER interrogations revealed that POWs had been involved in the construction of a new dam several kilometers downstream. The result was that the water basin had been quadrupled in size and its center shifted to several miles south of the steel plant. A mission using the original center of the lake as an intended impact point would essentially have missed the target.[10]

In the military area WRINGER interviews produced a wide variety of reports. The data involved subjects such as the Soviet use of television for military purposes; developments in the field of rockets and missiles; mechanics and manufacturing technology for gear reduction equipment in propeller-driven aircraft; the technology of Soviet synthetic fuel plants, water control and storage facilities of key Soviet cities; flight test data on new Soviet aircraft; and jet engine construction technology. Data on the physical vulnerability and the defenses of some targets were sufficient, in some cases, to permit SAC war planners to divide their list of important targets into priority groupings.[11]

As was to be expected, WRINGER would not be a perpetual operation. As more individuals were interviewed, it became more likely that new interviews would result in repetitive data. Further, as time passed the POWs' experiences in the Soviet Union became less and less relevant to what was happening there. In addition, Air Force and Navy reconnaissance missions were bringing back harder data in a number of areas. By 1953 the continued value of WRINGER was brought into question. Thus, whereas in 1950 the Air Force Director of Intelligence wrote that "in light of collection potential which WRINGER demonstrated . . . immediate steps should be taken to expand WRINGER activities in Europe," in 1953 an analyst stated that "WRINGER reports are subject to the law of diminishing returns."[12] Shortly afterward the WRINGER operation was concluded.

Faced with a dearth of information about the Soviet Union immediately after World War II, particularly potential targets in the Soviet heartland, the Air Force turned in all directions to gather whatever information might be available. One source was only miles from the Pentagon.

Located on Capitol Hill was the Library of Congress. As its title and location suggested, one of its purposes was to provide library services for congressmen and their staffs, although just as frequently it is used by thousands of researchers who need access to its book, periodical, and government document holdings. It occurred to Air Force officials that a massive amount of material on the Soviet Union—including information on its cities, industry, and terrain—might be in that library, waiting to be tapped by researchers. As a result, in 1948 the Air Force established Project TREASURE ISLAND for the "exploitation of open source material at the Library of Congress."[13]

The project involved the creation of an Air Research Division in the Library of Congress and controlled by the Air Force Directorate of Intelligence. The Directorate, in requesting funds for the creation of such a unit, stated:

> The required basic work on Urban Areas selected as priority targets for the various commands will necessitate research studies which will coordinate the findings of the photographic interpreters with the economic work done in the Strategic Vulnerability Branch, Air Intelligence Division, and must also include pertinent comments on the relative vulnerability of these areas as targets from the psychological (including sociological and political) points of view. These overlaps require the work of both highly trained analysts and abstractors who must devote their entire time to this work.[14]

The writer went on to note that the Air Force would have to hire sixty-one additional personnel and that the Library of Congress could provide the space necessary to undertake the program plus "its vast collection of pertinent documents."[15]

Over the years, of course, reliance on the Library of Congress to provide targeting information became unnecessary with the development of technical collection systems such as the U-2, KH-4, and RHYOLITE. The photographs and electronic signals they produced were employed for targeting. However, the idea of open source data being used in the analysis of foreign military capabilities did not become irrelevant, and the Air Research Division became the Federal Research Division, under the supervision of the Defense Intelligence Agency.

In 1953 Eskimos informed members of the Air Force that foreign debris was being washed ashore on St. Lawrence Island.

Studies of the Bering Sea currents indicated that flotsam from Japanese and Siberian waters could easily find its way to Alaska's beaches. The Russian-language inscriptions on some of the earliest items confirmed the theoretical calculations.[16]

As a result, a yearly collection operation—Operation BEACHCOMBER—was instituted by Air Force Intelligence. The concept was a simple one: Assign people to walk the Alaskan beaches to collect any material of Soviet origin that might wash up on those beaches. Whatever might wash up was considered of potential interest. The rationale was expressed in an *Alaskan Air Command Intelligence Review* article that stated, "Data stencilled on a packing crate, or a manufacturer's part numbers, have always been excellent sources of intelligence information. Resupply routes, factory locations, production figures, unit strengths and positions—details such as these can be pieced together from the patient, long-term examination of such material."[17]

Operation BEACHCOMBER I took place in the summer of 1953, required two months, involved four officers and nine airmen, and covered 704 miles of beaches. The areas selected for patrolling included the shoreline of St. Lawrence Island, around the Seward Peninsula from Nome to Cape Espenberg, and the coast of the Chukchi Sea from Sheshalik to Point Hope. Coverage was broken down into seven legs, which were to be covered in two phases, with the first phase concentrating on the mainland and the second on the island. Three four-man teams were formed for the first phase, then planned to regroup for the four legs of the island search. To assist the teams in screening out items of no value, Russian-language translators and technical intelligence personnel were assigned to the teams.[18]

The entire group was airlifted to Nome, and two teams continued by air to Kotzebue. The first phase proceeded essentially as planned, but the Espenberg-to-Wales team was delayed when the Eskimo boat crew refused to make the trip. The situation was further complicated when after the team took ten days to find a replacement boat it was found to be unsuitable for rough water operation.[19]

All teams were delayed by the weather and sea conditions. Thus the Chukchi Sea group had to pass up a short stretch of beach that was inaccessible due to drifting ice. To counteract the climate, the teams evolved a system of "leapfrog walking" in which part of a team would patrol the beach while the other would ride in the boat, carrying supplies. If an obstacle was reached by the walkers, the boat would drop off the second group of walkers past the obstacle and pick up the first team. The technique allowed the teams to cover far more than the planned ten miles a day.[20]

The search of St. Lawrence Island was conducted in the same manner, although without the Espenberg-to-Wales team, which never resolved its boat problems. Thus the search involved three teams of three men each. Two of the teams were airlifted to Gambell Island and one to the Northeast Cape. One of the Gambell teams was to proceed around the southern side of the island, patrol the beaches to Cape Chithak, then proceed directly to the Northeast Cape. The other team planned to cover the northern shoreline either all the way to the Northeast Cape or until it met the still missing team. Since the other team never arrived, one team covered the entire northern side of the island.[21]

The team at Northeast Cape walked westward along the southern shore to Cape Chithak, where its planned rendezvous with a team from Gambell was missed. After continuing a short distance beyond the rendezvous point they were forced by a dwindling food supply to return directly to the Northeast Cape. By the time the Gambell team that had been scheduled to rendezvous with the Northeast Cape team arrived, the area had been searched, and they headed directly to the Cape. All teams then returned to Elmendorf.[22] The teams turned up a total of 115 items of foreign origin.[23]

The BEACHCOMBER operation was repeated in the summer of 1954. Since summer on Alaska's northwestern shore meant exposure to a cold, windy climate, all the participants underwent a rugged six-week training course consisting of a series of twenty-mile hikes while carrying weight equal to the weight (sixty-five to seventy-five pounds) of the equipment they would be carrying on an actual mission.[24]

A total of five teams were involved in BEACHCOMBER II—

two to search St. Lawrence Island's beaches, and three to explore the mainland's beaches. Each team consisted of one officer and three airmen, except that one of the St. Lawrence teams also had a Navy intelligence officer from Kodiak Naval Station. Altogether the teams covered 660 miles on foot, with supplies and the items recovered being carried by Eskimo skin boats with native crews. A total of sixty-three items of foreign origin were recovered, including a radiosonde that utilized a new type of tube and thus elicited the interest of the Air Technical Intelligence Center.[25]

The year 1955 saw Operation BEACHCOMBER III begin on August 1 with the airlift of twenty-five officers and airmen and their equipment from Elmendorf AFB to Nome and then on to their starting points. By August 16 the last team had returned to the main base at Elmendorf, completing the operation in half the time it had taken the previous two years—despite the large stretches of beach that still were covered with snow on August 1.[26]

The effort produced coverage of 546 miles of beach, leading to the recovery of eighty items of Soviet origin. The bulk of these items consisted of parts of wooden boxes, barrels, and so on, with Soviet manufacturing and shipping data. Also included were some electrical equipment and "a bottle with an unquotable message (no intelligence value) in Russian inside."[27]

Operation BEACHCOMBER IV began on July 14, 1956. Over four hundred miles of beach were searched on foot and produced 148 items of foreign origin. Once again the majority of the items were parts of wooden boxes, barrels, and wood products bearing Russian manufacturing and shipping data. Other items discovered included electrical equipment, radio and vacuum tubes, bottles, oil drums, fuel samples, and life rings.[28]

As with the other BEACHCOMBER operations, the climatic conditions were far from ideal, and obstacles prevented continuous coverage of the beaches. The leapfrog walking method again was used, with two men walking for thirty minutes or until the first obstacle was reached. The other two members of the team who had been riding in the accompanying boat then went ashore and started walking down the beach while the boat waited to pick up the first pair of beachcombers approaching the obstacle.

Using this procedure, about twenty to thirty miles were covered per day. In one case a team was stormbound on an isolated beach for five days and had to be resupplied by air.[29]

Operation BEACHCOMBER V began on July 16, 1957, with three officers and eight airmen. Four beaches were patrolled: Cape Prince of Wales to Espenberg; Shesvalek to Point Hope; Gambell to Northeast Cape; St. Lawrence Island; and Wainwright to Cape Lisburne. Each team was able to cover twenty-five to forty miles per day. In addition to looking for objects of Soviet origin, the beachcombers also sought "to accomplish the essential task of effecting liaison at each village in an effort to refurbish the consciousness in the natives of the importance of reporting items of Russian origin which they might locate along the beach at any time of the year. . . ."[30]

The 252 items considered to be of "intelligence value" resulted in the production of reports such as "Life Preserver Rings of Soviet Origin," "Serum Bottle," and "FOLSAM of Possible Soviet Origin found near Kivilina, Alaska."[31]

New York City also served as home for an operation whose objective was the collection of information about the Soviet Union. The project originated in the spring of 1952, when the Soviet Russia Division of the CIA proposed an operation involving scanning the exteriors of all letters to the Soviet Union and recording, by hand, the names and addresses of the correspondents. Opening the mail was not part of the original proposal, but it was noted as an option for the future.[32]

The project, with Post Office concurrence, began on a full-time basis in February 1953. Among its objectives was to "produce intelligence information when read in the light of other known factors and events." From February 1953 to March 1956 the operation involved almost exclusively the examination of the exteriors of the letters, although some letters were opened without knowledge of the Post Office "on a completely surreptitious basis . . . [by] swiping a letter, processing it at night and returning it the next day."[33]

In a November 21, 1955, memorandum to Richard Helms, Assistant Director of the Plans Directorate, James Jesus Angleton, chief of the Directorate's Counterintelligence Staff, proposed that the CIA "gain access to all mail traffic to and from the U.S.S.R. which enters or transits the United States through the Port of New York." In addition he suggested that the "raw information acquired be recorded, indexed and analyzed and various components of the Agency furnished items of information which would appear to be helpful to their respective missions."[34]

Angleton further suggested a shift in emphasis from mail covers to mail opening. He wrote that "[i]t is estimated that it will be possible to make discreet interior examination and photograph the contents of approximately two percent of all incoming communications for the U.S.S.R., or approximately 400 per month."[35] In addition to positive intelligence information, Angleton anticipated that the mail openings also would provide useful counterintelligence information. Since the Soviets would assume that the mail was safe from unauthorized openings, the operation would provide "an entirely new avenue of information in the field of counterespionage."[36]

Angleton's suggestions were approved on December 7, 1955, and operation HT/LINGUAL, as it was known within the Plans Directorate, began in 1956 when the operation moved from the General Post Office in Manhattan to a secure room at LaGuardia Airport.[37] Until 1962, when the operation moved to Idlewild (Kennedy) International Airport, mail to and from the Soviet Union was delivered each day by a postal clerk to the LaGuardia facility. A team of four CIA agents, working five days a week, would sort through the five thousand to fifteen thousand items of correspondence delivered each day. The exteriors of as many items as possible were photographed with a Diebold machine, and from thirty-five to seventy-five letters would be selected for opening daily.[38]

Agents who were to be assigned the task of opening mail prepared by attending the one-week "flaps and seals" course run by the Plans Directorate's Technical Services Division. The basic method of opening the mail was extraordinarily simple: The glue on the envelopes was softened by steam from a kettle, and with the aid of a narrow stick, the flap was pried open and the letter removed. It took approximately five to fifteen seconds to open a single letter. Experimentation with a steam "oven" capable of handling about one hundred letters simultaneously proved unsuccessful, and the CIA returned to the more traditional method. In addition to reading opened mail, the agents brought some of it to a TSD laboratory so it might be subjected to further chemical and other technical examination for secret writing and censorship techniques. Opened letters were returned to the airport the next morning and reinserted into the mail flow.[39]

Letters were selected for opening in one of two ways: on a random basis or by reference to a watch list. About 75 percent of the opened letters were chosen at random as of 1961, although the balance may have become more even in the later years of the project.[40] One agent involved in the program stated that there were no criteria for opening mail to or from people not on the watch list, that selection might occur "according to individual taste, if you will, your own reading about current events. . . . [Y]ou never knew what you would hit. . . . We would try to get a smattering of everything, maybe the academic field or travel agencies or something. . . . I don't recall a specific instruction. I kind of place that under our individual tastes."[41]

The watch list was originated in the mid-1950s and at first involved no more than ten to twenty names. It grew rapidly, however, with the Soviet Russia Division, the Counterintelligence Staff, the Office of Security, and the FBI all contributing names. By the end of the project it had grown to six hundred names. In 1957 a CIA memorandum had suggested five categories of names for the list:

1. former agents or covert contract personnel who originally came from "the Denied Areas" in Europe, were utilized by the Agency, and have now been resettled in the United States or Canada
2. defectors from "the Denied Areas" in Europe who were under the control or auspices of the

Agency and who have now been resettled in the United States or Canada

3. repatriates from the United States or Canada who were originally brought to the United States or Canada under the auspices of the Agency and who have now returned or will return to the U.S.S.R.

4. suspected Soviet agents or other individuals either temporarily or permanently residing in the United States, who are known or suspected of being engaged in counterespionage or counterintelligence activities on behalf of the U.S.S.R. and

5. foreign nationals, originally from the U.S.S.R. and satellite countries, now residing in the United States and presently being utilized by the Agency in any capacity[42]

Shortly thereafter, however, the watch list expanded considerably, coming to include the names of individuals who were in contact with individuals on the watch list. Among those who came to be included on the list were the American Friends Service Committee, the Federation of American Scientists, Edward Albee, John Steinbeck, and Praeger Publishers, to name just a few.[43]

Despite two internal reviews that questioned the value of the program, including one that stated that the "positive intelligence from this source is meager," the project continued until 1973.[44] The project was terminated in 1973 by new DCI, James Schlesinger, in face of an ultimatum by Chief Postal Inspector William Cotter to withdraw U.S. Postal Service support unless presidential authorization was obtained, and the conclusion of Deputy Director for Operations William Colby that the "substantial political risk of revelation was not justified by the operation's contribution to foreign intelligence and counterintelligence collection."[45]

*   *   *

Yet another method of attacking the Soviet target abroad has focused on the Soviet embassies and missions distributed throughout the world and the individuals who staff them. While penetration of a Soviet embassy or mission, especially if it is in a backwater, is not of the same value as the penetration of the Ministry of Foreign Affairs or a design bureau, it still can provide valuable information. Soviet diplomats can report on policies under consideration, particularly with regard to the country they are stationed in, as well as gossip concerning personalities and power struggles in the Ministry of Foreign Affairs. A Soviet military adviser can provide information on future arms deliveries to a particular country as well as intelligence on weapons systems. Thus former CIA officer Harry Rositzke has written that "even a one- or two-year penetration of a Soviet embassy can provide classified information going far beyond the parochial concerns of the embassy itself; broad policy reports from the Soviet foreign office; party correspondence from the Central Committee; new directives from KGB or GRU headquarters in Moscow. All roads do not lead to Moscow, but in a highly centralized and disciplined bureaucracy most spokes lead to the hub."[46]

Additionally, a Soviet embassy or mission is a far "softer" target than the Soviet Union. Although Soviet personnel are kept on a tight leash and the Soviet Colony section of the KGB Residency is looking for signs of disaffection, improper contacts, or even careless behavior, the control is not as strict or effective as if the employee were back in Moscow. Further, the representatives of the Soviet Bloc Division of the CIA Directorate of Operations will not have to operate against the full force of the KGB's Second Chief Directorate, as they would have to in Moscow. Indeed, in many cases the local security authorities will be working with them or at least not obstructing their activities.

In many countries, penetrating the Soviet establishment was the *primary* function of the CIA station. Thus one agent was told by his boss shortly before the agent was to depart for Austria that "the Austrian station has one real mission and a bucket of marginal responsibilities, many of them bilge. Your job is to recruit Russians. Until we've done that, we've failed. . . . Our basic job is to penetrate the Soviet establishment—that's the only way we'll get the answers the White House is screaming for."[47]

Thus the CIA has devoted a great deal of time and energy to seeking to penetrate Soviet embassies and missions throughout the world. According to one former CIA officer, complete penetration of such a facility would include: "at least one spy within, reporting on his own government; the ability to read the mail to and from the embassy; being able to listen to telephone calls; at least one microphone broadcasting secrets from within; the capability of obtaining photographs of everyone working in the embassy and nearly everyone who visited; and access to its trash."[48]

Over the past forty years the CIA has had varying levels of success in attaining such penetrations. The most successful penetration began in Vienna in 1953, when Lieutenant Colonel Peter Popov dropped a note into an American diplomat's car. Popov's note said: "I am a Russian officer attached to the Soviet Group of Forces Headquarters in Baden bei Wien. If you are interested in buying a copy of the new table of organization for a Soviet armored division, meet me on the corner of Dorotheergasse and Stallburgasse at 8:30 P.M., November 12. If you are not there I will return at the same time on November 13. The price is 3,000 Austrian schillings." After an initial meeting that followed up on his note, Popov, now code-named ATTIC, was introduced to his case officer, George Kisvalter. Kisvalter had been in St. Petersburg before the Revolution, spoke fluent Russian, French, German, and Italian, and joined the Soviet Russia Division in 1952.[49]

Popov identified himself as a graduate of the Military Diplomatic Academy assigned to the intelligence *rezidentura* of the GRU in Vienna, with an office in the Imperial Hotel. The Imperial had been Austria's largest and best hotel until seized by Soviet troops when they arrived in Vienna in April 1945. Popov also specified that he was a case officer working against the Yugoslav target. In exchange for money, Popov was willing to provide information.[50]

Before Popov's arrival the CIA station had been operating against the Soviet representatives from the outside. After weeks of experimentation a CIA officer found that if one parked "an artfully dilapidated Austrian-plated sedan in the right spot on the Ringstrasse—previously marked with an inconspicuous splash of paint to show exactly where the front wheels should be—the eye of the toy tiger (and the lens of the radio-operated camera concealed in the beast) had a perfect line of sight on the crosswalk most favored by the Russians hustling from the Imperial to the Grasse for lunch." From some distance away an officer with a concealed radio could trigger the camera whenever a likely target stepped onto the crosswalk. The photographs and data that resulted were sent to the Soviet Russia Division for further analysis.[51]

Popov's special knowledge now could be applied to the data. He was able to match names to faces, cover names to true names, and specify the officers' operational assignments. Popov's information thus produced a quantum leap in the state of knowledge of the Vienna CIA station concerning their GRU adversaries.[52]

Subsequently Popov was able to provide even more detail on the GRU. When in Baden bei Wien to receive his duty officer briefing he was asked by the Baden finance officer to bring the payroll sheets to Vienna. Listed on the sheets were the names of every GRU officer, technical and clerical person, and driver working in the Vienna *rezidentura* and in the Baden offices. The payroll list specified the rank, date of grade, pay, and allowances.[53]

More important than ATTIC's information on the GRU was his information on Soviet military doctrine and weapons. In one instance Popov was asked to satisfy one of the U.S. Army's highest-priority requirements—a copy of the 1947 Soviet Army field regulations. The manual was believed to be the first and only basic manual of Red Army organization and tactics issued after World War II. Popov informed his controllers that the 1947 manual had been withdrawn and replaced in 1951. Subsequently Popov and Kisvalter spent an entire meeting photocopying the 1951 manual, which Popov had removed from the GRU offices in the Imperial Hotel.[54]

In July 1954 Popov returned to the Soviet Union for home

leave and spent three weeks at the Kaliningrad rest center. Formerly the capital of East Prussia, it was in the area ceded to the Soviet Union after the war. A resort built for Gestapo personnel was turned into a rest area for KGB and GRU personnel as well as high-ranking officials from the atomic-weapons and guided-missile programs. While there he acquired information ranging from atomic submarine data to information on guided missiles—information he reported to Kisvalter upon his return to Vienna.[55]

As a result of the Soviet-Austrian Treaty of 1955 Popov was sent to Moscow and, without warning, transferred to the illegals support section of the GRU Opergruppe in East Berlin. From his new post he would process illegal agents passing through East Berlin on their way to their foreign assignments.[56] To inform the CIA of his transfer, Popov simply handed a letter explaining the situation to a member of the British military mission touring East Germany. In turn the officer passed it on to a SIS representative, who then passed it on to the CIA.[57]

Popov continued to report in person to Kisvalter, crossing into the Western sector from the East. His reports extended beyond information of interest to counterintelligence authorities and included a wide range of military information. The information came from the reserve officers' courses he attended on a regular basis as well as from conversations with high-ranking officers stationed with the Group of Soviet Forces Germany. The data included sensitive details concerning Soviet weapons systems and data on missiles and guidance systems.[58]

In December 1958 Popov was transferred back to Moscow. He returned to find himself under arrest, Soviet counterintelligence having tumbled onto his contact with the CIA. However, after interrogation he was allowed to resume contacts with the CIA in Moscow—under Soviet control, of course. Instead of passing true information, he was passing Soviet-designed disinformation. The charade was continued until October 16, 1959, when Popov and his Moscow case officer, Russell Langelle, were arrested by the KGB while exchanging a note on the Moscow bus.[59]

What exactly resulted in Popov's detection has been a subject of debate for many years. There have been suggestions that Popov was blown as early as 1955—that the note he passed to the British military officer also passed through British SIS officer George Blake, who also was a top Soviet penetration agent. Kisvalter, however, finds it unbelievable that Popov had been blown so early: "Judging from the quality of information we got from Popov long after Blake left Berlin, it couldn't have been Blake who blew Popov."[60]

An alternative explanation is that clumsy FBI surveillance of a Soviet agent immediately after her arrival in New York indicated a leak in the GRU's East Berlin apparatus that could be narrowed down to one of three people—one of whom was Popov. Another explanation is that Popov and Langelle were early victims of KGB "spy dust"—a chemical that can be used to track movements of individuals and determine their contacts. According to a KGB defector, Yuri Nosenko, who has been accused of being a false defector, Langelle's Russian maid dusted his shoes with the powder. Using a sniffer dog, the KGB tracked Langelle to a mailbox, where they found a note to Popov.[61] The last explanation, it should be noted, is inconsistent with Popov being arrested immediately upon his return to the Soviet Union.

As a result of the detection of Popov's activities and the arrest of Langelle, the latter was declared *persona non grata*. Popov subsequently was executed in a particularly horrific manner—being thrown alive into a furnace in the basement of GRU headquarters. The U.S. gain from Popov's sacrifice was large: Popov provided information that might have reduced defense R&D expenditures by one-half billion dollars. The information included specification of Soviet weapons, including tanks; tables of equipment for Soviet tank, mechanized, and rifle divisions; as well as a description of Soviet army tactics in the utilization of atomic weapons.[62]

Soviet missions in Latin America and Cuba also have been the target of CIA penetration attempts. The major target has been the Soviet embassy in Mexico City. During the 1960s the CIA station was running a wide variety of operations designed to penetrate the Soviet mission there. Two observation posts were established in front of the embassy to cover the entrances, while a third post, designated LI/CALLA, was placed opposite the back of the embassy to provide coverage of its gardens. LI/CALLA was located in one of five homes surrounding the Soviet embassy; the home was owned by the CIA station. All the observation posts were used for taking photos of personnel and visitors as well as the license plates of visitors' cars. At one point films were made of Soviets talking in the garden area, but lip-readers were unable to decipher the conversations. The front observation posts operated in concert with a surveillance team, LI/EMBRACE, maintaining radio contact and informing them when a particular surveillance target would leave the embassy.[63]

Other operations included LI/ENVOY, the monitoring of Soviet telephones; the acquisition of travel documents; and information on arrivals and departures. In addition, interception of Mexican diplomatic communications was exploited to reveal requests for Mexican visas by Soviet officials, including diplomatic couriers.[64] Access agents were also run against Soviet officials. During Philip Agee's stay in Mexico City, between fifteen and twenty such agents were operated. Included were the Secretary of the Foreign Press Association, Katherine Manjarrez, and her husband—both targeted against the Soviet press attaché and the TASS correspondent. A third was LI/COWL-1, the owner of a small grocery store in front of the embassy, where the Soviets would buy soft drinks and other items. One operation involving LI/COWL-1 was targeted against the embassy's administrative officer. During a visit to LI/COWL-1's establishment he was introduced to a Mexican girl recruited by the CIA station. An affair followed, as planned, with the CIA recording and photographing the events. The photographs obtained could have been exploited for blackmail or to provoke disruption by sending them to the embassy.[65]

The most recent CIA success against a Soviet mission occurred in New York at the United Nations. In 1974 Arkady Shevchenko, the Under Secretary General of the U.N. and a Soviet foreign ministry official, informed U.S. representatives of his desire to defect.[66] According to Shevchenko's account—which has been disputed by some and supported by others—CIA representatives asked him to remain in position temporarily and serve as an agent of the CIA.[67] Shevchenko, feeling he had little choice in the matter, agreed. He was assigned the CIA code name ANDY and told that they were not asking him to follow people or steal and photograph documents. Rather, they wanted the information Shevchenko already had access to—about policy matters, political decisions, and the decision-making process.[68]

Having been recruited, Shevchenko began his triple employment—for the U.N., the U.S.S.R., and the CIA. According to his account, "I read the code cables and other secret material arriving from Moscow via diplomatic pouch. In addition, officials from the Central Committee, the Foreign Ministry, and other branches of government and academic institutions, including friends from the embassy in Washington, visited New York. I was also following events and gossip in Moscow through the 'pocket post'—the stream of private letters carried back and forth by individual diplomats and other travelers to avoid the mandatory opening and checking by the KGB censors."[69]

As a result of his activities, Shevchenko was able to keep the CIA apprised of:

> What was going on in the Kremlin, particularly regarding the Brezhnev-Kosygin frictions over the future course of Soviet-American relations, about Moscow's instructions to Ambassador Anatoly Dobrynin in Washington, details of Soviet policy and the political rationale for many plans and events in various parts of the world. I told him about the Soviet positions on arms control negotiations—SALT and others—including fallback provisions contained in the instructions. I told him of specific Soviet plans for continuing the fight with movements in Angola that did not accept Moscow's role there. From officials in Moscow involved in economic matters, I passed on information that the original oil-fields in the

Volga-Ural region on the Ob River would soon decline and that in several years the Soviet Union
would have difficulty expanding oil production in
the smaller, less accessible fields.[70]

In 1976 Shevchenko returned to Moscow on vacation and for
consultations—which allowed him to gather information about
the thinking of Gromyko and other officials of the Foreign Ministry and Central Committee. He was also part of a group review-
ing Soviet policy in Africa.[71]

Late spring 1977 saw a security clampdown as a result of the
TRIGON affair, making Shevchenko's life more difficult. Among
the new measures was a roster, maintained by the mission
guards inside the entrance, in which the comings and goings of
senior officers were recorded as they entered or left the building.[72] Finally, in April 1978 Shevchenko bolted and came in from
the cold—turning from spy to defector.

An important source of information concerning Soviet military capabilities comes from the acquisition of new or used foreign weapons systems, communications, and other devices of
military significance. In many cases confirmation on small systems cannot be obtained by signals intelligence or satellite photography. Further, possession of the actual system adds
significant new information to whatever is already possessed.
The acquisition and analysis—the material exploitation—of such
systems allows scientists to determine not only the capabilities of
the system but also how such capabilities were achieved. Such
knowledge then can be exploited to improve U.S. systems as well
as to develop countermeasures against foreign systems.

Acquisition of such systems is a high-priority intelligence objective and is attained by a variety of methods. In Indonesia in
the 1960s the CIA conducted an operation designated HA/
BRINK. In one phase of the operation, CIA operatives entered a
warehouse holding SAM-2 missiles that Indonesia acquired from
the Soviet Union, removed the guidance system for one, and
took it with them. HA/BRINK also obtained the designs and

workings of numerous Soviet weapons—the surface-to-surface Styx naval missile, the W Class submarine, Komar guided-missile patrol boats, the Riga Class destroyer, the Sverdlov cruiser, the TU-16 (Badger) bomber, and a Kennel air-to-surface missile.[73]

The United States can acquire advanced Soviet aircraft from the defection of pilots or by purchasing the aircraft. Once obtained, the aircraft is examined thoroughly by Foreign Technology Division (FTD) officers and scientists. Thus when Viktor Belenko landed his MiG-25 in Japan in 1975, a high priority of U.S. Intelligence was the examination of the airplane. Before being returned to the Soviet Union, after insistent Soviet requests, the entire MiG-25 was disassembled at Hyakuri Air Base in Japan. The engines, radar, computer, electronic countermeasures, automatic pilot, and communications equipment were placed on blocks and stands for mechanical, metallurgical, and photographic analysis.[74]

Examination of the plane, as well as debriefing of the pilot, sharply altered Western understanding of the plane and its missions. Among the discoveries was a radar more powerful than that ever installed in any interceptor or fighter, and the use of vacuum tubes rather than transistors.[75] Vacuum tubes, although they represent a more primitive technology than transistors, are resistant to electromagnetic pulse (EMP) created by nuclear detonations.

The MiG-25 was far from the first MiG obtained for exploitation purposes. In early 1951 the Allied Force commander in Korea was asked to make any effort to obtain a complete MiG-15 for analysis. As a result of the request, a MiG that was shot down and crashed off Korea was retrieved within a short time. Portions of another MiG were retrieved by helicopter. Air Technical Intelligence Center personnel landed, ran up to the crashed plane, threw grenades into it to separate assemblies small enough to carry, and left under hostile fire. In 1953 a defecting North Korean pilot flew an intact MiG-15 to South Korea.[76]

In other instances crashed planes, ships, or other items have been recovered from the ocean. In 1970 the United States recovered a nuclear weapon from a Soviet aircraft that crashed in the Sea of Japan; in 1971 the Navy recovered electronic eaves-dropping equipment from a sunken trawler; and in 1972 a joint U.S.-British operation recovered electronic gear from a Soviet plane that had crashed earlier that year into the North Sea.[77]

A continuous recovery operation, SAND DOLLAR, involved the recovery of Soviet test warheads that landed in the Pacific Broad Ocean Area at the conclusion of long-range ICBM tests. U.S. radars tracked the warheads to determine the precise impact point. What appeared to be civilian drilling ships then were sent to the Pacific test range after the tests had been completed to recover nose cones whose self-detonation mechanisms had failed to operate. Ships were guided to the proper locations by comput-ers coordinated with U.S. satellites, and the objects were located by sonar and magnetometer devices. Scientists at the FTD who analyzed the captured nose cones learned how the Soviets de-signed and constructed each part.[78]

The most elaborate of all the recovery operations cost over a hundred million dollars and involved four thousand people plus the CIA and Howard Hughes. The operation, conducted in 1974, had its genesis in 1968. On April 11, 1968, a Soviet Golf (G Class) submarine in the northwestern Pacific surfaced to recharge its batteries. Instead, a massive explosion occurred, sending the ship and its entire crew to the bottom. The Soviets began sur-veillance of all possible disaster sites, listening for radio transmis-sions and sending out their own. Mid-May saw the Soviets abandon their round-the-clock trawler fleet activity and simply try to achieve radio contact while mid-June saw the abandon-ment of even that attempt. While the Soviet Navy was unable to locate its lost ship, the U.S. Navy did. A set of ocean-bottom hydrophones code-named SEA SPIDER and part of the Navy's Sound Surveillance System (SOSUS) was able to locate the sub-marine to within a ten-square-mile area.[79]

The advantage to be gained by salvaging the submarine and its contents was considered obvious by intelligence officials. On board the submarine would be an array of coding and decoding devices. It also was believed that the submarine was armed with three nuclear missiles—either the 350-mile range SS-N-4 Sark or the seven-hundred-mile-range SS-N-5 Serb—and possibly some nuclear-tipped torpedoes. In addition, documents concerning Soviet nuclear targeting policy also might be on board.[80]

Examination of the warheads would provide the United States with an insight into the state of Soviet nuclear technology—particularly the reliability, accuracy, and detonation mechanisms of the missiles. Recovery also would allow naval analysts a chance to examine Soviet torpedoes for the first time.[81] Examining the homing devices incorporated into the design of the torpedo would be a valuable help to those assigned the task of developing countermeasures to cause the torpedo to miss its intended target. It would allow analysts to subject the steel used in the hulls to metallurgical analysis, allowing for a determination of the depth to which Soviet subs could dive.[82]

At the time a prize of great value was considered to be the cipher machines and Soviet code manuals that might be stored in watertight safes. Subsequently, some intelligence experts played down the value on the grounds that Soviet (as U.S.) code machines are constructed to permit the operator to reset circuits and insert new coding and encoding discs at random.[83]

Before further action could be taken, it was necessary to determine the exact position of the submarine. A secret Navy research ship, the *Mizar*, was sent to the general vicinity, where it put overboard an array of sensing devices: sonar, electronic scanners, cameras equipped with powerful strobe lights, and a magnetic sensor to detect the presence of metal on the seabed. The *Mizar* then spent two months towing the equipment across the ten-square-mile area until it had located and obtained a variety of data, including photographs of the submarine resting on the seabed.[84]

Richard Helms, Director of the CIA at the time the Soviet sub sank, reacted negatively to the suggestion of Deputy Director for Science and Technology Carl Duckett to raise the sub, but soon changed his mind. With approval from the White House, the CIA proceeded to contact Howard Hughes. A CIA official explained the reason for the choice of Hughes: "The Hughes organization had the technical know-how for a project of that difficulty, and moreover Hughes has a passion for secrecy, which frankly was what we had in mind." Further, the new President of Hughes Aircraft, A. D. "Bud" Wheelon, was a former CIA Deputy Director for Science and Technology.[85] Hence Hughes and the CIA began work on Project AZORIAN.[86]

Hughes, in alliance with Lockheed and Global Marine, Inc., developed a design for a new ship—thirty-six thousand tons, 618 feet in length, and 115.5 feet in the beam—that would serve as a floating, highly stable platform. Amidships a high derrick would pass piping directly through the "moon pool" in the ship's hull, which could be opened or closed.[87] The moon pool was a two-hundred-foot-long, sixty-five-foot-wide pool into which an object could be lifted from the sea.[88] A companion to the ship was to be a huge submersible barge roughly the size of a football field, which would be covered by an oval roof. The barge would carry the gigantic retrieval claws that would grapple for the submarine and raise it. The roof would prevent Soviet satellites from photographing the cargo.[89]

The ship, to be christened the *Glomar Explorer*, and the barge, the *HMB-1*, were constructed by Sun Shipbuilding and Dry Dock, Inc., under the supervision of Global Marine and the National Steel and Shipbuilding Company. The construction of such an unusual ship, particularly when done for Hughes, could not be expected to go unnoticed—either by the industry or by Soviet reconnaissance satellites. To provide a cover, Hughes claimed that the ships were going to be involved in mining the ocean floor for precious metals such as titanium, manganese, uranium, copper, and nickel.[90]

On November 4, 1972, the *Glomar Explorer* was launched with a 170-man crew picked by the CIA. Of the 170, forty men constituted the mining staff and knew of the ship's secret mission. According to one account, it tested its detection equipment and some of its recovery systems at the site of the 1968 accidental explosion of the U.S. nuclear-powered submarine *Scorpion*, which went down near the Azores in about ten thousand feet of water.[91]

Returning to Los Angeles, the *Glomar Explorer* rendezvoused with the *HMB-1* and headed for the open sea on June 20, 1974, to conduct the retrieval mission.[92] At that point Project AZORIAN became Project JENNIFER.[93] By the middle of July the submarine site was reached and the *Glomar Explorer* proceeded with its work, with the guidance of a computer and bottom-placed transducer so as to stray no more than fifty feet in any direction. The barge was maneuvered directly beneath the *Glomar*'s moon pool and held in place by stanchions from the mother ship. Pipe from the ship was attached to the giant grappling claws, which resembled a series of six interconnected ice tongs hanging from a long platform. The ship's crew then began to feed length after length of pipe through the hole. By the time the claw reached the Soviet submarine sixteen thousand feet below, the pipe itself weighed more than four hundred thousand pounds. Claw operators used television cameras equipped with strobe lights to see what they were doing.[94]

According to one account, as the claw began to encircle the sub, two or three prongs became entangled in the seabed. The claws were pulled through the seabed to encircle the submarine, but in the process some of the prongs were bent out of shape and thus were unable to support the submarine fully. At five thousand feet the rear two thirds of the submarine, which included the conning tower, three missiles, and the vessel's code room, broke off and sank back to the seabed. The front third was raised into the moon pool.[95] Among the items recovered, according to William Colby, were two nuclear torpedoes and the body of a Soviet nuclear expert along with his personal journal.[96] The *Glomar* returned on August 12, 1974.[97]

Several accounts challenged the version of events that suggested that the entire submarine was not recovered. It was noted that the moon pool of the specially constructed *Glomar Explorer* was two hundred feet—120 feet shorter than the length of a Golf submarine. In addition, it was claimed that the ship's lifting capacity was 450 tons short of being able to pick up the sunken submarine in one piece. In addition, it was argued that the speed of the submarine's fall would have been comparable to that of an airliner crashing to the ground, and it would be almost impossible for a submarine to have survived intact. The cases of the *Thresher* and the *Scorpion,* two U.S. Navy submarines that had sunk, were pointed to; in both cases the subs had broken into at least three components, with metallic debris scattered over a wide area.[98] At least one of the contradictions appears to be resolved by the fact that the CIA had intended to cut off part of the sub while it was raised but before bringing it into the moon pool.[99]

Even if only one third of the submarine was recovered, the CIA was able to gather some information from the effort. It discovered that the subs used wooden two-by-fours in the building of some compartments—an extremely crude method. It also was determined that the exterior welding of the hull was uneven and pitted, with the hull itself not being of constant thickness. Hatch covers and valves also were constructed crudely when compared with those on U.S. submarines. Two torpedoes recovered were determined to be powered by electric motors, while another two were steam-powered, which indicated that the submarine's firing tubes were not interchangeable. Several books and journals were recovered, some of whose pages could be deciphered after chemical treatment. Apparently included was a partial description of the Soviet cryptographic codes in effect in 1968.[100]

Apparently plans to salvage the remainder of the submarine, Project MATADOR, were canceled in light of public disclosure of the operation.

XI.

Legacy

*I*n the forty-two years since the beginning of the Cold War the United States has built up an enormous intelligence apparatus to collect and analyze information concerning military, economic, and foreign policy and domestic and sociological developments with regard to the Soviet Union and other countries. This apparatus involves well over twenty-five intelligence organizations that collectively spend about twenty billion dollars per year. A substantial portion of the twenty billion dollars is spent on high-tech collection systems: reconnaissance satellites and aircraft; signals intelligence ships and submarines; ground stations to intercept signals or detect underground nuclear tests. At the same time, significant attention is devoted to other means—human intelligence, open sources, and the acquisition of military hardware. While the apparatus focuses on countries other than the Soviet Union, the U.S.S.R. is without doubt the primary target, with over half of the national intelligence budget going toward collection and analysis concerning the Soviet target.[1]

To augment its own collection activities, the United States also is involved in a variety of intelligence-sharing arrangements with foreign countries, especially with regard to the collection of signals intelligence. Since 1947 the United States has been a participant in the UKUSA Agreement, which links the United States, Britain, Australia, Canada, and New Zealand in a highly formalized arrangement for the collection and sharing of signals intelligence. A similar arrangement exists among those countries with regard to ocean surveillance.[2] Likewise, Japan—as demonstrated by the KAL 007 incident—collects large amounts of signals intelligence that is shared with the United States. Israel has also been a particularly valuable source of data, providing the United States with Soviet weapons captured as a result of its conflicts with its Arab neighbors. And, as already discussed, Norwegian- and Chinese-run SIGINT stations produce information of great value to the United States concerning, among other things, Soviet missile testing.

The present array of U.S. intelligence assets includes the traditional human sources. As demonstrated by the Tolkachev case, the CIA is at least on occasion able to penetrate the formidable security barriers thrown up by the KGB and acquire valuable information on Soviet military programs. What other human sources the CIA may have in design bureaus, GOSPLAN, or the Ministry of Foreign Affairs is not known.

Of course, the technical collection systems now serve as the core of the U.S. intelligence apparatus directed at the Soviet Union. Until replaced or augmented by the KH-12, the KH-11 launched on December 4, 1984, will serve as the only U.S. imaging satellite—overflying the Soviet Union eleven times a day and producing real-time imagery of Soviet installations, both military and civilian. Sometime after the KH-12 is placed in orbit, a radar-imaging satellite will join the U.S. inventory of imaging satellites, largely sweeping away the problem of cloud cover as the KH-12 will reduce the problem of obtaining useful nighttime photography.

The SR-71A, operational for over twenty years, still is used for peripheral missions that allow imagery along the Soviet periphery—imagery produced either by use of visible light sensors or the aircraft's high-resolution radar system. As noted earlier, the plane also has a substantial SIGINT role.

In addition to the SR-71, several other aircraft are involved in SIGINT collection. The most important of these are the RC-135 planes in their three different versions—COMBAT SENT, RIVET JOINT, and COBRA BALL. The EP-3E and various ARIA planes also serve as SIGINT platforms.

The most secret of the SIGINT assets are, of course, the satellite systems. Beyond what residual capabilities, if any, are left in the RHYOLITE/AQUACADE satellites launched at the end of the 1970s, the United States has the MAGNUM and CHALET satellites in geosynchronous orbit as well as the highly elliptically orbiting JUMPSEAT satellite, which "hovers" over the Soviet Arctic. In addition, an occasional ferret satellite stills monitors the emissions of Soviet radar systems.

After deemphasizing SIGINT collected from surface ships, the United States now employs both destroyers and frigates against a variety of target countries, including the Soviet Union. More covertly, HOLYSTONE missions continue under the code name BARNACLE; these missions take submarines near or even into Soviet territorial waters to collect intelligence by a variety of means.

The United States still maintains an extensive worldwide network of listening posts. Those operating in England, Norway, China, Japan, Turkey, and Alaska continue to be the most important in terms of monitoring Soviet military activities—via their combination of communications and telemetry interception equipment as well as radars for tracking missile warheads in flight. In addition, a separate set of ground stations run by AFOAT-1's successor—the Air Force Technical Applications Center—is responsible for monitoring the nuclear detonations from Soviet test sites at Semipalatinsk and Novaya Zemlya.

In 1987 the United States also finds itself with an extensive and sophisticated system for monitoring Soviet naval movements, especially those of Soviet submarines. From space the Navy and NRO continue to operate the WHITE CLOUD ocean surveillance satellites to monitor Soviet surface ships, while from the air P-3C Orion planes are used to monitor Soviet submarines. Ground stations such as the one in Edzell also produce data on

Soviet naval movements. Additionally, the initial CAESAR ocean-bottom arrays have grown into a fifty-array network that locates Soviet submarines as they emerge from their home ports.

These assets can be turned to monitor Soviet developments in a variety of areas. For example, when the Strategic Rocket Forces conduct a test of a solid-fuel SS-24 from Plesetsk to the target area on Kamchatka, a large number of U.S. collection systems focus on the event. First indication of an impending test may come from KH-11 imagery, which may reveal a variety of preparations for a test—the movement of the missile to the launch site, preparation of the launch facility, and the setting up of any special monitoring equipment. Additional warning may come from an increased flow of communications traffic, which may be intercepted by a geosynchronous satellite, a Norwegian ground station, or an electronically equipped ship in the North Sea.

As a result of such indications, the Defense Special Missile and Astronautics Center at Fort Meade, Maryland—a joint National Security Agency-Defense Intelligence Agency operation—would inform U.S. signals intelligence assets of a forthcoming test. The countdown could be monitored by a variety of intelligence systems: the Vardo ground station, a frigate or destroyer in the White Sea, or a satellite such as MAGNUM or CHALET.

Detection of the actual launch would come from a number of sources: those listening to the countdown, and from the Defense Support Program early-warning satellites that can detect a missile launch by the infrared plume of the rocket.

If the launch had been from Tyuratam in the central Soviet Union—the launch site for liquid fuel missiles—the Turkish and Chinese ground stations would constitute the primary land-based facilities for monitoring the countdown and the telemetry from the initial stages of the test. Again, the geosychronous-orbit SIGINT and early-warning satellites would play their respective roles in telemetry interception and launch detection.

In the case of an IRBM test from Kapustin Yar to the Lake Baikal/Irkutsk area, the Turkish sites again would play a major role in the monitoring of launch preparations, of the countdown, of the launch, and of the initial telemetry. During the later stages of such an IRBM test, one would expect that the Chinese sites would play a significant role in intercepting the telemetry being transmitted by the reentry vehicle or vehicles.

In the postboost phase, where the missile separates from the postboost vehicle or MIRVs separate from the bus, radars and telemetry interception equipment will begin to follow the movements of the delivery vehicle or MIRV bus and in the case of the latter will monitor the number of objects (either dummy warheads or decoys) released and the total number of release maneuvers. Questions concerning the number of warheads that may be deployed on the SS-18 stem from such data, indicating that in one test the SS-18 may have performed up to fourteen release maneuvers.[3]

During the last stage of the missile test, a final set of reconnaissance assets go to work. The COBRA DANE and COBRA JUDY radars track the flight of the warhead or warheads, with COBRA JUDY being able to pick up its targets earlier than COBRA DANE and continue monitoring them almost to the end of the test. Due to line-of-sight constraints, COBRA DANE's coverage terminates prior to that of COBRA JUDY. Additionally, a COBRA BALL aircraft will fly figure eights parallel to the Soviet coast that will allow the aircraft to intercept telemetry as well as to photograph the warheads as they descend to earth.

Subsequent to the conclusion of the test, the KH-11 would photograph the impact area to determine the exact location where the warheads struck. In the case of a test failure, the KH-11 would provide information on the nature and consequences of the failure. Thus U.S. monitoring of an April 1986 test of the planned successor to the ten-warhead SS-18 revealed that it had ended in failure and that the missile possibly had exploded. It was reported, on the basis of U.S. monitoring activities, that the missile had emerged from its silo during the test, malfunctioned, and never left the flight test area. In addition, it was reported that there had been an explosion and that some of the test facilities had been damaged.[4]

The United States also can monitor Soviet nuclear weapons

tests. As with ICBM tests, the first sign of an impending nuclear weapons test may come from overhead photography—specifically, that of a KH-11 passing over the Soviet nuclear test sites Semipalatinsk and Novaya Zemlya. Preparation for a nuclear test involves a variety of activities, such as implanting the device. It was reported in March 1986 that the Soviet Union had begun preparations for the possible resumption of nuclear weapons testing. KH-11 imagery revealed the digging of holes and tunnels in which nuclear explosives could be placed as well as the moving of monitoring equipment into the test area.[5]

An increase in communications traffic as well as the content of that traffic—intercepted by the CHALET and MAGNUM satellites—also could reveal the plan for a forthcoming test. Communications from the test site to the relevant ministries in Moscow would be necessary to allow discussion concerning the specifics of the test as well as travel plans for officials planning to be at the site.

Both overhead imagery and SIGINT satellites would continue to be used to monitor the sequence of events leading to the actual detonation of the device.

Once the device has been detonated, the seismic ground stations have the crucial role in collecting data that allows the United States to estimate the yield of a particular test. The seismometers at seismic stations such as NORSAR, NORESS, and Belbasi will pick two types of waves produced by the nuclear explosion, each of which has two subtypes. There are two types of body waves (waves that pass through the body of the earth): P and S waves. Likewise, there are two varieties of surface waves: Rayleigh and Love waves; these are differentiated by the differing motions of elements of the earth's surface as the wave passes by. Readings of the magnitude of these waves picked up at stations such as Belbasi and NORSAR are then transformed into estimates concerning the yield of the explosion—a process that is far from unambiguous and that has resulted in considerable controversy.[6]

Detection of the venting of any radioactive debris outside Soviet frontiers may be detected by either airborne or ground systéms. AFTAC can employ the various aircraft it possesses for air sampling operations to determine if the air moving out of the U.S.S.R. contains radioactive debris. Alternatively, many of the AFTAC ground sites possess air sampling equipment that can be similarly employed.

While the technological capabilities of the U.S. intelligence community are impressive, the most important function of an intelligence network is not to collect massive amounts of data and develop highly sophisticated collection systems but to provide the data and analysis required to address the most important issues of foreign, economic, and defense policy. One can question whether, in fact, the U.S. intelligence community has been doing this as fully as it might.

As noted earlier, the initial buildup of U.S. intelligence activity after World War II—particularly in the area of technical collection—was in response to fear of the Soviet Union. Thus the main objects of the collection effort using human and technical sources was to obtain early warning of any impending Soviet attack, to develop a target base for U.S. bomber forces to attack, and to collect electronic intelligence that would allow the bombers to neutralize the Soviet early-warning and air-defense system.

Since that time there have been numerous changes in the international scene and in U.S.-Soviet relations. The inevitable war that many on both sides feared (or in some cases hoped for) has been shown to be less than inevitable. Both nations have built up immense nuclear arsenals, and the advantage to be obtained by a surprise attack appears significant only to those who treat nuclear war as a computer game and not an event that would physically and psychologically shatter both superpowers beyond repair. Even a conventional war between the United States and the U.S.S.R. would be devastating for both sides in terms of the loss of people and materiel. Further, a *conventional* war could put severe strains on Soviet control of dissident nationalities and East European nations such as Poland.

Under such circumstances it makes sense to question whether the basic nature of the intelligence effort should be the same in 1985 as it was in 1945; whether highly detailed intelligence about the Soviet military should be given the same priority it had forty years ago; and whether intelligence for war planning should by given as high a priority as previously.

Clearly, certain items of military intelligence continue to be of significant importance. The Soviet military R&D effort is important to monitor because the information obtained can warn of impending breakthroughs that could, at least in theory, upset the rather robust strategic balance. The nature of Soviet strategic capabilities and conventional forces also merits attention, for several reasons—as support for arms-control negotiations and verification and for force planning. However, it is questionable whether the great amount of detailed information now being collected is truly useful: Is it important to develop a profile of the deputy chief of logistics at each level of the Soviet military, to monitor the communications from minor facilities, or to develop a massive target data inventory of five hundred thousand Soviet installations from which war planners can choose the forty-thousand-item National Strategic Target List and then the Single Integrated Operational Plan?[7]

The need to collect such information is driven by a variety of factors. The nuclear targeting doctrines in the Carter and Reagan administrations and codified in Presidential Directive 59 and National Security Decision Directive 13 (both titled "Nuclear Weapons Employment Policy") required an even greater set of targets than existed previously, including targets such as KGB facilities.[8] Second, as long as there is significant military control over the organizations that run the technical collection program—the National Reconnaissance Office and the National Security Agency—their collection activities will be weighted in the military's favor. Quite naturally, the military will seek to acquire as much information as it considers useful. To the commander every detail about the military forces he may oppose is potentially useful.

The U.S. intelligence focus on the Soviet Union is not strictly military. Significant attention has been devoted not only to questions concerning Soviet foreign policy but also to domestic subjects such as energy and the economy.[9] At the same time, the balance may still be too heavily in favor of military intelligence. For if one believes that war is not really inevitable or even probable, then it may be wise to rethink intelligence collection and analysis priorities—both with regard to different aspects of Soviet life and with regard to the entire world.

The Soviet Union clearly is a markedly different society than the United States in terms of its internal policies and its treatment of its European allies. But in the world arena it can be viewed more as a competitor of the United States than a likely military opponent—if only because the cost of being a military opponent would be so great. Thus it may be more important than before that the intelligence effort focus more on foreign and domestic economic, political, and sociological forces that may affect the Soviet position at home and abroad.

Some of this intelligence—that concerning sociological and political factors—may be produced from open sources and via, in the words of Stansfield Turner, "good, hard analysis."[10] For example, the Soviet Union is a huge, multinational empire. It consists of sixteen nominally independent Soviet Socialist Republics, with each republic being the homeland of a major national group. There are fifty-three ethnically defined political and administrative units in the Soviet Union.[11] Altogether there are more than one hundred distinct nationalities. The ethnic groups have their own language and culture and often resent the Great Russian control exerted over their lives.

One particular ethnic problem that has emerged is the "yellowing" of the Soviet population—the growing percentage of Asians who make up the U.S.S.R. due to the higher birth rates of the Asian groups. This may cause serious problems for the Soviet military, as the Asian troops are considered less capable and less reliable than those drawn from the Russian Soviet Federated Socialist Republic, the Ukraine, or Byelorussia. As a result, Moscow may be forced to alter its long-standing prohibition against assigning troops to the same region they come from for fear they will not act against their fellow natives or will resort to some degree of liberalization. Alternatively, increased repression might be the result.[12] Additionally, such a yellowing may reduce the leadership's confidence in the reliability of troops that might be sent into countries such as Czechoslovakia, Poland, and Afghanistan.[13]

How such a situation affects the Soviet Union's actions in the absence of a conflict with the United States may be of more importance than the implications in the event of war. Clearly, the ethnic problem can be exploited in a wartime situation to reduce the effectiveness of the Soviet military. But it also may be more important for U.S. leaders to understand how the Soviet leadership is responding to the ethnic problem in the absence of war.

The Soviet economy is another area where greater emphasis might be placed. Here much of the information has to be acquired by covert means, including signals intelligence, due to Soviet secrecy. A shift in the use of technical collection resources might be necessary if capabilities were not to be expanded. But the prime focus should not be on how to damage the Soviet economy fatally in the event of war but rather on how Soviet economic needs and performance—in agriculture, energy, and other areas—will affect Soviet domestic, military, and international policies, and the projected impact on the United States.

With regard to Eastern Europe, the main priority may not most wisely be the establishment of the order of battle in fine detail or day-to-day monitoring of the entire Warsaw Pact establishment, but the internal situation in those countries and their changing relationships with the Soviet Union. If the major threat comes not from a willful Soviet/Warsaw Pact invasion but the Soviet response to a Hungarian-type rebellion or a Prague Spring leading to an accidental conflict, it becomes more important to understand the forces that may trigger such events than the military forces that would be involved—since understanding the former may allow one to help prevent such an outcome.

Also of importance is the requirement to improve U.S. understanding of the Third World and of the conflicts created by poverty, disease, hunger, famine, repression, and racism—even to the point of shifting some intelligence resources away from the Soviet target. A deeper understanding of such conflicts might prevent the automatic assumption that they are Soviet- or Communist-inspired and allow the United States to frame an intelligent policy to deal with such situations when they arise, and when possible to prevent them from occurring.

The prime use of U.S. intelligence assets with respect to the Soviet Union and other countries should be to facilitate the maintenance of peace—not simply through a mindless "prepare for war to ensure peace" strategy but through the collection of information that truly serves the cause of ensuring a stable and free world.

ACRONYMS,

ABBREVIATIONS, AND CODE NAMES

AFOAT-1	Office of the Air Force Assistant for Atomic Energy, Section 1
AFSCF	Air Force Satellite Control Facility
AFTAC	Air Force Technical Applications Center
AGER	Auxiliary General—Environmental Research (Ship)
AGTR	Auxiliary General—Technical Research (Ship)
ALEXANDER	code name of Oleg Penkovskiy
AQUACADE	second code name for RHYOLITE satellites
AQUATONE	code name for project to build the U-2
ARGONAUT	code name of Yalta Conference of February 1945
ARGUS	intended follow-on to RHYOLITE
ARIS	Advanded Range Instrumentation Ship
ARPA	Advanced Research Projects Agency
BARNACLE	code name for certain submarine intelligence-gathering operations
BIOGRAPH	code name for U.S. Air Forces Europe peripheral electronic intelligence missions in the 1950s

BLACK KNIGHT   Air Force program to procure
                       RB-57D
BOLLARD   code name for certain submarine
                       intelligence-gathering operations
CAESAR   code name for first SOSUS array off
                       U.S. East Coast
CENTERING (Project)   code name for Air Force's Long
                       Range Detection Program of nuclear
                       explosions
CHALET   code name for a class of geo-
                       synchronous-orbit SIGINT satellites
CIA   (U.S.) Central Intelligence Agency
CLASSIC WIZARD   code name for U.S. space ocean
                       surveillance team
CLICKBEETLE   signals intelligence patrols in the
                       Sea of Japan
COBRA DANE   phased array radar on Shemya Is-
                       land, Alaska
COBRA JEAN   employment (until 1983) of ad-
                       vanced-range instrumentation ships
                       to monitor Soviet missile tests
COBRA JUDY   phased array radar on U.S.N.S.
                       Observation Island
COBRA MIST   over-the-horizon radar operated in
                       England between 1971 and 1973
COBRA SHOE   U.S. intelligence radar, possibly lo-
                       cated at Pirinclik
COLOSSUS   SOSUS array deployed along U.S.
                       Pacific coast
COMINT   communications intelligence
CORONA   code name for first CIA photo-
                       graphic reconnaissance satellite
COTTONSEED (Proj-   code name for Air Force's Long
ect)   Range Detection Program of nuclear
                       explosions
DEFSMAC   (U.S.) Defense Special Missile and
                       Astronautics Center

DISCOVERER	name for satellite program that provided a cover for CORONA
EAM	(Greek) National Liberation Front
ELAS	(Greek) National Popular Liberation Army
FIELD MOUSE, Project	first nickname for installation of electronic intelligence equipment on AGER ships
FISHBOWL	code name for 1962 nuclear test series
FLTSATCOM	Fleet Satellite Communications satellite
FROTH	code name that indicated data on Soviet air movements obtained by SIGINT
GAMBIT	code name for the KH-8
GAMMA GUPPY	U.S. intelligence operation involving the interception of radiotelephone conversations of Soviet Politburo members
GENETRIX	code name for Air Force balloon reconnaissance project
GOPHER	code name for Air Force balloon reconnaissance project
GRANDSON	code name for Air Force balloon reconnaissance project
GREYBACK	code name for Air Force balloon reconnaissance project
GRU	Chief Intelligence Directorate (Soviet General Staff)
HEXAGON	code name for the KH-9
HOLYSTONE	code name for certain submarine intelligence-gathering operations
IDEALIST	code name for the U-2
IVY BELLS	implantation of induction device to intercept communications transmitted on underseas cable

JUMPSEAT	elliptically orbiting SIGINT satellite
KENNAN	code name for the KH-11
KEYHOLE	general code name for U.S. photographic reconnaissance satellites
KGB	(Soviet Union) Committee for State Security
KKE	Greek Communist Party
LEOPARD	code name for peripheral photographic reconnaissance missions conducted by Alaskan Air Command in late 1940s
LF	low frequency
MAGNUM	code name for RHYOLITE/AQUACADE follow-on
MERINO	code name for Pine Gap facility
MIDAS	Missile Defense Alarm System
MOL	Manned Orbiting Laboratory (KH-10)
NACA	National Advisory Committee on Aeronautics
NAVFACs	Naval Facilities
NORSAR	Norwegian Seismic Array
NRO	National Reconnaissance Office
NRPCs	Naval Regional Processing Facilities
NSA	(U.S.) National Security Agency
OVERCALLS	code name for peripheral photographic reconnaissance missions conducted by Alaskan Air Command in late 1940s
OVERSALT	code name for Far East Air Force peripheral electronic intelligence missions
OXCART	code name for SR-71
PEEA	(Greek) Political Committee of National Liberation
PINKROOT	mission schedule for U.S.S. *Banner* and U.S.S. *Pueblo*

PINNACLE	code name for certain submarine intelligence-gathering operations
REDSKIN	CIA program to collect intelligence from nonofficial travelers to U.S.S.R.
REDSOX	code name for CIA operation infiltrating agents into U.S.S.R.
RHYOLITE	code name for U.S. geosynchronous signals-intelligence satellite first launched in 1970
RICKRACK	code name for peripheral photographic reconnaissance missions conducted by Alaskan Air Command in late 1940s
RTS	Remote Tracking Station
SALT	Strategic Arms Limitation Talks
SAMOS	Satellite and Missile Observation System
SAVAK	(Iran) National Security and Intelligence Organization (under Shah)
SDS	Satellite Data System
SEA LION, Operation	use of Japan-based RB-57D's for SIGINT and aerial sampling operations
SEA SPIDER	SOSUS array deployed around Hawaiian Islands
SENTRY	original code name for first Air Force photographic reconnaissance satellite
SIS	(U.K.) Secret Intelligence Service
SOD HUT, Project	second nickname for installation of electronic intelligence equipment on AGER ships
SOSUS	Sound Surveillance System
STARFISH PRIME	1.4-megaton device exploded as part of FISHBOWL series
STONEWORK	code name for peripheral photo-

	graphic reconnaissance missions conducted by Alaskan Air Command in late 1940s
TERMINAL	code name for Potsdam Conference of July 1945
TREASURE ISLAND	creation of Air Research Unit at Library of Congress in 1948
TRESSCOMM	Technical Research Ship Communications
TRIGON	code name of Alexsandr Dmitrevich Ogorodnik
UNRRA	United Nations Relief and Reconstruction Administration
VLF	Very Low Frequency
WHITE CLOUD	code name for space segment of CLASSIC WIZARD
WRSP	Weather Reconnaissance Squadron, Provisional

NOTES

Chapter I:
A NEW ENEMY

1. James Bamford, *The Puzzle Palace: A Report on NSA, America's Most Secret Agency* (Boston, Mass.: Houghton-Mifflin, 1982), pp. 36–37.

2. Ronald Lewin, *The American Magic: Codes, Ciphers and the Defeat of Japan* (New York: Farrar, Straus & Giroux, 1982), p. 46; Desmond Ball, "Allied Intelligence Cooperation Involving Australia During World War II," *Australian Outlook* 32, 4 (1978), 299–309.

3. Gordon W. Prange, *Miracle at Midway* (New York: McGraw-Hill, 1982), pp. 45–46.

4. William E. Burrows, *Deep Black: Space Espionage and National Security* (New York: Random House, forthcoming), Chap. 2.

5. Alfred Price, *The History of U.S. Electronic Warfare, Volume I: The Years of Innovation—Beginnings to 1946* (Washington, D.C.: Association of Old Cross, 1984), pp. 49, 52.

6. Ibid., pp. 52–53

7. Mario de Arcangelis, *Electronic Warfare: From the Battle of Tsushima to the Falklands* (Dorset, England: Bradford Press, 1985), p. 96.

8. "The Archangel Is Illuminated," *Journal of Electronic Defense* (February 1984), pp. 24, 68.

9. Price, op. cit., *Volume I*, pp. 48, 147.

10. See George F. Kennan, *The Decision to Intervene* (New York: Norton, 1984); Lloyd Gardner, *Safe for Democracy: Anglo-American Response to Revolution, 1913–1923* (New York: Oxford University Press, 1984);

Rhodri Jeffreys-Jones, *American Espionage: From Secret Service to CIA* (New York: The Free Press, 1977), pp. 87–101.

11. George F. Kennan, *Memoirs 1925–1950* (Boston: Little, Brown, 1967), p. 56.

12. Hugh DeSantis, *The Diplomacy of Silence: The American Foreign Service, The Soviet Union and the Cold War, 1933–1947* (Chicago: University of Chicago Press, 1980), pp. 33–35; Kennan, op. cit., p. 72.

13. George C. Herring, Jr., *Aid to Russia 1941–1946: Strategy, Diplomacy, the Origins of the Cold War* (New York: Columbia University Press, 1973), p. xiii.

14. Memo to the President from Richmond B. Keech, administrative assistant, Subject: Report of War Aid Furnished by U.S. to U.S.S.R., December 28, 1946 (Harry S. Truman Library: President's Secretaries Files, Subject File Box 181, Folder Russia 1945–1948).

15. Quoted in Alexander Werth, *Russia at War 1941–1945* (New York: E. P. Dutton, 1964), p. xi.

16. Robert Beitzell, *The Uneasy Alliance: America, Britain and Russia, 1941–1943* (New York: Alfred A. Knopf, 1972), pp. 303–65; see also Keith Eubank, *Summit at Teheran: The Untold Story* (New York: William Morrow, 1985); Keith Sainsbury, *The Turning Point: Roosevelt, Stalin, Chruchill and Chiang Kai-shek, 1943: The Moscow, Cairo and Teheran Conferences* (New York: Oxford University Press, 1985).

17. John Lewis Gaddis, *The United States and the Origins of the Cold War* (New York: Columbia University Press, 1972), pp. 137–38.

18. Quoted in Lawrence S. Wittner, *American Intervention in Greece, 1943–1949* (New York: Columbia University Press, 1982), p. 6.

19. Ibid., pp. 6–7.

20. Bruce Robellet Kuniholm, *The Origins of the Cold War in the Near East: Great Power Conflict and Diplomacy in Iran, Turkey and Greece* (Princeton, N.J.: Princeton University Press, 1980), p. 115; Albert Reiss, "The Churchill-Stalin Secret 'Percentages' Agreement on the Balkans," *American Historical Review* 83, 2 (1978):368–87.

21. Gaddis, op. cit., p. 161.

22. Lynn Etheridge Davis, *The Cold War Begins* (Princeton, N.J.: Princeton University Press, 1974), pp. 177–79.

23. Ibid., pp. 182–83.

24. Gaddis, op. cit., p. 163.

25. Walter La Feber, *America, Russia, and the Cold War 1945–1975,* 3rd ed. (New York: John Wiley, 1976), p. 15.

26. Gaddis, op. cit., p. 163.

27. Ibid., p. 241.

28. La Feber, op. cit., p. 26.

29. Quoted in Gaddis, op. cit., pp. 263–64.

30. Davis, op. cit., p. 294.

31. Quoted in Daniel Yergin, *Shattered Peace: The Origins of the Cold War and the National Security State* (Boston: Houghton Mifflin, 1978), p. 124.

32. Ibid., p. 130.

33. Davis, op. cit., pp. 315–16.

34. Gaddis, op. cit., p. 280.

35. Kennan, op. cit., p. 284.

36. Vojtech Mastny, *Russia's Road to the Cold War: Diplomacy, Warfare and the Politics of Communism 1941–1945* (New York: Columbia University Press, 1979), p. 255.

37. Ibid., p. 256.

38. Yergin, op. cit., p. 180.

39. Ibid., pp. 183–88.

40. Ibid., pp. 187–90.

41. Trevor Barnes, "The Secret Cold War: The CIA and American Foreign Policy in Europe, 1946–1956, Part II," *The Historical Journal* 25, 3 (1982): 649–70.

42. Yergin, op. cit., p. 319.

43. Ibid., p. 315.

44. La Feber, op. cit., p. 61.

45. Ibid., p. 19.

46. Yergin, op. cit., p. 326.

47. La Feber, op. cit., p. 71.

48. Yergin, op. cit., p. 312.

49. La Feber, op. cit., p. 73.

50. Yergin, op. cit., p. 347.

51. Ibid., p. 348.

52. La Feber, op. cit., p. 36.

53. Ibid., pp. 36–37; Wittner, op. cit., p. 55.

54. La Feber, op. cit., pp., 36–37.

55. Kuniholm, op. cit., p. 86; Yergin, op. cit., p. 289.

56. Yergin, op. cit., p. 289.

57. Kuniholm, op. cit., p. 90.

58. Ibid., pp. 91–95.

59. Ibid., pp. 221–22.

60. Ibid., pp. 225–26, 250–52.

61. Ibid., pp. 399–400.

62. Ibid., p. 400.

63. Hannes Adomeit, *Soviet Risk-Taking and Crisis Behavior: A Theoretical and Empirical Analysis* (Boston: George Allen & Unwin, 1982), p. 93.

64. La Feber, op. cit., p. 76.

65. Quoted in Adomeit, op. cit., p. 79.

66. Ibid., pp. 80–81.

67. Quoted in ibid., p. 90.

68. Ibid., p. 92.

69. Quoted in ibid.

70. Ibid., p. 94.

71. Yergin, op. cit., p. 377; La Feber, op. cit., p. 78.

72. Yergin, op. cit., p. 396.

73. Quoted in La Feber, op. cit., p. 39.

74. Quoted in ibid.

75. Kennan, op. cit., p. 292.

76. Gaddis, op. cit., p. 316.

77. George F. Kennan, "Moscow Embassy Telegram #511" in Thomas H. Etzold and John Lewis Gaddis, *Containment: Documents on American Policy and Strategy, 1945–1950* (New York: Columbia University Press, 1978), p. 61.

78. Quoted in La Feber, op. cit., p. 65.

79. Kennan, *Memoirs, 1925–1950*, p. 294.

80. Clark Clifford, "American Relations with the Soviet Union. A Report to the President by the Special Council to the President, September 1946 (TOP SECRET)," Appendix A in Arthur Krock, *Memoirs: Sixty Years on the Firing Line* (New York: Funk & Wagnalls, 1968), p. 428.

81. Central Intelligence Agency, "Threats to the Security of the United States," ORE 60–48 (September 28, 1948), HSTL, PSF, Box 266.

82. Yergin, op. cit., pp. 210–11.

83. Clifford, op. cit., p. 425.

84. Quoted in Daniel Ford, *The Button: The Pentagon's Strategic Command and Control System* (New York: Simon & Schuster, 1985), p. 106.

85. David Alan Rosenberg, "The Origins of Overkill: Nuclear Weapons and American Strategy, 1945–1960," *International Security* 7, 4 (1983): 3–71.

Chapter II:
HUMINT

1. Kemp Tolley, *Caviar and Commissars: The Experience of a U.S. Naval Officer in Stalin's Russia* (Annapolis, Md.: Naval Institute Press, 1983), pp. 75, 189, 261–65.

2. Bradley F. Smith, *The Shadow Warriors: O.S.S. and the Origins of the CIA* (New York: Basic Books, 1983), p. 127.

3. Anthony Cave Brown, *The Last Hero: Wild Bill Donovan* (New York: Times Books, 1982), p. 149.

4. Ibid., p. 420.

5. Ibid., p. 422.

6. Jeffery M. Dorwart, *Conflict of Duty: The U.S. Navy's Intelligence Dilemma, 1919–1945* (Annapolis Md.: Naval Institute Press, 1983), pp. 224–25.

7. Thomas G. Paterson, *Soviet-American Confrontation: Postwar Reconstruction and the Origins of the Cold War* (Baltimore, Md.: Johns Hopkins University Press, 1973), pp. 61, 96.

8. Harry Rositzke, *The CIA's Secret Operations: Espionage, Counterespionage and Covert Action* (New York: Reader's Digest Press, 1977), p. 27.

9. Ibid., pp. 17, 21.

10. Philip Agee, *Inside the Company: A CIA Diary* (New York: Stonehill, 1975), p. 68.

11. Rositzke, op. cit., pp. 19–20.

12. Ibid., p. 55.

13. Ibid., p. 25.

14. Ibid., pp. 32–33.

15. Ibid., p. 38.

16. Peer de Silva, *Sub Rosa: The CIA and the Uses of Intelligence* (New York: Times Books, 1978), p. 58.

17. Ibid., p. 58.

18. Ibid., p. 59.

19. Ibid.

20. Of course, assumptions were involved, and a crucial wrong assumption could invalidate the analysis. See John Prados, *The Soviet Estimate: U.S. Intelligence Analysis and Russian Military Strength* (New York: Dial, 1982), pp. 38–50.

21. Letter from H. M. McCoy to Chief of Staff, United States Air Force 23 November 1948, Subject: Photographic Equipment for 1 May 1949 USSR Air Show, RG 341 Entry 214, File 2-5400 to 2-5499, Modern Military Branch (MMB), National Archives (NA).

22. Letter from Colonel Malcom D. Seashore, chief, Air Technical Intelligence Center, to AFOIN-C/AA, Subject: (Secret) Procurement and Development of Photographic Equipment for Air Attachés, 27 February 1952, RG 341, Entry 214, File 2-22000 through 2-22099, MMB, NA.

23. Letter from H. M. McCoy, op. cit.

24. "Air Intelligence Information Report 140–49: Soviet Air Day Show," July 19, 1949, RG 341 Entry 267, File 2-8566 MMB, NA.

25. Letter from Edward G. Davis, Collection Branch, Air Intelligence Requirements Division, to United States Air Attaché, Moscow, Subject: Request for Additional Information on the Air Craft Flown in the May Day, RG 341, Entry 214, File No. 2-7900 through 2-7999, MMB, NA.

26. Letter from Colonel Emmett B. Cassady, Chief, Air Attaché Branch, Collection Division, Directorate of Intelligence, USAF, to U.S. Air Attaché American Embassy, Moscow, Subject: Use of Classified Equipment (Secret), June 17, 1952 RG 341, Entry 214, File 2-23800 to 2-23900, MMB, NA.

27. Telegram from USAIRA, Moscow to Chief of Staff, U.S. Air Force, July 31, 1953, RG 341, Entry 214, File 3-2900 through 3-2999, MMB, NA.

28. "Air Intelligence Information Report 90-50: Anti-Aircraft and Radar Emplacements—Vicinity of Moscow," May 9, 1950, RG 341, Entry 267, File 2-13152, MMB, NA.

29. "Air Intelligence Information Report IR 40-53: Radar Signal Emanations," March 10, 1953, RG 341, Entry 267, File 3-1000 through 3-1099, MMB, NA.

30. USAF, Directorate of Intelligence, *History of AFOIN-1, 1 July 1954 thru 31 December 1954*, RG-341, Entry 214, File 5-530, MMB, NA.

31. Ibid.

32. "Air Intelligence Information Report IR 193–55: Observations of Travelers in U.S.S.R.," October 14, 1955, RG 341, Entry 267, File 5-2500, MMB, NA.

33. Ibid.

34. Ibid.

35. Agee, op. cit., p. 68; Rositzke, op. cit., p. 57.

36. Rositzke, op. cit., p. 57.

37. Ibid., pp. 57–58.

38. Ibid., p. 60.

39. Ibid., pp. 58–59.

40. Ibid., p. 59.

41. Ibid., pp. 59–60.

42. Ibid., p. 59.

43. Oleg Penkovskiy, *The Penkovskiy Papers* (Garden City, N.Y.: Doubleday, 1965), pp. 30–31; Greville Wynne, *The Man from Odessa: The Secret Career of a British Agent* (London: Granada, 1983), p. 203. *The Penkovskiy Papers* generally are agreed to be a CIA-constructed work based on, at most, information passed on by Penkovskiy, rather than being actual memoirs. Much of the book consists of commentary by Frank Gibney. Information from portions attributed to Penkovskiy hereafter are cited as "Penkovskiy, op. cit.," while information from portions written by Gibney are cited as "Gibney, op. cit."

44. Penkovskiy, op. cit., pp. 31, 52; Gibney, op. cit., p. 61.

45. Penkovskiy, op. cit., pp. 31, 54.

46. Ibid., pp. 28–29; Wynne, op. cit., p. 203; Gibney, op. cit., p. 7.

47. Wynne, op. cit., p. 206.

48. Ibid.

49. Ibid., p. 207.

50. Ibid., p. 208.

51. Ibid., pp. 214–16. Penkovskiy also demanded that no one in the British Security Service (MI5) be informed of his activities because the KGB had placed an agent at the very highest level of MI5.

52. Nigel West, *The Circus: MI5, 1945–1972* (Briarcliff Manor, N.Y.: Stein and Day, 1983), p. 86.

53. Ibid., p. 87.

54. Gibney, op. cit., p. 197.

55. Wynne, op. cit., p. 230.

56. Ibid., pp. 230–39, 246–47.

57. Penkovskiy, op. cit., pp. 261–62.

58. West, op. cit., p. 88.

59. Ibid.

60. Ibid., pp. 88–89.

61. Gibney, op. cit., pp. 2, 379–80.

62. West, op. cit., p. 89.

63. Greville Wynne, *The Man from Moscow* (London: Hutchinson, 1967), p. 7.

64. Ibid., p. 7–9.

65. John Ranelagh, *The Agency: The Rise and Decline of the CIA* (New York: Simon & Schuster, 1986), pp. 401–402.

66. Chapman Pincher, *Their Trade Is Treachery* (London: Sidgwick and Jackson, 1981) pp. 69, 147, 152, 157; West, op. cit., p. 89; Thomas Powers, *The Man Who kept the Secrets: Richard Helms and the CIA* (New York: Alfred A. Knopf, 1979), p. 283.

67. Powers, op. cit. p. 283.

68. John Barron, *KGB Today: The Hidden Hand* (New York: Reader's Digest Press, 1983), p. 428.

69. Ibid., p. 428; Jimmy Carter, *Keeping Faith: Memoirs of a President* (London: Collins, 1982), p. 147.

70. Barron, op. cit., p. 428; Ernest Volkman, *Warriors of the Night: Spies, Soldiers and American Intelligence* (New York: William Morrow, 1985), p. 224; Arkady N. Shevchenko, *Breaking with Moscow* (New York: Alfred A. Knopf, 1985), p. 314.

71. Barron, op. cit., p. 428; Volkman, op. cit., p. 224.

72. Volkman, op. cit., pp. 224–25.

73. Barron, op. cit., p. 428.

74. Ibid., pp. 428–29.

75. Ibid., p. 429.

76. Shevchenko, op. cit., p. 314.

77. Volkman, op. cit., p. 275; David Martin, "A CIA Spy in the Kremlin," *Newsweek* (July 21, 1980), pp. 69–70; Daniel Schorr, "The Trigon Caper," *First Principles* (December 1980), pp. 11, 13, 15; Jack Anderson, "Mystery Kissinger-Dobrynin Meeting," *Washington Post* (December 16, 1980), p. B15.

78. Philip Taubman, "Capital's Rumor Mill: The Death of an Agent and the Talk It Started," *The New York Times* (September 23, 1980), pp. A1, A4; Schorr, op. cit.; Anderson, op. cit.

79. Henry Hurt, *Shadrin: The Spy Who Never Came Back* (New York: McGraw-Hill/Reader's Digest Press, 1981) p. 254n.; Anderson, op. cit.

80. Stansfield Turner, *Secrecy and Democracy: The CIA in Transition* (Boston: Houghton Mifflin, 1985), p. 50; Martin, op. cit.; Myra Mac-Pherson, "The Good Neighbor Who Came in from the Cold," *Washington Post* (June 21, 1978), pp. B1, B4.

81. David K. Shipler, "Soviet, Retaliating Publicizes Case Against Women Linked to C.I.A.," *The New York Times* (June 13, 1978), p. A12.

82. Schorr, op. cit.

83. Taubman, op. cit.; Martin, op cit.; Turner, op. cit., p. 53; Barron, op. cit., p. 429; Shevchenko, op. cit., p. 314.

84. Barron, op. cit., pp. 429–30.

85. Foreign Broadcast Information Service, "PRAVDA: KGB Arrests CIA-Controlled Moscow Spy," *Daily Report: Soviet Union* (September 24, 1985), p. A1.

86. Patrick E. Tyler, "Soviet Seized as U.S. Spy Exposed by Howard," *Washington Post* (October 18, 1985), p. A10; Stephen Engelberg, "U.S. Indicates Ex-CIA Officer Helped Soviet Capture a Russian," *The New York Times* (October 18, 1985), p. A18.

87. William Kucewicz, "KGB Defector Confirms Intelligence Fiasco," *Wall Street Journal* (October 17, 1985).

88. Ibid.

89. Steven Strasser et al., "Reagan's Secrecy Campaign," *Newsweek* (September 26, 1983), p. 38; "SS-16 Deployment Raises Senate Questions," *Aviation Week and Space Technology* (September 24, 1979), p. 24; Drew Middleton, "Soviet Fleet, Hurt by Blast, May Lie Low," *The New York Times* (June 26, 1984), p. A5.

90. "Soviets Arrest Four Scientists on Spying Charges," *Washington Post* (September 28, 1982), p. A10.

91. Robert Gillette, "Soviets Ousting U.S. Diplomat as a Spy," *Los Angeles Times* (March 11, 1983), p. 4. Seth Mydans, "Soviet Expels a U.S. Diplomat for 'Major Espionage Action,'" *The New York Times* (June 15, 1985), p. 3; Dusko Doder, "U.S. Official Expelled From Moscow As Spy," *Washington Post* (June 15, 1985), p. A17.

92. Foreign Broadcast Information Service, "Ukrainian Paper Accuses U.S. Diplomats of Spying," *Daily Report: Soviet Union* (October 22, 1985), p. A2.

93. Bernard Gwertzman, "U.S. Intelligence in the Dark About Andropov," *The New York Times* (December 29, 1983), p. A9.

94. Robert C. Toth, "Gromyko Visit a Sign of Infighting at Kremlin," *Los Angeles Times* (September 14, 1984), p. 16.

Chapter III:
GROUND STATIONS

1. Technical Sergeant George L. Parson, *History of Alaskan Air Command (1 July to 31st December 1950).* Headquarters, USAF, 1951 p. 37.

2. Ibid., p. 36.

3. Ibid., p. 37.

4. Ibid.

5. SRH-139, *Unit History of 3rd Radio Squadron Mobile, U.S. Air Force Security Service,* January 1 to December 31, 1950, Modern Military Branch, National Archives.

6. James Bamford, *The Puzzle Palace: A Report on NSA, America's Most Secret Agency* (Boston: Houghton Mifflin, 1982), p. 163.

7. SRH-139, op. cit.

8. *Monthly Status Report of the 37th Radio Squadron Mobile,* July 1952, pp. 1–2; interview.

9. Ibid.; interview.

10. *Monthly Status Report of the 37th Radio Squadron Mobile,* October 1952, pp. 2, 9.

11. Vessie E. Hardy, *Historical Data Report for the 37th Radio Squadron Mobile,* April 1, 1953 to June 30, 1953. Prepared for the Historical Office, 37th Radio Squadron Mobile., p. 2.

12. Interview.

13. Robert N. Strickland and Forrest L. Tackett, *Historical Data Report for the 37th Radio Squadron, Mobile,* October 1, 1953 to December 31, 1953, HQ 37th RSM, p. 19; Robert N. Strickland and Forrest L. Tackett, *Historical Data Report for the 37th Radio Squadron Mobile* January 1, 1954 to March 31, 1954, Historical Office, 37th Radio Squadron Mobile, p. 2.

14. Interview.

15. Interview.

16. Interview.

17. Duncan Campbell, *The Unsinkable Aircraft Carrier: American Military Power in Britain* (London: Michael Joseph, 1984), pp. 160–61.

18. Ibid., p. 153.

19. Ibid., p. 154.

20. Memorandum for Mr. Bill Moyers, Assistant to the President, Subject: Weekly Report for the President, May 12, 1964.

21. Campbell, op. cit., p. 155; "British MP Accuses U.S. of Electronic Spying," *New Scientist* (August 5, 1976), p. 268.

22. Campbell, op. cit., p. 155.

23. Malcom Spaven, *Fortress Scotland: A Guide to the Military Presence* (London: Pluto Press, 1983), p. 105.

24. House Appropriations Committee, *Military Construction Appropriations for 1986, Part 2* (Washington, D.C.: U.S. Government Printing Office, 1985), p. 1301.

25. Spaven, op. cit., p. 106.

26. Ibid., pp. 106–107.

27. Campbell, op. cit., p. 170.

28. Duncan Campbell, "New Spy Station to Look Inside USSR," *New Statesman* (December 21–28, 1984), p. 6.

29. F. G. Samia, "The Norwegian Connection: Norway (Un)willing Spy for the U.S.," *Covert Action Information Bulletin* 9 (June 1980), pp. 4–9.

30. Ibid.; R. W. Apple, Jr., "Norwegians, Ardent Neutralists, Also Want Their Defense Strong," *The New York Times* (August 5, 1978), p. 2.

31. Owen Wilkes and Nils Petter Gleditsch, *Intelligence Installations in Norway: Their Number, Location, Function and Legality* (Oslo, Norway: PRIO, 1979), pp. 18–19.

32. Ibid., p. 25; Seymour Hersh, *"The Target Is Destroyed": What Really Happened to Flight 007 and What America Knew About It* (New York: Random House, 1986), p. 4.

33. Wilkes and Gleditsch, op. cit., p. 32.

34. Ibid., p. 35; Hersh, op. cit., p. 42.

35. Wilkes and Gleditsch, op. cit., p. 20.

36. Ibid., p. 48.

37. Ibid., pp. 48–49.

38. Ibid., pp. 52–56; Svein Mykkeltveit, "Seismological Facilities in Norway," in *Workshop on Seismological Verification of a Comprehensive Nuclear Test Ban* (Oslo, Norway: Norwegian Ministry of Foreign Affairs, 1985), pp. 2–5.

39. Glenn Zorpette, "Monitoring the Tests," *IEEE Spectrum* (July 1986), pp. 57–66.

40. Letter from Colonel Conrad J. Herlick, Deputy, Commitments and Priorities, Operations & Commitments Division, Directorate of Operations to the Director of Requirements DCS/D, Subject: (TS) Establishment of Ground Based ECM Unit in Turkey, October 2, 1951, RG 341, Entry 214, File 2-23500–2-23599, Modern Military Branch, National Archives.

41. Wilham Dacko and Arthur Langenkamp, *Historical Data Report for Project Penn.*, January 1, 1953 through March 31, 1953, Air Force Historical Office, Chap. I.

42. "Planned Deployment of the 75th RSM," May 29, 1953, RG 341, Entry 214, File No. 2-2100 to 2-10199, MMB, NA; "USAFSS Rights Required, Turkey," RG 341 Entry 214, File No. 4-415 to 4-569, MMB, NA.

43. Interview.

44. Interview.

45. Interview.

46. House Committee on International Relations, *United States Military Installations and Objectives in the Mediterranean* (Washington, D.C.: U.S. Government Printing Office, 1977) pp. 43–44; Michael K. Burns, "U.S. Reactivating Bases in Turkey," *Baltimore Sun* (October 21, 1978), pp. 1, 23; TUSLOG Detachment 28, *Command History, 1 January–30 September 1977*, 1977.

47. "How U.S. Taps Soviet Missile Secrets," *Aviation Week* (October 21, 1957), pp. 26–27; John Prados, *The Soviet Estimate: U.S. Intelligence Analysis and Russian Military Strength* (Garden City, N.Y.: Doubleday/Dial, 1982), p. 35.

48. "How the U.S. Taps Soviet Missile Secrets," op. cit.

49. Ibid.

50. Marvine Howe, "U.S. and Turks Monitor Soviet at Isolated Post," *The New York Times* (January 4, 1981), p. 7.

51. Ibid.; Michael Getler, "U.S. Intelligence Facilities in Turkey Get New Attention After Iran Turmoil," *Washington Post* (February 9, 1979), p. A15; Senate Foreign Relations Committee, *Fiscal Year 1980 International Security Assistance Authorization* (Washington, D.C.: U.S. Government Printing Office, 1979), p. 365; House Committee on International Relations, op. cit., p. 39.

52. "U.S. Electronic Espionage: A Memoir," *Ramparts* (August 1972), pp. 35–50.

53. Burns, op. cit.

54. Getler, op. cit.

55. Burns, op. cit.; Henry S. Bradsher, "U.S. Upgrades Spy Equipment at Turkish Sites," *Washington Star* (April 11, 1980), p. 7.

56. Getler, op. cit.

57. Senate Foreign Relations Committee, *Fiscal Year 1980 International Security Assistance Authorization*, p. 365.

58. House Committee on International Relations, op. cit., p. 44.

59. Senate Foreign Relations Committee, loc. cit.

60. "U.S. and Turkey Sign Pact on Aid and Bases," *The New York Times* (March 30, 1980), p. 1.

61. "U.S. to Help Turkey Make Arms in Exchange for Intelligence Bases," *Los Angeles Times* (November 22, 1979), Part XI, p. 3.

62. House Committee on International Relations, op. cit., p. 46.

63. Burns, op. cit.

64. "Memorandum for the Record," January 14, 1953, RG 341, Entry 214, File 4-6A to 4-191, MMB, NA.

65. Joint Message Form, from: HQ USAF AFOIN to: USAIRA Tehran, Iran Subject: B/65, July 30, 1952, RG 341 Entry 214 File No. 2-24400 to 2-24499 MMB, NA; Memorandum for: Deputy Chief of Staff, Operations, Subject: (Top Secret), AFOAT-1 Operations in Iran Aug 1, 1952, RG 341, Entry 214, File No. 2-24400 to 2-24499, MMB, NA.

66. Eliot Marshal, "Senate Skeptical on SALT Verification," *Science* (July 27, 1979), pp. 373–76.

67. Senate Foreign Relations Committee, op. cit., p. 366.

68. Dial Torgeson, "U.S. Spy Devices Still Running at Iran Post," *International Herald Tribune* (March 7, 1979), pp. A1, A8.

69. Hedrick Smith, "U.S. Aides Say Loss of Post in Iran Impairs Missile-Monitoring Ability," *The New York Times* (March 2, 1979), pp. A1, A8.

70. Torgeson, op. cit.

71. William Sullivan, *Mission to Iran* (New York: W. W. Norton, 1981), pp. 21–22.

72. Torgeson, op. cit.

73. Ibid.

74. Cyrus Vance, *Hard Choices: Critical Years in America's Foreign Policy* (New York: Simon & Schuster, 1983), p. 342.

75. "Soviets Tighten Grip on Iran," *Jane's Defence Weekly* (November 23, 1985), p. 1125.

76. Smith, op. cit.

77. Vance, op. cit., pp. 354–55.

78. Philip Taubman, "U.S. and Peking Jointly Monitor Russian Missiles," *The New York Times* (June 18, 1981), pp. A1, A14.

79. Murrey Marder, "Monitoring: Not So-Secret-Secret," *Washington Post* (June 19, 1981), p. 10.

80. Robert C. Toth, "U.S. China Jointly Track Firings of Soviet Missiles," *Los Angeles Times* (June 18, 1981), pp. 1, 9; David Bonavia, "Radar Post Leak May Be Warning to Soviet Union," *The Times* (London) (June 20, 1981), p. 5.

81. Taubman, op. cit.

82. Walter Pincus, "U.S. Seeks A-Test Monitoring Facility," *Washington Post* (March 19, 1986), p. A8.

83. Hersh, op. cit., p. 47.

84. Keyes Beech, "Secret U.S. Base Keeps Eye on Far East," *Los Angeles Times* (January 20, 1980), p. 17.

85. Hersh, op. cit., pp. 47, 49, 51.

86. William Arkin and Richard Fieldhouse, *Nuclear Battlefields: Global Links in the Arms Race* (Cambridge, Mass.: Ballinger, 1985), p. 225.

87. Dr. E. Michael del Papa, *Meeting the Challenge: ESD and the Cobra Dane Construction Effort on Shemya Island* (Bedford, Mass.: Electronic Systems Division, Air Force Systems Command, 1979), p. 4.

88. Ibid., p. 3.

89. Ibid.

90. Ibid.

91. Ibid.

92. Eli Brookner, "Phased-Array Radars," *Scientific American* 252, 2 (April 1985), pp. 94–103.

93. del Papa, op. cit., p. 35.

94. Philip J. Klass, "USAF Tracking Radar Details Disclosed," *Aviation Week and Space Technology* (October 25, 1976), pp. 41–46.

95. del Papa, op. cit., p. 38.

96. Klass, op. cit.

97. Laurence Stern, "U.S. Tapped Top Russian's Car Phones," *Washington Post* (December 5, 1973), pp. A1, A16; Ernest Volkman, "U.S. Spies Lend an Ear to Soviets," *Newsday* (July 12, 1977), p. 7.

98. Stern, op. cit.

99. Ibid.

100. Ibid; Jack Anderson, "CIA Eavesdrops on Kremlin Chiefs," *Washington Post* (September 16, 1971), p. F7.

Chapter IV:
PATROLLING THE PERIPHERY

1. W. Stuart Symington, "Memorandum for General Spaatz," April 5, 1948, Department of the Air Force.

2. "Limit of Offshore Distance for Reconnaissance Flights in Pacific Areas," July 27, 1948, RG 341, Entry 214, File 2-3003 through 2-3099, Modern Military Branch (MMB), National Archives (NA).

3. *Study on Electronic and Other Aerial Reconnaissance, Appendix B*, November 10, 1949, RG 341, Entry 267, File 2-10102, MMB, NA.

4. Routing and Record Sheet for Memorandum from Major General George C. McDonald, Director of Intelligence, WAF, to Director of Plans and Operations, April 23, 1948, Subject: Photographic Coverage—Chukotski Peninsula Airfields, RG 341, Entry 214, File 3-3000 through 3-3099, MMB, NA.

5. "Memorandum for the Record," n.d., RG 341, Entry 214, File 2-3000 to 2-3099, MMB, NA; "Limit on Offshore Distance for Reconnaissance Flights in Pacific Areas."

6. Tab A to Letter from Major General C. P. Cabell, Acting Director of Intelligence, Deputy Chief of Staff, Operations, to Chief of Staff, Subject: Photographic Coverage—Chukotski Peninsula Airfields, May 7, 1948, RG 341, Entry 214, File 2-1500 to 2-1599, MMB, NA.

7. Letter from Brigadier General Ernest Moore, Acting Director of Intelligence, Deputy Chief of Staff, Operations, to Director of Training and Requirements, Subject: Photographic Coverage—Chukotski Peninsula Airfields, August 16, 1948, RG 341, Entry 214, F16 2-3300 through 2-3399, MMB, NA.

8. "Memorandum for the Record," March 15, 1949, RG 341, Entry 214, File 6700 to 6799, MMB, NA: Major General C. P. Cabell, Director of Intelligence, USAF, to Major General Budway, Alaskan Air Command, December 27, 1948, RG 341, Entry 214, File 2-5400 through 2-5499, MMB, NA.

9. Colonel H. M. Monroe, Chief of Staff, Alaskan Air Command to Chief of Staff, USAF, "Importance of Long-Range Photography to Alaskan Theater," n.d., RG 341, Entry 214, File 2-5400 through 2-5499, MMB, NA.

10. Frank A. Armstrong, Commanding General, AAC, to Chief of Staff, USAF, Subject: Photographic Coverage of Northeastern Siberia, November 4, 1949, RG 341, Entry 214, File 2-10000 through 2-10099, MMB, NA.

11. Memorandum of Photographic Reconnaissance of USSR, RG 341, Entry 267, File 2-10103, MMB, NA.

12. "Memorandum for the Record," October 24, 1949, RG 341, Entry 214, File 2-9600 through 2-9699, MMB, NA; letter from Colonel A. Hansen, Chief, Reconnaissance Branch, Air Intelligence Requirements Division, Directorate of Intelligence, to Aeronautical Chart Service, Subject: Transmittal of Photo Intelligence Reports, October 25, 1949, RG 341, Entry 214, File 2-9600 through 2-9699, MMB, NA.

13. "Memorandum for the Record," June 19, 1951, RG 341, Entry 214, File 2-20200 through 2-20299, MMB, NA.

14. Colonel C. J. Stattler, Jr., Deputy Assistant Chief of Staff/A-2 to Director of Intelligence, USAF, Subject: (Uncl.) "Pie Face Project," March 6, 1953, RG 341, Entry 214, File 3-900 to 3-999, MMB, NA.

15. *Supplement to the History of 91st Strategic Reconnaissance Squadron Photo (M), 1 May 1951 to 31 May 1951* (Yokota AB, Japan: 91st SRS Photo [M], 1951), p. 4.

16. Ibid., p. 8.

17. Ibid.

18. *History of the 91st Strategic Reconnaissance Squadron, Medium, Photo, 1 October 1951 through 31 October 1951* (Yokota AB, Japan: 91st SRS, Medium, Photo 1951), p. 24.

19. Ibid., p. 30.

20. "Memorandum for the Record," February 12, 1952, RG 341, Entry 214, File 3-300 through 399, MMB, NA.

21. "Memorandum for the Record," September 12, 1953, RG 341, Entry 214, File 3-3300 through 3-3399, MMB, NA.

22. Letter from Carl Espe, Director of Naval Intelligence, to Major General J. A. Samford, Director of Intelligence, U.S. Air Force, Subject: Request for Photography, May 25, 1954, RG 341, Entry 214, File 4-1114 to 4-1290, MMB, NA.

23. "Memorandum for the Record," July 14, 1948, RG 341, Entry 214, File 2-3000 through 2-3099, MMB, NA.

24. Letter from Major General C. P. Cabell, Director of Intelligence, USAF, to Commanding General, Alaskan Air Command, Subject: ECM Ferret Program—Alaskan Air Command, July 26, 1948, RG 341, Entry 214, File 2-3000 through 2-3099, MMB, NA.

25. "USAF Intelligence Requirements for Electronic Reconnaissance," tab C to letter to Commanding General, Strategic Air Command,

July 21, 1947, RG 341, Entry 214, File 2-8100 through 2-8199, MMB, NA.

26. Study on Electronic and other Aerial Reconnaissance, Appendix A.

27. Letter from Major General C. P. Cabell, "Subject: ECM Ferret Program."

28. Letter from Richard J. Meyer, 1985.

29. Letter from Lieutenant Farley A. Latta, Assistant Adjutant General, AAC, to Director of Intelligence, USAF, Subject: Cover Story for Forced Landing in the Far Eastern U.S.S.R., August 24, 1949, RG 341, Entry 214 File 2-8999, MMB, NA.

30. "Memorandum for the Record," October 31, 1949, RG 341, Entry 214, File No. 2-19600 through 2-19699, MMB, NA; letter from Richard R. Klocko, Director of Intelligence, to Commanding General, United States Air Forces in Europe, July 13, 1949, RG 341, Entry 214, File 2-8300 through 2-8399, MMB, NA.

31. Omar N. Bradley, Memorandum for the Secretary of Defense, Subject: Special Electronic Airborne Search Operations (SESP), May 5, 1950, HSTL, PSF.

32. Evaluation Division, DI/USAF-ONI, "Analysis of Navy Ferret Mission in the Baltic," *Air Intelligence Information Report* TC-9-52, March 21, 1952, RG 341, Entry 267, File 2-23033 to 2-23099, MMB, NA.

33. Dick van der Aart, *Aerial Espionage: Secret Intelligence Flights by East and West* (New York: Arco/Prentice Hall Press, 1986), pp. 9, 56–59.

34. Duncan Campbell, *The Unsinkable Aircraft Carrier: American Military Power in Britain* (London: Michael Joseph, 1984), pp. 127, 131.

35. Ibid., pp. 128–29.

36. Interview.

37. "Memorandum for the Record," December 8, 1953, RG 341, Entry 214, MMB, NA.

38. Letter to Commanding General, Strategic Air Command, July 21, 1949, RG 341, Entry 214, File 2-8100 through 2-8199, MMB, NA. While the JCS represented the highest military authority, the ferret operations—also known as Special Electronic Search Projects (SESP)—were of great concern to the President, Secretary of Defense, and the State Department, since those operations simulta-

neously represented potential sources of immensely valuable information and of one or more international incidents. See Louis N. Johnson, Memorandum to the President, Subject:`Special Electronic Search Operations (SESP), May 24, 1950, HSTL. PSF; Omar N. Bradley, Memorandum for the Secretary of Defense, Subject: Special Electronic Airborne Search Operations, July 22, 1950, HSTL, PSF; Omar N. Bradley, Memorandum for the Secretary of Defense, Subject: Special Electronic Airborne Search Operations (SESP), May 5, 1950, HSTL, PSF.

39. *Supplement to the History of the 91st Strategic Reconnaissance Squadron Photo(M), 1 March thru 31 March 1951,* p. 4; *Supplement to the History of the 91st Strategic Reconnaissance Squadron, Medium, Photo—History of the 91st Strategic Reconnaissance Squadron, Medium, Photo, Yokota Air Force Base, Japan, 1 August 1951 through 31 August 1951,* p. 7.

40. *Supplement to the History of the 91st Strategic Reconnaissance Squadron, Photo, Medium, 1 September 1951 through 31 September 1951—History of the 91st Strategic Reconnaissance Squadron, Medium, Photo, Yokota Air Force Base, Japan, 1 September 1951 through 31 September 1951,* pp. 8–9.

41. Ibid., p. 12.

42. Letter from Colonel Charles M. Townsend, Chief, Supplemental Research Branch, Directorate of Intelligence, USAF, to Director of Operations, USAF, Subject: (Restricted) Airborne Intercept Program, October 22, 1953, RG 341, Entry 214, File 3-25000 through 3-25099, MMB, NA.

43. "Memorandum for the Record," November 10, 1953, RG 341, Entry 214, File 3-4000 through 3-4099; Letter from Major General John A. Samford, Director of Intelligence to Director of Operations, USAF, Subject: (Unclassified) Request for Operational Directive, November 20, 1953, RG 341, Entry 214, File 3-4000 through 3-4099, MMB, NA.

44. Richard G. Hewlett and Francis Duncan, *Atomic Shield 1947–1952* (Volume II of *A History of the Atomic Energy Commission*) (University Park, Pa.: The Pennsylvania State University Press, 1969), pp. 130–31.

45. Ibid.

46. Office of Research and Evaluation, "Soviet Capability for the Development and Production of Certain Types of Weapons and Equipment," ORE 3/1, October 31, 1946, "CIA" Box, USJCS Records,

MMB, NA cited in Gregg Herken, *The Winning Weapon: The Atomic Bomb in the Cold War 1945–1950* (New York: Vintage, 1982), p. 391, n. 51.

47. Lewis L. Strauss, *Men and Decisions* (Garden City, N.Y.: Doubleday, 1962), p. 202.

48. Hewlett and Duncan, op. cit., p. 131.

49. Strauss quoting the directive in Strauss, op. cit., p. 204.

50. Omar N. Bradley and Clay Blair, *A General's Life* (New York: Simon & Schuster, 1983), p. 514.

51. Letter from Arnold Ross, April 1, 1985.

52. Ibid.

53. Robert J. Donovan, *Tumultuous Years: The Presidency of Harry S. Truman, 1949–1953* (New York: W. W. Norton, 1982), p. 98.

54. Ibid., p. 98.

55. Peter King and H. Friedman, "Collection and Identification of Fission Products of Foreign Origin," Naval Research Laboratory, September 22, 1949, HSTL, PSF, Box 199; R. W. Spence, "Identification of Radioactivity in Special Samples," Los Alamos Scientific Laboratory, October 4, 1949, HSTL, PSF, Box 199.

56. Donovan, op. cit., p. 99.

57. Herbert York, *The Advisors: Oppenheimer, Teller and the Superbomb* (San Francisco: W. H. Freeman, 1976), p. 33.

58. Memorandum by the Chief of Staff, U.S. Air Force, to the Secretary of Defense on Long-Range Detection of Atomic Explosions, HSTL, PSF, Box 199.

59. Kenneth W. Condit, *The History of the Joint Chiefs of Staff: The Joint Chiefs of Staff and National Policy Volume II, 1947–1949* (Washington, D.C.: Historical Division, Joint Secretariat, JCS, 1964), p. 526.

60. Interview with Herbert Scoville, McLean, Va., May 14, 1984.

61. Memorandum for General Maude, Subject: Proposed U.S./U.K. Cooperation within Area 5 of the Technical Cooperation Program, May 4, 1951, RG 341 Entry 214, MMB, NA.

62. Interview with Herbert Scoville.

63. Jay Miller, *Lockheed U-2* (Austin, Tex.: Aerofax, 1983), p. 16.

64. Ibid.

65. Harvey Kinney and Bob Trimble, "Flying the Stratosphere," *Air Classics* 9, 10 (1973), pp. 26–34, 72–73.

66. "Memorandum for Director of Intelligence, DCS/O Subject: (Uncl.) Determination of Proper Security Classification," November 26, 1954, RG 341, Entry 214, File 4-4459 through 4-4592, MMB, NA.

67. Embassy of the Union of Soviet Socialist Republics, "Soviet Note No. 261," January 5, 1948, RG 341, Entry 214, File 2-900 through 2-999, MMB, NA.

68. Letter from Francis B. Stevens, Acting Chief, Division of Eastern European Affairs, Department of State, to Colonel F. C. Gideon, January 16, 1948, RG 341, Entry 214, File 2-900 through 2-999, MMB, NA.

69. "Memorandum for the Record," February 20, 1948, RG 341, Entry 214, File 2-900 through 2-999, MMB, NA.

70. Lennart Bern, "Soviet and Warsaw Pact Air Incidents," *Jane's Defence Weekly* (January 12, 1985), p. 58.

71. John M. Carroll, *Secrets of Electronic Espionage* (New York: E. P. Dutton, 1966), p. 136.

72. Ibid.; Duncan Campbell, op. cit., p. 128.

73. Bern, op. cit.

74. Ibid.; Richard Fitts (ed.), *The Strategy of Electromagnetic Conflict* (Los Altos, Calif.: Peninsula Press, 1980), p. 62.

75. Omar N. Bradley, chairman, JCS, "Memorandum for the Secretary of Defense, Subject: Special Electronic Airborne Search Operations," July 22, 1950, HSTL, PSF; Omar N. Bradley, "Memorandum for the Secretary of Defense, Subject: Special Electronic Airborne Search Operations," May 5, 1950, HSTL, PSF.

76. Major General C. P. Cabell, Director of Intelligence, USAF, "Memorandum for the Secretary of the Air Staff, Subject: (TS) B-29 Intercepted, July 20, 1950, RG 341, Entry 214, File 2-14300 through 2-14399, MMB, NA.

77. National Security Agency, "Incidents Involving U.S. Recon Missions," n.d.; Joint Electronic Warfare Center, untitled list of incidents involving U.S. or Western aircraft; Bern, op. cit.; Fitts (ed.), loc. cit.

78. National Security Agency, op cit.; Air Force Security Service, Air Force Special Communications Center, Special Research Study 1-59, "Review of Reactions to Reconnaissance Flights Since 1952," January 27, 1959, p. 4.

79. JEWC, untitled list; National Security Agency, op. cit.; Air Force Security Service, Air Force Special Communications Center, "Résumé of 'Incidents' or 'Shoot Downs' Related to U.S. Ferret Flights Near Communist Territory," September 14, 1956, p. 5.

80. "Memorandum for the Record," November 10, 1953, RG 341, Entry 214, File 3-4000 through 3-4099 MMB, NA. The quoted material is quoted by the memorandum and attributed to AFOOP-OC-R, letter, Subject: (Restricted) USAF Electronic Reconnaissance Peacetime Program, June 17, 1953.

81. JEWC untitled list; National Security Agency, op. cit.; *History of the Fifth Air Force 1 July 1954–31 December 1954*, Volume II (Far East Air Forces, USAF), pp. 478–79.

82. National Security Agency, op. cit.; Air Force Security Service, Air Force Special Communications Center, op. cit., p. 7; Carroll, op. cit., p. 169.

83. Fitts (ed.), loc. cit.; Air Force Security Service, Air Force Special Communications Center, op. cit., p. 7; Carroll, op. cit., p. 169.

84. A. J. Goodpaster, "Memorandum for the Record," September 9, 1958, DDEL: DDEP: WHO: Office of Staff Secretary: Subject Series, Alphabetical Subseries b, 14,f: Intel Matters (6).

85. "6 U.S. Fliers Lost in Plane Downed in Soviet Armenia," *The New York Times* (September 13, 1958), pp. 1, 6.

86. A. J. Goodpaster, "Memorandum for the Record."

87. Carroll, op. cit., p. 169.

88. Ibid.

89. "How they Died," *Time* (February 16, 1959), pp. 17–18.

90. Carroll, op. cit., p. 170; Osgood Caruthers, "U.S. Fliers Downed in '58 Held in Soviet, Moscow Journal Hints," *The New York Times* (January 24, 1961), pp. 1, 2.

91. Air Force Security Service, Air Force Special Communication Centers, "Review of Reactions to Reconnaissance Flights Since 1952," pp. 2–3.

92. Fitts (ed.) op. cit., p. 63.

Chapter V:
OVERFLIGHTS

1. Colonel Edward Barber, Directorate of Intelligence, to Director of Requirements, Subject: Use of Free Balloons to Secure Electronic Information, October 25, 1950, RG 341, Entry 214, File 2-16600 to 2-16699, Modern Military Branch (MMB), National Archives (NA).

2. W. W. Rostow, *Open Skies: Eisenhower's Proposal of July 21, 1955* (Austin, Tex.: University of Texas Press, 1982), p. 6.

3. Dwight D. Eisenhower, *Mandate for Change, 1953–1956* (Garden City, N.Y.: Doubleday, 1963), p. 521.

4. Ibid., p. 522.

5. John T. Bohn, *History of the 1st Air Division, Activation 22 April 1955 to Inactivation 20 May 1956* (SAC Historical Study No. 62) (Offutt AFB, Neb.: Strategic Air Command, November 1956), p. 1.

6. "Memorandum for the Record," October 3, 1950, RG 341, Entry 214, File 2-16200 to 2-16299, MMB, NA.

7. Ibid.

8. "Memorandum for the Record," April 5, 1951, RG 341, Entry 214, File 2-19000 to 2-19099, MMB, NA.

9. Major General D. L. Pott, director of Research and Development, DCS/R&D, to Commanding General, Air Material Command, Subject: (Top Secret), Photographic Reconnaissance Balloons, November 6, 1950, RG 341, Entry 214, File 2-16200 to 2-16299, MMB, NA; Colonel W. W. Homes, Chief, Equipment Division, D/R&D, DCS/O to Director of Intelligence, DCS/O, Subject: Requirement for a Reconnaissance Capability by Recoverable Free Balloons, November 7, 1950, RG 341, Entry 214, File 2-16200 to 2-16299, MMB, NA.

10. "Memorandum for the Record," April 5, 1951, RG 341, Entry 214, File 2-19000 to 2-19099, MMB, NA.

11. "Memorandum for the Record," December 12, 1951, RG 341, Entry 214, File 2-22000 to 2-22099, MMB, NA.

12. Colonel R. E. Koon, Deputy Director of Operations, DCS/O, to Brigadier General G. E. Price, Director of Requirements, DCS/D and Major General R. H. Ramey, Director of Operations, DCS/O, Subject: (Uncl.) Future Development Action—GOPHER Project, April 17, 1953, RG 341, Entry 214, File 3-2200 to 3-2299, MMB, NA.

13. Brigadier General John Ackerman, Directorate of Intelligence to Directorate of Research & Development, DCS/O, Subject (Uncl.) Future Development Action GOPHER Project, June 17, 1953, RG 341, Entry 214, File 3-2200 to 3-2299, MMB, NA.

14. Colonel C. C. Roger, Directorate of Intelligence, "Memorandum for Mr. Ayer. Subject: Status of GRANDSON," September 24, 1953, RG 341, Entry 214, File 3-3500 to 3-3599, MMB, NA.

15. Paul Worthman, note 3 in Rostow, op. cit., pp. 191–92.

16. Ibid.

17. *1st Air Division (Meteorological Survey), Final Report, Project 119L*, p. 8. The assignment came in the form of a letter titled "Assignment of Additional Mission to Strategic Air Command."

18. Ibid.; Frank Chappell, Directorate of Intelligence, Memorandum for Director of Requirements, DCS/O Subject: (Uncl.) Requirement for Special Electronic Equipment, November 2, 1954, RG 341, Entry 214, File 4-4231 to 4-4293, MMB, NA.

19. *1st Air Division (Meteorological Survey), Final Report Project 119L*, p. 8.

20. Ibid., pp. 8, 12.

21. Ibid., p. 12.

22. Ibid.; Colonel James F. Setchell, Directorate of Intelligence, to Commanding General, U.S. Air Force Security Service, Subject: (Uncl.) Assignment of Additional Mission to USAF Security Service, September 18, 1952, RG 341, Entry 214, File 2-35300 to 2-35299, MMB, NA, and "Functions Concerning Mission and Functions of the Balloon Launching Squadron" attachment.

23. *1st Air Division (Meteorological Survey), Final Report Project 119L*, p. 9.

24. Ibid., p. 11.

25. Ibid., p. 12.

26. Tom D. Crouch, *The Eagle Aloft: Two Centuries of the Balloon in America* (Washington, D.C.: Smithsonian Institution Press, 1983), p. 644.

27. *1st Air Division (Meteorological Survey), Final Report Project 119L*, p. 16.

28. Ibid., pp. 16, 19.

29. Ibid., p. 16.

30. Ibid.

31. Deputy Director for Collection and Dissemination, Directorate of Intelligence, to Director of Requirements, Directorate of Research & Development, Subject: (Secret) Special Reconnaissance Operations, October 23, 1953, RG 341, Entry 214, File 3-3700 to 3-3799, MMB, NA.

32. Welles Hangen, "Russia Charges Balloon Forays by U.S. and Turks," *The New York Times* (February 6, 1956), pp. 1, 3.

33. Attachment to "Memorandum for Colonel A. J. Goodpaster, The White House" (February 8, 1956), Dulles Papers, DDEL.

34. "Russians Display Balloons of U.S.," *The New York Times* (February 10, 1956), pp. 1, 3.

35. John Foster Dulles, "Memorandum of Conversation with the President, February 6, 1956," Meetings with the President, Jan.–July 56(5) Box 4, J. F. Dulles Papers, White House Library, DDEL.

36. Attachment to "Memorandum for Colonel A. J. Goodpaster, the White House," op. cit.

37. *1st Air Division (Meteorological Survey), Final Report 119L*, pp. 25, 27.

38. Ibid., p. 25.

39. Ibid., pp. 22, 25.

40. Ibid., p. 27.

41. A. J. Goodpaster, "Memorandum for the Record, Conference of the Joint Chiefs of Staff with the President, 10 February 1956," February 10, 1956.

42. Crouch, op. cit., p. 647.

43. Donald E. Welzenbach, "Observation Balloons and Reconnaissance Satellites," *Studies in Intelligence* (Spring 1986), pp. 21–28.

44. Interviews with Richard Bissell and Herbert Scoville.

45. Oral history interview with Robert Amory, Jr. (February 9, 1966), (Washington, D.C.: JFK Library), pp. 112–13.

46. Ibid., pp. 113–14.

47. Thomas Powers, *The Man Who Kept the Secrets: Richard Helms and the CIA* (New York: Alfred A. Knopf, 1979), p. 95; Leonard Mosley, *Dulles: A Biography of Eleanor, Allen and John Foster and their Family Network* (New York: Dial, 1978), p. 365.

48. A. J. Goodpaster, "Memorandum of Conference with the President, 0810, 24 November 1954," November 24, 1954, ACW Diary, Nov. 54, Bx. 3, ACWD, ACWF, DDE Papers as President, DDEL.

49. Powers, op. cit., pp. 95–96.

50. Quoted in Kelly Johnson with Maggie Smith, *More Than My Share of It All* (Washington, D.C.: Smithsonian Institution Press, 1985), p. 122.

51. Oral history interview with Richard M. Bissell, Jr., Columbia University (1973), p. 42.

52. Interview with Richard M. Bissell, Jr., by Dr. Thomas Soapes, oral historian, DDEL (November 9, 1976), p. 5.

53. Ibid., p. 8.

54. Ibid., p. 4.

55. Powers, op. cit., pp. 95–96; Johnson with Smith, op. cit., p. 125. For detailed accounts of the first flights see Skip Holm, "Spyplane: The First U-2 Flights," *Air Progress Aviation Review* (June 1986), pp. 24ff.

56. Powers, *The Man Who Kept the Secrets*, p. 96; "U.S. to Continue U-2 Flights Over Soviet," *Aviation Week* (May 16, 1960), pp. 26–27; William E. Burrows, *Deep Black: Space Espionage and National Security* (New York: Random House, forthcoming), Chapter 3.

57. Dwight D. Eisenhower, *Waging Peace, 1956–1961* (Garden City, N.Y.: Doubleday, 1965), p. 41.

58. Ibid., p. 545.

59. Jay Miller, *Lockheed U-2* (Austin, Tex.: Aerofax, 1983), p. 25.

60. Ibid., pp. 26–27.

61. Michael R. Beschloss, *Mayday: Eisenhower, Khrushchev and the U-2 Affair* (New York: Harper & Row, 1986), pp. 111–12.

62. Ibid., p. 120.

63. Mosley, op. cit., p. 368; Miller, op. cit., p. 26.

64. Miller, op. cit., pp. 26–30; Mosley, op. cit., p. 368.

65. "Soviet Note No. 23," July 10, 1956, White House Corr., Gen. 1956(3), Box 3, JFD Papers, WH Memoranda, DDEL.

66. Interview with Richard M. Bissell, Jr. (June 6, 1984), Farmington, Conn.

67. Mosley, op. cit., p. 368.

68. Ibid., p. 369.

69. Miller, op. cit., pp. 27, 30; Francis Gary Powers, *Operation Overflight* (New York: Holt, Rienhart & Winston, 1970), pp. 61–62; Beschloss, op. cit., pp. 147, 155.

70. Quoted in John Ranelagh, *The Agency: The Rise and Decline of the CIA* (New York: Simon & Schuster, 1986), p. 317.

71. "Testimony of Allen Dulles," *Executive Sessions of the Senate Foreign Relations Committee (Historical Series), Vol. XII, Eighty-sixth Congress— Second Session, 1960* (Washington, D.C.: U.S. Government Printing Office, 1982) p. 284.

72. Soapes interview with Richard M. Bissell, Jr., pp. 45–46.

73. Interview with Richard M. Bissell, Jr. (March 16, 1984), Farmington, Conn.

74. Ibid.

75. Beschloss, op. cit., p. 147.

76. Powers (Francis Gary), op. cit., p. 46.

77. Ibid., p. 47.

78. Interview with Richard M. Bissell, Jr. (March 16, 1984).

79. Miller, op. cit., p. 30.

80. Ibid., p. 28; Soapes interview with Richard M. Bissell, Jr., p. 47.

81. "Memorandum for the Record," March 7, 1958, DDEP: WHO: Office of Staff Secretary: Subject Series, Alphabetical Subseries b, 14, f: Intel Matters (5), DDEL. Four months later Eisenhower gave approval to a new balloon program, WS-461L. With its new camera system it was believed it could produce photographs from a sufficiently high altitude to be undetectable. A July 7 launching was followed within the month by Soviet protests—causing Eisenhower to cancel the program. See Welzenbach, op. cit.

82. John S. D. Eisenhower, "Memorandum of Conference with President," December 16, 1958, *DDRS*, 1982–001388.

83. John S. D. Eisenhower, "Memorandum for the Record," February 12, 1959, *DDRS* 1981-662A.

84. A. J. Goodpaster, "Memorandum for the Record," March 4, 1959, DDEP: WHO: Office of Staff Secretary, Subject Series, Alphabetical Subseries, 6, 15, f1. Intelligence Matter (4); A. J. Goodpaster, "Memorandum of Conference with the President, April 7, 1959, *DDRS*, 1982-001389.

85. Beschloss, op, cit., p. 237.

86. A. J. Goodpaster, "Memorandum for the Record," February 8, 1960 *DDRS*, 1981-623A.

87. Beschloss, op. cit., p. 237.

88. Ibid., pp. 241–42; Miller, op. cit., p. 30.

89. Beschloss, op. cit., pp. 241–42.

90. A. J. Goodpaster, "Memorandum for the Record," April 25, 1960, WHO St. Sec., Subject Series, Alphabetical Subseries, Box 15, Intelligence Matters-14, March–May 1960, DDEL.

91. "U.S. to Continue U-2 Flights Over Soviet," *Aviation Week*; Beschloss, op. cit., p. 241.

92. Nikita Khrushchev, *Khrushchev Remembers: The Last Testament* (New York: Bantam, 1976), p. 504.

93. Beschloss, op. cit., p. 39.

94. "Testimony of Allen Dulles," p. 285.

Chapter VI:
RECONNAISSANCE AT SEA

1. Letter from Major General George Budway, Director of Intelligence, AAC, to Major General C. P. Cabell, Director of Intelligence, USAF, November 17, 1948, RG 341, Entry 214, File No. 2-5400 through 2-5499, Modern Military Branch (MMB), National Archives (NA).

2. Peer de Silva, *Sub Rosa: The CIA and the Uses of Intelligence* (New York: Times Books, 1978), pp. 58–59.

3. CINCLANTFLT, "Northern Cruise, Intelligence Requirements for, Project No. 53-714," RG 341, Entry 214, File 3-2499, MMB, NA.

4. Quoted in James Bamford, *The Puzzle Palace: A Report on NSA, America's Most Secret Agency* (Boston: Houghton Mifflin, 1982), p. 213.

5. Ibid.

6. Ibid., pp. 213–14.

7. Ibid., p. 214.

8. Ibid., pp. 215, 231.

9. Bamford, op. cit., p. 219.

10. Trevor Armbrister, *A Matter of Accountability: The True Story of the Pueblo Affair* (New York: Coward-McCann, 1970), pp. 81–82.

11. Ibid., pp. 83–85.

12. Ibid., pp. 85–86.

13. Bamford, op. cit., p. 231.

14. House Armed Services Committee, *Inquiry into the U.S.S. Pueblo and EC-121 Plane Incidents* (Washington, D.C.: U.S. Government Printing Office, 1969), p. 698.

15. Ibid., pp. 762–63.

16. Ibid., p. 763.

17. Armbrister, op. cit., p. 87.

18. Bamford, op. cit., p. 232.

19. Ibid.

20. House Armed Services Committee, op. cit., p. 766.

21. Armbrister, op. cit., pp. 4, 21.

22. House Armed Services Committee, op. cit., p. 763.

23. Bamford, op. cit., p. 235.

24. Seymour Hersh, "Submarines of U.S. Stage Spy Missions Inside Soviet Waters," *The New York Times* (May 25, 1975), pp. 1, 42.

25. Seymour Hersh, "A False Navy Report Alleged in Sub Crash," *The New York Times* (July 6, 1975), pp. 1, 26.

26. Hersh, "Submarines of U.S. Stage Spy Missions Inside Soviet Waters."

27. Ibid.

28. Ibid.

29. Ibid.

30. Hannes Adomeit, *Soviet Risk-Taking and Crisis Behavior* (London: George Allen & Unwin, 1982), p. 242.

31. Hersh, "Submarines of U.S. Stage Spy Missions Inside Soviet Waters."

32. Ibid.

33. Ibid.

34. Hersh, "A False Navy Report Alleged in Sub Crash."

35. Ibid.

36. Ibid.

37. Ibid.

38. Ibid.

39. *Jane's Fighting Ships, 1983–1984* (London: Jane's Publishing Co., 1983), p. 639.

40. Private information.

41. Fred Kaplan and Walter V. Robinson, "Pelton's 'Top Secret' Intelligence Not So Secret," *Boston Globe* (June 5, 1986), pp. 1, 16–17.

42. Susan Schmidt and Patrick E. Tyler, "FBI Says Pelton Reported Soviet Interest in Satellites: Agents Detail Talks with Alleged Spy," *Washington Post* (May 29, 1986), pp. A1, A14–A15.

43. Kaplan and Robinson, op. cit.; Office of the Chief of Naval Operations, *Navy Special Warfare Master Plan (NSWP) 1984* (Washington, D.C.: OCNO, 1984), pp. xi, xv, I-1.

44. Norman Polmar, "The Deep Submergence Vehicle Fleet," *Proceedings of the U.S. Naval Institute* (June 1986), pp. 119–20.

45. Susan Schmidt and Patrick E. Tyler, "Pelton Map Designation Held Wrong," *Washington Post* (May 31, 1986), pp. A1, A12.

46. Richard Burt, "Technology Is Essential to Arms Verification," *The New York Times* (August 14, 1979), pp. C1, C2.

47. Murray Sayle, "KE 007: A Conspiracy of Circumstance," *The New York Review of Books* (April 25, 1985), pp. 44–54.

48. *Jane's Fighting Ships, 1983–1984*, p. 681.

49. *Jane's Fighting Ships, 1983–1984*, p. 674; private information.

50. Private information.

51. William Arkin and Richard Fieldhouse, *Nuclear Battlefields: Global Links in the Arms Race* (Cambridge, Mass.: Ballinger, 1985), p. 255.

52. Ibid., p. 258; private information.

53. Richard Halloran, "2 U.S. Ships Enter Soviet Waters Off Crimea to Gather Intelligence," *The New York Times* (March 19, 1986), pp. A1, A11; George C. Wilson, "Soviet Ships Shadowed U.S. Vessels' Transit," *Washington Post* (March 20, 1986), p. A33.

54. Halloran, op. cit.

55. Private information.

56. Halloran, op. cit.; Wilson, op. cit.

57. Senate Committee on Appropriations, *Department of Defense Appropriations FY 1973, Part 4* (Washington, D.C.: U.S. Government Printing Office, 1972), p. 363; *Jane's Fighting Ships, 1983–1984*, p. 714.

58. Kenneth J. Stein, "Cobra Judy Phased Array Radar Tested," *Aviation Week and Space Technology* (August 10, 1981), pp. 70–73.

59. Ibid.

60. "X-Band Expands Cobra Judy's Repertoire," *Defense Electronics* (January 1985), pp. 43–44.

61. Thomas S. Burns, *The Secret War for the Ocean Depths: Soviet-American Rivalry for Mastery of the Seas* (New York: Rawson, 1978), p. 154.

62. Owen Wilkes, "Strategic Anti-Submarine Warfare and Its Implications for a Counterforce First Strike," *SIPRI Yearbook 1979* (London: Taylor & Francis, 1979), p. 430.

63. House Appropriations Committee, *Department of Defense Appropriations for Fiscal Year 1977, Part 5* (Washington, D.C.: U.S. Government Printing Office, 1976), p. 1255; Drew Middleton, "Expert Predicts Big U.S. Gain in SubWarfare," *The New York Times* (July 18, 1979), p. A5.

64. Defense Market Survey, "Sonar-Sub-surface-Caesar," *DMS Market Intelligence Report* (Greenwich, Conn.: DMS, 1980), p. 1; Clyde W. Burleson, *The Jennifer Project* (Englewood Cliffs, N.J.: Prentice-Hall, 1977), p. 18; Joel Wit, "Advances in Antisubmarine Warfare," *Scientific American* 244, 2 (February 1981): 36ff.

65. Howard B. Dratch, "High Stakes in the Azores," *The Nation* (November 8, 1975), pp. 455–56; "NATO Fixed SONAR Range Commissioned," *Armed Forces Journal* (August 1972), p. 29; "Atlantic Islands: NATO Seeks Wider Facilities," *International Herald Tribune* (June 1981), p. 75; Richard Timsar, "Portugal Bargains for U.S. Military Aid with Strategic Mid-Atlantic Base," *The Christian Science Monitor* (March 24, 1981), p. 9.

66. Wit, op. cit.

67. Arkin and Fieldhouse, op. cit., Appendix A.

68. Desmond Ball, "The U.S. Air Force Satellite Communications

(AFSATCOM) System: The Australian Connection" (Canberra: Strategic & Defense Studies Centre, March 1982); private information.

69. Walter Sullivan, "Can Submarines Stay Hidden?," *The New York Times* (December 11, 1984), pp. C1, C9.

70. Paul Bracken, *The Command and Control of Nuclear Forces* (New Haven, Conn.: Yale University Press, 1983), p. 14.

71. Burns, op. cit., p. 156.

72. Robert Aldridge, *First Strike: The Pentagon's Strategy for Nuclear War* (Boston, Mass.: South End Press, 1983), p. 165.

73. Melinda C. Beck with David C. Martin, "The War Beneath the Seas," *Newsweek* (February 8, 1982), pp. 37–38.

74. Department of Defense, *Soviet Military Power 1985* (Washington, D.C.: Department of Defense, 1985), p. 96.

75. A. Preston, "SOSUS Update Aims to Keep Track of Alfa," *Jane's Defence Weekly* 1, 2 (January 21, 1984), p. 60.

76. Robert P. Berman and John C. Baker, *Soviet Strategic Forces: Requirements and Responses* (Washington, D.C.: Brookings Institution, 1982), pp. 106–7.

Chapter VII:
KEYHOLES AND FERRETS

1. Gerald M. Steinberg, *Satellite Reconnaissance: The Role of Informal Bargaining* (New York: Praeger, 1983), p. 23; Bruno W. Augenstein, *Evolution of the U.S. Military Space Program, 1945–1960: Some Key Events in Study, Planning and Program Development* (Santa Monica, Calif.: RAND, 1982), p. 5; Philip Klass, *Secret Sentries in Space* (New York: Random House, 1971), p. 76.

2. Memorandum for Deputy Chief of Staff, Development, Subject: (Deleted) Satellite Vehicles, December 18, 1952, RG 341, Entry 214, File 2-36300 through 2-36399, Modern Military Branch (MMB), National Archives (NA).

3. Ibid.

4. Steinberg, loc. cit.; Augenstein, loc. cit.; Klass, loc. cit.

5. Memorandum for Deputy Chief of Staff, Development, Subject (Deleted) Satellite Vehicles.

6. Ibid.

7. Ibid.

8. Ibid.

9. Paul Stares, *The Militarization of Space: U.S. Policy, 1945–1984* (Ithaca, N.Y.: Cornell University Press, 1985), p. 30.

10. Herbert F. York and G. Allen Greb, "Strategic Reconnaissance," *Bulletin of the Atomic Scientists* 33, 4 (April 1977): 33–41.

11. Anthony Kenden, "U.S. Reconnaissance Satellite Programs," *Spaceflight* 20, 7 (1978): 243ff.

12. Letter from Neil McElroy to Dwight David Eisenhower, January 29, 1959, *DDRS* 1982-001538.

13. "USAF Pushes Pied Piper Space Vehicle," *Aviation Week* (October 14, 1957), p. 26.

14. *Briefing on Army Satellite Program*, November 10, 1957, *DDRS* 1977-101B.

15. John Prados, *The Soviet Estimate: U.S. Intelligence Analysis and Russian Military Strength* (New York: Dial, 1982), pp. 195–96.

16. Interview with Richard Bissell; Thomas Powers, *The Man Who Kept the Secrets: Richard Helms and the CIA* (New York: Alfred A. Knopf, 1979), p. 97.

17. National Security Council, "U.S. Policy on Outer Space," NSC 5814, June 20, 1958.

18. Kenden, op. cit.; "Work on Pied Piper Accelerated: Satellite Has Clam-Shell Nose Cone," *Aviation Week* (June 23, 1958), pp. 18–19.

19. Office of the Director of Defense Research and Engineering, *Military*

Space Projects (Report No. 10) (Washington, D.C.: Department of Defense, 1960), p. 1, *DDRS* 1980-36C.

20. Leonard Mosley, *Dulles: A Biography of Eleanor, Allen and John Foster and Their Family Network* (New York: Dial, 1978), p. 432.

21. Office of the Director of Defense Research and Engineering, op. cit., pp. 27–28.

22. Kenden, op. cit.

23. Ibid.

24. Ibid.

25. Ibid.; interview.

26. Mosley, loc. cit.

27. Ibid.; Office of the Director of Defense Research and Engineering, *Military Space Projects* (Report No. 11) (Washington, D.C.: Department of Defense, 1960), *DDRS* 1980-36D; Larry Booda, "First Capsule Recovered from Satellite," *Aviation Week* (August 22, 1960), pp. 33–35.

28. John Nammack, "C-119's Third Pass Snares Discoverer," *Aviation Week* (August 29, 1960), pp. 30–31; "Space Capsule is Caught in Mid-Air by U.S. Plane on Re-entry from Orbit," *The New York Times* (August 20, 1960), pp. 1, 7.

29. Lawrence Freedman, *U.S. Intelligence and the Soviet Strategic Threat* (Boulder, Colo.: Westview, 1977), p. 73.

30. Ibid.

31. Kenden, op. cit.

32. House Committee on Science and Astronautics, *Science, Astronautics and Defense* (Washington, D.C.: U.S. Government Printing Office, 1961), p. 63.

33. Kenden, "U.S. Satellite Reconnaissance Programs."

34. "SAMOS II Fact Sheet" (Washington, D.C.: Department of Defense, 1961).

35. Kenden, op. cit.

36. Klass, op. cit., pp. 104–6.

37. Ibid.

38. Howard Simons, "Our Fantastic Eye in the Sky," *Washington Post* (December 8, 1963), pp. E1, 5.

39. Freedman, op. cit., p. 72.

40. Interview with Herbert Scoville.

41. Kenden, op. cit.

42. Ibid.

43. Samuel Glasstone and Philip J. Dolan, *The Effects of Nuclear Weapons,* 3rd ed. (Washington, D.C.: DOD/DOE, 1977), pp. 45–47.

44. Interview with Herbert Scoville.

45. Thomas Karas, *The New High Ground: Strategies and Weapons of Space-Age War* (New York: Simon & Schuster, 1983), p. 30.

46. Roger A. Jernigan, *Air Force Satellite Control Facility: Historical Brief and Chronology 1954–1981* (Sunnyvale, Calif.: AFSCF History Office, 1982), p. 113.

47. Russell Hawkes, "USAF's Satellite Test Center Grows," *Aviation Week* (May 30, 1960), pp. 57–63.

48. Ibid.

49. Senate Appropriations Committee, *Department of Defense Appropriations FY 1974, Part 4* (Washington, D.C.: U.S. Government Printing Office, 1973), p. 481.

50. Jernigan, op. cit., p. 113.

51. Jernigan, loc. cit.

52. Lee Bowen, *The Threshold of Space: The Air Force in the National Space Program, 1945–1959* (Washington, D.C.: USAF Historical Division Liaison Office, September 1960), p. 26.

53. Ibid., p. 27.

54. Ibid., pp. 27, 30.

55. Ibid., pp. 32–33.

56. House Committee on Science and Astronautics, *Defense Space Interests* (Washington, D.C.: U.S. Government Printing Office, 1961), pp. 113–14.

57. Carl Berger, *The Air Force in Space Fiscal Year 1961* (Washington, D.C.: USAF Historical Division Liaison Office, 1966), p. 34.

58. Ibid., p. 35.

59. George B. Kistiakowsky, *A Scientist in the White House: The Private Diary of President Eisenhower's Special Assistant for Science and Technology* (Cambridge, Mass.: Harvard University Press, 1976), pp. 382–83.

60. Ibid., pp. 394–95.

61. Jay Miller, *Lockheed U-2* (Austin, Tex.: Aerofax, 1983), p. 12.

62. Interview.

63. Secretary of the Air Force Order No. 115.1, August 31, 1960, Subject: Organization and Functions of the Office of Missile and Satellite Systems.

64. Secretary of the Air Force Order No. 116.1, August 31, 1960, Subject: The Director of the SAMOS Project.

65. As in Senate Armed Services Committee, *Inquiry into Satellite and Missile Programs,* Part I (Washington, D.C.: U.S. Government Printing Office, 1958), pp. 1974–75; House Committee on Government Operations, *Air Force Ballistic Missile Management (Formation of Aerospace Corporation)* (Washington, D.C.: U.S. Government Printing Office, 1961), pp. 19, 41; Senate Committee on Aeronautical and Space Sciences, *Missiles, Space and Other Defense Matters* (Washington, D.C.: U.S. Government Printing Office, 1960), p. 63.

66 Steinberg, op. cit., pp. 30, 42.

67. Ibid., p. 40.

68. Ibid., p. 27.

69. Ibid., p. 39.

70. Ibid., p. 42.

71. Arthur Sylvester, "Memorandum for the President, White House, Subject: SAMOS II Launch," January 26, 1961, *DDRS* 1981-364B.

72. Ibid.

73. Steinberg, op. cit., p. 43.

74. Ibid.

75. Ibid.

76. Ibid., p. 44.

77. Ibid., pp. 53–54.

78. Ibid., p. 43; "Space Secrecy Muddle," *Aviation Week and Space Technology* (April 23, 1962), p. 21.

79. JFK Library, National Security Files/Box 336, Sanitized Version of September 27, 1983.

80. Prados, op. cit., p. 173.

81. Kenden, op. cit.

82. Ibid.

83. Klass, op. cit., p. 194.

84. Kenden, "U.S. Reconnaissance Satellite Programs."

85. Ibid.

86. Seymour M. Hersh, *"The Target Is Destroyed": What Really Happened to Flight 007 and What America Knew About It* (New York: Random House, 1986), p. 38; private information.

87. Philip Klass, "Military Satellites Gain Vital Data," *Aviation Week and Space Technology* (September 15, 1969), pp. 55–60.

88. Launch data are based on Kenden, op. cit.

89. David Baker, *The Shape of Wars to Come* (Briarcliff Manor, N.Y.: Stein and Day, 1982), p. 61.

90. Launch data are based on Kenden, op. cit.

91. Klass, *Secret Sentries*, p. 167; Barry Miller, "USAF Planning Space Data Link System," *Aviation Week and Space Technology* (April 11, 1966), p. 65ff.

92. "Recon Satellite in Orbit Covering Mideast," *Aviation Week and Space Technology* (August 31, 1970), p. 13.

93. Freedman, op. cit., pp. 164–65.

94. D. G. King-Hele et. al., *The RAE Tables of Earth Satellites, 1957–1980* (Farnborough, Eng.: Royal Aircraft Establishment, 1981), p. 114; "Space Reconnaissance Dwindles," *Aviation Week and Space Technology* (October 6, 1980), pp. 18–20.

95. Jeffrey T. Richelson, *United States Strategic Reconnaissance: Photographic/Imaging Satellites* (Los Angeles: ACIS Working Paper No. 38, May 1983), Appendix, Table 6.

96. "Space Reconnaissance Dwindles."

Chapter VIII:
PARPRO AND THE SOVIET TARGET

1. Interview with Richard Bissell.

2. Scott D. Sagan "Nuclear Alerts and Crisis Management" *International Security*, 9, 4 (1985), pp. 99–139.

3. John Prados, *The Soviet Estimate: U.S. Intelligence and Russian Military Strength* (New York: Dial, 1982), p. 175.

4. William E. Burrows, *Deep Black: Space Espionage and National Security* (New York: Random House, forthcoming), Chap. 6.

5. Kelly L. Johnson, "Development of the Lockheed SR-71 Blackbird," *Lockheed Horizons* (1981), pp. 1–7.

6. Ibid.

7. Ibid.

8. Jay Miller, *The Lockheed A-12/YF-12/SR-71 Story* (Austin, Tex.: Aerofax, 1983), p. 3.

9. Ibid.

10. Andrew W. Waters, *All the U.S. Air Force Airplanes 1907–1983* (New York: Hippocrene Books, 1983), p. 302; Miller, op. cit., p. 2.

11. Burrows, loc. cit.

12. Miller, op. cit., p. 2.

13. Kelly Johnson with Maggie Smith, *More Than My Share of It All* (Washington, D.C.: Smithsonian Institution Press, 1985), pp. 136, 144.

14. Donald E. Fink, "U-2s, SR-71s Merged in One Wing," *Aviation Week and Space Technology* (May 10, 1976), p. 83; Miller, op. cit., p. 5.

15. Bill Yenne, *SAC: A Primer of Modern Strategic Airpower* (Novato, Calif.: Presidio Press, 1985), p. 34.

16. Ibid.

17. Ibid.

18. Miller, op. cit., p. 3.

19. Burrows, loc. cit.; Yenne, loc. cit.; Johnson with Smith, op. cit., p. 195.

20. Fink, op. cit.

21. Johnson with Smith, op. cit., p. 144.

22. Private information.

23. Martin Streetly, "U.S. Airborne ELINT Systems, Part 4: The Lockheed SR-71A," *Jane's Defence Weekly* (April 13, 1985), pp. 634–35; Joint Chiefs of Staff, *JCS 1982 Posture Statement* (Washington, D.C.: U.S. Government Printing Office, 1981), p. 198.

24. "Second SR-71 Deployed to England," *Aviation Week and Space Technology* (January 31, 1983), p. 59.

25. Colonel Asa Bates, "National Technical Means of Verification," *Royal United Services Institute Journal* 123, 2 (June 1978): 64–73.

26. Benjamin Schemmer, *The Raid* (New York: Harper & Row, 1975), p. 169.

27. Colonel William V. Kennedy, *Intelligence Warfare* (New York: Crescent, 1983), p. 105.

28. David Binder, "Radar Detector Aboard SR-71 Alerted Pilot to Missile's Attack," *The New York Times* (August 29, 1981), p. 3; Burrows, loc. cit.

29. Binder, loc. cit.

30. Burrows, loc. cit.

31. Ibid.

32. "SR-71," U.S. Air Force Fact Sheet 82-36, Secretary of the Air Force, Office of Public Affairs.

33. William Arkin, "Current Intelligence Collection: Its Effect on Crisis Management and Policy Formulation" presented at International Studies Association, March 5–9, 1985, Washington, D.C.; Dick Van der Art, *Aerial Espionage: Secret Intelligence Flights by East and West* (New York: Arco/Prentice-Hall, 1984), p. 71.

34. "Electronic Environment Sampled Regularly," *Aviation Week and Space Technology* (May 10, 1976), pp. 90–92.

35. Duncan Campbell, "Spy in the Sky," *New Statesman* (September 9, 1983), pp. 8–9.

36. John Barron, *MiG Pilot: The Final Escape of Lt. Belenko* (New York: Avon, 1980), p. 174.

37. "An Exercise in Restraint," *Newsweek* (April 28, 1969), pp. 27–31; "A New Lesson in the Limits of Power," *Time* (April 25, 1969), pp. 15–17.

38. Andrew W. Waters, op. cit., pp. 151–52.

39. "An Exercise in Restraint," loc. cit.

40. House Armed Services Committee, *Inquiry into the U.S.S. Pueblo and EC-121 Plane Incidents* (Washington, D.C.: U.S. Government Printing Office, 1969), p. 907.

41. "The Spy Planes: What They Do and Why," *Time* (April 25, 1969), p. 17.

42. Untitled memo, *DDRS* 1982-001583.

43. House Appropriations Committee, *Department of Defense Appropriations for 1984,* Part 8 (Washington, D.C.: U.S. Government Printing Office, 1983), p. 384.

44. Martin Streetly, "U.S. Airborne ELINT Systems, Part 3: The Boeing RC-135 Family," *Jane's Defence Weekly* (March 16, 1985), pp. 460–65.

45. Seymour M. Hersh, *"The Target Is Destroyed": What Really Happened to Flight 007 and What America Knew About It* (New York: Random House, 1986), p. 9.

46. Private information; William A. Arkin and Richard Fieldhouse, *Nuclear Battlefields: Global Links in the Arms Race* (Cambridge, Mass.: Ballinger, 1985), pp. 257–58.

47. Ibid., p. 260; Hersh, op. cit., pp. 9–10.

48. George C. Wilson, "U.S. RC-135 Was Assessing Soviet Air Defense," *Washington Post* (September 7, 1983), p. A-12; Philip Taubman, "U.S. Says Intelligence Plane Was on a Routine Mission," *The New York Times* (September 5, 1983), p. 4; Hersh, op. cit., p. 220.

49. Private information.

50. Private information.

51. Streetly, "U.S. Airborne ELINT Systems, Part 3."

52. *6 SWR 55-2: Operations, Aircrew, and Staff Procedures* (September 30, 1983), Department of the Air Force, Headquarters, 6th Strategic Wing, pp. 4–11.

53. Private information.

54. Private information.

55. T. Edward Eskelson and Tom Bernard, "A Personal View," *Baltimore News-American* (September 15, 1983), p. 8.

56. *6 SWR 55-2: Operations, Aircrew, and Staff Procedures*, pp. 3–14.

57. Charles W. Corddry and Albert Schlstedt, Jr., "Plane's Covert Role Is to Monitor Soviet Space Flights, Missile Tests," *Baltimore Sun* (May 1, 1981), p. 1.

58. Ibid.

59. House Appropriations Committee, *Military Construction Appropriations for 1985*, Part 3 (Washington, D.C.: U.S. Government Printing Office, 1984), pp. 105–6.

60. Brendan M. Greeley, Jr., "USAF Readies Range Instrumentation Aircraft for First Flight," *Aviation Week and Space Technology* (February 25, 1985), pp. 23–24.

61. Ibid.

62. Ibid.

63. Ibid.

64. Lori A. McClelland, "Versatile P-3C Orion Meeting Growing ASW Challenge," *Defense Electronics* (April 1985), pp. 132–41.

65. David Miller, *An Illustrated Guide to Modern Sub Hunters* (New York: Arco, 1984), p. 125.

66. George A. Wilmoth, "Lockheed's Antisubmarine Aircraft: Watching the Threat," *Defense Systems Review* 3, 6 (1985): 18–25.

67. Miller, loc. cit.

68. Ibid., p. 124; Wilmoth, op. cit.

69. McClelland, op. cit.

70. Miller, loc. cit.

71. *P-3C Orion Update Weapon System* (Burbank, Calif.: Lockheed, n.d.), p. 17.

72. Ibid., p. 18; McClelland, op. cit.; Nicholas M. Horrock, "The Submarine Hunters," *Newsweek* (January 23, 1984), p. 38.

73. Jeffrey T. Richelson and Desmond Ball, *The Ties That Bind: Intelligence Cooperation Between the UKUSA Countries* (London: George Allen & Unwin, 1985), p. 220.

74. McClelland, op. cit.

75. Horrock, op. cit.

76. Private information.

77. Van der Art, op. cit., pp. 53–54.

78. Ibid.

Chapter IX:
RHYOLITE, KENNAN, AND BEYOND

1. Interviews with Herbert Scoville and Richard Bissell.

2. U.S. Congress, Senate Select Committee to Study Governmental Operations with Respect to Intelligence Activities, *Supplementary Detailed Staff Reports*, Book IV (Washington, D.C.: U.S. Government Printing Office, 1976), p. 75.

3. Robert B. Giffen, *U.S. Space System Survivability: Strategic Alternatives for the 1990s* (Washington, D.C.: National Defense University, 1982), p. 8.

4. Farooq Hussain, "The Future of Arms Control: The Impact of Weapons Test Restrictions," *Adelphi Papers* 165 (1981): 29.

5. Desmond Ball, *A Suitable Piece of Real Estate: American Installations in Australia* (Sydney: Hale & Iremonger, 1980), p. 73.

6. Robert Lindsey, *The Falcon and the Snowman: A True Story of Friendship and Espionage* (New York: Simon & Schuster, 1979), pp. 54–58.

7. Philip J. Klass, "U.S. Monitoring Capability Impaired," *Aviation Week and Space Technology* (May 14, 1979), p. 18.

8. Desmond Ball, "The Rhyolite Program" (Canberra: Australian National University, 1982), mimeograph.

9. Lindsey, op. cit., p. 111.

10. Ball, "The Rhyolite Program."

11. Klass, op. cit.

12. D. C. King-Hele et al., *The RAE Table of Earth Satellites, 1957–1980* (New York: Facts on File, 1981), p. 324.

13. Ball, "The Rhyolite Program."

14. Lindsey, op. cit., p. 57.

15. Ball, "The Rhyolite Program."

16. Ibid.

17. Victor Marchetti in the film *Allies* (a Grand Bay film directed by Marian Wilkinson and produced by Sylvie LeClezio, Syndey, 1983).

18. See Lindsey, op. cit., for a book-length account. On the renaming of RHYOLITE see William E. Burrows, *Deep Black: Space Espionage and National Security* (New York: Random House, forthcoming), Chap. 8; Glenn Zorpette, "Monitoring the Tests," *IEEE Spectron* (July 1986), pp. 57–66.

19. Lindsey, op. cit., pp. 345–46.

20. Jeffrey T. Richelson and William M. Arkin, "Spy Satellites: Secret But Much Is Known," *Washington Post* (January 6, 1985), pp. C1–C2.

21. Ball, *A Suitable Piece of Real Estate*, p. 59.

22. Ball, "The Rhyolite Program."

23. Ibid.

24. Ibid.

25. Ibid.

26. Ibid.

27. Ibid.

28. Ball, *A Suitable Piece of Real Estate*, p. 65.

29. Paul Stares, *The Militarization of Space: U.S. Policy, 1945–1984* (Ithaca, N.Y.: Cornell University Press, 1985), p. 160; Curtis L. Peebles, "The Guardians," *Spaceflight* (November 1978), pp. 38ff.; private information.

30. Philip J. Klass, *Secret Sentries in Space* (New York: Random House, 1971), pp. 147–48; Donald E. Fink, "CIA Control Bid Slowed Decision on MOL," *Aviation Week and Space Technology* (September 20, 1965), pp. 26–27.

31. Klass, *Secret Sentries in Space,* p. 147.

32. Fink, op. cit.; private information.

33. Stares, loc. cit.; Peebles, op. cit.; Klass, *Secret Sentries in Space,* p. 169.

34. Klass, *Secret Sentries in Space,* p. 169.

35. Private information.

36. "Big Bird: America's Spy in Space," *Flight International* (January 27, 1977),; Philip Klass, *Secret Sentries in Space;* pp. 170–71. "Space Reconnaissance Dwindles," *Aviation Week and Space Technology* (October 6, 1980), pp. 18–20.

37. King-Hele et al., op. cit. and subsequent issues.

38. King-Hele et al., p. 612; D.C. King-Hele et al., *The RAE Table of Earth Satellites, 1981–82* (Farnborough, Eng.: Royal Aircraft Establishment, 1983).

39. D.C. King-Hele et al., *The RAE Table of Earth Satellites, 1983–85* (Farnborough, Eng.: Royal Aircraft Establishment, 1986), pp. 740, 790.

40. Private information.

41. Jeffrey Richelson, *United States Strategic Reconnaissance: Photographic/Imaging Satellites* (Los Angeles: UCLA ACIS Working Paper No. 38, 1983), Appendix, Table 11.

42. Jeffrey Richelson, "The Satellite Data System," *Journal of the British Interplanetary Society* 37, 5 (1984): 226–28; Burrows, op. cit., Chap. 9; Seymour Hersh, *"The Target Is Destroyed": What Really Happened to Flight 007 and What America Knew About It* (New York: Random House, 1986), p. 4.

43. Jeffrey Richelson, "The Keyhole Satellite Program," *Journal of Strategic Studies* 7, 2 (1984): 121–54.

44. Lindsey, op. cit., p. 58.

45. Klass, "U.S. Monitoring Capability Impaired."

46. Richard Burt, "U.S. Plans New Way to Check Soviet Missile Tests," *The New York Times* (June 29, 1979), p. A3.

47. Hussain, op. cit., p. 42.

48. "Navy Ocean Surveillance Satellite Depicted," *Aviation Week and Space Technology* (May 24, 1976), p. 22.

49. "Expanded Ocean Surveillance Effort Set," *Aviation Week and Space Technology* (June 10, 1978). pp. 22–23.

50. Ibid.

51. Ibid.

52. William Arkin and Richard Fieldhouse, *Nuclear Battlefields: Global Links in the Arms Race* (Cambridge, Mass.: Ballinger, 1985), p. 192.

53. Jeffrey T. Richelson, *The U.S. Intelligence Community* (Cambridge, Mass.: Ballinger, 1985), pp. 142–43.

54. Burrows, op. cit., Chap. 11.

55. Interview.

56. Interview.

57. King-Hele et al., *The RAE Table of Earth Satellites, 1957–1980*, p. 474.

58. Curtis L. Peebles, "Satellite Photograph Interpretation," *Spaceflight* (October 1982), pp. 161–63.

59. John Pike, "Reagan Prepares for War in Outer Space," *CounterSpy* 7, 1 (September–November 1982): 17–22; James Bamford, "America's Supersecret Eyes in Space," *The New York Times Magazine* (January 13, 1985), pp. 39ff.

60. Correspondence from Anthony Kenden (May 23, 1985).

61. Bamford, op. cit.

62. George Lardner, Jr., "Satellite Unchanged from Manual Bought by Soviets, U.S. Officials Say," *Washington Post* (October 10, 1985), p. A20.

63. Jack Anderson and Dale Van Atta, "The Games Soviets Play," *Washington Post* (April 21, 1985), p. K7.

64. "Inside the Rescue Mission," *Newsweek* (July 12, 1982), p. 19.

65. "Soviet Strategic Bomber Photographed at Ramenskoye," *Aviation Week and Space Technology* (December 14, 1981), p. 17.

66. Max White, "U.S. Satellite Reconnaissance During the Falklands Conflict," Earth Satellite Research Unit, Department of Mathematics, University of Aston.

67. "Satellite Pictures Show Soviet CVN Towering Above Nikolaiev Shipyard," *Jane's Defence Weekly* (August 11, 1984), pp. 171–73.

68. Lardner, op. cit.

69. "Satellite Pictures Show Soviet CVN Towering Above Nickolaiev Shipyard."

70. Michael R. Gordon, "U.S. Says Soviet Complies on Some Arms Issues," *The New York Times* (November 24, 1985), p. 18.

71. Private information.

72. "How Satellites May Help Sell SALT," *U.S. News and World Report* (May 21, 1978), pp. 25–26; "Missile Disguise," *Aviation Week and Space Technology* (September 29, 1980), p. 17.

73. "Soviets Build Directed Energy Weapon," *Aviation Week and Space Technology* (July 28, 1980), pp. 47–50.

74. "Industry Observer," *Aviation Week and Space Technology* (September 9, 1985), p. 150; "Titan 34D Booster Failed Following Premature Shutdown of Aerojet Engine," *Aviation Week and Space Technology* (November 18, 1985), p. 26.

75. Jack Cushman, "Space Shuttle Explosion Throws Military Programs into Disarray," *Defense Week* (February 3, 1986), pp. 2–4.

76. William J. Broad, "Titan Loss May Force Early Use of Shuttle," *The New York Times* (April 22, 1986), pp. C1, C3; William J. Broad, "Titan Rocket Explodes over California Base," *The New York Times* (April 19, 1986), pp. 1, 7; Walter Andrews, "Reconnaissance Gap Feared in Wake of Titan Explosion," *Washington Times* (April 21, 1986), p. 2A.

77. "Titan Failure: 'We Don't Think There's a Crisis,'" *Aerospace Daily* (April 29, 1986), p. 161; private information.

78. "KH-12 Reconnaissance Satellite Planned for Kennedy Launch," *Aviation Week and Space Technology* (June 23, 1986), p. 17.

79. Jack Anderson, "Hiding Behind the Flag?," *Washington Post* (February 10, 1985), p. D8; John Noble Wilford, "Shuttle Launched on Secret Mission," *The New York Times* (January 25, 1985), pp. A1–A2.

80. Burt, op. cit.

81. Klass, "U.S. Monitoring Capability Impaired."

82. Craig Covault, "Defense Managers Cancel Shuttle Mission 10,"

Aviation Week and Space Technology (June 13, 1983), pp. 16–18; Thomas O'Toole, "Oil Leak Blamed for Flawed Satellite," *Washington Post* (July 13, 1983), p. A2.

83. James Gerstenzang, "Shuttle Lifts Off with Spy Cargo," *Los Angeles Times* (January 25, 1985), pp. 1, 11.

84. William J. Broad, "Experts Say Satellite Can Detect Soviet War Steps," *The New York Times* (January 25, 1985), p. A12.

85. Walter Andrews, "Defense Aide Confirms U.S. Satellites Jammed," *Washington Times* (June 21, 1984), p. 1.

86. Walter Pincus and Mary Thornton, "U.S. to Orbit 'SIGINT' Craft from Shuttle," *Washington Post* (December 19, 1984), pp. A1, A8, A9.

87. "KH-11 Overruns Said to Slow Development of Follow-On Spacecraft," *Aerospace Daily* (January 23, 1984), pp. 16–17.

88. Deborah G. Meyer, "DOD Likely to Spend $250 Billion on C^{3}I Through 1990," *Armed Forces Journal International* (February 1985), pp. 72–84; Pat Ohlendorf, "The New Breed of High-Tech Peacekeeper," *MacLean's* (January 23, 1984), pp. 52–53.

89. Walter Pincus, "Hill Conferees Propose Test of Space Arms," *Washington Post* (July 11, 1984), pp. A1–A3.

90. "New Payload Could Boost Shuttle Cost," *Aviation Week and Space Technology* (August 14, 1978), pp. 16–17.

91. Andrew Cockburn, *The Threat: Inside the Soviet Military Machine* (New York: Random House, 1983), p. 19.

92. Paul E. Sherr, Arnold H. Glasser, James C. Barnes, and James H Willand, *Worldwide Cloud Cover Distributions for Use in Computer Simulations* (Concord, Mass.: Allied Research Associates, 1968), p. 5.

93. Philip Klass, "U.S. Scrutinizing New Soviet Radar," *Aviation Week and Space Technology* (August 22, 1983), pp. 19–20.

94. "Space Reconnaissance Dwindles"; "Navy Will Develop All-Weather Ocean Monitor Satellite," *Aviation Week and Space Technology* (August 28, 1978), p. 50; Craig Covault, "USAF, NASA Discuss Shuttle Use for Satellite Maintenance," *Aviation Week and Space Technology* (December 17, 1984), pp. 14–16.

95. "Washington Roundup," *Aviation Week and Space Technology* (June 4,

1979), p. 11; Robert C. Toth, "Anaheim Firm May Have Sought Spy Satellite Data," *Los Angeles Times* (October 10, 1982), pp. 1, 32.

96. Wayne Biddle, "U.S Planning Satellite to Spy on Laser Weapons in Soviet," *The New York Times* (July 11, 1984), p. A13; Pincus, op. cit.

Chapter X:
THE SOVIET TARGET ABROAD

1. Ernest Volkman, *Warriors of the Night: Spies, Soldiers and American Intelligence* (New York: William Morrow, 1985), pp. 36–37.

2. Ibid., p. 37.

3. Ibid., p. 38.

4. James M. Erdmann, "The Wringer in Postwar Germany: Its Impact on United States-German Relations and Defense Policies," in Clifford L. Egan and Alexander Knott (eds.), *Essay in Twentieth-Century American Diplomatic History Dedicated to Professor Daniel M. Smith* (Lanham Md.: University Press of America, 1982), pp. 159–91.

5. Ibid.

6. Ibid.

7. Ibid.

8. Ibid.

9. Ibid.

10. Ibid.

11. Ibid.

12. Ibid.; Major General C. P. Cabell, Memorandum to Assistant for Production, Subject: Expansion of WRINGER Intelligence Collection Activities, November 1, 1950, RG 341, Entry 214, File 2-16800 to 2-16899, Modern Military Branch (MMB), National Archives (NA).

13. "Requirements for Expansion of the Air Intelligence Effort to Accelerate and Improve the Air Defense of the United States and Alaska," October 29, 1949, RG 341, Entry 214, File 2-9800 to 2-9899, MMB, NA.

14. Major General George C. McDonald, "Allocation of Funds for the Establishment of an Air Research Unit in the Library of Congress," February 24, 1948, RG 341, Entry 214, File 2-1300 to 2-1399, MMB, NA.

15. Ibid.

16. Alaskan Air Command, *History of the Alaskan Air Command, July–December 1953* (Elmendorf AFB, Alaska: AAC, 1954), p. 234.

17. "Operation Beachcomber," *AAC Intelligence Review* 53, 6 (December 1953): 20–23.

18. Ibid.

19. Ibid.

20. Ibid.

21. Ibid.

22. Ibid.

23. "Operation Beachcomber II," *AAC Intelligence Review* 55, 1 (February 1955): 23–28.

24. Ibid.

25. Ibid.

26. "Operation Beachcomber III," *AAC Intelligence Review* 55, 5 (October 1955): 24–29.

27. Ibid.

28. Robert M. Yates, *History of the 5004th Air Intelligence Squadron, 1 July–31 December 1956* (Elmendorf AFB, Alas.: 5004th AISS, AAC, April 1957), p. 36.

29. Ibid., p. 36.

30. 5004th Air Intelligence Squadron, *Operation Beachcomber V, Quarterly Unit Historical Data Report, 1 July 1957 to 1 April 1958* (Elmendorf AFB, Alas.: AFHRC, 1958), p. 3.

31. Ibid.

32. Senate Select Committee to Study Governmental Operations with Respect to Intelligence Activities (hereinafter Senate Select Committee), *Supplementary Detailed Staff Reports on Intelligence Activities and the Rights of Americans*, Book III (Washington, D.C.: U.S. Government Printing Office, 1976), p. 567.

33. Ibid., p. 570.

34. Ibid., pp. 569–70.

35. Quoted in David Martin, *Wilderness of Mirrors* (New York: Harper & Row, 1979), p. 69.

36. Ibid.

37. Senate Select Committee, *Supplementary Detailed Staff Reports on Intelligence Activities and the Rights of Americans*, Book III, p. 570.

38. Ibid., pp. 571–72.

39. Ibid., p. 572.

40. Ibid., p. 574.

41. Ibid., pp. 574–75.

42. Ibid., p. 573.

43. Ibid., pp. 573–74.

44. Ibid., p. 577.

45. Ibid., p. 603.

46. Harry Rositzke, *The CIA's Secret Operations* (New York: Reader's Digest Press, 1977), p. 82.

47. William Hood, *Mole* (New York: W. W. Norton, 1982), p. 28.

48. David Atlee Phillips, *The Night Watch* (New York: Ballantine, 1982), p. 146.

49. Nigel West, *The Circus: MI 5 Operations, 1945–1972* (Briarcliff Manor, N.Y.: Stein and Day, 1983), p. 64; Hood, op. cit., pp. 26, 104.

50. Hood, op. cit., pp. 63–64, 74.

51. Ibid., p. 76.

52. Ibid., p. 77.

53. Ibid., p. 106.

54. Ibid., p. 127.

55. Ibid., pp. 170, 173.

56. Ibid., p. 210.

57. West, loc. cit.

58. Hood, op. cit., p. 251.

59. Martin, op. cit., p. 94.

60. Quoted in ibid., pp. 102–3.

61. Jack Anderson and Dale van Atta, "Soviets Sprinkled 'Spy Dust' for Years," *Washington Post* (September 16, 1985), p. B13.

62. John Prados, *The Soviet Estimate: U.S. Intelligence Analysis and Russian Military Strength* (New York: Dial, 1982), p. 148; Rositzke, op. cit., pp. 68–69.

63. Philip Agee, *Inside the Company: A CIA Diary* (New York: Stonehill, 1975), p. 528.

64. Ibid.

65. Ibid., p. 529

66. Arkady N. Shevchenko, *Breaking with Moscow* (New York: Alfred A. Knopf, 1985), p. 10.

67. Ibid.; Edward Jay Epstein, "The Spy Who Came in to Be Sold," *The New Republic* (July 15 and 22, 1983), pp. 35–42; David Remnick, "Shevchenko: The Saga Behind the Best Seller," *Washington Post* (June 6, 1985), pp. B1, B6.

68. Shevchenko, op. cit., p. 25.

69. Ibid., p. 34.

70. Ibid.

71. Ibid., pp. 268–70.

72. Ibid., p. 313.

73. John Barron, *KGB Today: The Hidden Hand* (New York: Reader's Digest Press, 1983), pp. 233–34; "Statement of Facts, United States of America *v.* David Henry Barnett," K80-0390, U.S. District Court, Maryland, 1980.

74. John Barron, *MiG Pilot* (New York: Avon, 1981), pp. 169–86.

75. Ibid.

76. Foreign Technology Division, *FTD 1917–1967* (Dayton, Ohio: FTD, 1967), p. 24.

77. Clyde W. Burleson, *The Jennifer Project* (Englewood Cliffs, N.J.: Prentice-Hall, 1977), p. 47.

78. Roy Varner and Wayne Collier, *A Matter of Risk* (New York: Random House, 1977), p. 26.

79. "The Great Submarine Snatch," *Time* (March 31, 1975), pp. 20–27; Burleson, op. cit., p. 18.

80. Ibid.

81. Burleson, op. cit., p. 33.

82. "The Great Submarine Snatch."

83. Ibid.

84. Ibid.

85. Ibid.

86. Varner and Collier, op. cit., p. 39.

87. "The Great Submarine Snatch."

88. Seymour Hersh, "Human Error Is Cited in '74 Glomar Failure," *The New York Times* (December 9, 1976), pp. 1, 55.

89. "The Great Submarine Snatch."

90. Ibid.

91. Ibid.

92. Ibid.

93. Varner and Collier, op. cit., p. 134.

94. "The Great Submarine Snatch."

95. Hersh, op. cit.

96. Burleson, op. cit., p. 112.

97. Ibid., p. 133.

98. See "The Great Submarine Snatch"; Burleson, op. cit., pp. 21, 28, 107–9.

99. Hersh, op. cit.

100. Ibid.

Chapter XI:
LEGACY

1. Scott Breckinridge, *The CIA and the U.S. Intelligence System* (Boulder, Colo.: Westview, 1986), p. 56.

2. See Jeffrey T. Richelson and Desmond Ball, *The Ties That Bind: Intelligence Cooperation Between the UKUSA Countries* (London: George Allen & Unwin, 1985), pp. 174–89.

3. Richard Burt, "Soviet Reported to Add to Load Missile Can Fire," *The New York Times* (March 14, 1979), pp. A1, A7.

4. Michael R. Gordon, "U.S. Reports Failure in Recent Soviet Test of Big New Missile," *The New York Times* (April 15, 1986), pp. A1, A8.

5. Michael R. Gordon, "Soviet Reported Acting to Begin New Atom Tests," *The New York Times* (March 18, 1986), pp. A1, A4.

6. See Jeffrey Richelson, "Old Surveillance, New Interpretations," *Bulletin of the Atomic Scientists* (February 1986): 18–23.

7. See Desmond Ball, "Targeting for Strategic Deterrence," *Adelphi Papers* 185 (1983).

8. Ibid., p. 31.

9. For example, see the CIA studies in Joint Economic Committee, *U.S.S.R.: Measures of Economic Growth and Development, 1950–1980* (Washington, D.C.: U.S. Government Printing Office, 1982); CIA and DIA, *The Soviet Economy Under a New Leader* (1986).

10. Telephone interview.

11. Ralph S. Clem, "Ethnicity and Its Implications," *Bulletin of the Atomic Scientists* 38, 6 (June 1982): 53–58.

12. See S. Enders Wimbush, *The Ethnic Factor in the Soviet Armed Forces* (Santa Monica, Calif.: The RAND Corporation, 1982).

13. Jeremy Azrael, *Emergent Nationality Problems in the U.S.S.R.* (Santa Monica, Calif.: The RAND Corporation, 1977), p. 31.

BIBLIOGRAPHY

DOCUMENT COLLECTIONS

Air Force Security Service/Electronic Security Documents released under the Freedom of Information Act.

Alaskan Air Command Documents released under the Freedom of Information Act.

Declassified Documents Reference System (DDRS).

Dwight David Eisenhower Library (DDEL).

National Security Agency Documents released under the Freedom of Information Act.

National Security Council Documents released under the Freedom of Information Act.

91st Strategic Reconnaissance Squadron Photo (M) Documents available at the Air Force Office of History, Bolling AFB, Washington, D.C.

President's Secretaries Files, Harry S. Truman Library.

Record Group 341 (Air Force Intelligence), Entries 214 and 267, Modern Military Branch, National Archives.

Record Group 457 (National Security Agency), Modern Military Branch, National Archives.

Secretary of the Air Force Documents released under the Freedom of Information Act.

Strategic Air Command declassified documents released under the Freedom of Information Act.

GOVERNMENT DOCUMENTS

Berger, Carl. *The Air Force in Space Fiscal Year 1961.* Washington, D.C.: USAF Historical Division Liaison Office, 1966.

Bowen, Lee. *The Threshold of Space: The Air Force in the National Space Program, 1945–1959.* Washington, D.C.: USAF Historical Division Liaison Office, September 1960.

Central Intelligence Agency. "Threats to the Security of the United States," ORE 60-48, September 28, 1948, HSTL, PSF, Box 266.

Condit, Kenneth W. *The History of the Joint Chiefs of Staff: The Joint Chiefs of Staff and National Policy, Volume II, 1947–1949.* Washington, D.C.: Historical Division, Joint Secretariat, JCS, 1964.

del Papa, Dr. E. Michael. *Meeting the Challenge: ESD and the Cobra Dane Construction Effort on Shemya Island.* Bedford, Mass.: Electronic Systems Division, Air Force Systems Command, 1979.

Department of Defense. *Soviet Military Power 1985.* Washington, D.C.: DOD, 1985.

Foreign Technology Division. *FTD 1917–1967.* Dayton, Ohio: FTD, 1967.

Glasstone, Samuel, and Dolan, Philip J. *The Effects of Nuclear Weapons,* 3rd ed. Washington, D.C.: DOD/DOE, 1977, pp. 45–47.

Jernigan, Roger A. *Air Force Satellite Control Facility: Historical Brief and Chronology, 1954–1981.* Sunnyvale, Calif.: AFSCF History Office, 1982.

Office of the Chief of Naval Operations. *Navy Special Warfare Master Plan (NSWMP).* Washington, D.C.: OCNO, 1984.

"SAMOS II Fact Sheet." Washington, D.C.: Department of Defense, 1961.

6th Strategic Wing. *R 55-2 Operations: Aircrew and Staff Procedures*, September 30, 1983. Department of the Air Force Headquarters.

U.K. Royal Aircraft Establishment. *RAE Table of Earth Satellites*, various issues.

U.S. Congress, House Appropriations Committee. *Department of Defense Appropriations*, various years.

—————. *Military Construction Appropriations*, various years.

U.S. Congress, House Armed Services Committee. *Inquiry into the U.S.S. Pueblo and EC-121 Plane Incidents*. Washington, D.C.: U.S. Government Printing Office, 1969.

U.S. Congress, House Committee on Government Operations. *Air Force Ballistic Missile Management (Formation of Aerospace Corporation)*. Washington, D.C.: U.S. Government Printing Office, 1961.

U.S. Congress, House Committee on International Relations. *United States Military Installations and Objectives in the Mediterranean*. Washington, D.C.: U.S. Government Printing Office, 1977.

U.S. Congress, House Committee on Science and Astronautics. *Science, Astronautics and Defense*. Washington, D.C.: U.S. Government Printing Office, 1961.

—————. *Defense Space Interests*. Washington, D.C.: U.S. Government Printing Office, 1961.

U.S. Congress, Senate Appropriations Committee. *Department of Defense Appropriations*, various years.

U.S. Congress, Senate Armed Services Committee. *Inquiry into Satellite and Missile Programs, Part I*. Washington, D.C.: U.S. Government Printing Office, 1958.

U.S. Congress, Senate Committee on Aeronautical and Space Sciences, *Missile, Space and Other Defense Matters*. Washington, D.C.: U.S. Government Printing Office, 1960.

U.S. Congress, Senate Foreign Relations Committee. *Fiscal Year 1980 International Security Assistance Authorization*. Washington, D.C.: U.S. Government Printing Office, 1979.

—————. *Executive Sessions of the Senate Foreign Relations Committee (Historical Series), Vol. XII, Eighty-sixth Congress, Second Session, 1960*. Washington, D.C.: U.S. Government Printing Office, 1982.

U.S. Congress, Senate Select Committee to Study Governmental Operations with Respect to Intelligence Activities. *Supplementary Detailed Staff Reports on Intelligence Activities and the Rights of Americans*, Book III. Washington, D.C.: U.S. Government Printing Office, 1976.

——. *Supplementary Detailed Staff Reports*, Book IV. Washington, D.C.: U.S. Government Printing Office, 1976.

U.S. Joint Chiefs of Staff. *JCS 1982 Posture Statement*. Washington, D.C.: U.S. Government Printing Office, 1981.

Workshop on Seismological Verification of a Comprehensive Test Ban. Oslo: Norwegian Ministry of Foreign Affairs, 1985.

BOOKS AND REPORTS

Adomeit, Hannes. *Soviet Risk-Taking and Crisis Behavior: A Theoretical and Empirical Analysis*. Boston: George Allen & Unwin, 1982.

Agee, Philip. *Inside the Company: A CIA Diary*. New York: Stonehill, 1975.

Aldridge, Robert. *First Strike: The Pentagon's Strategy for Nuclear War*. Boston: South End Press, 1983.

Arkin, William, and Fieldhouse, Richard. *Nuclear Battlefields: Global Links in the Arms Race*. Cambridge, Mass: Ballinger, 1985.

Armbrister, Trevor. *A Matter of Accountability: The True Story of the Pueblo Affair*. New York: Coward-McCann, 1970.

Augenstein, Bruno W. *Evolution of the U.S. Military Space Program, 1945–1960: Some Key Events in Study, Planning and Program Development*. Santa Monica, Calif: RAND, 1982.

Baker, David. *The Shape of Wars to Come*. Briarcliff Manor, N.Y.: Stein and Day, 1982.

Ball, Desmond. *A Suitable Piece of Real Estate: American Installations in Australia*. Sydney: Hale & Iremonger, 1980.

Bamford, James.*The Puzzle Palace: A Report on NSA, America's Most Secret Agency*. Boston: Houghton Mifflin, 1982.

Barron, John. *MiG Pilot: The Final Escape of Lt. Belenko*. New York: Avon, 1980.

————. *KGB Today: The Hidden Hand*. New York: Reader's Digest Press, 1983.

Beitzell, Robert. *The Uneasy Alliance: America, Britain and Russia, 1941–1943*. New York: Alfred A. Knopf, 1972.

Berman, Robert P., and Baker, John C. *Soviet Strategic Forces: Requirements and Responses*. Washington, D.C.: Brookings Institution, 1982.

Beschloss, Michael R. *Mayday: Eisenhower, Khrushchev and the U-2 Affair*. New York: Harper & Row, 1986.

Bracken, Paul. *The Command and Control of Nuclear Forces*. New Haven, Conn.: Yale University Press, 1983.

Bradley, Omar N., and Blair, Clay. *A General's Life*. New York: Simon & Schuster, 1983.

Breckinridge, Scott. *The CIA and the U.S. Intelligence System*. Boulder, Colo.: Westview, 1986.

Brown, Anthony Cave. *The Last Hero: Wild Bill Donovan*. New York: Times Books, 1982.

Burleson, Clyde W. *The Jennifer Project*. Englewood Cliffs, N.J.: Prentice-Hall, 1977.

Burns, Thomas S. *The Secret War for the Ocean Depths: Soviet-American Rivalry for Mastery of the Seas*. New York: Rawson, 1978.

Burrows, William E. *Deep Black: Space Espionage and National Security*. New York: Random House, forthcoming.

Campbell, Duncan. *The Unsinkable Aircraft Carrier*. London: Michael Joseph, 1984.

Carroll, John M. *Secrets of Electronic Espionage*. New York: E. P. Dutton, 1966.

Carter, Jimmy. *Keeping Faith: Memoirs of a President*. London: Collins, 1982.

Cockburn, Andrew. *The Threat: Inside the Soviet Military Machine.* New York: Random House, 1983.

Crouch, Tom D. *The Eagle Aloft: Two Centuries of the Balloon in America.* Washington, D.C.: Smithsonian Institution Press, 1983.

Davis, Lynn Etheridge. *The Cold War Begins.* Princeton, N.J.: Princeton University Press, 1974.

de Arcangelis, Mario. *Electronic Warfare: From the Battle of Tsushima to the Falklands.* Dorset, Eng.: Bradford Press, 1985.

De Santis, Hugh. *The Diplomacy of Silence: The American Foreign Service, the Soviet Union and the Cold War, 1933–1947.* Chicago: University of Chicago Press, 1980.

de Silva, Peer. *Sub Rosa: The CIA and the Uses of Intelligence.* New York: Times Books, 1978.

Donovan, Robert J. *Tumultuous Years: The Presidency of Harry S. Truman, 1949–1953.* New York: W. W. Norton, 1982.

Dorwart, Jeffrey M. *Conflict of Duty: The U.S. Navy's Intelligence Dilemma.* Annapolis, Md.: Naval Institute Press, 1983.

Eisenhower, Dwight D. *Mandate for Change, 1953–1956.* Garden City, N.Y.: Doubleday, 1963.

———. *Waging Peace, 1956–1961.* Garden City, N.Y.: Doubleday, 1965.

Etzold, Thomas, and Gaddis, John Lewis (ed.). *Containment: Documents on American Policy and Strategy, 1945–1950.* New York: Columbia University Press, 1978.

Eubank, Keith. *Summit at Teheran: The Untold Story.* New York: William Morrow, 1985.

Fitts, Richard (ed.). *The Strategy of Electromagnetic Conflict.* Los Altos, Calif.: Peninsula Press, 1980.

Ford, Daniel. *The Button: The Pentagon's Strategic Command and Control System.* New York: Simon & Schuster, 1985.

Freedman, Lawrence. *U.S. Intelligence and the Soviet Strategic Threat.* Boulder, Colo.: Westview, 1977.

Gaddis, John Lewis. *The United States and the Origins of the Cold War.* New York: Columbia University Press, 1972.

Gardner, Lloyd. *Safe for Democracy: Anglo-American Response to Revolution, 1913–1923.* New York: Oxford University Press, 1984.

Giffen, Robert B. *U.S. Space System Survivability: Strategic Alternatives for the 1990s.* Washington, D.C.: National Defense University, 1982.

Herken, Gregg. *The Winning Weapon: The Atomic Bomb in the Cold War, 1945–1950.* New York: Vintage, 1982.

Herring, George C., Jr. *Aid to Russia, 1941–1946: Strategy, Diplomacy, the Origins of the Cold War.* New York: Columbia University Press, 1973.

Hersch, Seymour M. *"The Target Is Destroyed": What Really Happened to Flight 007 and What America Knew About It.* New York: Random House 1986.

Hewlett, Richard G., and Duncan, Francis. Atomic Shield, 1947–1952 (Volume II of *A History of the Atomic Energy Commission*). University Park Pa.: Pennsylvania State University Press, 1969.

Hood, William. *Mole.* New York: W. W. Norton, 1982.

Hurt, Henry. *Shadrin: The Spy Who Never Came Back.* New York: McGraw-Hill/Reader's Digest Press, 1981.

Jane's Fighting Ships, 1983–1984. London: Jane's Publishing Co., 1983.

Jeffreys-Jones, Rhodri. *American Espionage: From Secret Service to CIA.* New York: The Free Press, 1977.

Johnson, Kelly, with Smith, Maggie. *More Than My Share of It All.* Washington, D.C.: Smithsonian Institution Press, 1985.

Karas, Thomas. *The New High Ground: Strategies and Weapons of Space-Age War.* New York: Simon & Schuster, 1983.

Kennan, George F. *Memoirs, 1925–1950.* Boston: Little, Brown, 1967.

———. *The Decision to Intervene.* New York: W. W. Norton, 1984.

Kennedy, Colonel William V. *Intelligence Warfare.* New York: Crescent, 1983.

Krushchev, Nikita. *Krushchev Remembers: The Last Testament.* New York: Bantam, 1976.

King-Hele, D. C., et al. *The RAE Table of Earth Satellites, 1957–1980.* Farnborough, Eng.: Royal Aircraft Establishment, 1981.

Kistiakowsky, George. *A Scientist in the White House: The Private Diary of President Eisenhower's Special Assistant for Science and Technology*, Cambridge, Mass.: Harvard University Press, 1976.

Klass, Philip. *Secret Sentries in Space*. New York: Random House, 1971.

Krock, Arthur. *Memoirs: Sixty Years on the Firing Line*. New York: Funk & Wagnalls, 1968.

Kuniholm, Bruce Robellet. *The Origins of the Cold War in the Near East: Great Power Conflict and Diplomacy in Iran, Turkey and Greece*. Princeton, N.J.: Princeton University Press, 1980.

La Feber, Walter. *America, Russia and the Cold War, 1945–1975*, 3rd ed. New York: John Wiley, 1976.

Lewis, Ronald. *The American Magic: Codes, Ciphers and the Defeat of Japan*. New York: Farrar, Straus & Giroux, 1982.

Lindsey, Robert. *The Falcon and the Snowman: A True Story of Friendship and Espionage*. New York: Simon & Schuster, 1979.

Martin, David. *Wilderness of Mirrors*. New York: Harper & Row, 1979.

Mastny, Vojtech. *Russia's Road to the Cold War: Diplomacy, Warfare and the Politics of Communism, 1941–1945*. New York: Columbia University Press, 1979.

Miller, David. *An Illustrated Guide to Modern Sub Hunters*. New York: Arco, 1984.

Miller, Jay. *The Lockheed A-12/YF-12/SR-71 Story*. Austin, Tex.: Aerofax, 1983.

———. *Lockheed U-2*. Austin, Tex.: Aerofax, 1983.

Mosley, Leonard. *Dulles: A Biography of Eleanor, Allen and John Foster and Their Family Network*. New York: Dial, 1978.

P-3C Orion Update Weapon System. Burbank, Calif.: Lockheed, n.d.

Paterson, Thomas G. *Soviet-American Confrontation: Postwar Reconstruction and the Origins of the Cold War* Baltimore: Johns Hopkins University Press, 1973.

Penkovskiy, Oleg. *The Penkovskiy Papers*. Garden City, N.Y.: Doubleday, 1965.

Phillips, David Atlee. *The Night Watch*. New York: Ballantine, 1982.

Pincher, Chapman. *Their Trade Is Treachery*. London: Sedgwick and Jackson, 1981.

Powers, Francis Gary. *Operation Overflight*. New York: Holt, Rinehart & Winston, 1970.

Powers, Thomas. *The Man Who Kept the Secrets: Richard Helms and the CIA*. New York: Alfred A. Knopf, 1979.

Prados, John. *The Soviet Estimate: U.S. Intelligence Analysis and Russian Military Strength*. Garden City, N.Y.: Doubleday/Dial, 1982.

Prange, Gordon W. *Miracle at Midway*. New York: McGraw-Hill, 1982.

Price, Alfred. *The History of U.S. Electronic Warfare, Volume I: The Years of Innovation—Beginnings to 1946*. Washington, D.C.: Association of Old Crows, 1984.

Ranelagh, John. *The Agency: The Rise and Decline of the CIA*. New York: Simon & Schuster, 1986.

Richelson, Jeffrey T. *United States Strategic Reconnaissance: Photographic/Imaging Satellites*. Los Angeles: UCLA Center for International & Strategic Affairs, 1983.

———. *The U.S. Intelligence Community*. Cambridge, Mass.: Ballinger, 1985.

———. and Desmond Ball. *The Ties That Bind: Intelligence Cooperation Between the UKUSA Countries*. London: George Allen & Unwin, 1985.

Rositzke, Harry. *The CIA's Secret Operations: Espionage, Counterespionage and Covert Action*. New York: Reader's Digest Press, 1977.

Rostow, Walt W. *Open Skies: Eisenhower's Proposal of July 21, 1955*. Austin, Tex.: University of Texas Press, 1982.

Sainsbury, Keith. *The Turning Point: Roosevelt, Stalin, Churchill and Chiang Kai-shek, 1943: The Moscow, Cairo and Teheran Conferences*. New York: Oxford University Press, 1985.

Sherr, Paul E.; Glasser, Arnold H.; Barnes, James C.; and Willand, James H. *Worldwide Cloud Cover Distributions for Use in Computer Simulations*. Concord, Mass.: Allied Research Associates, 1968.

Shevchenko, Arkady N. *Breaking with Moscow*. New York: Alfred A. Knopf, 1985.

Smith, Bradley F. *The Shadow Warriors: O.S.S. and the Origins of the CIA*. New York: Basic Books, 1983.

Spaven, Malcolm. *Fortress Scotland: A Guide to the Military Presence* London: Pluto Press, 1983.

Stares, Paul. *The Militarization of Space: U.S. Policy, 1945–1984*. Ithaca, N.Y.: Cornell University Press, 1985.

Steinberg, Gerald M. *Satellite Reconnaissance: The Role of Informal Bargaining*. New York: Praeger, 1983.

Strauss, Lewis L. *Men and Decisions*. Garden City, N.Y.: Doubleday, 1962.

Sullivan, William. *Mission to Iran*. New York: W. W. Norton, 1981.

Tolley, Kemp. *Caviar and Commissars: The Experiences of a U.S. Naval Officer in Stalin's Russia*. Annapolis, Md.: U.S. Naval Institute Press, 1983.

Turner, Stansfield. *Secrecy and Democracy: The CIA in Transition*. Boston: Houghton Mifflin, 1985.

Vance, Cyrus. *Hard Choices: Critical Years in America's Foreign Policy*. New York: Simon & Schuster, 1983.

Van der Art, Dick. *Aerial Espionage: Secret Intelligence Flights by East and West*. New York: Arco/Prentice-Hall Press, 1986.

Varner, Roy, and Collier, Wayne. *A Matter of Risk*. New York: Random House, 1977.

Volkman, Ernest. *Warriors of the Night: Spies, Soldiers and American Intelligence*. New York: William Morrow, 1985.

Waters, Andrew W. *All the U.S. Air Force Airplanes, 1907–1983*. New York: Hippocrene, 1983.

Werth, Alexander. *Russia at War, 1941–1945*. New York: E. P. Dutton, 1964.

West, Nigel. *The Circus: MI5, 1945–1972*. Briarcliff Manor, N.Y.: Stein and Day, 1983.

Wilkes, Owen, and Gleditsch, Nils Petter. *Intelligence Installations in Norway: Their Number, Location, Function and Legality*. Oslo: PRIO, 1979.

Wittner, Lawrence S. *American Intervention in Greece, 1943–1949*. New York: Columbia University Press, 1982.

Wynne, Greville. *The Man from Moscow*. London: Hutchinson, 1967.

———. *The Man from Odessa: The Secret Career of a British Agent*. London: Granada, 1983.

Yenne, Bill. *SAC: A Primer of Modern Strategic Airpower*. Novato, Calif.: Presidio Press, 1985.

Yergin, Daniel. *Shattered Peace: The Origins of the Cold War and the National Security State*. Boston: Houghton Mifflin, 1978.

York, Herbert. *The Advisors: Oppenheimer, Teller and the Superbomb*. San Francisco: W. H. Freeman, 1976.

ARTICLES

"A New Lesson in the Limits of Power," *Time* (April 25, 1969), pp. 15–17.

"An Exercise in Restraint," *Newsweek* (April 28, 1969) pp. 27–31.

Anderson, Jack. "CIA Eavesdrops on Kremlin Chiefs," *Washington Post* (September 16, 1971), p. F7.

———. "Mystery Kissinger-Dobrynin Meeting," *Washington Post* (December 16, 1980), p. B15.

———. "Hiding Behind the Flag?," *Washington Post* (February 10, 1985), p. D8.

———. and Van Atta, Dale. "The Games Soviets Play," *Washington Post* (April 21, 1985), p. K7.

———. "Soviets Sprinkled 'Spy Dust' for Years," *Washington Post* (September 16, 1985), p. B13.

Andrews, Walter. "Defense Aides Confirm U.S. Satellites Jammed," *Washington Times* (June 21, 1984), p. 1.

————. "Reconnaissance Gap Feared in Wake of Titan Explosion," *Washington Times* (April 21, 1986), p. 2A.

Apple, R. W., Jr., "Norwegians, Ardent Neutralists, Also Want Their Defense Strong," *New York Times* (August 5, 1978), p. 2.

Arkin, William. "Current Intelligence Collection: Its Effect on Crisis Management and Policy Formation," presented at International Studies Association (March 5–9, 1985), Washington, D. C.

"Atlantic Islands: NATO Seeks Wider Facilities," *International Herald Tribune* (June 1981), p. 7S.

Ball, Desmond. "Allied Intelligence Cooperation Involving Australia During World War II," *Australian Outlook* 32, 4 (1978): 299–309.

————. "The U.S. Air Force Satellite Communications (AFSATCOM) System: The Australian Connection." Canberra: Strategic and Defence Studies Centre, March 1982.

————. "The Rhyolite Program." Canberra: Australian National University, 1982.

Bamford, James. "America's Supersecret Eyes in Space," *The New York Times Magazine* (January 13, 1985), pp. 39ff.

Barnes, Trevor. "The Secret Cold War: The C.I.A. and American Foreign Policy in Europe, 1946–1956, Part II," *The Historical Journal* 25, 3 (1982): 649–70.

Bates, Colonel Asa. "National Technical Means of Verification," *Royal United Services Institute Journal* 123, 2 (June 1978): 64–73.

Beck, Melinda C., with Martin, David C. "The War Beneath the Seas," *Newsweek* (February 8, 1982), pp. 37–38.

Beech, Keyes. "Secret U.S. Base Keeps Eye on Far East," *Los Angeles Times* (January 20, 1980), p. 17.

Bern, Lennart. "Soviet and Warsaw Pact Air Incidents," *Jane's Defence Weekly* (January 12, 1985), p. 58.

Biddle, Wayne. "U.S. Planning Satellite to Spy on Laser Weapons in Soviet," *The New York Times* (July 11, 1984), p. A13.

"Big Bird: America's Spy in Space," *Flight International* (January 27, 1977).

Binder, David. "Radar Detector Aboard SR-71 Alerted Pilot to Missile's Attack," *The New York Times* (August 29, 1981), p. 3.

Bonavia, David. "Radar Post Leak May Be Warning to Soviet Union," *The Times* (London) (June 20, 1981), p. 5.

Booda, Larry. "First Capsule Recovered from Satellite," *Aviation Week* (August 22, 1960), pp. 33–35.

Bradsher, Henry S. "U.S. Upgrades Spy Equipment at Turkish Sites," *Washington Star* (April 11, 1980), p. 7.

"British MP Accuses U.S. of Electronic Spying," *New Scientist* (August 5, 1976), p. 268.

Broad, William J. "Experts Say Satellite Can Detect Soviet War Steps," *The New York Times* (January 25, 1985), p. A12.

———. "Titan Rocket Explodes Over California Base," *The New York Times* (April 19, 1986), pp. 1, 7.

———. "Titan Loss May Force Early Use of Shuttle," *The New York Times* (April 22, 1986), pp. C1, C3.

Brookner, Eli. "Phased-Array Radars," *Scientific American* 252, 2 (February 1985): 94–103.

Burns, Michael K. "U.S. Reactivating Bases in Turkey," *Baltimore Sun* (October 21, 1978), pp. 1, 28.

Burt, Richard. "Soviet Reported to Add to Load Missile Can Fire," *The New York Times* (March 14, 1979), pp. A1,A7.

———. "U.S. Plans New Way to Check Soviet Missile Tests," *The New York Times* (June 29, 1979), p. A3.

———. "Technology Is Essential to Arms Verification," *The New York Times* (August 14, 1979), pp. C1,C2.

Campbell, Duncan. "Spy in the Sky," *New Statesman* (September 9, 1983), pp. 8–9.

———. "New Spy Station to Look Inside U.S.S.R.," *New Statesman* (December 21 and 28, 1984), p. 6.

Caruthers, Osgood. "U.S. Fliers Downed in '58 Held in Soviet, Moscow Journal Hints," *The New York Times* (January 24, 1961), pp. 1, 2.

Clem, Ralph. "Ethnicity and its Implications," *Bulletin of the Atomic Scientists* 38, 6 (June 1982): 53–58.

Corddry, Charles W., and Schlstedt, Albert, Jr., "Plane's Covert Role Is to Monitor Soviet Space Flights, Missile Tests," *Baltimore Sun* (May 1, 1981), p. 1.

Covault, Craig. "USAF, NASA Discuss Shuttle Use for Satellite Mainte-nance," *Aviation Week and Space Technology* (December 17, 1984), pp. 14–16.

Cushman, Jack. "Space Shuttle Explosion Throws Military Programs into Disarray," *Defense Week* (February 3, 1986), pp. 2–4.

Doder, Dusko. "U.S. Official Expelled from Moscow as Spy," *Washington Post* (June 15, 1985), p. A17.

Dratch, Howard B. "High Stakes in the Azores," *The Nation* (November 8, 1975), pp. 455–56.

"Electronic Environment Sampled Regularly," *Aviation Week and Space Technology* (May 10, 1976), pp. 90–92.

Engelberg, Stephen. "U.S. Indicates ex-CIA Officer Helped Soviet Cap-ture a Russian," *The New York Times* (October 18, 1985), p. A18.

Epstein, Edward Jay. "The Spy Who Came in to Be Sold," *The New Republic* (July 15 and 22, 1983), pp. 35–42.

Erdmann, James M. "The Wringer in Postwar Germany: Its Impact on United States-German Relations and Defense Policies," in Clifford L. Egan and Alexander Knott (eds.), *Essays in Twentieth-Century American Diplomatic History Dedicated to Professor Daniel M. Smith* (Lanham, Md.: University Press of America, 1982) pp. 159–91.

"Expanded Ocean Surveillance Effort Set," *Aviation Week and Space Tech-nology* (June 10, 1978), pp. 22–23.

Fink, Donald E. "U-2's, SR-71's Merged in One Wing," *Aviation Week and Space Technology* (May 10, 1976), p. 83.

Gerstenzang, James. "Shuttle Lifts Off With Spy Cargo," *Los Angeles Times* (January 25, 1985), pp. 1, 11.

Getler, Michael. "U.S. Intelligence Facilities in Turkey Get New Atten-tion After Iran Turmoil," *Washington Post* (February 9, 1979), p. A15.

Gillette, Robert. "Soviets Ousting U.S. Diplomat as Spy," *Los Angeles Times* (March 11, 1983), p. 4.

Gordon, Michael R. "Soviet Reported Acting to Begin New Atom Tests," *The New York Times* (March 18, 1986), pp. A1, A4.

Greeley, Brendan M., Jr. "USAF Readies Range Instrumentation Air-craft for First Flight," *Aviation Week and Space Technology* (February 25, 1985), pp. 23–24.

Gwertzman, Bernard. "U.S. Intelligence in the Dark About Andropov," *The New York Times* (December 29, 1983), p. A9.

Halloran, Richard. "2 Ships Enter Soviet Waters Off Crimea to Gather Intelligence," *The New York Times* (March 19, 1986), p. A1, A11.

Hangen, Welles. "Russia Charges Balloon Forays by U.S. and Turks," *The New York Times* (February 6, 1956), pp. 1, 3.

Hawkes, Russell. "USAF's Satellite Test Center Grows," *Aviation Week* (May 30, 1960), pp. 57–63.

Hersh, Seymour. "Submarines of U.S. Stage Spy Missions Inside Soviet Waters," *The New York Times* (May 25, 1975), pp. 1, 42.

———. "A False Navy Report Alleged in Sub Crash," *The New York Times* (July 6, 1975), pp. 1, 26.

———. "Human Error Is Cited in '74 Glomar Failure," *The New York Times* (December 9, 1976), pp. 1, 55.

Holm, Skip. "Spyplane: The First U-2 Flights," *Air Progress Aviation Review* (June 1986), pp. 24ff.

Horrock, Nicholas M. "The Submarine Hunters," *Newsweek* (January 23, 1984), p. 38.

"How Satellites May Help Sell SALT," *U.S. News and World Report* (May 21, 1978), pp. 25–26.

"How They Died," *Time* (February 16, 1959), pp. 17–18.

"How U.S. Taps Soviet Missile Secrets," *Aviation Week* (October 21, 1957), pp. 26–27.

Howe, Marvine. "U.S. and Turks Monitor Soviet at Isolated Post," *The New York Times* (January 4, 1981), p. 7.

Hussain, Farooq. "The Future of Arms Control: The Impact of Weapons Test Restrictions," *Adelphi Papers* 165 (1981).

"Industry Observer," *Aviation Week and Space Technology* (September 9, 1985), p. 15.

"Inside the Rescue Mission," *Newsweek* (July 12, 1982), p. 19.

Johnson, Kelly. "Development of the Lockheed SR-71 Blackbird," *Lockheed Horizons* (1981), pp. 1–7.

Kaplan, Fred, and Robinson, Walter V. "Pelton's 'Top-Secret' Intelligence Not So Secret," *Boston Globe* (June 5, 1986), pp. 1, 16, 17.

Kenden, Anthony. "U.S. Reconnaissance Satellite Programs," *Spaceflight* 20, 7 (1978): 243ff.

"KH-11 Overruns Said to Slow Development of Follow-On Spacecraft," *Aerospace Daily* (January 23, 1984), pp. 16–17.

"KH-12 Reconnaissance Satellite Planned for Kennedy Launch," *Aviation Week and Space Technology* (June 23, 1986), p. 17.

Kinney, Harvey, and Trimble, Bob. "Flying the Stratosphere," *Air Classics* 9, 10 (1973): 26ff.

Klass, Philip. "Military Satellites Gain Vital Data," *Aviation Week and Space Technology* (September 15, 1969), pp. 55–60.

———. "U.S. Monitoring Capability Impaired," *Aviation Week and Space Technology* (May 14, 1979), p. 18.

———. "U.S. Scrutinizing New Soviet Radar," *Aviation Week and Space Technology* (August 22, 1983), pp. 19–20.

Kucewicz, William. "KGB Defector Confirms U.S. Intelligence Fiasco," *The Wall Street Journal* (October 17, 1985).

Lardner, George, Jr. "Satellite Unchanged from Manual Bought by Soviets, U.S. Officials Say," *Washington Post* (October 10, 1985), p. A20.

MacPherson, Myra. "The Good Neighbor Who Came in from the Cold," *Washington Post* (June 21, 1978), pp. B1, B4.

Marder, Murrey. "Monitoring: Not So-Secret-Secret," *Washington Post* (June 19, 1981), p. 10.

Marshal, Eliot. "Senate Skeptical on SALT Verification," *Science* (July 27, 1979), pp. 373–76.

Martin, David. "A Spy in the Kremlin," *Newsweek* (July 21, 1980), pp. 69–70.

McClelland, Lori A. "Versatile P-3C Orion Meeting Growing ASW Challenge," *Defense Electronics* (April 1985), pp. 132–41.

Meyer, Deborah G. "DOD Likely to Spend $250 Billion on C³I Through 1990," *Armed Forces Journal International* (February 1985), pp. 72–84.

Middleton, Drew. "Soviet Fleet, Hurt by Blast, May Lie Low," *The New York Times* (June 26, 1984), p. A5.

Miller, Barry. "USAF Planning Space Data Link System," *Aviation Week and Space Technology* (April 11, 1966), pp. 65ff.

"Missile Disguise," *Aviation Week and Space Technology* (September 29, 1980), p. 17.

Mydans, Seth. "Soviet Expells a U.S. Diplomat for 'Major Espionage Action,'" *The New York Times* (June 15, 1985), p. 3.

Namack, John. "C-119's Third Pass Snares Discoverer," *Aviation Week* (August 29, 1960), pp. 30–31.

"NATO Fixed SONAR Range Commissioned," *Armed Forces Journal* (August 1972), p. 29.

"Navy Ocean Surveillance Satellite Depicted," *Aviation Week and Space Technology* (May 24, 1976), p. 22.

"Navy Will Develop All-Weather Ocean Monitor Satellite," *Aviation Week and Space Technology* (August 28, 1978), p. 50.

"New Payload Could Boost Shuttle Cost," *Aviation Week and Space Technology* (August 14, 1978), pp. 16–17.

Ohlendorf, Pat. "The New Breed of High-Tech Peacekeeper," *MacLean's* (January 23, 1984), pp. 52–53.

O'Toole, Thomas. "Oil Leak Blamed for Flawed Satellite," *Washington Post* (July 13, 1983), p. A2.

Peebles, Curtis L. "The Guardians," *Spaceflight* (November 1978), pp. 38ff.

———. "Satellite Photograph Interpretation," *Spaceflight* (October 1982), pp. 161–63.

Pike, John. "Reagan Prepares for War in Outer Space," *Counter Spy* 7, 1 (September–November 1982): 17–22.

Pincus, Walter. "Hill Conferees Propose Test of Space Arms," *Washington Post* (July 11, 1984), pp. A1–A3.

———. "U.S. Seeks A-Test Monitoring Facility," *Washington Post* (March 19, 1986), p. A8.

———. and Thornton, Mary. "U.S. to Orbit 'SIGINT' Craft from Shuttle," *Washington Post* (December 19, 1984), pp. A1, A8–A9.

Polmar, Norman. "The Deep Submergence Vehicle Fleet," *U.S. Naval Institute Proceedings* (June 1986), pp. 119–20.

Preston, A. "SOSUS Update Aims to Keep Track of Alfa," *Jane's Defence Weekly* 1, 2 (January 21, 1984): 60.

"Recon Satellite in Orbit Covering Mideast," *Avaition Week and Space Technology* (August 31, 1970), p. 13.

Reiss, Albert. "The Churchill-Stalin Secret 'Percentages' Agreement on the Balkans," *American Historical Review* 83, 2 (1978): 368–87.

Remnick, David. "Shevchenko: The Saga Behind the Best Seller," *Washington Post* (June 6, 1985), pp. B1, B6.

Richelson, Jeffrey. "The Satellite Data System," *Journal of the British Interplanetary Society* 37, 5 (1984): 226–28.

———. "The Keyhole Satellite Program," *Journal of Strategic Studies* 7, 2 (1984): 121–54.

———. "Old Surveillance, New Interpretations," *Bulletin of the Atomic Scientists* (February 1986), pp. 18–23.

———, and Arkin, William M. "Spy Satellites: Secret But Much Is Known," *Washington Post* (January 6, 1985), pp. C1–C2.

Rosenberg, David Alan. "The Origins of Overkill: Nuclear Weapons and American Strategy, 1945–1960," *International Security* 7, 4 (1983): 3–71.

"Russians Display Balloons of U.S.," *The New York Times* (February 10, 1956), pp. 1, 3.

Sagan, Scott. "Nuclear Alerts and Crisis Management," *International Security* 9, 4 (1985), pp. 99–139.

Samia, F. G. "The Norwegian Connection: Norway (Un)willing Spy for the U.S.," *Covert Action Information Bulletin* 9 (June 1980): 4–9.

"Satellite Pictures Show Soviet CVN Towering Above Nikolaiev Shipyard," *Jane's Defence Weekly* (August 11, 1984), pp. 171–73.

Sayle, Murray. "KE 007: A Conspiracy of Circumstance," *The New York Review of Books* (April 25, 1985), pp. 44–54.

Schmidt, Susan, and Tyler, Patrick E. "FBI Says Pelton Reported Soviet Interest in Satellites: Agents Detail Talks with Alleged Spy," *Washington Post* (May 24, 1986), pp. A1, A14–A15.

———. "Pelton Map Designation Held Wrong," *Washington Post* (May 31, 1986), pp. A1, A12.

Schorr, Daniel. "The Trigon Caper," *First Principles* (December 1980), pp. 11, 13, 15.

"Second SR-71 Deployed to England," *Aviation Week and Space Technology* (January 31, 1983), p. 59.

Shipler, David. "Soviet, Retaliating, Publicizes Case Against Woman Linked to C.I.A.," *The New York Times* (June 13, 1978), p. A12.

Simons, Howard. "Our Fantastic Eye in the Sky," *Washington Post* (December 8, 1963), pp. E1, E5.

"6 U.S. Fliers Lost in Plane Downed in Soviet Armenia," *The New York Times* (September 13, 1958), pp. 1, 6.

Smith, Hedrick. "U.S. Aides Say Loss of Post in Iran Impairs Missile-Monitoring Ability," *The New York Times* (March 2, 1979), pp. A1, A8.

"Soviet Strategic Bomber Photographed at Ramenskoye," *Aviation Week and Space Technology* (Dec 14, 1981), p. 17.

"Soviets Build Directed Energy Weapon," *Aviation Week and Space Technology* (July 28, 1980), pp. 47–50.

"Space Capsule Is Caught in Mid-Air by U.S. Plane on Re-entry from Orbit," *The New York Times* (August 20, 1960), pp. 1, 7.

"Space Reconnaissance Dwindles," *Aviation Week and Space Technology* (October 6, 1980), pp. 18–20.

"Space Secrecy Muddle," *Aviation Week and Space Technology* (April 23, 1962), p. 21.

"SR-71," United States Air Force Fact Sheet 82-36, Secretary of the Air Force, Office of Public Affairs.

Stein, Kenneth J. "Cobra Judy Phased Array Radar Tested," *Aviation Week and Space Technology* (August 10, 1981), pp. 70–73.

Streetly, Martin. "U.S. Airborne ELINT Systems, Part 3: The Boeing RC-135 Family," *Jane's Defence Weekly* (March 16, 1985), pp. 460–65.

———. "U.S. Airborne ELINT Systems, Part 4: The Lockheed SR-71A," *Jane's Defence Weekly* (April 13,1985), pp. 634–35.

"Soviets Arrest Four Scientists on Spying Charges," *Washington Post* (September 28, 1982), p. A10.

"Soviets Tighten Grip on Iran," *Jane's Defence Weekly* (November 23, 1985), p. 1125.

"SS-16 Deployment Raises Senate Questions," *Aviation Week and Space Technology* (September 24, 1979), p. 24.

Stern, Laurence. "U.S. Tapped Top Russians' Car Phones," *Washington Post* (December 5, 1973), pp. A1, A16.

Strasser, Stephen, et al. "Reagan's Secrecy Campaign," *Newsweek* (September 26, 1983), p. 38.

Sullivan, Walter. "Can Submarines Stay Hidden?" *The New York Times* (December 11, 1984), pp. C1, C9.

Taubman, Philip. "Capital's Rumor Mill: The Death of an Agent and the Talk It Started," *The New York Times* (September 23, 1980), pp. A1, A4.

———. "U.S. and Peking Jointly Monitor Russian Missiles," *The New York Times* (June 18, 1981), pp. A1, A14.

———. "U.S. Says Intelligence Plane Was on a Routine Mission," *The New York Times* (September 5, 1983), p. 4.

"The Archangel Is Illuminated," *Journal of Electronic Defense* (February 1984), pp. 24ff.

"The Great Submarine Snatch," *Time* (March 31, 1975), pp. 20–27.

"The Spy Planes: What They Do and Why," *Time* (April 25, 1969), p. 17.

Timsar, Richard. "Portugal Bargains for U.S. Military Aid with Strategic Mid-Atlantic Base," *The Christian Science Monitor* (March 24, 1981), p. 9.

"Titan 34D Booster Failed Following Premature Shutdown of Aerojet Engine," *Aviation Week and Space Technology* (November 18, 1985), p. 26.

Torgeson, Dial. "U.S. Spy Devices Still Running at Iran Post," *International Herald Tribune* (March 7, 1979), pp. A1, A8

Toth, Robert C. "Anaheim Firm May Have Sought Spy Satellite Data," *Los Angeles Times* (October 10, 1982), pp. 1, 32.

———."Gromyko Visit a Sign of Infighting in Kremlin," *Los Angeles Times* (September 14, 1984), p. 16.

Tyler, Patrick. "Soviet Seized as U.S. Spy Said Exposed by Howard," *Washington Post* (October 18, 1985), p. A10.

"USAF Pushes Pied Piper Space Vehicle," *Aviation Week* (October 14, 1957), p. 26.

"U.S. and Turkey Sign Pact on Aid and Bases," *The New York Times* (March 30, 1980), p. 1.

"U.S. Electronic Espionage: A Memoir," *Ramparts* (August 1972), pp. 35–50.

"U.S. to Continue U-2 Flights Over Soviet," *Aviation Week* (May 16, 1960), pp. 26–27.

"U.S. to Help Turkey Make Arms in Exchange for Intelligence Bases," *Los Angeles Times* (November 22, 1979), Part XI, p. 3.

Volkman, Ernest. "U.S. Spies Lend an Ear to Soviets," *Newsday* (July 28, 1977), p. 7.

"Washington Roundup," *Aviation Week and Space Technology* (June 4, 1979), p. 11.

Welzenbach, Donald. "Observation Balloons and Reconnaissance Satellites," *Studies in Intelligence* (Spring 1986), pp. 21–28.

White, Max. "U.S. Satellite Reconnaissance During the Falklands Conflict," Earth Satellite Research Unit, Department of Mathematics, University of Aston.

Wilford, John Noble. "Shuttle Launched on Secret Mission," *The New York Times* (January 25, 1985), pp. A1–A2.

Wilkes, Owen. "Strategic Anti-Submarine Warfare and Its Implications for a Counterforce First Strike" in *SIPRI Yearbook 1979*. London: Taylor & Francis, 1979.

Wilmoth, George A. "Lockheed's Antisubmarine Aircraft: Watching the Threat," *Defense Systems Review* 3, 6 (1985): 18–25.

Wilson, George C. "U.S. RC-135 Was Assessing Soviet Air Defense," *Washington Post* (September 7, 1983), p. A12.

———. "Soviet Ships Shadowed U.S. Vessels' Transit," *Washington Post* (March 20, 1986), p. A33.

Wit, Joel. "Advances in Antisubmarine Warfare," *Scientific American* 244, 2 (February 1981): 36ff.

"Work on Pied Piper Accelerated: Satellite Has Clam Shell Nose Cone," *Aviation Week* (June 23, 1958), pp. 18–19.

"X-Band Expands Cobra Judy's Repertoire," *Defense Electronics* (January 1985), pp. 43–44.

York, Herbert F., and Greb, G. Allen. "Strategic Reconnaissance," *Bulletin of the Atomic Scientists* 33, 4 (April 1977): 33–41.

Index

373